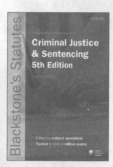

Core Text Series

- Written with authority by leading subject experts
- Takes a focused approach, leading law students straight to the heart of the subject
- Clear, concise, straightforward analysis of the subject and its challenges

Company Law: Alan Dignam and John Lowry

Constitutional and Administrative Law: Neil Parpworth

Criminal Law: Nicola Padfield

Employment Law: Robert Upex, Richard Benny, and Stephen Hardy

European Union Law: Margot Horspool and Matthew Humphreys

Evidence: Roderick Munday

Family Law: Mary Welstead and Susan Edwards

Intellectual Property Law: Jennifer Davis

Land Law: Kevin Gray and Susan Francis Gray

Medical Law: Jonathan Herring

The Law of Contract: Janet O'Sullivan and Jonathan Hilliard

The Law of Trusts: James Penner

The Legal System: Kate Malleson and Richard Moules

Tort: Stephen Hedley

For further information about titles in the series,
please visit www.oup.co.uk/series/cts

OXFORD
UNIVERSITY PRESS

CORE TEXT SERIES

Criminal Law

Ninth Edition

NICOLA PADFIELD

MA (Oxon), Dip Crim (Cantab), DES (Aix-Marseille) Barrister-at-Law,
Master of Fitzwilliam College and Reader in Criminal and Penal Justice,
University of Cambridge; Bencher of the Middle Temple.

OXFORD
UNIVERSITY PRESS

OXFORD
UNIVERSITY PRESS

Great Clarendon Street, Oxford, OX2 6DP,
United Kingdom

Oxford University Press is a department of the University of Oxford.
It furthers the University's objective of excellence in research, scholarship,
and education by publishing worldwide. Oxford is a registered trade mark of
Oxford University Press in the UK and in certain other countries

Published in the United States of America by Oxford University Press
198 Madison Avenue, New York, NY 10016, United States of America

British Library Cataloguing in Publication Data

Data available

Library of Congress Control Number: 2014938487

ISBN 978-0-19-870416-4

Printed in Great Britain by
Ashford Colour Press Ltd, Gosport, Hampshire

Preface to ninth edition

Since the Core Text Series was launched in the mid-1990s, our aim has been to produce a new edition of every book every two years. Our ambition has been to describe the law in a straightforward way, but without intellectual dishonesty and over-simplification. The challenge is to write at different 'levels' simultaneously, to strip the subject to its core while continuing to point out the intellectual challenges and difficulties within it. It is a 'core' law series in several senses:

(i) the books are relatively short;

(ii) they seek to identify the fundamental principles of the subject;

(iii) they concentrate on the most important, key topics within the subject.

This book therefore seeks to provide a different sort of criminal law textbook. The criminal law needs to be reduced to its core for a number of reasons. Parliament is in the habit of adding more and more offences to the statute book, and the core is in danger of being lost from sight. The subject is notoriously unclear, with appellate decisions appearing regularly to shift the already unsteady foundations of criminal liability. The book investigates the core of criminal law by looking at various central concepts and offences. I have sought to cover the subject in standard textbook fashion, but also to graft into it the elements of a case book: substantial statute and case law quotation should enable the student to get to the heart and core of the subject, and references to academic analyses and to law reform proposals are intended to point the student in the direction of the many challenges and difficulties of the subject. Inevitably some readers may take issue with the choice of material: given the constraints imposed by the need to produce a concise book, I have sought to omit everything outside the core issues in criminal law to ensure that this is a manageable and approachable text. In earlier editions I resisted the temptation to exclude entirely terrorism and crimes against the environment, because I felt (and still feel) that it is important that students remember that the criminal courts are concerned with a very broad range of offences. And these two areas are becoming ever more important. But for this edition I have been persuaded that a separate chapter on environmental crime is not really justified. Having accepted that, I maintain that identifying the 'core' of criminal law remains no easy matter.

The style of this book is deliberately brief and core-like. Certain abbreviations have been routinely used in order to save space and for ease of presentation. Where cases have been summarized, the text is slightly indented for ease of reference.

Sometimes after the name of the deciding court (SC, HL, CA, etc.), a judge's name is mentioned. This is because he (still sadly, and rarely, she!) gave the main or only judgment or speech. If a judge's name appears later in the summary, it is because I have chosen to highlight what was said by one judge in particular. I make no apology for frequent references to individual judges: it is, after all, the judges who are making and interpreting the law. The student may well find the large amount of knowledge she is required to digest easier to learn once she has 'got to know' judges individually: the subject comes alive when you are able to think, 'Aha, Baroness Hale again', or 'I'm not surprised that Lord Mustill held that, given his views in...'. It also impresses examiners if a candidate can say, 'as Lord Bingham said in *Kennedy (No. 2)* (2007)...', rather than the prosaic 'as the House of Lords said in *Kennedy (No. 2)*' or the rather feeble 'as *Kennedy No. 2* decided'. An examiner is more likely to give a candidate the benefit of the doubt when he is not sure if something has been understood, if the candidate has made it very clear elsewhere that she had an accurate understanding!

The additional reading at the end of each chapter is necessarily highly selective. Within the text there are also references to some of the leading textbooks. Students who have access to law reports and periodicals will be well rewarded if they keep up to date by browsing through new cases and articles as they appear. The main criminal law journal remains the Criminal Law Review: students are well advised to read monthly commentaries on recent cases: they provide excellent reviews of the key issues as well as pointers towards possible reforms and improvements. If, as a student, you can follow these arguments, you will know you are doing fine! As well, periodicals such as the Cambridge Law Journal, the Modern Law Review, the Law Quarterly Review, and the Journal of Criminal Law regularly publish short commentaries on key cases. The practitioners' short monthly newsletter Archbold Review (edited by this author; available on Westlaw) also gives up-to-date information. Another technique for understanding the criminal law: take this book and read it in the public gallery of your local Crown Court or magistrates' court: then you will not forget the impact and importance of the subject as it affects people's lives. This subject is about the application of the law to, and the punishment of, real people.

Inevitably, this book can only take a snapshot at one moment in time: it seeks to present and discuss the criminal law as it is at the beginning of February 2014. Please feel free to send comments and criticisms of this edition to the author at nmp21@cam.ac.uk.

Nicky Padfield
Fitzwilliam College,
Cambridge CB3 0DG
4 February 2014

New to this edition

This ninth edition covers all the essential developments in this dynamic area of law. New coverage includes:

- Up-to-date coverage of recent case law, including *Bristow* (2013), *Hughes* (2013), *Banfield* (2013), and *Oye* (2013).

- Fully revised discussion of insanity and automatism and the provisional reforms that address these issues.

- Improved author commentary guides students through the essential cases with clear and thought-provoking analysis.

- Revised structure makes the book as approachable and manageable as possible.

- Commentary on recent Law Commission reports, and other valuable academic articles published since the last edition of this book.

Author approach

The aim of the Core Text Series is to strip the subject to its core whilst simultaneously highlighting the intellectual challenges and difficulties within the law. This textbook helps you to explore and gain a solid understanding of the key issues and contentions that make up criminal law as we know it.

Familiarity with and understanding of key cases are integral to the learning of criminal law; directing and depicting the core principles and the issues of controversy in the law. The author provides succinct summaries of numerous carefully selected cases within the body of the text to help readers to get to the core of the subject.

Table of abbreviations

ABH	Actual bodily harm
A-G	Attorney General
CA	Court of Appeal (Criminal Division)
CAA	Criminal Attempts Act
CC	Crown Court
CCA	Court of Criminal Appeal
CCCR	Court of Crown Cases Reserved
CCRC	Criminal Cases Review Commission
CDA	Criminal Damage Act
CJA	Criminal Justice Act
C&JA	Coroners and Justice Act
CJIA	Criminal Justice and Immigration Act
CJPOA	Criminal Justice and Public Order Act
CLA	Criminal Law Act
CLRC	Criminal Law Revision Committee
CMAC	Courts Martial Appeals Court
CP(IUP)A	Criminal Procedure (Insanity and Unfitness to Plead) Act
CPS	Crown Prosecution Service
CYPA	Children and Young Persons Act
D	Defendant
DC	Divisional Court (of the Queen's Bench Division of the High Court)
DCC	Draft Criminal Code
DJ	District Judge
DJ(MC)	District Judge (Magistrates' Court)
DPP	Director of Public Prosecutions
DVCVA	Domestic Violence, Crime and Victims Act
ECHR	European Convention on Human Rights
ECtHR	European Court of Human Rights
EU	European Union
FD	Framework Directive
GBH	Grievous bodily harm
HA	Homicide Act
HC	High Court
HL	House of Lords
HRA	Human Rights Act

HSAWA	Health and Safety at Work etc. Act
JSB	Judicial Studies Board
KBD	King's Bench Division
Law Com	Law Commission
LCCP	Law Commission Consultation Paper
LCJ	Lord Chief Justice
LJ	Lord Justice
MC	Magistrates' Court
MHA	Mental Health Act
MHRT	Mental Health Review Tribunal
OAPA	Offences against the Person Act
OSA	Official Secrets Act
P	Prosecution
PC	Privy Council
POA	Public Order Act
QBD	Queen's Bench Division
RTA	Road Traffic Act
SC	Supreme Court
SOA	Sexual Offences Act
SO(A)A	Sexual Offences (Amendment) Act
TA	Theft Act
V	Victim

A number of leading textbooks are also referred to in the text:

Allen	Allen's *Textbook of Criminal Law* (7th edn, 2003)
PCL	Ashworth and Horder, *Principles of Criminal Law* (7th edn, 2013)
Ormerod	Ormerod, *Smith and Hogan's Criminal Law* (13th edn, 2011)
TCL	Glanville Williams' *Textbook on Criminal Law* (2nd edn, 1983)

Contents

Table of statutes

Paragraph references printed in **bold** type indicate where the Act is set out in part or in full.

Secondary legislation

Table of cases

Guide to the book

There are a number of features throughout the textbook designed to help you in your studies.

SUMMARY

This chapter examines various states of mir

Intention: intention is not the same as moti intent: an intent may be inferred when the from what D does, even if D did not want it

Knowledge and belief: wilful blindness ma

Recklessness: for many years recklessness w i.e. D is reckless if he consciously takes a risk

Chapter summaries highlight what will be addressed in each chapter, so you are aware of the key learning outcomes for each topic.

FURTHER READING

Ashworth, A., 'Defining Criminal Offences Law Essays (1987).

Glazebrook, P., 'Should We Have a Law of A

Harding, C, 'The Offence of Belonging: Ca [2005] Crim LR 690.

Law Commission, Assisting and Encouraging

At the end of each chapter is a list of recommended **further reading**. These suggestions include books and journal articles, and will help to supplement your knowledge, and develop your understanding of key topics.

SELF-TEST QUESTION

1   In a drunken fight, Dee stabs Phil in the she thought the knife was so blunt tha tunately she almost severs his finger ar Discuss Dee's liability.

2   Dee deliberately hits Phil on the heac foresee any harm resulting to him. Sur offence(s) has Dee committed?

Each chapter concludes with a selection of **self-test questions**. These allow you to check your understanding of the topics covered, and help you engage fully with the material in preparation for further study, writing essays, and answering exam questions.

1 Introduction

SUMMARY

This chapter seeks to put criminal law in its context: to look at the aims and ambit of the criminal law; and the criminal justice system within which it is applied. The student is encouraged to think about some key principles and values which will help in the evaluation of the offences and defences described later in the book.

1.1 At first sight, it seems relatively easy to distinguish criminal law from other areas of law: criminal law involves a description of the behaviour which makes a person liable to punishment by the state. But the lines are not always easy to draw. The civil law is also used to regulate behaviour (through measures such as injunctions and Anti-Social Behaviour Orders (ASBOs)). Nor is it always the state which runs prisons and other criminal justice agencies. But a crime is a legal wrong, which may result in punishment. Where does criminal law end and civil law take over? If I refuse to pay a plumber who mends my dripping tap, either he may sue me in the civil courts for non-payment of a civil debt, or he may try to get the police to initiate a criminal prosecution alleging that I obtained his services by fraud or deception. In other areas, the boundaries may be blurred because the extent to which someone should be held to be blameworthy is unclear: if a doctor treats you appallingly and causes your death, should she be prosecuted? Another example might be the meaning of the word 'dishonestly'. A person is not guilty of theft unless he or she acted 'dishonestly': are you dishonest if you see £50 in the street and you decide to keep it? Not all crimes are perceived to be immoral: some are merely 'regulatory', as is discussed particularly in Chapter 3 which looks at crimes of strict liability. In any case, it is difficult to agree on a 'shared morality'.

1.2 In order to identify the proper boundaries of the criminal law, it is useful to identify certain fundamental principles. Ashworth's *Principles of Criminal Law* (PCL) is a useful assessment of the criminal law through the identification of key principles. For Ashworth, the *principle of individual autonomy* lies at the foundation of criminal liability. Individuals in general have the capacity and free will to make meaningful choices, and this individual autonomy should be respected by others and the legal system. He also selects other key principles which should be at the heart of the criminal law:

- the principle of welfare, of upholding the common good;

- the principle of prevention of harm to others;

- the principle of minimal intervention: the law should not criminalize too much behaviour;

- the principle of social responsibility: society requires a certain level of cooperation between citizens;

- the principle of proportionate response: the response of the criminal law should be reasonably proportionate to the harm committed or threatened;

- the non-retroactivity principle: a person should not be convicted or punished except in accordance with a previously declared offence;

- the thin-ice principle: those who skate on thin ice can hardly expect to find a sign denoting the precise spot where they will fall in;

- the principle of maximum certainty: people should have fair warning about the criminal law;

- the principle of fair labelling: offences should be labelled so as to reflect the seriousness of the law breaking;

- the principle of strict construction: ambiguities in criminal law should be construed in favour of the defendant;

- the presumption of innocence: a principle of procedural fairness that D should be presumed innocent until proved guilty.

1.3 Elsewhere, Ashworth (2000, at p. 253) identified four interlinked principles which form the principled core of the criminal law:

Ashworth's principled core of the criminal law

- The criminal law should be used, and used only, to censure persons for substantial wrongdoing.

- Criminal laws should be enforced with respect for equal treatment and proportionality.

- Persons accused of substantial wrongdoing ought to be afforded the protections appropriate to those charged with criminal offences; i.e., at least the minimum protections declared by Articles 6.2 and 6.3 of the European Convention on Human Rights.

- Maximum sentences and effective sentence levels should be proportionate to the seriousness of the wrongdoing.

Throughout this book, the student is encouraged to think about the principles behind individual crimes. These principles sometimes clash and conflict, and they are often not openly acknowledged by the judges and commentators. But by applying the sort of approach that Ashworth suggests, you will find it much easier to judge and to evaluate the criminal law. 'General principles of criminal law' may include the general principles discussed in Chapters 2 and 3 of this book; they may also include the more fundamental principles of criminal justice discussed by Ashworth.

Purposes of criminal law

1.4 When you have read about people being prosecuted for anything from aiding and abetting suicide to outraging public decency, you may well want to ask some fundamental questions about what the criminal law is seeking to achieve. Here are some ideas.

The criminal law seeks:

- to enforce moral values;
- to punish those who deserve punishment;
- to protect the public from harm;
- to reform the offender;
- to deter offenders and potential offenders;
- to educate people about appropriate conduct and behaviour;
- to preserve order;
- to protect vulnerable people from exploitation and corruption.

Parliament set out the purposes of punishment in the Criminal Justice Act 2003, s 142:

(1) Any court dealing with an offender in respect of his offence must have regard to the following purposes of sentencing—

(a) the punishment of offenders,

(b) the reduction of crime (including its reduction by deterrence),

(c) the reform and rehabilitation of offenders,

(d) the protection of the public, and

(e) the making of reparation by offenders to persons affected by their offences.

Is this list useful? Some of the purposes seem somewhat contradictory. Many writers have sought to find a primary aim. However, it may be that you decide that the criminal law should seek to achieve a combination of these purposes, but giving different priorities to different aims in different contexts. Most law courses separate out the study of punishment from the study of criminal law, but the two are inevitably intertwined. You may find it useful to read a book on sentencing law or on theories of punishment (e.g. Ashworth (2010)).

The relationship between law and morals

1.5 The question whether the law should be used to penalize immoral behaviour has been endlessly debated. A classic example of the debate is that between Professor Hart and Lord Devlin in the 1960s, provoked by the recommendation of the Wolfenden Committee to decriminalize homosexual acts between consenting adults (which happened in the Sexual Offences Act (SOA) 1967). Devlin, a retired Law Lord, argued that society cannot live without morals, and that its morals are those standards of conduct of which the reasonable man approves. The law was needed to enforce morality. Hart, on the other hand, argued that not only was there no such thing as a moral consensus, but neither was there any evidence that those who deviate from conventional sexual morality are in other ways hostile to society. Devlin's stand depends on there being some common shared morality (which he thought could be found in the jury room). Yet current debates on some subjects, such as abortion or euthanasia, suggest that there is no easily accessible common thread of morality. It is also widely accepted that the criminal law should not criminalize certain activities that many might consider immoral as long as they don't happen in public. Yet is this distinction between that which happens in public and in private tenable? Domestic violence is certainly not acceptable because it happens in private!

1.6 Whose morality is to be enforced? It is likely to be the morality of the powerful. The enactment of new offences (such as criminal trespass, introduced in the Criminal Justice and Public Order Act (CJPOA) 1994; employing those without the right to work, in the Asylum and Immigration Act 1996; breach of an anti-social behaviour order, in the Crime and Disorder Act 1998; or the many new offences related to terrorism passed in recent years (see **9.34**)) reminds us that it is the Government of the day which has the power to define the limits of the criminal law. The role of the jury, magistrate, and judge is limited by the statutory framework within which they work. New crimes are often added to the statute book and few are removed. It is important for the student to consider whether there is too much criminal law, and an application of key principles allows an assessment of whether the body of criminal law needs to be stripped back to its core.

1.7 Useful illustrations of the Hart/Devlin debate are to be found in the speeches of the House of Lords (HL) in *Brown* (1993). What is instructive is the different attitude of the majority and minority judges to the question of whether the criminal law should be used to uphold morality:

Brown **(1993)** A group of sado-masochists committed acts of violence against each other for the sexual pleasure they got from giving and receiving pain. They were convicted of offences against the Offences against the Person Act (OAPA) 1861, s 20 and s 47 and received sentences of imprisonment.

HL (by a majority of 3 to 2): upheld the decision of the Court of Appeal (CA) to reject their appeals. Lord Templeman, in the majority, said:

> The violence of sado-masochistic encounters involves the indulgence of cruelty by sadists and the degradation of victims ... Society is entitled and bound to protect itself against a cult of violence. Pleasure derived from the infliction of pain is an evil thing. Cruelty is uncivilised.

Lord Mustill (dissenting) disagreed:

> The issue before the House is not whether [D]s' conduct is morally right, but whether it is properly charged under the Act of 1861. When proposing that the conduct is not rightly so charged I do not invite your Lordships' House to endorse it as morally acceptable ... What I do say is that these are questions of private morality; that the standards by which they fall to be judged are not those of the criminal law; and that if these standards are to be upheld the individual must enforce them upon himself according to his own moral standards.

Consider which way you would have decided this issue before reading on to **1.25**, which considers the approach taken by the European Court of Human Rights (ECtHR). We return to this case when considering the tricky question of consent (see **5.7**).

Grading crimes

1.8 So far we have discussed some of the difficulties involved in marking the outer limits of the criminal law. As difficult is the challenge of grading individual crimes according to their relative seriousness. This is equally important, since we seek to punish people appropriately according to the gravity of their offence. While we can easily agree that murder is more blameworthy than assault, is it necessarily 'worse' than manslaughter? There is no one scale of seriousness. A common measure is the seriousness of the harm caused. Thus, it can be argued that I am more culpable if I kill you than if I merely wound you, whatever my intent. Certainly, we seem to blame the drunk driver who kills someone more than we blame the drunk driver who happily doesn't happen to hit anyone. But how do you work out which harms are worse than others? Von Hirsch and Jareborg (1991) developed a scale based on the extent that the harm affects someone's living standards, but the complexities of real life suggest that there are other possible dimensions to help measure offence seriousness.

Another measure of culpability is the intent of the offender. I am more culpable if I intend to kill you and do so, than if I cause your death merely by being careless. Grading crimes according to what happens is somewhat arbitrary: concentrating on the state of mind of the offender may be fairer. This was the view of the Sentencing Guidelines Council, created in the Criminal Justice Act (CJA) 2003 with a statutory duty to provide sentencing guidelines to judges and magistrates. In their Guideline, *Overarching Principles: Seriousness* (2004), they stated:

> *The seriousness of an offence is determined by two main parameters: the culpability of the offender and the harm caused or risked being caused by the offence ... The culpability of the offender in the particular circumstances of an individual case should be the initial factor in determining the seriousness of an offence.*

Yet this too may be unfair as we cannot enter other people's minds—you are still likely to judge me by the external appearances of my act, whatever my innermost thoughts. The Sentencing Guidelines Council was replaced in April 2010 by a strengthened Sentencing Council. It is worth keeping your eye on their website.

1.9 When we come to look at individual crimes, we will see that they are graded in various ways by Parliament in different contexts and that different words are used to describe the required guilty state of mind (see Chapter 3). How narrowly should individual crimes be subdivided? For example, culpable homicides are currently divided into murder and manslaughter, but English law does not distinguish first degree and second degree murder or manslaughter. The Law Commission in 1996

(Law Com No. 237, see **8.33**) recommended that manslaughter should be subdivided into reckless killing and a more minor offence of killing by gross recklessness. Then (Report No. 304 (2006)) they suggested first degree and second degree murder (see **8.46**). Would subdivisions such as this be useful? One can argue that the law is already over-precise and there are trends in the opposite direction: see the extraordinarily broad new fraud offence (at **11.43**). Be alert to labelling issues and to the breadth of individual offence 'labels'.

1.10 You may decide too that other crimes may be too broadly defined: 'sexual assault' may include anything from forced penetration to bottom pinching (see **10.17**) and robbery includes 'mere' handbag snatching (see **11.22**): does this dilute too much an otherwise very serious offence? Decades ago, Glazebrook wrote a stimulating article (in (1969) 85 LQR 27) arguing that we could live without a law of attempt by defining substantive crimes more widely: thus rape would not be unlawful sexual intercourse, but an assault committed with sexual intent. Then there would be no need for a crime of attempted rape. There certainly seems to be a trend today towards more preparatory or inchoate offences: crimes such as fraud are committed without any requirement that D should actually have gained anything. (We could look too at recent offences targeted at would-be terrorists, which focus on acts of preparation.) This raises a question of fair labelling: since people understand rape to be unlawful sexual intercourse, there are compelling reasons to define it in law in this way. Is the same not true of fraud: should it be merely attempted fraud if you didn't actually gain anything?

Criminal law in context: the criminal justice process

1.11 The criminal law is not a neat theoretical system: it needs to work in practice. After reading this book you may conclude that the criminal law is in something of a state of chaos, because, in studying criminal law, we often concentrate on the most difficult and controversial areas. It is therefore worth reminding ourselves that courts up and down the country are today dealing with many criminal prosecutions with little difficulty. Most people plead guilty (since there are generous sentence discounts for those who plead guilty, particularly at an early stage in proceedings). And most disputes in contested criminal trials concern questions of fact, not questions of law (though distinguishing law from fact can be very difficult: see **5.27**) or questions of evidence or procedure.

Many crimes are never discovered or reported to the police. A high proportion of known offenders are never prosecuted, but may instead be formally or informally cautioned by the police, given a caution with conditions by the Crown Prosecution

Service (CPS), or served with a fixed penalty notice or penalty notice for disorder. If someone is to be prosecuted, then this prosecution is likely to be initiated by the police. Many of the difficulties in this subject are created by charging practices and policies. Thus, one of the difficulties we will explore is whether someone who tricks their victim into giving them possession of their goods is guilty of theft (see *Gomez* (1991) at **11.10**) as well as fraud. This difficulty would not have become an issue of criminal law if the police (or the CPS) charged such suspects with an offence of fraud and not with theft. Thus, the criminal law can be improved by better decisions by prosecutors and not just by clarification from appellate judges at the other end of the process. (But not all crimes are investigated by the police: many non-police agencies initiate prosecutions: see Padfield (2008).)

1.12 Most prosecutions are conducted by the CPS, which follows the guidance of the Code for Crown Prosecutors as well as its own policy manuals. Its website is a very useful source of guidance on the law. A case may be dropped because the CPS decides there is insufficient evidence to proceed to trial or because the public interest does not demand a prosecution: the offence may be trivial or there has been a long delay between the offence taking place and the date of the trial, for example. You may well be surprised when reading some of the cases discussed in this book that the case was prosecuted at all or you may wonder why a criminal charge was not amended at an early stage. The CPS has suffered criticism throughout its nearly 30-year life (see Padfield (2008)) and now, when it has gained a more confident role, it is of course suffering from dramatic budget cuts. Time will tell how this will affect practice in the criminal courts.

1.13 Criminal cases are tried in either a Crown Court (CC) or a magistrates' court (MC). Offences are categorized according to their mode of trial. Offences may be indictable (i.e. triable by a jury in a CC); summary (i.e. triable by magistrates (lay or stipendiary) in a MC); or triable either way. Proposals to remove the defendant's ability to elect for trial in the CC in either-way offences, making the decision instead one for the magistrates, a move aimed at saving money and cutting delays in the criminal justice process, have not been brought into force. But the categorization of offences should have little impact on the general principles of criminal liability, being most relevant to procedures before or at trial. However, it would be wrong to assume that these procedural differences have no effect on substantive issues of criminal law. Appeals from MCs are generally heard in the CC and are rarely reported and so there is little judicial guidance on the interpretation of, for example, driving offences or of minor assaults. A procedure exists for MCs or CCs to state a case for the opinion of the Divisional Court of the Queen's Bench Division (QBD) of the High Court, and this procedure is used not infrequently to clarify points of law, especially in cases heard in MCs (see **Table 1.1**).

Year	No. of appeals
1995	243
1998	188
2002	135
2004	97
2006	137
2008	78
2010	73
2012	80

Table 1.1 Appeals by way of case stated heard in the High Court
Source: *Judicial and Court Statistics* (published online).

1.14 Note which of the cases that you come across in this book were decided by the HL or Supreme Court (SC) and consider which party appealed and why. It may be that the highest courts do (did?) not take minor offences as seriously as they should, sometimes appearing to ignore the general principles that such cases may raise. Thus, Spencer (1984) 43 Camb LJ 10 suggested that cases such as *Lawrence* (1972, see **11.9**) and *Morris* (1984, see **11.9**) reflect the HL's opinion that theft was not sufficiently important to merit detailed consideration in the HL and this exacerbated the problems experienced in defining the word 'appropriation' (see **11.10**). The vast majority of cases you look at in criminal law are decisions of the CA, which deals with appeals from trials in CCs. Most cases reach the CA because the defendant appeals; some because the Attorney General (A-G) refers an acquittal (see **1.22**); and some important cases return to the CA because they are referred there by the Criminal Cases Review Commission (CCRC), under the Criminal Attempts Act (CAA) 1995, s 9 (see, e.g. *Kennedy (No. 2)* (2007, at **2.22**)). The only ground for allowing an appeal against conviction is that the conviction is 'unsafe' (CAA 1968, s 2 as amended by the CAA 1995). Thus the CA examines the way the trial judge summed up to the jury to see whether the conviction is 'safe': it does not substitute its own opinion on the facts.

The rules of procedure and evidence

1.15 This book ignores most rules of procedure and evidence. Yet it should not be forgotten that these rules may well have more influence on whether someone stands trial and indeed on whether they are convicted, than the substantive rules of criminal law. Bear in mind that, in practice, arguments about the admissibility of certain evidence (can a witness give oral evidence anonymously; is a statement inadmissible hearsay; was a confession gained by oppression and should it therefore be excluded; can the jury be told about D's previous convictions, etc?) may have crucial importance in securing an acquittal or a conviction. Similarly, rules of procedure (can the judge's view on a likely sentence be sought before D enters a plea, for example?) have enormous impact. Furthermore, questions about the burden of proof (who has to prove what) are crucial. This book follows the traditional pattern of criminal law courses in this country by leaving the study of evidence and procedure to other texts, but a wise and intellectually curious student should keep an eye on these wider issues. While studying criminal law, visit courts and consider what a small proportion of the court's time is spent in considering details of substantive criminal law.

The role of the jury

1.16 The most serious cases are tried by a judge and jury and it is worth considering the impact that trial by jury has had on the development of the criminal law generally. It is often suggested that it was the reluctance of juries to convict drivers who killed of manslaughter, which resulted in the creation of the more minor offence of causing death by reckless driving. Jackson and Doran (1995) compared the process of trial by judge alone with that of the trial by jury (in the context of the abolition of trial by jury for certain trials in Northern Ireland). They point out that trials throughout the common law world are still dominated by rules and practices designed for a lay fact-finding tribunal, even though many no longer have trials by jury. Even in England few cases result in jury trial: most cases which reach the CC result in guilty pleas and there is no trial (see **Table 1.2**).

1.17 Trial by jury can allow the law to be less precise than perhaps it should be. In **11.14** we examine the meaning of the word 'dishonesty' in the criminal context. Juries are told by judges that it is an ordinary word which should be given its ordinary meaning. Yet how is a jury to decide whether someone who keeps a £50 note, found in the street, is acting dishonestly? Should the jury merely decide questions of disputed fact (D is lying: he did not intend to tell the police the next day about the £50 note, otherwise why would he have already gone on a spending spree that afternoon?) or should they have some wider function as a barometer of public morality (is keeping property found lying in the street wrong?). There are ardent supporters of trial by jury: for example Devlin (1991) and Houlder (1997) who suggest that the jury provides a democratic veto on law enforcement. Can this

Year	No. of defendants dealt with	Not guilty pleas (%)	Those pleading not guilty acquitted (%)
1995	88,985	24	40
1998	77,794	39	64
2000	75,887	42	67
2002	77,495	43	63
2004	81,742	42	67
2006	83,730	34	59
2008	96,027	29	60
2010	112,702	29	64
2012	96,409	31	58

Table 1.2 Crown Court trials
Source: *Judicial Statistics and Court Statistics*

really be so in a system where less than 3 per cent of all criminal cases are tried in the CC and, even then, only a minority of these cases is contested?

Sentencing

1.10 In many ways it makes little sense to study criminal law without studying sentencing. In practice, the public (and the offender) are more interested to know the punishment imposed on an offender rather than the label applied to the offence: for example, in knowing that someone got three years' imprisonment, rather than in knowing the precise legal label applicable to their offence. However, this does not mean that the offences themselves should not be appropriately distinguished, as Ashworth's fair labelling and other principles make clear (see **1.2**).

1.19 Generally, Parliament lays down a statutory maximum sentence. Thus, the maximum penalty for rape is life imprisonment, for theft, seven years. When making charging decisions, prosecutors may be influenced as much by ideas about the suitable sentence as by the definition of the offence itself. Thus, since an offence under the OAPA 1861, s 20 (inflicting grievous bodily harm—GBH) has the same maximum penalty (five years) as an offence under s 47 (occasioning actual bodily harm—ABH), there is little reason for the prosecution to set out to prove the more serious offence. Since a life sentence of imprisonment is available for manslaughter as well as for murder, prosecutors may be happy to accept a guilty plea to manslaughter. Specific defences to murder, such as provocation and diminished responsibility, evolved at a time when the death penalty existed. It may be argued that if the penalty for murder were changed from a mandatory life sentence to a discretionary one, the debates on the borderline between murder and manslaughter would lose their urgency (see Chapter 8). This book therefore sometimes includes comments on the sentences imposed, as a key to understanding the definition of the offence itself.

Sources of criminal law

1.20   Most offences (especially recent offences) have been created by statute, but others have simply evolved through the common law. This means that definitions have evolved slowly through judgments stretching back over the centuries. The obvious example is murder: traditionally defined as 'unlawful killing with malice aforethought', the individual elements in this definition have to be explored by reference to many cases, some recent, some ancient. Judge-made law is derived from a small pool of cases: largely from appeals by those who have been convicted and who have chosen to appeal (see **Table 1.3**).

1.21   Until very recently, retrials were exceptionally rare in English law and they are still very unusual (see **Table 1.4**). It seems to have been accepted that it is wrong to

Year	No. of applications for leave to appeal against conviction	Appeals actually heard which were allowed (%)
1995	2,393	33
1998	2,099	42
2000	2,068	31
2002	1,914	34
2004	1,782	38
2006	1,596	46 (181 of 391 cases)
2008	1,588	43 (188 of 438 cases)
2010	1,488	31 (187 of 596 cases)
2012	1,697	38.5 (151 of 392 cases)

Table 1.3 Appeals against conviction to the Court of Appeal

Source: *Annual Judicial and Court Statistics*

Year	1990	1992	1994	1996	1998	2000	2002	2004	2006	2008	2010	2012
No. of retrials	3	12	51	53	73	72	50	66	58	72	56	39

Table 1.4 Number of retrials ordered by the Court of Appeal
Source: *Annual Judicial and Court Statistics*

make D face a retrial and, of course, it is very expensive and hard on both defendants and witnesses. Should retrials be more readily used, especially in cases where the CA feels D is probably guilty?

1.22 Other cases we look at will be Divisional Court (DC) decisions (appeals by way of case stated (see 1.13)). There are also a few A-G's References, where the prosecution refer an acquittal under the CJA 1972, s 36. Although the original acquittal will not be affected by the result of the appeal, the procedure allows the higher courts the opportunity to review a wider variety of case than simply those of aggrieved convicted offenders. It also allows them to 'sit on' a wrong ruling on a point of law before it becomes widespread.

1.23 The principle of non-retroactivity (see 1.2) means that people should only be found guilty of crimes which were known to be criminal at the time that D committed his offence. One of the dangers with judge-made law is its retroactive effect. Much of the controversy which surrounded the case of *R* (1992) (see 1.26 and 10.9) concerned the question whether the HL went too far in extending the law of rape to husbands who had sex with their wives without their consent. While few people would argue that such activity should not be criminal, many considered that it was more appropriate for Parliament rather than the judiciary to change the law: even though R might have argued that at the time when he raped his wife, his act was not an offence in English law, the HL was able to uphold a change in the law with retrospective effect.

1.24 Another danger is that some common law offences remain vaguely defined, perhaps offending against the principle of maximum certainty. Consider three examples concerning the offence of outraging public decency:

> *Gibson* (1990) D1 exhibited at D2's art gallery an exhibit of a model's head from which were hung earrings made out of (real) freeze-dried human foetuses (the message being that women allegedly wear their abortions as lightly as they wear their earrings). They were convicted of outraging public decency, contrary to the common law.
>
> CA: upheld their convictions. Despite the paucity of reported cases, there was undoubtedly a common law crime of outraging public decency.

Walker **(1995)** D exposed his penis to two girls in the sitting room of his house and was convicted of outraging public decency.

CA (Laws J): allowed his appeal. The act had not been committed in a place where there was a real possibility that members of the general public might witness it. A more appropriate charge might have been indecent assault (now sexual assault) or under the Indecency with Children Act 1960.

Hamilton **(2007)** D secretly videoed up women's skirts in supermarkets, by hiding a camera in a bag. The women were not identified: the offences came to light when the video films were seized. He was convicted of outraging public decency.

CA: dismissed appeal. It was necessary to prove two elements: (i) that the act was of such a lewd, obscene, or disgusting nature as to outrage public decency and (ii) that the act took place in a public place and was capable of being seen by two or more persons, even if they had not actually seen it. D's conduct was capable of being judged by a jury to be lewd, obscene, or disgusting and the jury was entitled to reach that conclusion, even if nobody saw him carrying out the filming. As regards the public element, that required the act to be done in a place that the public had access to or a place where what was done was capable of public view. D's filming in a supermarket clearly satisfied that part of the public element. Although nobody saw him filming, there was evidence from the videos that others were present. Accordingly, the jury had been entitled to convict.

Ashworth (at [2008] Crim LR 229) is critical of the CA's decision to extend the ambit of this offence (by deciding that no one needed to see the act). Indeed, should an offence such as outraging public decency exist? As Lord Bingham made clear in *Rimmington; Goldstein* (2005, see **3.31**), cases of public nuisance, the courts have no power to create new offences or to abolish old ones: it is nowadays accepted that Parliament is the appropriate body to create new offences. Parliament is democratically accountable and has the opportunity to seek expert advice (see **1.31**) prior to its debates. I would argue that there is no room at all for common law offences in the 21st century, let alone expanding them. It does seem that they are slowly disappearing: blasphemy was abolished in the Criminal Justice and Immigration Act (CJIA) 2008 and common law libel offences in the Coroners and Justice Act 2009. The Law Commission has also consulted on public nuisance and outraging public decency: only time will tell whether Parliament acts!

The Human Rights Act 1998

1.25 The European Convention on Human Rights (ECHR) was ratified by the UK Government in 1951, but until recently the aggrieved citizen had to pursue her claim in the ECtHR in Strasbourg. The Human Rights Act (HRA) 1998 incorporated the Convention into domestic law: and from 2 October 2000 these Convention rights became part of the underlying principles of our criminal law. Here are extracts from some relevant articles:

Article 6

(1) In the determination of his civil rights and obligations or of any criminal charge against him, everyone is entitled to a fair and public hearing within a reasonable time by an independent and impartial tribunal established by law ...

(2) Everyone charged with a criminal offence shall be presumed innocent until proved guilty according to law.

(3) Everyone charged with a criminal offence has the following minimum rights:

   (a) to be informed promptly, in a language which he understands and in detail, of the nature and cause of the accusation against him;

   (b) to have adequate time and facilities for the preparation of his defence;

   (c) to defend himself in person or through legal assistance of his own choosing or, if he has not sufficient means to pay for legal assistance, to be given it free when the interests of justice so require;

   (d) to examine or have examined witnesses against him and to obtain the attendance and examination of witnesses on his behalf under the same conditions as witnesses against him;

   (e) to have the free assistance of an interpreter if he cannot understand or speak the language used in court.

Article 7

No one shall be held guilty of any criminal offence on account of any act or omission which did not constitute a criminal offence under national or international law at the time when it was committed.

Article 8

Everyone has the right to respect of his private and family life, his home and his correspondence ...

Article 10

Everyone has the right to freedom of expression ...

Article 11

Everyone has the right to freedom of peaceful assembly ...

1.26 Even before the incorporation of the ECHR into domestic law (the HRA 1998 came into force in October 2000), the Court had an important influence. For example:

SW v United Kingdom; CR v United Kingdom **(1995)** Both applicants had been convicted of the rape/attempted rape of their wives before their marriages had been legally ended. They relied on Art 7, since at the time of their convictions it had been widely accepted that marital rape was not a crime (see *R* (1992) discussed at **1.23** and **10.9**).

ECtHR: held unanimously that the essentially debasing character of rape was so manifest that the results of the decisions of the CA and HL, that the applicants could be convicted of rape and attempted rape, could not be said to be at variance with the object and purpose of Art 7, namely to ensure that no one should be subject to arbitrary prosecution, conviction, or punishment. Furthermore, the abandonment of the unacceptable idea of a husband being immune against prosecution for the rape of his wife was in conformity with the fundamental objectives of the Convention, the very essence of which was respect for human dignity and human freedom.

Laskey, Jaggard and Brown v United Kingdom **(1997)** The applicants had been convicted of offences under the OAPA 1861 arising out of sado-masochistic acts (see **1.7**).

ECtHR: held unanimously that there had been no violation of Art 8.

> One of the roles which the state is unquestionably entitled to undertake is to seek to regulate, through the operation of the criminal law, activities which involve the infliction of physical harm. This is so whether the activities in question occur in the course of sexual conduct or otherwise. ... it is evident from the facts established by the national courts that the applicants' sado-masochistic activities involved a significant degree of injury or wounding which could not be characterised as trifling or transient ... the national authorities were entitled to consider that the prosecution and conviction of the applicants were necessary in a democratic society for the protection of health within the meaning of Art 8(2) of the Convention.

One judge, Judge Pettiti, wished to expand this first paragraph, by noting:

> ...to regulate and punish practices of sexual abuse that are demeaning even if they do not involve the infliction of physical harm.

The HRA 1998 resulted in a flood of litigation. However, its impact on substantive criminal law has been less marked than in the areas of evidence and procedure.

The European Union

1.27 Until recently, criminal lawyers tended to ignore the European Union, believing it to be concerned with economic and political matters only. But in reality, over the last 20 years, the EU has become increasingly interested in, and has involved itself in, criminal justice matters. Until the Treaty of Lisbon was ratified at the end of 2009, the EU could be represented by three pillars: the first pillar was the older European (Economic) Communities, but Title VI of the Treaty of European Union had developed the more recent 'third pillar', on 'Police and Judicial Cooperation in Criminal Matters', creating 'an area of freedom, security and justice'. There have been many framework decisions under this pillar, which leave to national Governments the detailed decisions on implementation. So far the impact of framework decisions has been more procedural than substantive, but there can be little doubt that with the post-Lisbon EU, more legislation will be driven by European as well as domestic political priorities (see Baker (2009)). An important question is whether the harmonization or approximation of the rules of criminal law throughout Europe is to be encouraged.

Reform and codification

1.28 Criminal law evolves slowly through the decisions of the courts. Key cases subtly shift the boundaries of the criminal law. Such change may be inadequate both because of its slow speed and because one has to wait for the 'accidents of history' which cause a relevant case to reach the higher courts. Imagine that the SC felt that the time had come to decide that women who have sex with men by deceit should be guilty of rape (at present, only men can commit rape as a principal offender): could the courts change the law? Not only would it be argued that such a fundamental change in the law could only be enacted by Parliament, but it would also be difficult (impossible?) to 'invent' a suitable case by which to change the law. We would need a woman to be prosecuted, so that an appeal could reach the higher courts. Perhaps the most interesting fact about *R* (1992) (see **1.23**) was that the husband was prosecuted in the first place, and that the jury convicted him, given that it was widely accepted at that time that the law did not penalize marital rape.

1.29 Law reform is no easy business. Choose a subject on which you have strong opinions: euthanasia, abortion, possession of cannabis: try and draw up a watertight proposal in the shape of a Bill that you would like to present to Parliament. A forerunner of the Law Commission was the Criminal Law Revision Committee (CLRC) set up in 1959, by the then Home Secretary, Lord Butler, 'to be a standing committee to examine such aspects of the criminal law of England and Wales as the Home Secretary may from time to time refer to the Committee, to consider whether the law requires revision and to make recommendations.' Its members gave their services voluntarily and part time and only dealt with topics specifically referred to them by the Home Secretary. When Lord Gardiner became Lord Chancellor in 1963, he took the post on condition that a Law Commission, a permanent body outside Government, be set up to keep the law up to date. The CLRC's Report on *Conspiracy to Defraud* (Cmnd 9873, 1986) was their final piece of work: they ceased to meet after that.

The Law Commission

1.30 The Law Commissions Act 1965, s 3(1) provides that the Law Commission was established to:

> … take and keep under review all the law … with a view to its systematic development and reform, including in particular the codification of such law, the elimination of anomalies, the repeal of obsolete and unnecessary enactments, the reduction of the number of separate enactments and generally the simplification and modernisation of the law.

1.31 There will be frequent references in this book to their reports and recommendations. Perhaps the most exciting project was the Draft Criminal Code (DCC), which was laid before Parliament in 1989. The Law Commission summarized the advantages of codification under the following heads:

   (i) the constitutional arguments for codification;

   (ii) accessibility and comprehensibility;

   (iii) consistency;

   (iv) certainty.

1.32 Although the DCC was not enacted, students may still find it useful to look at it. It was published in two volumes: the Code itself, plus a commentary. The Law Commission, and the small group of academic criminal lawyers who produced the first draft, tried to draw up a Code of what the law is rather than a Code of what the law should be. The task of reducing the principles of criminal law of England and Wales to one neat Bill was immense, and the Law Commission's frank comments on how they reached the definitions they did, provide a useful commentary on key issues in criminal law. The project had widespread support.

But Parliament's time is scarce and criminal law is politically controversial. The Government did not find the time (or the inclination?) to enact the DCC and so the Law Commission has since then produced a wealth of smaller Bills and recommendations dealing with parts of the criminal law, in the hope that Parliament may find the time to act on these less time-consuming Bills.

1.33 The normal practice for the Law Commission is to produce a Consultation Paper, to which interested people are encouraged to respond, and then a Report. Throughout this book there will be references to many of the more important papers and reports to emerge from the Law Commission since the 1989 DCC:

- Law Com No. 218 (1993) *Legislating the Criminal Code: Offences against the Person and General Principles*;

- Law Com Consultation Paper (LCCP) No. 131 (1993) *Assisting and Encouraging Crime*, eventually followed by Law Com Report No. 300 (2006) *Inchoate Liability for Assisting and Encouraging Crime*, which was enacted in the Serious Crime Act 2007 (see Chapter 7) and Report No. 305 (2007) *Participating in Crime*;

- LCCP No. 134 (1994) *Consent and Offences against the Person*;

- LCCP No. 139 (1995) *Consent in the Criminal Law*;

- Law Com No. 229 (1995) *Legislating the Criminal Code: Intoxication and Criminal Liability*;

- Law Com No. 237 (1996) *Legislating the Criminal Code: Involuntary Manslaughter*;

- LCCP No. 155 (1999) *Legislating the Criminal Code: Fraud and Deception* (followed by Law Com No. 276 (2002);

- Law Com No. 279 (2002) *Children: Their Non-Accidental Death or Serious Injury (Criminal Trials)—A Consultative Report*;

- LCCP No. 173 (2003) *Partial Defences to Murder* (followed by Law Com Report No. 290 (2004));

- LCCP No. 177 (2005) *A New Homicide Act for England and Wales?* (followed by Report No. 304 (2006) *Murder, Manslaughter and Infanticide*);

- LCCP No. 183 (2007) *Conspiracy and Attempts*;

- LCCP No. 185 (2007) *Reforming Bribery*, followed by Report No. 313 (2008) *Reforming Bribery*;

- Law Com No. 314 (2009) *Intoxication and Criminal Liability*;

- Law Com No. 318 (2009) *Conspiracy and Attempts*;

- LCCP No. 193 (2010) *Simplification of Criminal Law: Public Nuisance and Outraging Public Decency*;

- LCCP No. 195 (2010) *Criminal Liability in Regulatory Contexts*;

- LCCP No. 197 (2010) *Unfitness to Plead*;

- LCCP No. 200 (2011) *Simplification of Criminal Law: Kidnapping*.

In 2012, the Law Commission published a 'scoping paper' on insanity seeking to discover whether the current law causes problems in practice. Then in 2013 they published a 'discussion paper' on both insanity and automatism, which set out provisional proposals for reform of both defences, based on lack of capacity (but curiously stated that they did not invite responses). Students with enough time will find it useful to read these reports (and to respond to consultations): they include summaries of current difficulties and dilemmas. But in recent years, the Government has had little appetite for tidying up and improving the general principles of the criminal law, preferring to concentrate on procedural and sentencing matters. Important statutes such as the SOA 2003 and the Fraud Act 2006 have created complex novelties, but we are still a long way from having a Criminal Code.

1.34 This is in stark contrast with most other countries which have their criminal law in statutory or codified form. A Code may mean a coherent re-statement of a body of law or merely a compilation or collection of existing laws. In France, there has been a Code Pénal since 1810, though a new one, passed in 1992, came into force in 1994. Indeed, most European countries have a criminal/penal code: the penal codes of Denmark, Finland, France, Germany, Greece, Italy, Norway, Sweden, and Turkey are all discussed in Law Com No. 139. Students should keep an eye on developments within the European Union (see **1.27**).

1.35 Nowadays even most English-speaking (i.e. common law) countries have a codified system of criminal law, at least to the extent that there is a basic criminal statute. The first common law code to be enacted was Macaulay's Indian Penal Code produced in 1837 and enacted in 1860. In the USA, each state has its own criminal law, often much influenced by the American Law Institute's Model Criminal Code produced in 1985. Despite valiant attempts by the Law Commission, there is still little sign of a criminal code reaching the statute book in England and Wales. Many chapters in this book will re-echo this author's wish to see the Government act.

FURTHER READING

Ashworth, A., 'Is the Criminal Law a Lost Cause?' (2000) 116 LQR 225.

Ashworth, A., *Sentencing and Criminal Justice* (5th edn, 2010).

Ashworth, A. and Horder, J, *Principles of Criminal Law* (7th edn, 2013).

Ashworth, A. and Redmayne, M., *The Criminal Process* (4th edn, 2010).

Baker, E., 'The European Union's "Area of Freedom, Security and (Criminal) Justice" Ten Years On' [2009] Crim LR 833.

Devlin, P., *The Enforcement of Morals* (1965).

Devlin, P., 'The Conscience of the Jury' (1991) 107 LQR 398.

Glazebrook, P., 'Should We Have a Law of Attempted Crime?' (1969) 85 LQR 27.

Hart, H. L. A., *Law Liberty and Morality* (1963).

Houlder, J., 'The Importance of Preserving the Jury System' [1997] Crim LR 875.

Jackson, J. and Doran, S., *Judge without Jury: Diplock Trials in the Adversary System* (1995).

Padfield, N., *The Criminal Justice Process: Text and Materials* (4th edn, 2008).

von Hirsch, A. and Jareborg, N., 'Gauging Criminal Harms: A Living Standard Analysis' (1991) 11 OJLS 1.

SELF TEST QUESTIONS

1   What (if any) are the general principles underpinning the criminal law?

2   Can you explain the relationship between criminal law and morals? Is there any identifiable shared morality nowadays?

3   Why do you think that criminal law is usually studied independently of sentencing or of criminal procedure and evidence?

4   Is it the role of the Court of Appeal to re-think the jury's decision? If not, what is the function of an appellate court?

5   Consider the arguments for, and against, codification of the criminal law.

2 The conduct element of a crime

SUMMARY

Most crimes require a criminal 'act': what is a *voluntary* act (cf. automatism at 2.3 and 4.18)?

Acts and omissions. Why is a person generally not liable for her failure to act? Note carefully the exceptions to this general rule, particularly the cases where the courts recognize a *duty* to act (e.g. *Evans* (2009)).

A person may cause a consequence which was perhaps unintended and unforeseen. Both factual causation (*but for* causation) and legal (or imputable) causation must be proved. An important HL case: *Kennedy (No. 2)* (2007).

Not all offences require an act: the existence of a *state of affairs* may be sufficient to impose liability. Are such offences drafted too widely?

Actus reus and *mens rea*

2.1 It has been conventional to divide crimes into two elements: *actus reus* (Latin for guilty act) and *mens rea* (guilty mind), and any crime can be chopped into these elements. For example, murder is the intentional killing of a human being. The *actus reus* of murder is the killing and the *mens rea* is the intention. However, these ambiguous Latin terms may lead to confusion since the *actus reus* or guilty act may include:

    (i) a voluntary act, or omission, or a state of affairs;

    (ii) as well as particular consequences; and/or

    (iii) particular circumstances.

2.2 Thus murder is a crime which requires that D does an act which causes death (the prescribed *consequence*). Another example: A person is not guilty of having sex with a girl under 16 unless P proves the *circumstance* of the offence that she was indeed under 16. The problem of distinguishing the *actus reus* of a crime is discussed further in Chapter 5, which looks at the difficulty of distinguishing the offence (*actus reus*) elements of a crime from its defence elements. It is worth wondering for a moment why we group the circumstances and consequence requirements of an offence under the one label '*actus reus*'. Robinson (1993), for example, pointed out that by grouping them (as well as the supporting doctrines of causation, voluntary act, omission, and possession) under the same heading, we gain no special insight into a characteristic or function that the various doctrines may share. However, having acknowledged the limitations of the labels, this book will continue to use terms which most commentators have adopted as convenient shorthand. Different commentators will define and categorize crimes differently, but the student should be able to distinguish different sorts of criminal conduct:

- act or conduct crimes (those crimes which need no consequence, but are complete as soon as D does a certain act), e.g. wounding; rape;

- consequence or result crimes (the conduct must bring about a proscribed consequence), e.g. murder; criminal damage;

- situational crimes (where neither an act nor a consequence is necessary), e.g. possessing illegal drugs.

Voluntary acts

2.3 D's act must be conscious and voluntary. Chapter 4 considers the defences of insanity and automatism. D may argue that he is not guilty of a crime because his mind was not in control of his actions. From D's point of view, it is better to treat questions of automatism as relevant to the *actus reus*, not *mens rea*: if it is treated as a question of *mens rea*, then D's recklessness or negligence may negate any possible argument based on automatism. The same will not be true if automatism is seen as a way of proving that an essential part of the *actus reus* is missing. Defining a voluntary act is no easy business:

Broome v Perkins (1986) D, a diabetic, drove home for five miles very erratically in a hypoglycaemic state. There was evidence that he may not have known what he was doing. Magistrates dismissed a charge of driving without due care and attention against him on the grounds of automatism.

DC (Glidewell LJ): remitted the case to the magistrates with the direction to convict. Since D was exercising some control over his bodily movements, his actions were not 'automatic' and 'involuntary'. D had to adduce evidence that his mind was not controlling his limbs (i.e. of no control) before he could be acquitted.

***Antoine* (2000)** This was a case where D was charged with murder and it was argued that he was unfit to plead (see **4.6**).

HL: Lord Hutton (who gave the only speech) acknowledged the difficulties in this area:

> A number of learned authors have commented that it is difficult in some cases to distinguish precisely between the *actus reus* and the *mens rea* and that the *actus reus* can include a mental element. In Smith & Hogan, *Criminal Law*, 9th edn, p. 28, Professor Sir John Smith QC stated:
>
> > It is not always possible to separate *actus reus* from *mens rea*. Sometimes a word which describes the *actus reus*, or part of it, implies a mental element.

In his speech in *DPP for Northern Ireland v Lynch* [1975] AC 653 Lord Simon recognized the difficulties arising from what he termed 'the chaotic terminology' relating to the mental element in crime. Nevertheless, he recognized that *actus reus* and *mens rea* are useful terms and said, at p. 690:

> Both terms have, however, justified themselves by their usefulness; and I shall myself employ them in their traditional senses—namely, *actus reus* to mean such conduct as constitutes a crime if the mental element involved in the definition of the crime is also present (or, more shortly, conduct prohibited by law); and *mens rea* to mean such mental element, over and above volition, as is involved in the definition of the crime.

2.4 When the Law Commission were drawing up the DCC in 1989 (see **1.31**), they were concerned to find a formula which would lead to the acquittal of someone such as the D in *Broome v Perkins* (subject to the question of prior fault).

Clause 33(1), therefore, provided that:

A person is not guilty of an offence if—

(a) he acts in a state of automatism, that is, his act—

    (i) is a reflex, spasm or convulsion; or

    (ii) occurs while he is in a condition (whether of sleep, unconsciousness, impaired consciousness or otherwise) depriving him of effective control of his act; and

(b) the act or condition is the result neither of anything done or omitted with the fault required for the offence nor of voluntary intoxication.

The DCC test appears to be more 'lenient' than that of *Broome v Perkins*, under which D must be convicted if he shows some control over his actions. The DCC definition would lead to his acquittal if he did not have effective control over his actions. Would this allow the court to acquit him if they judged him not to need punishment?

Liability for omissions

2.5 The person who commits a crime by a failure to act may be as culpable as the person who deliberately acts. Yet English law has traditionally been reluctant to impose liability for omissions because of a fear that this would throw too wide the net of the criminal law. As Lord Diplock said in *Miller* (1983), referring to the parable in the Bible of the men who passed by on the other side of the road when they saw a man who had been left half-dead by robbers:

> The conduct of the parabolic priest and Levite on the road to Jericho may indeed have been deplorable but English law has not so far developed to the stage of treating it as criminal.

In **2.10** we will consider whether a bolder approach to liability should be applied, but first let's examine the situations in which D may (or may not) be guilty simply for a failure to act.

2.6 Crimes cannot be committed by omission if the statute creating the offence requires action:

> **Ahmad (1986)** A landlord made major structural alterations to a flat but then took no steps to complete them. He was convicted under the Protection from Eviction Act 1977 of 'doing acts calculated to interfere with [V's] peace and comfort'.
>
> CA: D's conviction was quashed since he had not done 'acts' merely by failing to finish the alterations and so leaving the premises uninhabitable.

Other statutes, on the other hand, make clear that the person will be guilty if he or she 'causes' a consequence to happen whether by act or omission. Thus, the Water Resources Act 1991, s 85(1) provides that:

> ...a person contravenes this section if he causes or knowingly permits any poisonous, noxious or polluting matter or any solid waste matter to enter any controlled waters.

The DCC deliberately defines homicide offences in terms of 'causing death', rather than 'killing', and specifies that under the Code such results may be caused by omission (see **8.7**).

2.7 With common law offences, the position is particularly difficult. Although the basic rule is that D is not generally liable for a failure to act, there are a number of ways of avoiding this limitation. One way is to describe a series of acts and events as one continuous act:

Fagan v Metropolitan Police Commissioner **(1969)** D stopped his car accidentally on a policeman's foot, but then refused to move it for several minutes. He was convicted of assaulting the police officer in the execution of his duty.

DC: upheld his conviction. D's conduct in driving the car on to the foot and leaving it there should be viewed as a continuous act: once he developed a guilty mind, the crime was committed. Note the dissenting judgment of Bridge J, who argued that D had done no act after driving on to the foot which could constitute an assault: allowing the wheel to remain on the foot was merely an omission for which there was no liability.

2.8 This case illustrates the principle that the *actus reus* and *mens rea* should be contemporaneous. In *Fagan*, D developed the guilty mind after he had done the culpable act. The problem may also arise where D no longer has the guilty mind when he does the relevant act:

Meli v R **(1954)** D beat up V in a hut, and then threw him over a cliff, believing him to be dead. Medical evidence showed that V died from exposure at the bottom of the cliff and not from the beating. D therefore argued that his act of causing death (throwing V over the cliff) was not accompanied by *mens rea*.

Privy Council (PC): upholding the conviction, the whole matter was one transaction which should be regarded as a single course of conduct.

Le Brun **(1992)** D hit his wife, V, on the jaw. She fell, unconscious. Attempting to carry her home, he dropped her and she died of a fractured skull caused when her head hit the pavement.

CA (Lord Lane CJ): dismissed his appeal from his conviction for manslaughter: 'The act which causes death and the necessary mental state to constitute manslaughter need not coincide in point of time.'

Duty to act

2.9 It is more common (and perhaps more appropriate) to justify liability for an omission by proving that D was under a duty to act. Such duties arise in the five different ways now detailed in this paragraph:

(i) A person who creates a dangerous situation may be under a duty to act to remove the danger:

Miller (1983) D fell asleep holding a lit cigarette. He was awoken by a small fire and merely moved to a different room without attempting to put out the fire.

HL: upheld his conviction for arson. Lord Diplock's main speech is worth studying. He deprecates the use of the expression *actus reus* and compares the different academic analyses which explain liability in these circumstances. Whilst he prefers J. C. Smith's 'duty theory' to Glanville Williams' 'adoption of the continuing act' theory, he suggests the term 'responsibility theory' as it may be easier to explain to a jury.

Few would disagree with the conclusion of this case, though Ashworth does ask whether it is objectionable on grounds of retroactivity and lack of warning (see PCL, p. 99, and **1.5**).

DPP v Santa-Bermudez (2003) The DPP appealed (by way of case stated) against a decision of the CC allowing an appeal against a conviction by the MC for an offence of assault occasioning actual bodily harm. V, a police officer, had approached D, who seemed to be a ticket tout, at an underground station. V told D that she intended to conduct a full body search. On request, D emptied his pockets of one or more syringes. V also asked him to pull out the linings of his jacket pockets, which he did with the exception of two small breast pockets that could not be pulled out. Asked whether he possessed any needles or sharps, he said he did not. V started her search, put her fingers into one of the breast pockets, and was pierced by a hypodermic needle. D removed another needle from a pocket in his trousers, shrugged his shoulders and smirked. The CC allowed D's appeal, concluding that this did not disclose a positive act by D and that an omission to act did not in law amount to an assault.

High Court (HC): allowed the DPP's appeal. Following *Miller*, where someone, by act or word or a combination of the two, created a danger and thereby exposed another to a reasonably foreseeable risk of injury that materialized, there was an evidential basis for the *actus reus* of an assault occasioning actual bodily harm, although it remained necessary for P to prove an intention or recklessness to assault. If D, by giving V a dishonest assurance about the contents of his pockets, had thereby exposed her to a reasonably foreseeable risk of injury that materialized, it was wrong for the court to conclude there was no basis for the *actus reus* of assault occasioning actual bodily harm.

Evans **(2009)** D had bought heroin and gave some to V, her 16-year-old half-sister, who later self-administered the drug. D noticed that V looked as if she had taken an overdose and decided to spend the night with her. D and her mother, D2, did not call for medical assistance, as D feared she would get into trouble. When D woke, V was dead. D (and her mother) were convicted of manslaughter by gross negligence. (D was sentenced to four years' imprisonment; her mother to two years. They did not appeal their sentences.)

CA (five judges, led by Lord Judge CJ): dismissed the appeal. D's criminal liability, if any, depended on manslaughter by gross negligence. Her involvement in the supply to her sister of the fatal dose of heroin could not found a conviction for manslaughter on the basis of her unlawful and criminal act (see *Kennedy (No. 2)* (2007, at **2.22** and **8.23**). The question of whether a duty of care existed was a question of law for the judge, not the jury.

> In our judgment, consistently with *Adomako* [1995, see **8.29**] and the link between civil and criminal liability for negligence, for the purposes of gross negligence manslaughter, when a person has created or contributed to the creation of a state of affairs which he knows, or ought reasonably to know, has become life threatening, a consequent duty on him to act by taking reasonable steps to save the other's life will normally arise (para. 31).

This case clearly takes the principle in *Miller* a stage further: D may be guilty not only if she has created a dangerous situation, but also if she has simply contributed to that dangerous situation. Is the 'reasonable foreseeability' test of *Santa-Bermudez* more appropriate?

(ii) A duty may arise from a special relationship, such as that of parent/child (which would explain why Evans' mother did not appeal (see (i), earlier)) or doctor/patient.

(iii) If D voluntarily undertakes a duty, then a failure to undertake that duty may result in liability.

Gibbins and Proctor **(1918)** V's father and his mistress starved him to death.

Court of Criminal Appeal (CCA): upheld their convictions for murder.

Stone and Dobinson **(1977)** Ds, a man and his mistress, made little attempt to seek medical attention for V, his sister, who died whilst a lodger in their care.

CA (Geoffrey Lane LJ): upheld their convictions for manslaughter. The jury were entitled to find that the duty to care had been assumed and, once V became helplessly infirm, they had a duty either to summon help or to care for her themselves.

If you want a wonderful critique of this decision, read Bibbings LJ's powerful (if apocryphal!) dissent: she is deeply sympathetic to the efforts made by John (Stone) and Gwendoline (Dobinson) in caring for a difficult relation, and is very critical of the failure of the state (and others) to support them (see Hunter et al (2010) in the Further Reading section).

   (iv) If a duty to act is created by statute, then failure to fulfil that duty will result in criminal liability. Thus a positive duty is imposed by the Children and Young Persons Act (CYPA) 1933, s 1, on parents and those who are legally responsible for children to provide food, clothing, medical aid, and lodging for their children, creating the offence of wilful neglect.

   (v) A contract with a third party may give rise to a general duty to act.

Pittwood **(1902)** A railway crossing guard opened the gates to let a vehicle through, but then forgot to shut them again. V, a man in a cart, was hit and killed by a later train.

Taunton Assizes (Wright J): there was clearly misfeasance since D directly contributed to the accident. A man may incur criminal liability from a duty arising out of a contract.

However, although this case is often quoted as illustrating contractual liability resulting in criminal liability for omissions, it could just as well be seen as an example of (i) (see earlier).

2.10 Distinguishing between an act and an omission can itself be difficult. Medical treatment is a good example: when a doctor turns off a life support machine he would appear to do an act which causes death, whereas if he doesn't replace an empty drip bag he merely omits to do something. Smith and Hogan, having asked whether the ending of a programme of dialysis is an omission, while switching off a ventilator is an act, conclude that 'it seems offensive if liability for homicide depends on distinctions of this kind; but it appears to be so' (at p. 49).

Airedale NHS Trust v Bland **(1993)** A patient had been in a persistent vegetative state (PVS) for more than two years, and his parents supported the hospital in its application to be allowed to turn off his life support machine.

HL: unanimously held that if the doctors did so in this case, they would not be criminally liable. Students might like to read Hoffmann LJ's judgment in the CA (he was the only judge to explore the moral issues in depth). The HL agreed that doctors were not

obliged to continue care and treatment where it was no longer in the patient's best
interests, accepting that nasal feeding was treatment. Indeed, three of the five Law
Lords called for parliamentary intervention in this area, but still none has yet been
forthcoming (see Helme and Padfield (1993) and the final report of the Commission
on Assisted Dying (2012) for further discussion of this difficult topic).

The HL's reasoning is not entirely convincing. Not only is the distinction between
causing death and allowing someone to die dubious (see *Re B* (1981) and *Re J* (1991));
the case does not explore the question of intent adequately. It might be more helpful if the courts were prepared to hold that a doctor in these circumstances has ful-
filled her duties, and that there is therefore no *actus reus* on which to base liability.

2.11 Is it time to widen liability for omissions? Ashworth (see (1989) 105 LQR 424) suggested that the law should move towards a 'social responsibility' view of criminal
liability, recognizing certain duties of citizenship and equally recognizing the
limits on what it is fair to ask of citizens. Thus he suggests that it is appropriate to
penalize those who fail to take steps towards law enforcement or who fail to assist
those in sudden peril. Glanville Williams responded (see (1991) 107 LQR 86) by
defending individualism. He believed that there is a moral distinction between
killing and letting die which the law should recognize. Later we shall see (at **11.41**)
that people can be deceived by silence—is this a form of liability by an omission?

Firth **(1989)**   D, a consultant obstetrician, omitted to inform his hospital that he had
been treating private patients at his NHS hospital and had therefore avoided being
billed for NHS beds and facilities.

CA (Lord Lane CJ): upheld his conviction for an offence under the Theft Act (TA) 1978,
s 2(1)(c). If it was incumbent upon him to give the information to the hospital and he
deliberately refrained from doing so, with the result that no charge was levied either
upon the patients or upon himself, the wording of the section is satisfied. 'It mattered
not whether it was an act of commission or omission.'

Causation

2.12 Many crimes require a certain consequence to have been caused by the criminal
act. Thus, in murder or manslaughter, the act must cause death. For how remote
a consequence of my act should I be held responsible? The rules have become
relatively clear in homicide offences, and can be applied generally throughout the
criminal law where *mens rea* is required. We will see later that some crimes do
not require *mens rea*. These 'strict liability' offences (see **3.38**) may deal differently

with the question of causation. This becomes particularly obvious in Chapter 13 which explores environmental offences.

2.13 First, factual causation must be established: it must be proved that the death would not have resulted 'but for' the accused's conduct.

White **(1910)** D was indicted for the murder of his mother having put cyanide in her drink intending to kill her. Medical evidence showed that she had died of heart failure before drinking the poisoned drink and he was convicted of attempted murder.

CA: dismissed his appeal (and upheld his sentence of penal servitude for life).

The case is a useful example of 'but for' causation: the cyanide did not kill her and so even though he intended to kill her, and she died, he could not be guilty of murder.

2.14 In manslaughter cases (see **8.22**) questions of factual causation are often swallowed up within a discussion of dangerousness. As we shall see, D is guilty of constructive manslaughter if he intentionally does an unlawful and dangerous act which causes death. It must be dangerous in the sense that all sober and reasonable people would realize that the act would subject the victim to the risk of harm. The question is often how much knowledge of the circumstances should be attributed to this fictional bystander: contrast these cases:

Dawson **(1985)** Three Ds wearing masks, one carrying a replica gun and another carrying a pickaxe handle, attempted to rob a petrol station. They fled when the attendant, V, pushed an alarm, but V later died of a heart attack.

CA (Watson LJ): quashed their convictions for manslaughter. A key element in the decision was the fact that it was not suggested that any of the Ds knew that V had a weak heart. (All three were also convicted of offences of robbery and attempted robbery and their sentences of seven-and-a-half to nine-and-a-half years' imprisonment were upheld.)

Watson **(1989)** Ds burgled the house of a man aged 87, who died of a heart attack 90 minutes later.

CA: upheld their conviction for manslaughter. Ds knew of the old man's frailty, even though they only discovered it once they had broken in.

Bristow **(2013)** D was one of a group of at least six men who burgled V's business, which was situated along a secluded track. V was run over and killed by one of the two vehicles used by the burglars when leaving the burglary.

CA: upheld D's conviction for manslaughter. This was not a case like *Dawson* or *Watson* 'where the circumstances demonstrating the risk of harm to the occupier of property did not arise until a point during the burglary or at all' (Treacy LJ at para. 34). Whilst burglary of itself is not a dangerous crime, a particular burglary may be dangerous because of the circumstances surrounding its commission. Features of this case were capable of making this burglary dangerous, when coupled with foresight of the risk of intervention to prevent escape. (An odd aspect of this case is that the CA seems to have accepted that all the burglars were secondary parties. The jury should have been directed that someone committed the killing as a principal, even if they could not be sure who: see Chapter 6.)

Legal (or imputable) causation

2.15 This 'but for' test often does not appear to be enough on its own, since it can lead to the conviction of the morally innocent: A invites B to her house and B is murdered on the way. Clearly A is not guilty of murder. The obvious reason is that she has no guilty mind or guilty intent. But the law seems to go further and seems to suggest that A has not even 'caused' B's death. There are several additions to the 'but for' test, often referred to as questions of legal, or as Glanville Williams would prefer, 'imputable' causation (see *Textbook on Criminal Law* (TCL), p. 381). As you read the following paragraphs, ask yourself why it is that causation is not established independently of culpability.

2.16 D must have performed a culpable act. Thus, in a 'result crime', the culpable act must have caused the result and, in a 'conduct crime', the culpable act must be the culpable element in the conduct.

Dalloway **(1847)** V, a child, ran in front of D's cart and was killed. D was not holding the reins, but had left them lying loosely on the horse's back. D was acquitted after Earle J had summed up to the jury that if they thought that he could not have saved the child by pulling the reins, they must acquit him: i.e. he was only guilty if his neglect in not holding the reins had been the cause of death. The presence of the cart caused the child's death, and not the negligent driving. There was no causal connection: the child would have been killed even if he had been driving carefully.

2.17 D's act must be more than a minimal cause of the result.

Cato **(1976)** D injected V with a heroin compound at her request. V died.

CA: upheld D's conviction for manslaughter. Lord Widgery CJ: 'As a matter of law, it was sufficient if the prosecution could establish that it was a cause, provided it was a

> cause outside the *de minimis* range, and effectively bearing upon the acceleration of
> the moment of the victim's death.'

Ashworth points out that the court in *Cato* may have been using causal arguments
to circumscribe the law of manslaughter: 'if the offence charged had been a crime
of intention in which D's intention had been proved, the court would probably
have taken a broader view' (PCL, p. 125). What is *de minimis*? In *Hennigan* (1971)
the CA held that the trial judge was wrong to direct the jury that D was not guilty
if he was less than one-fifth to blame.

> **Dyson (1908)** D's child, V, died of injuries he received from D more than a year
> before his death. V was dying of meningitis and would have died within a short time
> despite his injuries.
>
> CA: quashed D's conviction for manslaughter since V had not died within a year and
> a day of his injuries (this is no longer the law: see **8.4**). The fact that V's death was an
> imminent event was not the reason for quashing the conviction: D's act had acceler-
> ated death.

2.18 In clause 17(1), the DCC puts the test this way:

> … a person causes a result which is an element of an offence when—
>
> (a) he does an act which makes a more than negligible contribution to its
> occurrence; or
>
> (b) he omits to do an act which might prevent its occurrence and which he is
> under a duty to do according to the law relating to the offence.

Glanville Williams (1989) argued that this definition fails because it 'does not
give even the barest indication that a question of moral responsibility or justice
is involved' (at p. 397). For him, clause 17(a) is open to the criticism that it fails to
distinguish between factual and imputable causation. He preferred to redraft the
clause in the following way:

> (1) Subject to the other provisions of this section, a person causes a result
> which is an element of an offence when he does an act which
>
> (a) in fact causes or contributes to its occurrence, and
>
> (b) is not too remote, too trivial or too accidental to have a just bearing
> on the doer's liability or on the gravity of his offence.

To those who object to the word 'just' in this definition, he responds that it makes
clear that a question of justice is involved, which enables the tribunal to exercise a
degree of discretion. Do you agree?

2.19   These rules of imputable or legal causation have developed because of a reluctance to convict of a crime (often a homicide in the case law) someone who is not considered adequately blameworthy. Thus Glanville Williams writes:

> …when one has settled the question of but-for causation, the further test to be applied to the but-for cause in order to qualify it for legal recognition is not a test of causation but a moral reaction. The question is whether the result can fairly be said to be imputable to the defendant… If the term cause must be used, it can best be distinguished in this meaning as the 'imputable' or 'responsible' or 'blameable' cause, to indicate the value-judgment involved (TCL, p. 381).

Why should a value judgment be involved? As Norrie (1991) points out, causation can only be explained by taking into account the social context within which people act. But is this necessarily the case? If policy considerations are to affect criminal liability, they could as well be reserved for the *mens rea* element. Glanville Williams poses the troubling example of tobacco companies: can they be prosecuted for manslaughter in causing the death of smokers? His answer is clear: no, they do not 'cause' death. But even in manslaughter, liability does not necessarily follow just because causation is established: some kind of *mens rea* has to be proved, involving perhaps the running of an unjustifiable risk (see **8.25**). Largely for autonomy reasons perhaps, English law appears to say that the risks taken by tobacco companies are justifiable. But these policy questions could be dealt with as part of the *mens rea* of the offence, and need not necessarily be treated as questions of causation. To return to the example given earlier of A and B, A did not intend to kill, nor was it virtually certain that B would be killed when A invited her to visit her house. What is the problem with accepting that A's invitation was one of the causes of B's death? Commenting on the interaction of causation and culpability, Ashworth talks of 'the puissance of culpability over causation' (PCL, p. 125). Certainly, questions of culpability dominate even questions of causation: we will discuss the SC's decision in *Gnango* (2011) at **6.4**. The decision can be criticized not only for failing to distinguish the liability of perpetrators from that of accomplices: all but the dissenting judge fail to take the question of causation seriously.

Novus actus interveniens

2.20   Examples of a *novus actus interveniens* (a new intervening act) which absolves D of liability include:

(i) Naturally occurring unpredictable events

Allen (in his *Textbook on Criminal Law*, 9th edn, at p. 43) provides the example of D rendering V unconscious and leaving him in a building which then collapses in an earthquake. In this case, D will not be held to have caused V's death. (He points out that if D, on the other hand, leaves V unconscious on the beach with an incoming tide, he may be liable.)

(ii) Outrageously incompetent medical treatment

Jordan (1956) D stabbed V who died eight days later in hospital when the wound had largely healed but after V had been wrongly injected with a drug and a large quantity of liquid which caused his death.

CCA: D's conviction for manslaughter was quashed since the medical treatment was 'palpably wrong'.

Cheshire (1991) D shot V in the thigh and stomach whilst they were arguing in a fish and chip shop. V died not of the wounds, but of a tracheotomy performed whilst he was in hospital to help him breathe.

CA: upheld his conviction for murder. Even though negligence in the treatment of the victim was the immediate cause of his death, the jury should not regard it as excluding the responsibility of the accused unless the negligent treatment was so independent of his acts, and in itself so potent in causing death, that they regard the contribution made by his acts as insignificant (per Beldam LJ).

How does one reconcile these two cases? There is a clear hint in *Cheshire* that Ds should not avoid liability for the consequences of their acts just because of the actions of doctors. Why is this? In an appropriate case, D could in any event be found guilty of attempted murder (see **8.3**) or of wounding (see **9.8**).

(iii) Acts of the victim

Sometimes V's own act may be said to break the chain of causation. However, it is more common for the courts to hold that D 'must take his victim as he finds him', and apply the 'thin skull rule'. Thus even if there is something unusual about V's physical or emotional make-up such that the consequence is much more serious than D could have foreseen, he may still be liable:

Holland (1841) V refused to have his finger amputated after he had been wounded by D, despite a surgeon's advice that this was the best form of treatment. He died of lockjaw (tetanus).

King's Bench Division (KBD): convicted D of murder.

Blaue **(1975)** D stabbed a Jehovah's Witness, who refused a blood transfusion and died.

CA: upheld D's conviction for manslaughter. Lawton LJ:

> It has long been the policy of the law that those who use violence on other people must take their victims as they find them. This in our judgment means the whole man, not just the physical man. It does not lie in the mouth of the assailant to say that his victim's religious beliefs which inhibited him from accepting certain kinds of treatment were unreasonable. The question for decision is what caused her death. The answer is the stab wound. The fact that the victim refused to stop this end coming about did not break the causal connection between the act and the death.

Williams **(1992)** V, a hitch-hiker, having been threatened by Ds, jumped out of their car and died of his injuries.

CA (Stuart-Smith LJ): quashed D's conviction for manslaughter. D was guilty if V's attempted escape was proportionate to the threat, that is to say, that it was within the ambit of reasonableness and not so daft as to make it his own voluntary act which amounted to a *novus actus interveniens*. In judging whether V acted reasonably, the jury should take into account 'any particular characteristic of the victim and the fact that in the agony of the moment he may act without thought and deliberation'. (See also *Dear* (1996), where the CA dismissed an appeal against conviction for murder where V had refused all offers of assistance after he was stabbed.)

2.21 A number of recent cases have concerned a drug addict helping another, who then dies:

Dias **(2001)** D prepared a syringe of heroin and passed it to V, who injected himself and died as a result.

CA: quashed D's conviction for manslaughter. Self-injection was not an unlawful act. The jury should have been asked to decide whether they were satisfied that the chain of causation was not broken between the unlawful act and the death:

> Assistance and encouragement is not to be automatically equated with causation. Causation raises questions of fact and degree. The recipient does not have to inject the drug which he is encouraged to take. He has a choice. It may be that in some circumstances the causative chain will still remain. That is a matter for the jury to decide (per Keene LJ).

Rogers **(2003)** D held a tourniquet on the arm of V, a drug abuser, while V injected himself with heroin. V subsequently died. After the judge ruled that there was no defence to the charges, D pleaded guilty to manslaughter and to administering poison so as to endanger life, contrary to the OAPA 1861, s 23 (see **9.31**).

CA: dismissed D's appeal. By applying and holding the tourniquet, D had played a part in the mechanics of the injection which caused death and since he had committed the *actus reus*, he could have no defence to either offence. Although self-injection was not an unlawful act, it was artificial and unreal to separate the application of the tourniquet from the injection which caused death. Accordingly, it was immaterial whether the deceased was committing a criminal offence in injecting himself once it had been established that D was a participant in the giving of an injection which caused death.

2.22 The CCRC (see **1.14**) therefore referred the 1999 case of *Kennedy* back to the CA, which once again dismissed the appeal, but in the HL, D was successful:

Kennedy (No. 2) (CA, 2005; HL, 2007) D prepared a syringe of heroin and gave it to V ready for injection. V died as a result of injecting himself with heroin, and D was convicted of constructive (unlawful act) manslaughter.

CA: dismissed the further appeal, but certified the following point of law of general public importance:

> When is it appropriate to find someone guilty of manslaughter where that person has been involved in the supply of a class A controlled drug, which is then freely and voluntarily self administered by the person to whom it was supplied, and the administration of the drug then causes his death?

HL: allowed the appeal, answering the certified question 'In the case of a fully-informed and responsible adult, never'. As Lord Bingham said:

> The finding that the deceased freely and voluntarily administered the injection to himself, knowing what it was, is fatal to any contention that the appellant caused the heroin to be administered to the deceased or taken by him ... The appellant supplied the heroin and prepared the syringe. But the deceased had a choice whether to inject himself or not. He chose to do so, knowing what he was doing. It was his act (paras 18–19).

Lord Bingham also explored the approach the courts have taken to causation in environmental crimes, which had been explicitly rejected by the CA:

> Questions of causation frequently arise in many areas of the law, but causation is not a single, unvarying concept to be mechanically applied without regard to the context in which the question arises. That was the point which Lord Hoffmann, with the express concurrence of three other members of the House, was at pains to make in Environment Agency (formerly National Rivers Authority) v Empress Car Co

(Abertillery) Ltd (1999). The House was not in that decision purporting to lay down general rules governing causation in criminal law. It was construing, with reference to the facts of the case before it, a statutory provision imposing strict criminal liability on those who cause pollution of controlled waters. Lord Hoffmann made clear that (p. 29E–F) common sense answers to questions of causation will differ according to the purpose for which the question is asked; that (p. 31E) one cannot give a common sense answer to a question of causation for the purpose of attributing responsibility under some rule without knowing the purpose and scope of the rule; that (p. 32B) strict liability was imposed in the interests of protecting controlled waters; and that (p. 36A) in the situation under consideration the act of the defendant could properly be held to have caused the pollution even though an ordinary act of a third party was the immediate cause of the diesel oil flowing into the river. It is worth underlining that the relevant question was the cause of the pollution, not the cause of the third party's act (at para. 15).

2.23 The courts seem to take a different attitude to causation in crimes of strict liability (see **3.38**). Thus, in pollution cases, the courts have treated the word 'causing' in a much more straightforward way, perhaps because the courts are less interested in these cases with questions of blameworthiness than with the idea of making the polluter pay:

Alphacell Ltd v Woodward (1972) Pumps in a settling tank became blocked and the tank overflowed, allowing polluted water to escape into a stream. D, the company which operated the settling tanks, was convicted of causing polluting matter to enter a stream.

HL: upheld the conviction.

> I consider…that what or who has caused a certain event to occur is essentially a practical question of fact which can best be answered by ordinary common sense rather than abstract metaphysical theory (per Lord Salmon).

The HL's 'common sense' approach involved deciding whether someone 'causes' something when they do nothing. See also:

National Rivers Authority v Yorkshire Water Services Ltd (1994) D owned and operated sewage works, which operated largely by gravity: from the settlement tanks, sewage flowed through filter beds and settlement tanks until it was eventually discharged into a river. D had permission to discharge sewage in accordance with certain conditions. They in turn granted consent to their industrial customers to discharge effluent into the sewers. These conditions excluded the discharge of iso-octonal, which is very dangerous to river life. An unauthorized and undiscovered person made a large discharge of iso-octonal into the sewer. D was convicted by the magistrates of causing pollution; their appeal was allowed by the CC, which held that as a matter of law the water authority did not cause the iso-octonal to enter controlled waters.

DC (Buckley J): reversed decision of the CC, applying the 'common sense approach of the HL in *Alphacell*'.

HL (Lord Mackay): allowed D's appeal, since D had a due diligence defence under s 108(7) of the Act.

The case provides an excellent example of conflicting policy interests: the DC's judgment, whilst disappointing for those who care primarily for environmental control, had put an extraordinary burden on industry. The appeal in the DC turned on whether causation was a question of law or fact. Buckley J, applying *Brutus v Cozens* (1973, see **12.18**) held: 'I am satisfied that once the facts have been established, whether any party may be said to have "caused" a certain result is itself a factual conclusion for the tribunal.' Despite the fact that, as Buckley J pointed out, 'Yorkshire Water could not reasonably be expected to prevent the discharge of isooctonal into the sewer or indeed into the works', he concluded that the question of causation should simply be left to the jury or magistrates, allowing them to use their 'common sense'. But the decision of the HL may be hardly less satisfactory: many of the key questions were left unexplored. The Lord Chancellor held that Yorkshire Water Services could not reasonably have been expected to prevent the discharge of the isooctonal. They could not have known of its presence until it had entered the works, at the earliest. Thereafter its discharge into controlled water was 'inevitable'. With respect, this conclusion is surely open to challenge. Yorkshire Water could monitor all sewage entering its works, and could provide a shut-down system (albeit at great expense). Many of the key questions were left unexplored.

This case was superseded by another in which the magistrates, CC, DC, and HL all agreed:

Empress Car Co (Abertillery) Ltd v National Rivers Authority **(1999)** D company maintained a diesel tank in a yard. The tap to the tank was opened by a person unknown (who could have been an employee or a complete stranger) and the entire contents of the tank ran into a drum, overflowed into the yard, and passed down a drain into a river. D's defence to a charge under s 85 of the Water Resources Act 1991 was that 'causing' required some positive act and that the escape could not be said to have been caused by the company.

HL (Lord Hoffmann): dismissed D's appeal. It was open to the magistrates to hold that D caused the oil to enter the controlled waters. It is wrong and distracting to ask 'what caused the pollution?' The only question is 'did D cause the pollution?'

> One cannot give a common sense answer to a question of causation for the purpose of attributing responsibility under some rule without knowing the purpose and scope

of the rule … If D did something which produced a situation in which the polluting matter could escape but a necessary condition of the actual escape which happened was also the act of a third party or a natural event, the justices should consider whether that act or event should be regarded as a normal fact of life or something extraordinary. If it was in the general run of things a matter of ordinary occurrence, it will not negative the causal effect of D's acts, even if it was not foreseeable that it would happen to that particular D or take that particular form. If it can be regarded as something extraordinary, it will be open to the justices to hold that D did not cause the pollution.

Express Ltd (t/a Express Dairies Distribution) v Environment Agency (2003) Ds appealed by way of case stated against their conviction for causing or knowingly allowing polluting matter to enter controlled waters contrary to the Water Resources Act 1991, s 85. Their vehicle had been coupled to a tanker trailer of milk. A tyre blew out on the trailer, the delivery pipe had sheared, and a large quantity of milk had escaped. The driver had pulled on to the motorway hard shoulder where the milk discharged into two drains and subsequently entered controlled waters. Ds submitted that the sequence of events had been so uncommon and extraordinary that there had been a break in the chain of causation so that the offence was not committed at all and that the defence under s 89(1) of the 1991 Act applied as the milk had been discharged in an emergency to avoid danger to life and health.

Admin Ct: allowed D's appeal. Everything that had happened flowed from the operation of the tanker on the road and there had been no break in the chain of causation. The defence under s 89(1) of the Act applied. The question was whether the act which caused the entry of the pollutant was done in an emergency in order to avoid danger to life or health. Causing entry was a broad concept and answers to questions of causation depended on why the questions were being asked. It was in order to provide a defence to an otherwise absolute offence where Parliament had recognized that some of those acting in an emergency should be excused. Clearly, the blowout was not caused in order to prevent danger to life or health, but pulling in to the side of the road, where drains into the brook were located, could well have been said to be for that purpose.

(Do not muddle this case with *Express Ltd (t/a Express Dairies Distribution) v Environment Agency* (2005) which concerned the liability of the landlord for his tenant's act.)

2.24 Contrast this 'common sense' approach to causation with that taken in homicide cases. At **2.15** we distinguished factual causation from legal or imputable causation. There the conclusion was that the main justification for these complicated rules on causation was the law's concern to say that D only 'caused' a death if he was blameworthy. We noted at **2.22** the comments of both the CA and the HL in *Kennedy (No. 2)* (2007) on the *Empress* (1999) approach to causation. Why do the courts not have the same concerns in this area of the law? Which approach do you prefer?

2.25 Another area of controversy concerns motorway pile-ups, caused by dangerous drivers:

Barnes **(2008)** D drove with a sofa unsecured on the back of his pick-up truck. The sofa fell off the back and D parked to go back and recover the sofa from the road. V, on a motorbike, avoided the sofa but drove into D's vehicle and was killed.

CA: upheld D's conviction for causing death by dangerous driving.

> We accept that, in principle, the distinction between dangerous driving which creates the circumstances of a fatal collision and dangerous driving which is the actual cause of a death may not be an easy concept to grasp. There may well be circumstances in which it would be preferable if a judge went into a little more detail than the judge did here. However, we note that on the facts of this case the stark issue was whether or not the cause of [V]'s death was his own driving. That issue was left fairly and squarely to the jury. The judge directed them specifically that they had to be sure that if they found the appellant drove dangerously with an insecure load they should consider the second element. Was the dangerous driving with a load that might work itself free and flip out onto the road a cause of [V]'s death which was more than just trivial? (Hallett LJ at para. 17).

Girdler **(2009)** D collided with V1's taxi, propelling it into the fast lane of a three-lane highway, leaving it broadside on to the traffic going in the same direction. V2 then drove into V1 and both were killed. D's case was that V2 was solely responsible for the accident that caused the deaths. He was convicted of causing the death by dangerous driving of V1 (and the jury failed to reach a verdict in relation to V2).

CA: quashed D's conviction (and ordered a retrial, at which he was convicted on both counts).

> Questions of causation frequently arise in many areas of the law, but causation is not a single, unvarying concept to be mechanically applied without regard to the context in which the question arises (para. 15).

> We are of the view that the words 'reasonably foreseeable' whilst apt to describe for a lawyer the appropriate test, may need to be reworded to ease the task of a jury. We suggest that a jury could be told, in circumstances like the present where the immediate cause of death is a second collision, that if they were sure that the defendant drove dangerously and were sure that his dangerous driving was more than a slight or trifling link to the death(s) then:

> > D will have caused the death(s) only if you are sure that it could sensibly have been anticipated that a fatal collision might occur in the circumstances in which the second collision did occur.

> The judge should identify the relevant circumstances and remind the jury of the prosecution and defence cases. If it is thought necessary it could be made clear to the jury that they are not concerned with what D foresaw (para. 43).

Parliament has now created a strict liability offence of causing death by driving without insurance and without a licence, contrary to the Road Traffic Act 1988, s 3ZB (added by the Road Safety Act 2006):

> **Williams (2010)** D drove his car without a driving licence or insurance. He knocked down and killed a man (V), who was crossing a dual-carriageway and had stepped out immediately in front of D's car. The jury were directed on the basis that P did not have to prove that there was any fault in the manner of D's driving; that the offence was proved if V's death had been caused by D's driving without insurance or a licence and that the cause had to be more than merely minimal or negligible. D was convicted of causing death by driving without insurance and without a licence.
>
> CA: dismissed D's appeal. It is sufficient for the commission of this offence that there is a factual causal link between D being unlawfully on the road and the fatality, the nature and quality of the driving being irrelevant. There is no requirement to prove any culpable state of mind or negligence as to the death. The judge was right therefore to explain to the jury that what was necessary was a cause that was more than minute or negligible, as that is what Parliament clearly intended. D's act may significantly contribute to the occurrence of a result even though his act is not the sole or main cause of the result.

Hirst (2008) wrote (before this decision) that:

> *Lack of sympathy for disqualified or uninsured drivers should not however blind us to the fact that this new offence corrupts the usual principles governing causation. It appears that D may be convicted of 'causing' death without his actual driving being at fault. If D's uninsured car is involved in a collision with V's motorcycle and V is killed, D will automatically be guilty, even if the accident was entirely V's fault. It is clear from the authorities that D may still be 'driving' even when his vehicle is stationary. It may be no defence, therefore, that D was waiting patiently at traffic signals when V rode into the back of his car (at p. 344).*

2.26 Luckily, the SC has bravely brought some common sense to this area: the decision in *Girdler* was recently overruled:

> **Hughes (2013)** D was convicted of 'causing death by driving while unlicensed, disqualified or uninsured' under the RTA 1988, s 3ZB (inserted by the Road Safety Act

2006). He had been driving well and was crashed into by V, a dangerous driver, being a tired heroin user.

CA: allowed P's appeal.

SC: allowed D's appeal. There was no logical or satisfactory intermediate position between holding (a) that the law imposed guilt of homicide whenever the unlicensed, etc, motorist was involved in a fatal accident and (b) that he, or she, was guilty of causing death only when there was some additional feature of the driving which was causative on a common sense view, and the latter entailed there being something in the manner of the driving which was open to proper criticism, that is, involved some element of fault, which contributed more than minimally to the death.

It is a relief that the Court found that there must be something more than 'but for' causation before someone can be convicted of this offence. Otherwise, it is extraordinarily harsh. Lord Hughes and Toulson (together delivering the judgment of the Court!) said that:

> Juries should thus be directed that it is not necessary for the Crown to prove careless or inconsiderate driving, but that there must be something open to proper criticism in the driving of D, beyond the mere presence of the vehicle on the road, and which contributed in some more than minimal way to the death (para. 33).

Now the s 3ZB offence will only rarely apply: dangerous drivers are charged with dangerous driving and careless drivers with careless driving. The SC gave as possible examples: driving slightly in excess of a speed limit or breach of a construction and use regulation falling short of careless driving (e.g. driving 34 mph in a 30 mph zone or driving with an under-inflated tyre).

State of affairs

2.27 Some offences require neither an act nor an omission, but merely a status or a state of affairs.

Larsonneur (1933) D was deported from Ireland and brought reluctantly into this country by the police.

CCA: upheld her conviction for 'being found in the UK', contrary to the Aliens Order 1920.

Winzar v Chief Constable of Kent (1983) The police removed D from a hospital where he was found drunk and put him in a police car on the street. He was then taken to the police station and charged with 'being found drunk on the highway' (see s 12 of the Licensing Act 1872, still in force).

DC: upheld his conviction. Although his presence on the highway was momentary and not of his own volition, he fell within the terms of the offence.

These cases have been widely criticized: what act of D's caused him or her to commit the crime? But it is the wide drafting of the offence which is at fault rather than its interpretation by the courts. Similarly with drug possession offences, which normally require only that D possessed the substance voluntarily. Thus the Misuse of Drugs Act 1971, s 5 provides simply that 'it is an offence for a person to have a controlled drug in his possession'.

2.28   Even where no knowledge is required in respect of the nature of what D possesses, D must know that he possesses something:

Warner v Metropolitan Police Commissioner **(1969)**   D was charged with possessing drugs contrary to the Drugs (Prevention of Misuse) Act 1964. She believed the stuff she possessed was scent.

HL: upheld her conviction (by a majority and all give different reasons). Lord Wilberforce: the jury must make the decision whether, in addition to physical control, D has, or ought to have, imputed to him the intention to possess, or knowledge that he does possess, what is in fact a prohibited substance. If he has this intention or knowledge, it is not additionally necessary that he should know the nature of the substance.

Deyemi **(2007)**   Ds had been stopped and searched. An electrical stun gun had been found. D's evidence was that they had believed it to be a torch. The judge found that D did not know that it was a stun gun but ruled that the offence was one of strict liability (see **3.38**). D then pleaded guilty, and appealed against the decision that the offence of possessing a prohibited weapon contrary to the Firearms Act, s 5(1)(b) was one of strict liability.

CA: dismissed their appeal. To prove an offence under s 5 of the 1968 Act, P merely had to prove possession of the object in question, and the fact that the object was a firearm or other weapon prohibited by the 1968 Act; P did not have to prove that D either knew, or could have known, it was a weapon prohibited by the 1968 Act.

However, in many crimes, the state of affairs or surrounding circumstances are only one part of the *actus reus*. There will be an 'act' as well. For example, the SOA 2003, s 5 concerns the rape of a child under 13 years of age. Here the surrounding circumstance is that the child must be under 13. The guilty act narrowly defined is the 'rape' of the child. As detailed in Chapter 3, different *mens rea* requirements may apply to different elements of the *actus reus*.

FURTHER READING

Commission on Assisted Dying, Report (2012) available at http://www.demos.co.uk/publications/thecommissiononassisteddying.

Helme, T. and Padfield, N., 'Setting Euthanasia on the Level' (1993) 15 *Liverpool Law Review* 75.

Hirst, M., 'Causing Death by Driving and Other Offences: A Question of Balance' [2008] Crim LR 339.

Hunter, R., McGlynn, C., and Rackley, E. (eds), *Feminist Judgments: From Theory to Practice* (2010).

Norrie, A., 'A Critique of Criminal Causation' (1991) 54 MLR 685.

Ormerod, D. and Fortson, R., 'Drug Suppliers as Manslaughterers (again)' [2005] Crim LR 819.

Padfield, N., 'Clean Water and Muddy Causation' [1995] Crim LR 683.

Robinson, P., 'Should the Criminal Law Abandon the *Actus Reus–Mens Rea* Distinction?' in S. Shute, J. Gardner, and J. Horder (eds), *Action and Value in Criminal Law* (1993).

Rogers, J., 'Death, Drugs and Duties' [2009] 6 *Archbold News* 6.

Williams, G., 'Finis for *Novus Actus*?' [1989] Camb LJ 391.

Williams, G., 'Gross Negligence Manslaughter and Duty of Care in "Drugs" Cases: *R v Evans*' [2009] Crim LR 631.

SELF-TEST QUESTIONS

1   As Dee sneezes, she hits Phil in the face. He develops a black eye: would English law say that Dee 'caused' the injury?

2   The parents of a severely handicapped baby instruct the doctors in the hospital where she is born to give her no treatment. They say that if she is not allowed to die, they will not take her home and care for her. The doctors agree to withdraw treatment, and the baby dies. Consider the criminal liability of both the parents and the doctors.

3   Dee stabs Phil causing him serious, but not necessarily fatal, injuries. A surgeon gives him an experimental form of treatment which fails to stop the bleeding.

Phil dies. Medical experts say that with the benefit of hindsight the treatment was probably wrong. Discuss Dee's criminal liability.

4   David rapes Violet who is a member of a religious group which emphasizes the value of virginity at marriage. Overcome by shame, Violet commits suicide. Discuss the criminal liability of David.

5   Dee, an electrician, is asked by Vera to re-wire her sitting room. Before the job is completed, Dee is called off to deal with an emergency elsewhere. Vera, who knows that Dee has left the room in a hazardous state, turns on a light and is electrocuted. She dies later that day, in hospital.

3

Criminal states of mind

SUMMARY

This chapter examines various states of mind which may lead to criminal liability:

Intention: intention is not the same as motive. Distinguish direct intent from inferred intent: an intent may be inferred when the consequence is virtually certain to follow from what D does, even if D did not want it to happen (*Nedrick/Woollin*).

Knowledge and belief: wilful blindness may constitute knowledge.

Wilfulness: Particularly in the context of 'wilful' neglect.

Recklessness: for many years recklessness was interpreted subjectively (*Cunningham*), i.e. D is reckless if he consciously takes a risk; then the concept was interpreted objectively in some contexts (e.g. criminal damage: *Caldwell*): D was objectively reckless if he gave no thought to an obvious risk. But *Caldwell* was overruled in *G* (2004). So currently a subjective interpretation.

Negligence: distinguish gross negligence from mere negligence, i.e. carelessness.

Strict liability: common in 'regulatory' offences, this means that D may be guilty even though he did not know that he was doing wrong.

3.1 The criminal law should penalize the blameworthy. Chapter 2 looks particularly at those harms, or acts, which may lead to criminal liability. The emphasis of this chapter is on the mental element in crimes, often known by the Latin expression *mens rea* or guilty mind. *Mens rea* means something very different in relation to different crimes. As Lord Simon said in *DPP v Majewski* (1977):

> … the mens rea is … the state of mind stigmatised as wrongful by the criminal law which, when compounded with the relevant prohibited conduct, constitutes a particular offence.

Some crimes require intention as the *mens rea*, some recklessness, others a different state of mind (or none at all). In some crimes, the relevant *mens rea* extends to the whole of the *actus reus*, in others to only part. Different elements of a crime may have different *mens rea* requirements and some concepts may be interpreted differently in different contexts. The key question to be kept in mind throughout this chapter is whether the criminal law gets it right: decide whether you believe the 'right' people are considered blameworthy.

Intention

3.2 Intention is used in relation to consequences: thus, a person may be said to intend the consequence of his actions if he wants them to happen. This is true whether or not it is likely to happen. For example, liability for criminal attempts depends on intent (see **7.8**). If you shoot at me wanting to kill me and miss, you will still be guilty of attempted murder whether you were standing next to me or a hundred metres away. This meaning of intent is often referred to as 'direct intent'.

3.3 A person's motive, or reason, for doing something is usually not relevant to liability (though good motives may result in lower sentences).

Steane **(1947)** D, a British subject, broadcast propaganda for the Germans during the Second World War. He said he had done it simply to save his wife and children who were still in Germany. He was convicted of intentionally doing acts likely to assist the enemy.

CCA (Lord Goddard): allowed D's appeal. If on the totality of the evidence there is room for more than one view as to D's intent, the jury should be directed that it is for P to prove the intent to the jury's satisfaction. They would not be entitled to presume a criminal intent if circumstances were consistent with an innocent intent such as a desire to save his wife and children.

This case has been much criticized because the court appeared to quash the conviction on the ground that D may have lacked *mens rea*. Would it be more appropriate to say that he did have the necessary intent, but that he had the benefit of the defence of duress (see **5.15**)?

3.4 The following case (which was not a criminal one) also poses problems in distinguishing motive from intent:

Gillick v West Norfolk and Wisbech Area Health Authority **(1985)** P sought judicial review of a Department of Health memorandum which said that in exceptional cases a doctor could prescribe contraceptive pills to a girl under the age of 16 without informing her parents.

HL: held that the memorandum was not unlawful. A child becomes increasingly independent as she grows older and the law does not recognize any rule of absolute parental authority until a fixed age. The bona fide exercise by a doctor of his clinical judgment negated the *mens rea* which would be an essential ingredient of an offence under s 6 (intercourse with a girl under 16) or s 28 (causing or encouraging under-age sex) of the SOA 1956 (now repealed and replaced by similar offences under the SOA 2003: see Chapter 10).

This decision was upheld in *R (Axon) v Secretion of State for Health* (2006). The main interest of the case lies in the failure of the judges to be very clear as to why any such doctor would not be aiding and abetting unlawful sexual intercourse (i.e. intentionally helping the boyfriend commit the offence). Is it because:

(i) the doctor has a defence of necessity? or because

(ii) the 'intent' necessary for aiding and abetting is a different sort of 'direct intent'?

The case is discussed further at **5.22** and **6.18**.

3.5 Another example of the relationship between intent and motive is found at **7.20**: in *Yip Chiu-Cheung* (1994) the PC decided that a drug dealer could be guilty of conspiring with an undercover drug enforcement officer: even where the undercover agent is acting courageously and with the best of motives (trying to break a drugs ring), he nonetheless 'intends' to commit the offence of importing illegal drugs through customs. Lord Griffiths made clear that a good motive is not itself a defence given that all the ingredients of the offence are present. The distinction between intention and purpose can be seen in:

Zafar et al (2008) Five Ds, four of whom were students at Bradford University, were found to possess ideological propaganda and other material which P alleged showed that they planned to go to Pakistan for terrorist training in Afghanistan. They were convicted of offences of 'possessing articles for a purpose connected with the commission, preparation or instigation of an act of terrorism', contrary to s 57 of the Terrorism Act 2000.

CA: quashed their convictions. The Lord Chief Justice (LCJ) held that:

…if s. 57 is to have the certainty of meaning that the law requires, it must be interpreted in a way that requires a direct connection between the object possessed and the act of terrorism. The section should be interpreted as if it reads:

A person commits an offence if he possesses an article in circumstances which give rise to a reasonable suspicion that he intends it to be used for the purpose of the commission, preparation or instigation of an act of terrorism.

The trial judge's directions to the jury were inadequate as they did not tell the jury that they had to be satisfied that each D intended to use the relevant articles to incite his fellow planners to fight in Afghanistan.

But see also the HL's decision in another terrorism-related case, *G* (2009), at **5.6**: to what extent can your motive give you a 'reasonable excuse'?

Oblique intent

3.6 Someone may 'intend' the consequence of his act even if he does not necessarily want it to happen, where he knows that the consequence is virtually certain to happen. His culpability may be as great: if I blow up an aeroplane simply to claim insurance on the cargo, not caring whether or not the pilot is killed, do I intend to kill the pilot? A little statutory help is to be found in the CJA 1967, s 8:

> s 8 A court or jury, in determining whether a person has committed an offence—
>
> (a) shall not be bound in law to infer that he intended or foresaw a result of his actions by reason only of its being a natural and probable consequence of those actions; but
>
> (b) shall decide whether he did intend or foresee that result by reference to all the evidence, drawing such inferences from the evidence as appear proper in the circumstances.

3.7 Many of the difficult cases have arisen in the context of murder, where D is only guilty if she intends to kill or to cause grievous bodily harm (see also **8.2**).

> *Hyam v DPP* **(1975)** D poured petrol through the letterbox of the house of her rival and set fire to it. In the resulting house fire, two girls were killed.
>
> HL (by a majority of 3 to 2): upheld her conviction for murder, though the three judges in the majority appeared to give different reasons for their decision. According to Lord Cross, mere foresight of probability was enough to allow the jury to infer intent, whereas Viscount Dilhorne felt that foresight of high probability was more appropriate. Lord Hailsham stated that foresight of probability or high probability was too vague and he concluded that D could be said to intend death if she 'intended to create a risk of death or serious bodily harm'. Lords Diplock and Kilbrandon dissented.

3.8 This case caused a decade of uncertainty, exacerbated by the fact that there were five separate speeches in the HL. It also seemed for a while after *Hyam* that intention might mean different things in different contexts. Two cases reveal the CA's attempts to limit the application of the wide definition of *Hyam*:

Mohan **(1976)** D drove his car at V, a policeman, in order to escape. V jumped out of the way, but D was charged with, and convicted of, attempting to cause bodily harm to the police officer.

CA: quashed his conviction. In order to prove an attempt to commit a crime (see **7.4**), P has to prove a specific intent, i.e. a decision by D to bring about, so far as it lay within his power, the commission of the offence which it was alleged that he had attempted to commit. It was not sufficient to establish that he knew or foresaw that the consequences of his act would be likely to be the commission of the completed offence: a reckless state of mind was not sufficient.

Belfon **(1976)** D attacked V with a razor causing him serious injury and was convicted of wounding with intent to do grievous bodily harm contrary to the OAPA 1861, s 18 (see **9.4**).

CA: quashed his conviction on the basis that the fact that D had foreseen that serious harm was likely to result from his acts, or that he had been reckless whether such harm would result, did not constitute the necessary intent.

3.9 Even in murder cases, there was much disquiet, though the issue was not faced again by the HL for another decade.

Moloney **(1985)** D shot V, his stepfather, dead in a drunken game. He was convicted of murder.

HL: unanimously agreed that the murder conviction should be replaced by one of manslaughter. Lord Bridge, giving the leading speech, held that murder is a crime of intention only. Intention should have the same meaning throughout the criminal law and a judge should leave it where possible to the jury's good sense to decide whether D acted with the necessary intent without any elaboration or paraphrase of what is meant by intent. D's foresight of the probability of a consequence does not of itself amount to intention but may be evidence of it. D could be said to intend death where (i) death was a natural consequence of D's voluntary act and (ii) D foresaw that consequence as being a natural consequence of his act.

This decision had the advantage of getting rid of the confusion between probability and intention, but was itself very ambiguous. What is or is not a natural consequence of shooting at someone? It was hardly surprising that within a year the HL had revisited the issue:

Hancock and Shankland (1986) Ds, on strike during a miners' strike, dropped a concrete block off a motorway bridge intending to frighten V, a taxi driver taking strike breakers to work. V was killed and Ds were convicted of murder.

HL (Lord Scarman gave the only speech): upheld CA's decision to substitute a manslaughter verdict. Lord Scarman suggested that the 'natural consequence' test of *Moloney* was too wide, concluding that the guidelines to juries require a reference to probability. They also require an explanation that the greater the probability of a consequence the more likely it is that the consequence was foreseen and that if that consequence was foreseen the greater the probability is that that consequence was also intended. But juries also require to be reminded that the decision is theirs to be reached upon a consideration of all the evidence.

3.10 The CA seemed to reach a workable definition in *Nedrick* and the point did not reach the HL again for another decade (*Woollin*).

Nedrick (1986) D poured paraffin through the letterbox of the house of a woman against whom he had a grudge and set fire to it. A child was killed and D was convicted of murder.

CA: quashed his murder conviction, substituting manslaughter. Lord Lane CJ held that:

(A) When determining whether the defendant had the necessary intent, it may therefore be helpful for a jury to ask themselves two questions.

  (1) How probable was the consequence which resulted from the defendant's voluntary act?

  (2) Did he foresee that consequence? If he did not appreciate that death or serious harm was likely to result from his act, he cannot have intended to bring it about. If he did, but thought that the risk to which he was exposing the person killed was only slight, then it may be easy for the jury to conclude that he did not intend to bring about that result. On the other hand, if the jury are satisfied that at the material time the defendant recognized that death or serious harm would be virtually certain (barring some unforeseen intervention) to result from his voluntary act, then that is a fact from which they may find it easy to infer that he intended to kill or do serious bodily harm, even though he may not have had any desire to achieve that result.

(B) Where the charge is murder and in the rare cases where the simple direction is not enough, the jury should be directed that they are not entitled to infer the necessary intention, unless they feel sure that death or serious bodily harm was a virtual certainty (barring some unforeseen intervention) as a result of the defendant's actions and that the defendant appreciated that such was the case.

(C) Where a man realizes that it is for all practical purposes inevitable that his actions will result in death or serious harm, the inference may be irresistible that he intended that result, however little he may have desired or wished it to happen. The decision is one for the jury to be reached upon a consideration of all the evidence (lettering added by Lord Steyn in *Woollin* (see **3.11**)).

3.11 Buxton (1988) called the position post-*Nedrick* an 'admittedly fragile equilibrium'. It was more than ten years before the HL revisited 'intention':

Woollin **(1999)** D was convicted of the murder of his three-month-old baby. P's case had been that in throwing the baby against something hard he must have realized that what he was doing was virtually certain to cause serious injury.

HL: allowed his appeal:

In my view Lord Lane's judgment in *Nedrick* provided valuable assistance to trial judges. The model direction is by now a tried-and-tested formula. Trial judges ought to continue to use it … First, I am persuaded by the speech of my noble and learned friend, Lord Hope of Craighead, that it is unlikely, if ever, to be helpful to direct the jury in terms of the two questions set out in (A). I agree that these questions may detract from the clarity of the critical direction in (B). Secondly, in their writings … Glanville Williams, J. C. Smith and Andrew Ashworth observed that the use of the words 'to infer' in (B) may detract from the clarity of the model direction. I agree. I would substitute the words 'to find'. Thirdly, the first sentence of (C) does not form part of the model direction. But it would always be right for the judge to say, as Lord Lane put it, that the decision is for the jury upon a consideration of all the evidence in the case (Lord Steyn).

Matthews and Alleyne **(2003)** V was assaulted and robbed outside a nightclub. Ds tried unsuccessfully to obtain money from a cashpoint with V's stolen bank card. V lost his glasses in the attack and was then forced into a car, driven to a bridge, and thrown into the river below. V had informed the attackers that he could not swim and subsequently drowned. P's case was that Ds had been determined to silence V by drowning him to prevent him identifying them as robbers, or appreciated that at the time V was thrown from the bridge his death was a virtual certainty. Ds maintained that they had dropped out after the assault and knew nothing about subsequent events. They were convicted of murder.

CA: dismissed the appeals. The law had not yet reached a definition of intent in murder in terms of appreciation of virtual certainty. *Woollin* (1999) was not regarded as yet reaching or laying down a substantive rule of law. *Woollin* as a whole found that *Nedrick* (1986) had been derived from existing case law at the time and the critical direction in *Nedrick* had been approved subject to the change of the word 'infer' to 'find'. The trial judge's direction went further than the law permitted him to go by redrafting the *Nedrick* and *Woollin* direction into a form where the jury were directed to find the necessary intent proved provided they were satisfied in the case of any D that there was an appreciation of the virtual certainty of death. The proper direction should have been in the terms that the jury were 'not entitled to find the necessary intention unless they felt sure that death, or serious bodily harm, was a virtual certainty as a result of D's actions and that the defendant appreciated that this was the case'. There was very little to choose between a rule of evidence and one of substantive law. If the jury were sure that the Ds appreciated the virtual certainty of V's death when they threw him off the bridge and also that they then had no intention of saving him from such death, it was impossible to see how a jury could not have found that they intended V to die. The trial judge had, throughout his summing up, constantly repeated the need for an intent to kill. Thus, whilst the judge's direction had amounted to a rule of substantive law, that was a misdirection, that misdirection was immaterial.

We will see later that when judges are summing up to juries on the meaning of the word 'dishonestly' (see **11.14**), they advise them to give the word its ordinary meaning, without further help. But here, the trial judge may give a more complex direction along the lines suggested in *Woollin*. Kaveny (2004) is very critical of the *Woollin* test. She argues that:

> *First, some conceptual clarity is in order. Foresight and intention are quite distinct mental states. No degree or type of foresight can be equated with intention, and—equally important but much less widely understood or even considered—no degree of foresight can, by itself, be the basis of a reliable inference of intention. Secondly, and again contrary to what is usually imagined, in difficult cases, it is not generally simpler to determine a particular defendant's foresight than his intent. Thirdly, English law should acknowledge that acting with the purpose to cause death or serious bodily harm and acting with a sufficient degree of foresight that one will cause death or serious bodily harm are two different ways of satisfying the mens rea requirement for murder. To my mind, the most coherent approach was presented some years ago in this journal by Lord Goff of Chieveley, who argued that English law should adopt the Scottish concept of 'wicked recklessness' as a distinct prong of the mens rea of murder.*

Clause 18(b)(ii) of the DCC (1989) stated that for Code purposes:

> ...a person acts ... 'intentionally' with respect to—
>
> (i)   a circumstance when he hopes or knows that it exists or will exist;

(ii) a result when he acts either in order to bring it about or being aware that it will occur in the ordinary course of events.

Does this sum up the position today, or is this a wider definition than that to be found in *Nedrick/Woollin*? The issue still raises its head from time to time (see *Royle* (2013)), but the current state of the law is relatively clear: judges are advised that they should avoid unnecessary elaboration on a simple direction on intent.

Specific intent

3.12 As well as referring to direct and oblique intent, students will find many references to specific intent, particularly in the context of crimes in respect of which drunkenness may be a 'defence'. In essence, drunkenness may be used to show that D did not have the required *mens rea* in crimes of specific intent (see **4.18**). But beware: the terms specific and direct intent are not magic formulae and you may find some judges/writers using them interchangeably.

Ulterior intent

3.13 A final form of intent is referred to as ulterior intent: where there is an additional *mens rea* requirement of the crime which is not directly related to an ingredient of the *actus reus*. For example:

(i) the OAPA 1961, s 18. causing grievous bodily harm with intent to do grievous bodily harm or with intent to resist arrest: see **9.4**;

(ii) the SOA 2003, ss 61–3: administering a substance with intention of stupefying or overpowering someone so as to enable any person to engage in sexual activity that involves them (s 61); committing an offence with intent to commit a sexual offence (s 62); and trespass with intent to commit a sexual offence (s 63): see **10.30**;

(iii) the TA 1968, s 9(1)(a): burglary by entering a building with intent to steal, inflict grievous bodily harm, or cause damage: see **11.25**;

(iv) the new law of fraud under the Fraud Act 2006 is entirely inchoate: D dishonestly does an act (or omission) with the intent of making a gain for himself or another. He does not have to make the gain, but simply to intend to do so: see **11.46**.

Here the word 'intent' bears the same meaning as it does in murder (see **3.6–3.11**).

Knowledge and belief

3.14 Many crimes require that D should 'knowingly' do something. Even 'wilful blindness' may constitute 'knowledge': English law treats someone as knowing something if, being pretty sure that it is so, he deliberately avoids asking questions which might confirm the fact. D must normally be judged on the facts as he believes them to be (though some mistakes must be reasonable if they are to absolve D from liability: see **5.30**).

> **Taaffe (1984)** D thought he was importing illegal currency into England. Importing currency was not at the time illegal, but D was in fact importing cannabis. He pleaded guilty to 'being knowingly concerned in the importation of cannabis resin, contrary to s 170(2) of the Customs and Excise Management Act 1979' after the judge ruled that he would have to direct the jury to convict.
>
> HL: upheld the decision of the CA to allow the appeal. D was to be judged on the facts as he believed them to be, i.e. that he was importing currency. His mistake of fact that importing currency was unlawful could not convert an innocent act into a criminal offence.

The *Taaffe* defence rarely works in practice:

> **Forbes (2001)** D was arrested at Heathrow Airport in possession of two videotapes that contained indecent photographs of children under 16 years of age and was convicted of being 'in any way knowingly concerned in any fraudulent evasion … of any prohibition' on the importation of goods contrary to the Customs and Excise Management Act 1979, s 170(2)(b). D's defence (rejected by the jury) was that he was carrying the films for someone else and did not know that they were prohibited.
>
> HL: upheld his conviction. It was not a pre-requisite that he knew or believed that he was importing indecent images of children. The burden of proof on P would be unrealistically high if it had to prove the precise nature of the prohibited goods. It was sufficient, therefore, to satisfy the offence, that D knew simply that he was importing prohibited goods.
>
> > It was, of course, open to D to say, if this was the fact, that he believed the videos to contain indecent photographs of adults and that he acted as he did because he believed, contrary to the fact, that they were prohibited. The line of defence which was approved in *Taaffe* (1984) ensures the acquittal of people who genuinely believe that they are importing indecent photographs of adults which are not obscene, when they are in fact photographs of children. But it is for D to put forward that defence. P does not have to prove what D knew the goods were which he was seeking to import knowing that they were prohibited goods (Lord Hope at para. 31).

3.15 Clause 18 of the DCC (1989) provided that:

…a person acts—

(a) knowingly with respect to a circumstance not only when he is aware that it exists or will exist, but also when he avoids taking steps that might confirm his belief that it exists or will exist.

To illustrate this test, the Law Commission gives the example of D who is handed a packet by E. The packet contains heroin. D chooses not to open the packet and therefore does not see what it contains. If D believes it to contain heroin, he is 'knowingly' in possession of heroin. Knowledge and belief are obviously close relations, but knowledge implies that the belief is correct whereas a belief may be mistaken. Thus, a belief that the goods are stolen is a necessary ingredient in the offence of handling stolen goods, contrary to the TA 1968, s 22 (see **11.52**). Boreham J said in *Hall* (1985):

Belief, of course, is something short of knowledge. It may be said to be the state of mind of a person who says to himself: 'I cannot say I know for certain that these goods are stolen, but there can be no other reasonable conclusion in the light of all the circumstances, in the light of all that I have heard and seen.'

Wilfulness

3.16 Section 44 of the Mental Capacity Act 2005 provides that:

(1) Subsection (2) applies if a person ("D")—

(a) has the care of a person ("P") who lacks, or whom D reasonably believes to lack, capacity,

(b) is the donee of a lasting power of attorney, or an enduring power of attorney (within the meaning of Schedule 4), created by P, or

(c) is a deputy appointed by the court for P.

(2) D is guilty of an offence if he ill-treats or wilfully neglects P.

(3) A person guilty of an offence under this section is liable—

(a) on summary conviction, to imprisonment for a term not exceeding 12 months or a fine not exceeding the statutory maximum or both;

(b) on conviction on indictment, to imprisonment for a term not exceeding 5 years or a fine or both.

There have been a number of appeals arising out of the prosecution of nurses for 'willfully' neglecting patients in their care. For example:

Patel **(2013)** D was a registered nurse working in a nursing home reserved for elderly patients who were mentally ill. V was a patient who lacked capacity within the meaning of the Mental Capacity Act 2005. D, who was in charge of the home, was told that V was becoming ill. His breathing was shallow and his pulse was faint. D apparently panicked. She did not perform cardiac pulmonary resuscitation (CPR) and, although she called for an ambulance, V had died by the time it arrived. A post mortem revealed that V had been suffering from pneumonia which caused a respiratory arrest, which in turn caused a cardiac arrest. There was a low survival rate from that kind of cardiac arrest and CPR would have been unlikely to have saved his life. D argued that V had not had a viable chance of survival, so her failure to carry out CPR had not caused his death and that any neglect on her part had not been wilful. The judge directed the jury on the meaning of neglect, directing that it was no defence to say that V would have died whether or not CPR had been administered. He also directed them on the meaning of the word 'wilfully', telling them that D could not escape liability by arguing that her failure to act had been borne out of stress or panic.

CA: dismissed her appeal. Section 44 of the 2005 Act had to be construed in accordance with its obvious meaning and the *actus reus* of the offence was complete if D neglected to do that which ought to have been done in the treatment of the patient. She could not escape liability on the basis that, even if she had administered the treatment in question, it would have made no difference to the patient. The judge was right to direct that the offence of wilful neglect was made out even if the failure to act was the result of panic. Neglect was wilful if a nurse or medical practitioner knew that it was necessary to administer a piece of treatment but deliberately decided not to do so because she could not face it. If D had been acting at a time of stress that would be a matter which the judge could take into account in sentencing.

Turbill and Broadway **(2013)** D2, a lead carer in a care home, had asked a staff member to put V to bed early because he was agitated. When D1 arrived on duty, D2 had told her that V had been agitated. D1 did not pass that information on to another staff member or check on V. In the morning V was found on the floor, semiconscious and partially hypothermic, and did not appear to have been put to bed. The judge directed the jury that the word 'wilful' was at the heart of the case, but he did not define it. He expressed P's case as being that Ds had failed to visit V out of a grossly careless lack of concern for such duty as they had to him, reflecting a 'couldn't care less attitude'. T and B argued that the directions had not been sufficiently clear.

CA: allowed the appeals. The test for wilfulness was subjective rather than objective. Recklessness, or failing to do what a careful and competent practitioner would do, was not enough. The term 'wilfully' meant deliberately refraining from acting, or refraining from acting because of not caring whether action was required or not. In parts of the summing up, the judge had appeared to equate carelessness, or negligence, with wilful neglect. They were not the same. Parliament had decreed that neglect was not enough to constitute a criminal offence, even of a vulnerable patient. The neglect had to be 'wilful' and that meant something more was required than a duty and what a reasonable person would regard as a reckless breach of that duty. The judge had used a variety of expressions: he used 'reckless' without defining it and without directing the jury that it was not simply an objective test; he used 'careless', 'carelessness' and 'grossly careless' as if they necessarily equated to a 'couldn't care less attitude', which they did not. Even 'gross carelessness' would not, of itself, be sufficient to amount to wilful neglect. The cumulative effect was to cause real doubt about whether the jury would have understood the essential elements of the offence.

Recklessness

3.17 Someone is reckless if he or she takes unjustified risks. Recklessness is the necessary *mens rea* for many offences: criminal damage, arson, assault, wounding . . . Perhaps it is simply the huge variety of offences which rely on recklessness as the basis of the necessary guilty mind which has given rise to the difficulties in its definition. The degree of risk will vary from offence to offence, and a person may be reckless in respect of acts, circumstances, or consequences (see **2.2**).

Subjective recklessness

3.18 This is the least controversial interpretation of the word:

Cunningham (1957) D tore a gas meter from the wall of an unoccupied house in order to steal the money in the meter. Escaping gas seeped through the wall to the next-door house where V was partially asphyxiated. D was convicted of maliciously administering a noxious thing contrary to the OAPA 1861, s 23 (see **9.31**).

CCA: quashed his conviction. The Court specifically adopted Professor Kenny's statement that in any statutory definition of a crime 'malice' must be taken not in the old vague sense of 'wickedness' in general, but as requiring either (i) an actual intention to do the particular kind of harm that in fact was done or (ii) recklessness as to whether such harm should occur or not (i.e. the accused has foreseen that the particular kind of harm might be done and yet has gone on to take the risk of it). It is not limited to, nor does it indeed require, any ill will towards the person injured.

3.19 Another illustration of this test at work is *Stephenson,* though this case was probably overruled by *Caldwell* (see **3.22**: now itself overruled):

***Stephenson* (1979)** D went to sleep in a haystack and lit a fire to keep warm. He was charged with arson under the Criminal Damage Act 1971, s 1. The only evidence for the defence was a consultant psychiatrist who said that D had a long history of schizophrenia and was quite capable of lighting a fire to keep warm without taking the danger into account.

CA (Geoffrey Lane LJ): quashed his conviction. D was in a mental condition which might have prevented him from appreciating the risk which would have been obvious to any normal person and this should have been left clearly to the jury.

3.20 The HL in *Savage* (1991) confirmed that this is the test which is applied to all offences under the OAPA 1861 which specify 'maliciously' (see **9.10**). It also used to apply to rape where, before the SOA 2003, D had to be proved to have been reckless whether the victim was consenting: *Satnam Singh* (1983). However, the word 'reckless' is not in the SOA 2003: the main offences, as detailed in Chapter 10, are now crimes of intent. Thus, for rape, P must prove an intention to penetrate, an absence of consent, and an absence of reasonable belief in consent.

3.21 The Law Commission in Consultation Paper No. 177 (2005) argued that 'recklessness' in the *Satnam Singh* sense can be known as 'reckless indifference' (i.e. recklessness manifesting a 'couldn't care less' attitude) and can be distinguished from 'simple recklessness' (reckless stupidity which is really just a kind of gross negligence): see paras 3.55 and 3.149 of their paper, where they explain why they thought that killing by reckless indifference should constitute 'second degree murder'. But, as detailed in Chapter 8, in their Report No. 304 (2006) they decide to avoid the word reckless, concluding that 'the term "reckless" has an unhappy history in the context of homicide. Although the House of Lords brought some welcome clarity to the definition of that term in another context [in *G* (2003); see **3.27**], we now believe that the law of homicide is better off without it' (at para. 3.57). This author doesn't agree: subjective recklessness would provide a wise test for manslaughter (see Chapter 8).

Objective recklessness

3.22 One of the difficulties in applying a subjective test is that D may well lie and it is impossible for a jury to enter his mind. Sometimes, too, D may not see obvious risks which the jury may well think that he should have seen. For these reasons, it seems, the HL developed an alternative view of recklessness in some offences:

Metropolitan Police Commissioner v Caldwell (1981) D, who was very drunk, set fire to a hotel and was convicted of arson under the Criminal Damage Act (CDA) 1971, s 1(2) (see **12.6**).

HL: upheld his conviction (though note Lord Edmund Davies' dissent, with which Lord Wilberforce concurred). Lord Diplock (in the majority):

> … a person charged with an offence under s 1(1) of the CDA 1971 is 'reckless as to whether any such property would be destroyed or damaged' if (1) he does an act which in fact creates an obvious risk that property will be destroyed or damaged and (2) when he does the act he either has not given any thought to the possibility of there being any such risk or has recognised that there was some risk involved and has nonetheless gone on to do it … Neither state of mind seems to me to be less blameworthy than the other; but if the difference between the two constituted the distinction between what does and what does not in legal theory amount to a guilty state of mind for the purpose of a statutory offence of damage to property, it would not be a practicable distinction for use in a trial by jury.

3.23 This test was clearly not intended to apply only to criminal damage since Lord Diplock applied it in a case of causing death by reckless driving (which is no longer an offence: see **8.37**) on the very same day:

Lawrence (1982) D drove his motorbike at 80 mph on a busy urban road and was convicted of causing death by reckless driving.

HL (Lord Diplock): upheld CA's decision to quash his conviction.

> An appropriate instruction to the jury on what is meant by driving recklessly would be that they must be satisfied of two things: first, that the defendant was in fact driving the vehicle in such a manner as to create an obvious and serious risk of causing physical injury to some other person who might happen to be using the road or of doing substantial damage to property; and second, that in driving in that manner the defendant did so without having given any thought to the possibility of there being any such risk or, having recognised there was some risk involved, had nonetheless gone on to take it.

3.24 The key difference to *Caldwell* was simply that in *Lawrence* the risk was required to be 'serious' as well as 'obvious'. To which other crimes did *Caldwell* recklessness apply? For a time, it formed part of the test for manslaughter (see the discussion of the HL's decision in *Seymour* (1983) and that of the PC in *Kong Cheuk Kwan v R* (1985) at **8.27**), but since Lord Mackay's speech in the HL in *Adomako* (1994) there must be some doubt as to whether recklessness is any longer an appropriate *mens rea* concept to apply in manslaughter cases (see **8.29**).

3.25 This objective test of recklessness could be extraordinarily harsh in its operation:

Elliott v C **(1983)** D, a 14-year-old girl with learning difficulties, poured white spirit in a shed and lit it. Magistrates acquitted her, holding that the risk of destroying the shed was not obvious to her.

DC (Goff LJ): while admitting that D's conduct was not reckless in the ordinary sense, said that the test was whether the risk was obvious to a reasonably prudent person.

> This is a case where it appears that the only basis upon which the accused might be held to have been reckless would be if the appropriate test to be applied was purely objective—a test which might in some circumstances be thought justifiable in relation to certain conduct (e.g. reckless driving), particularly where the word 'reckless' is used simply to characterise the relevant conduct. But such a test does not appear at first sight to be appropriate to a crime such as that under consideration in the present case, especially as recklessness in that crime has to be related to a particular consequence.

Goff LJ went on to consider the proposed qualification to Lord Diplock's *Caldwell/ Lawrence* principle that Professor Glanville Williams had made in (1981) 40 Camb LJ 252, that D should only be regarded as having acted recklessly by virtue of his failure to give any thought to an obvious risk that property would be destroyed or damaged, where such risk would have been obvious to him if he had given any thought to the matter. However, Goff LJ concluded that it would not be consistent with Lord Diplock's reasoning to impose any such qualification.

3.26 Perhaps a more just interpretation of *Caldwell* would have been Glanville Williams' approach, sometimes called a 'conditionally subjective' approach or a *via media*: the court would ask whether D had the capacity to make himself aware of the risk. The issue was discussed again in:

Stephen Malcolm R **(1984)** D, a 15-year-old boy, threw home-made petrol bombs outside a girl's bedroom, intending to frighten her.

CA (Ackner LJ): upheld his conviction under the CDA 1971, s 1(2)(b) for criminal damage 'being reckless as to whether life was endangered'. Because the HL had not given leave to appeal in *Elliott's* case, they should be taken to have rejected the argument that it would be right to inquire whether a person of D's age and with his characteristics would have appreciated the relevant risk. Since the risk would have been obvious to the reasonable man, it was irrelevant that D did not know of the risk.

3.27 Eventually (and at long last!) the decision in *Caldwell* was overruled:

G and another (2003) In the early hours of the morning, D1 and D2, aged 11 and 12, set fire to newspapers with a lighter and threw some of the papers under a large plastic wheelie-bin, which was in the yard behind a shop. They then left and the resulting fire caused approximately £1 million worth of damage. It was accepted that neither boy appreciated that there was any risk whatsoever of the fire spreading in the way that it did. They were convicted of arson, contrary to the CDA 1971, s 1 (see **12.6**), the judge having ruled that he was bound to direct the jury in accordance with *Caldwell* (1981).

HL: quashed their convictions and unanimously overruled the majority decision of the HL in *Caldwell*. Lord Bingham, giving the fullest speech, explored the historical background to *Caldwell*, including the Law Commission's Report on Offences of Damage to Property (Law Com No. 29 (1970)). He concluded that, in treating *Cunningham* (**3.18**) as irrelevant to the construction of 'reckless':

> … the majority [in *Caldwell*] fell into understandable but clearly demonstrable error. No relevant change in the *mens rea* necessary for the proof of the offence was intended and in holding otherwise the majority misconstrued section 1 of the [CDA 1971] (para. 29).

This was not the end of the question: Lord Bingham then outlined four reasons for overruling *Caldwell*, emphasizing the requirement for *mens rea*, fairness, academic and judicial criticisms of *Caldwell*, and the need to correct a misinterpretation which 'is offensive to principle and apt to cause injustice' (para. 35). He adopted the definition of the DCC of 1989 (see **3.29**). Lord Steyn described Ds' target of persuading the HL to depart from a previous decision as 'ambitious' but concluded that the very high threshold for departing from a previous decision of the HL had been satisfied. Under the sub-heading 'Justice and policy', he concluded that the norm created by the Convention on the Rights of the Child on its own justified a reappraisal of *Caldwell*. Lord Rodger stated that because the decision in *Caldwell* involved a legitimate choice between two legal policies, he was initially doubtful whether it would be appropriate for the House to overrule it. But he put particular emphasis on the dissenting speech of Lord Edmund-Davies in *Caldwell* when agreeing with his peers to 'set the law back on the track that Parliament originally intended it to follow'. Lord Browne-Wilkinson and Lord Hutton agreed.

3.28 Few will regret the departure of *Caldwell*. Perhaps it is surprising that the authority lasted as long as it did: a monument to the reluctance of the HL to cause uncertainty in the criminal law. Perhaps we should also be concerned that it was considered appropriate to try the boys in the CC before a jury: both judge and jury in this case were evidently uncomfortable with the trial. After the jury had retired, the judge had made clear to the boys that, even if the jury convicted, 'nothing unpleasant' awaited them. The jury perceptively returned to ask the judge, after they had retired, why they should consider the risk as perceived by a reasonable person or layman. The sentence, now quashed of course, was a one-year supervision order in each case. If prosecution was appropriate, was the Youth Court not a more appropriate venue for such a case?

Reform

3.29   Will the problems associated with defining recklessness now disappear? Given the fine distinctions discussed earlier, it is perhaps not surprising that the drafters of the DCC (1989) preferred a subjective definition of recklessness. Clause 18 provides that:

> ...a person acts– ...
>
>   (c) 'recklessly' with respect to–
>
>   (i)   a circumstance when he is aware of a risk that it exists or will exist;
>
>   (ii) a result when he is aware of a risk that it will occur; and it is, in the circumstances known to him, unreasonable to take the risk.

But the DCC is now 20 years old and times move on. Many recent offences have been drafted to require an ulterior intent, which removes the need for recklessness. Others are based on negligence.

Negligence

3.30   It can be argued that negligence is not a state of mind since it is merely a failure to comply with the standards of the reasonable man, but since it is the fault element required for some offences, it falls to be considered here. For example, the Road Traffic Act (RTA) 1988, s 3 defines the offence of 'driving without due care and attention', an offence clearly based on negligence. The Road Safety Act 2006 creates the new offence of 'causing death by dangerous driving': see 8.37. The offence under the Domestic Violence, Crime and Victims Act (DVCVA) 2004, s 5 (causing or allowing the death of a child or vulnerable adult) is also based on negligence (see 8.36). Negligence provides an objective standard which does not vary according to D's individual characteristics. Some statutes provide a 'no-negligence' defence, with the consequence that negligence will satisfy the requirements of the offence. An offence created where D 'did not know and had no reason to suspect' in effect penalizes D for negligence: Ashworth and Blake in [1996] Crim LR 306 point out that such offences raise important questions in relation to the burden of proof and the presumption of innocence.

3.31 Negligence is also the *mens rea* requirement of some common law offences:

Rimmington; Goldstein **(2005)** R was alleged to have caused a public nuisance by posting strongly racist communications to numerous people. He unsuccessfully challenged the indictment preferred against him at a preparatory hearing and his appeal to the CA was heard with that of G, who had been convicted of causing a public nuisance, having admitted sending a small quantity of salt through the post to a friend. A small quantity of salt had leaked on to the hands of a postal worker and the sorting office had been temporarily closed. Both appeals were dismissed by the CA.

HL: unanimously allowed both appeals. Lord Bingham gave the main speech, providing a detailed review of the history of the offence and of the authorities. Just as the courts have no power to create new offences, so they have no power to abolish existing offences. The two guiding common law principles—that no one should be punished under a law unless it is sufficiently clear and certain to enable him to know what conduct is forbidden before he does it; and that no one should be punished for any act which was not clearly and ascertainably punishable when the act was done—are entirely consistent with Art 7(1) of the ECHR (see **1.25**):

> A legal adviser asked to give his opinion in advance would ascertain whether the act or omission contemplated was likely to inflict significant injury on a substantial section of the public exercising their ordinary rights as such: if so, an obvious risk of causing a public nuisance would be apparent; if not, not (para. 36).

The 'state of mind' test laid down by the CA in *Shorrock* (1994), that D is responsible for a nuisance which he knew, or ought to have known (because the means of knowledge were available to him), would be the consequence of what he did or omitted to do, was correct. So in G's case, it had not been proven that he knew or should reasonably have known that the salt would escape into the sorting office or in the course of the post.

3.32 Most importantly, 'gross' negligence can be the basis for liability for manslaughter. The following test was laid down by Lord Hewart CJ in *Bateman* (1925):

> …the facts must be such that, in the opinion of the jury, the negligence of the accused went beyond a mere matter of compensation between subjects and showed such disregard for the life and safety of others as to amount to a crime against the State and conduct deserving punishment.

It seemed during the 1980s that this test of 'gross negligence' was going to be replaced in manslaughter cases by a test of objective recklessness (see *Seymour*

(1983); *Kong Cheuk Kwan v R* (1985) at **8.27**), but the HL later confirmed that gross negligence may be sufficient:

> **Adomako (1994)** D, an anaesthetist, failed to notice that an oxygen tube had become disconnected and V, the patient, died. P alleged that D had been grossly negligent in not noticing the obvious signs of disconnection and in failing to see that the alarm on the ventilator was not switched on.
>
> HL: upheld D's conviction for manslaughter. Lord Mackay:
>
>> In cases of criminal negligence involving a breach of duty it is a sufficient direction to the jury to adopt the gross negligence test … it is not necessary to refer to the definition of recklessness in *Lawrence* (1982), although it is perfectly open to the trial judge to use the word 'reckless' in its ordinary meaning as part of his exposition of the law if he deems it appropriate in the circumstances of the particular case … The essence of the matter which is supremely a jury question is whether, having regard to the risk of death involved, the conduct of the defendant was so bad in all the circumstances as to amount in their judgment to a criminal act or omission.

Thus Lord Mackay wished to leave a value judgment in the hands of juries: was this behaviour bad enough to justify a manslaughter conviction? We will return to this case at **8.29** in the context of an analysis of the law of manslaughter. Do you think that the key ingredient of such a serious offence should be defined more clearly?

Transferred malice

3.33 If a person by mistake or bad judgment causes injury to the wrong person or property, he may still be guilty of the offence he intended. Thus there is no problem in convicting D of the murder of A when he intended to kill B, or of wounding C when he intended to wound E: the doctrine of transferred malice or transferred intent applies:

> **Latimer (1886)** D aimed a blow at X with a belt, but by mistake hit V.
>
> Court of Crown Cases Reserved (CCCR) (Lord Coleridge CJ): upheld his conviction for unlawful wounding, under the OAPA 1861, s 20. 'He had an intent to do an unlawful act and in carrying out that intent he did injure a person; and the law says that, under such circumstances, a man is guilty of maliciously wounding the person actually wounded.'

Mitchell **(1983)** D assaulted a man aged 72 in a Post Office queue. The man fell on to V, an elderly lady of 89 who died of the injuries she suffered.

CA: upheld his conviction for manslaughter. Staughton LJ: 'We can see no reason of policy for holding that an act calculated to harm A cannot be manslaughter if it in fact kills B.'

A-G's Reference (No. 3 of 1994) **(1997)** D stabbed his girlfriend who he knew to be pregnant. The girlfriend recovered, but V, her baby, was born prematurely as a result of the wound and died after 120 days. The trial judge held that D could not be convicted of murder or manslaughter and ordered D's acquittal.

HL: D was rightly acquitted of murder. Since there was no evidence that D intended to injure the foetus or the child, it would be straining the concept of transferred malice too far to apply it in these circumstances: it would require the malice to be transferred not once but twice, namely from the mother to the foetus and from the foetus to the child. (However, manslaughter could have been committed: see **8.3**; **8.25**.)

3.34   These cases cause no problem because the definition of the offence is wide enough to cover the situation in hand: in *Latimer*, D wounded someone and it doesn't matter that he was striking out at someone else. However, *mens rea* will not necessarily transfer from one offence to a different one:

Pembliton **(1874)** D picked up a large stone to throw it at someone with whom he was fighting and broke a window.

CCCR (Lord Coleridge CJ): quashed his conviction for malicious damage. The jury had found that he had intended to hit someone, but this was not adequate *mens rea* for malicious damage, which required foresight of damage to property, not foresight of damage to people:

> …as they have found that he threw the stone at the people he had been fighting with intending to strike them and not intending to break the window, I think that the conviction must be quashed.

Ellis **(1986)** Ds were participating in importing large quantities of cannabis in secret compartments in cars and were charged with being knowingly concerned in the fraudulent evasion of the prohibition on the importation of a controlled drug. Their defence was that they thought they were importing prohibited pornography.

CA: dismissed their appeal. An intention to import a prohibited substance is sufficient *mens rea* for importing both a controlled drug of class A, and for the separate offence of importing a class B drug, and this would extend to an intention to import other prohibited substances such as pornography.

3.35 What is important is an analysis of the precise fault required for the offence charged. This problem is discussed in Chapter 6 which looks at the liability of accomplices. If the accomplice encourages violence against a particular victim and the principal deliberately chooses another victim not contemplated by the accessory, the accessory will not be liable. If the accomplice encourages violence against a particular victim, and the principal misfires, then the accomplice will still be liable because the principal has tried to do what the accomplice encouraged. The doctrine of transferred malice applies (see *Gnango* (2011) at **6.4**).

Vicarious liability

3.36 Generally, criminal liability is personal. This can be contrasted with the position in tort, where employers are usually liable for the torts of their employees committed in the course of their employment (see Hedley, *Tort* (7th edn, 2010)). In criminal law, one person is not generally liable for crimes committed by another:

> *Huggins* **(1730)** The warden of Fleet prison was acquitted of murder when V's death had been caused by his incarceration in an unhealthy cell.

Thus, in criminal law vicarious liability is exceptional. The exceptions include:

(i) Rare common law offences: for example, public nuisance and criminal libel. Whether such offences should continue to exist was raised at **1.24** and indeed the common law libel offences were at last abolished in the Coroners and Justice Act 2009. Public nuisance is being reviewed by the Law Commission.

(ii) 'Extensive' or 'extended' construction of statutes. This normally occurs in employer/employee situations where the employer is held to be strictly liable for the offence. Thus words such as 'sell', 'use', or 'possess' may be interpreted as applying both to the person who actually sells and to the principal on behalf of whom he is acting. This is further discussed at **3.39**.

(iii) The delegation principle: this is found most frequently in cases relating to licensees. The courts have interpreted some offences requiring knowledge so as to permit the conviction of the manager of premises on the basis of the acts of someone to whom he has delegated responsibility.

***Allen v Whitehead* (1930)** D employed a manager to run a café in London. He instructed the manager not to allow prostitutes to gather on the premises, but was convicted of knowingly permitting prostitutes to remain in a place of refreshment contrary to the Metropolitan Police Act 1839, s 44, even though his manager had flouted his instructions.

3.37 This 'delegation principle' was regarded as anomalous by the HL in *Vane v Yiannopoullos* (1965). Certainly it is extraordinarily harsh on a D who has done all that he can to comply with the law. The DCC (1989) would have abolished it. The CA in *St Regis Paper Co Ltd* (2011, see **4.34**) do not want to extend it beyond the *Allen v Whitehead*-type situation.

Strict liability

3.38 Those offences which do not require proof of *mens rea* in respect of one or more elements of the *actus reus* are known as crimes of strict liability. Liability is rarely absolute: general defences will normally apply. Common law offences of strict liability are very rare today, but they are not unknown:

***R v Lemon; Whitehouse v Gay News* (1979)** The editor and publishers of *Gay News* published a poem which described homosexual acts done with the body of Christ after his death and described his alleged homosexual practices in his lifetime. They were convicted of blasphemy.

HL: dismissed their appeal. The harm was done by the intentional publication, whether or not D intended to blaspheme. Lord Diplock dissented, arguing that there was no justification on grounds of public order or public morals for arguing that the common law offence of blasphemy should impose strict liability. (See also *Rimmington; Goldstein* (2005) at **3.31**.) But note that the offence of blasphemy was abolished by s 79 of the CJIA 2008.

3.39 Most examples of strict liability offences are of course statutory and they are numerous. Ashworth and Blake (1996) consider that of the 540 serious offences dealt with in *Archbold* (the practitioner's main guide to criminal pleading, evidence, and practice) in 1995, 123 had a strict liability element. Most such offences are considered to be regulatory, applying to particular trades for example, but many can result in significant periods of imprisonment. Ashworth and Blake comment that if Parliament is free to impose strict liability as and when it wishes, the presumption of innocence rings hollow: they point out that the Canadian courts have invalidated most strict liability offences for which imprisonment is a possible penalty.

The following two cases are traditional illustrations of the difficulties which the courts face in this area:

***Cundy v Le Cocq* (1884)** The Licensing Act 1872, s 13 made it an offence for any licensed person to sell intoxicating liquor to a drunken person. D was convicted even though he was not aware that the person he was serving was intoxicated.

QBD: upheld his conviction. The words of the section amounted to an absolute prohibition on the sale of alcohol to the drunk and the existence of a bona fide mistake as to the condition of the person served was no answer to the charge, but only a matter for the mitigation of the penalty imposed.

***Sherras v de Rutzen* (1895)** The Licensing Act 1872, s 16(2) prohibits a licensed victualler from supplying liquor to a police constable who is on duty. D was convicted, although he reasonably believed that the police constable was off duty.

QBD: quashed the conviction. It would be straining the law to say that a D who was acting in the bona fide belief that the constable was off duty, and who had reasonable grounds for that belief, was guilty of an offence for which he was liable both to a penalty and to have his licence endorsed.

3.40   Another leading case on strict liability for more than a century was:

***Prince* (1875)** D was convicted of taking an unmarried girl under the age of 16 out of the possession of her parents. It was accepted that he had reasonable grounds for believing that she was over 16.

CCCR (16 judges!): the conviction was upheld since strict liability applied in relation to the girl's age. However, Bramwell B (with whom six other judges agreed) said that his judgment gave full scope to the doctrine of *mens rea*: had D believed that he had the father's permission, or that she was in no one's possession, then he would have had no *mens rea*.

This authority lasted until:

***B (a minor) v DPP* (2000)** D, aged 15, sat next to V, a 13-year-old girl, on a bus. He asked her several times to perform oral sex with him and she repeatedly refused. His defence was that he honestly believed she was over 14, but when the magistrates ruled that this was no defence to a charge under s 1 of the Indecency with Children Act 1960, he changed his plea to guilty.

HL (unanimously): allowed D's appeal. Where Parliament failed to specify the mental element required, it was not a necessary implication that it was the intention of Parliament that liability should be strict so that an honest belief as to the age of the child would not be a defence. *Prince* (1875) was a 'relic from an age dead and gone' (Lord Hutton) and could be ignored as concerning a different offence and a different statute. P must prove that D knew that, or was reckless whether, the child was under 14.

Although this case concerned the Indecency with Children Act 1960, it had important implications for other possible offences of strict liability:

K **(2001)** D, a man of 26, was charged with indecent assault against a girl under the age of 14, contrary to the SOA 1956, s 14. His defence was that the activity was consensual and that he believed that she was over 16. The trial judge ruled as a preliminary issue that P had to prove the absence of a genuine belief that V was over 16

CA: P's appeal allowed; an absence of a genuine belief did not have to be proved.

HL: reversed CA. Indecent assault on a consenting child under 16, contrary to the SOA 1956, s 14 or 15 was not an offence of strict liability. Lord Bingham stated that the 1956 and 1960 Acts should be treated as a single code and described *Prince* as 'discredited'.

Whilst the courts' acknowledgement of a clear presumption of *mens rea* was welcome, there was a snag, as J. C. Smith pointed out at [2002] Crim LR 993: because of the HL's 'new readiness' to ignore the obvious intention of Parliament, we can no longer take the words of a statute at face value. As detailed in Chapter 10, the SOA 2003 has created a very strict new set of laws. Thus, it is clear that a mistaken belief as to age will be no defence when the child is under 13 (see *G* (2008) at **10.21**). When the child is under 16, but over 13, a reasonable and mistaken belief as to the child's age may provide a defence. But there are other strict liability sexual offences too: s 14 of the Policing and Crime Act 2009 inserted a new offence into s 53A of the SOA 2003: paying for the sexual services of a prostitute subjected to force, threats or any other form of coercion, or any form of deception (committed by a third person). This is strict liability: there is no need for D to know that the prostitute has been coerced: see the Home Office's public information poster 'Walk in a punter. Walk out a criminal': see <http://toomuchtosayformyself.com/2010/04/01/walk-in-a-punter-walk-out-a-criminal/>.

3.41 Strict liability in the sexual arena reflects a strict approach to offending. When it comes to many other offences, it is often difficult to decide whether strict liability applies.

Sweet v Parsley **(1970)** D rented a farmhouse, but sub-let it to students. Police found cannabis at the farm and she was charged and convicted of 'being concerned in the management of premises used for the purpose of smoking cannabis resin', contrary to the Dangerous Drugs Act 1965, s 5(b).

HL: quashed her conviction. Lord Reid: 'Whenever a section is silent as to *mens rea* there is a presumption that, in order to give effect to the will of Parliament, we must read in words appropriate to require *mens rea*.' He distinguished quasi-criminal offences, where the presumption of *mens rea* might be more easily rebutted, from truly criminal acts where the stigma attached to conviction was greater.

3.42 This decision did not, of course, sound the death knell of strict liability:

Pharmaceutical Society of Great Britain v Storkwain **(1986)** D pharmacists dispensed prescribed drugs to someone who gave a forged prescription. D acting in good faith and on reasonable grounds, believed the prescriptions were valid. They were convicted of selling medicines without an appropriate prescription, contrary to the Medicines Act 1968, s 58.

HL: upheld the conviction since it was clear from the 1968 Act that Parliament must have intended that the presumption of *mens rea* was inapplicable to s 58(2).

It can be difficult to anticipate when the courts will decide that an offence is one of strict liability. One of the difficulties arises from the courts' attempts to distinguish between truly criminal acts and those which are illegal only because the public welfare so demands, so-called 'regulatory offences'.

Harrow London Borough Council v Shah **(1999)** D's shop assistant sold a lottery ticket to a person who he reasonably believed to be 16, but who was in fact under that age.

Div Ct (Mitchell J): upheld his conviction. This was not a 'truly criminal act' but one which in the public interest was prohibited under a penalty. The offence imposed strict (and vicarious) liability.

In other cases, the courts avoid the problem by concentrating on some other issue. Thus, in **2.23** the problems of causation were raised. The 'common sense' approach of the HL to questions of causation in *Alphacell Ltd v Woodward* (1972) distracted from the need for a discussion of strict liability.

L **(2008)** During building work at a golf club (an unincorporated body), an underground pipe taking heating oil from a storage tank to a boiler was fractured and some 1,500 litres of oil escaped and polluted a nearby watercourse. The Environment Agency initiated a prosecution against the chairman and treasurer of the club. The judge agreed to quash the indictment as the club itself could, and should, have been prosecuted.

CA: the judge had erred in ruling that the individual Ds could not be prosecuted. The correct position was that a prosecution under s 85 of the 1991 Act could be brought against either the club or against individual members.

Ormerod comments at [2009] Crim LR 381:

> ...given the enormous number of strict liability offences that organisations might transgress in the course of performing their usual business the prospect of personal liability of all members seems astounding ... No better example than the present case is needed to demonstrate the potential harshness of the law. An individual member of the club with no responsibility for organisation and in no way at fault can be convicted on the basis of strict liability offence coupled with the strict Empress approach to causation [see **2.23**] and the wide interpretation of liability for unincorporated association members.

3.43 There are many arguments for creating offences of strict liability:

- Protectionism/social defence.
- People who run businesses should do so properly.
- Guilty people should not escape conviction because of lack of proof/ evidence.
- Strict liability offences are easier to enforce.
- People may be deterred by the knowledge that offences are strict liability.
- It obliges people to adopt high standards.
- It saves court time: people plead guilty.
- A person who creates a risk and takes a profit from that risk should also pay for the adverse consequences.

However, there are perhaps stronger counter-arguments:

- Liability should not be imposed on those who are not blameworthy.
- It is wrong to penalize those who have taken all proper care.
- It is inefficient, merely delaying an analysis of fault until the sentencing stage.
- There is no evidence that it raises standards.
- It may put small business at an unfair risk.

3.44 The arguments were summed up well by Thomas (1978):

> The effect of imposing strict liability is not necessarily to eliminate fault as a require-
> ment of liability, but to delegate to the enforcer both the responsibility of deciding
> what kind of fault will in general justify a prosecution (with the certainty of convic-
> tion) and the right to determine whether in the circumstances of the particular case
> that degree of fault is present. The main objections to the concept of strict liability
> are thus procedural rather than substantive, and the questions to be addressed to the
> proponent of a statute creating an offence of strict liability are: 'Why is it not possible
> to incorporate into the definition of the offence the nature of the fault which is likely
> in practice to be required as a condition precedent to prosecution, and why is it not
> possible for the existence of this fault to be determined in accordance with the normal
> process of law?'

As discussed again in Chapter 13, on crimes against the environment, one consequence of the law's tough stance in imposing strict liability is that wide discretion is then given to the prosecuting body: despite the appearance of a law
which imposes liability without fault, in practice a prosecution may be unlikely
to take place unless the company is perceived to be genuinely blameworthy. Yet
the case of *L* (2008) shows how harsh the law can be when all members of a golf
club can be held guilty of an offence of strict liability. The arguments against
strict liability imposed on individuals seem strong, but there may be different arguments applicable to corporate liability, a subject which is discussed in
Chapter 4.

Reform

3.45 The DCC (1989) accepted that *mens rea* should be presumed in clause 20:

> (1) Every offence requires a fault element of recklessness with respect to each of
>   its elements other than fault elements, unless otherwise provided.

This clumsy clause means that strict liability can only be imposed if Parliament
expressly or by necessary implication so provides. In the Commentary to clause
20, the Law Commission said that they thought it would be inappropriate to
make the presumption displaceable only by express provision. There is no
guidance on when the courts should decide that Parliament 'plainly implied'
that an offence is one of strict liability. The Law Commission gave the example
of an offence of causing polluting matter to enter a watercourse created after
the Code comes into force. In the absence of any provision to the contrary the
offence requires (a) an intention to cause the matter to enter the watercourse
or recklessness whether it will do so, and (b) knowledge that the matter is a

pollutant or recklessness whether it is. This puts a heavy onus on parliamentary draftsmen to make their message clear. Perhaps today there is less discussion about the 'unprincipled' use of strict liability because the increasing use of fixed penalty notices, conditional cautions, and other diversionary measures means that many less serious offences are dealt with outside the formal criminal courts, and most often beyond the gaze of the appellate courts. But it is a very important topic!

FURTHER READING

Ashworth, A. and Blake, M., 'The Burden of Proof and the Presumption of Innocence' [1996] Crim LR 306.

Buxton, R., 'Some Simple Thoughts on Intention' [1988] Crim LR 484.

Duff, A., *Intention, Agency and Criminal Liability* (1990).

Goff, Lord, 'The Mental Element in the Crime of Murder' (1988) 104 LQR 30.

Kaveny, M. C., 'Inferring Intention from Foresight' (2004) 120 LQR 81.

Leigh, L., *Strict and Vicarious Liability* (1982).

Norrie, A., 'Between Orthodox Subjectivism and Moral Contextualism' [2006] Crim LR 486.

Simester, A. (ed.), *Appraising Strict Liability* (2005).

Thomas, D., 'Form and Function in the Criminal Law' in P. Glazebrook (ed.), *Reshaping the Criminal Law* (1978).

Williams, G., 'The Unresolved Problem of Recklessness' (1988) 8 LS 74.

SELF-TEST QUESTIONS

1   Dee bakes Phil a birthday cake. Intending to kill him, she puts poison in the cake. Phil takes the cake home and eats it. Dee then has second thoughts and goes to Phil's home where she finds him seriously ill. She calls an ambulance, but Phil dies before it arrives. Discuss Dee's liability.

2   Dee wishes to collect the insurance money on her house, so sets fire to it knowing that Phil might be asleep upstairs. Would English law say that she intended to kill Phil?

3   Dee is sleeping rough and spends three nights in an old barn. She is freezing cold and sets fire to a pile of old rubbish in the barn. The fire gets out of control so Dee leaves to find somewhere else to sleep. The barn is destroyed. Medical evidence says that Dee has a mental age of 8. Is she reckless?

4   If a patient dies due to medical incompetence, how incompetent does a doctor have to have been before a jury may judge him to have been grossly negligent and therefore guilty of manslaughter?

5   Is the imposition of strict liability ever justified?

4

Incapacitating conditions

SUMMARY

Childhood: children under the age of 10 cannot be convicted of a crime. The Crime and Disorder Act 1998 abolished the doctrine of *doli incapax* which had allowed a sliding scale of responsibility for those aged 10 to 14: that the Act really did this was confirmed in *T* (2009).

Insanity: *M'Naghten Rules:* D is not guilty by reason of insanity if he has 'a defect of reason, from disease of the mind, as not to know the nature and quality of the act he was doing; or, if he did know it, that he did not know he was doing what was wrong'. Note the problem of providing satisfactory legal/medical definitions of mental disorder.

Intoxication: conflicting policy issues: D is guilty of most crimes if he commits them when drunk, but his drunkenness may show he did not have the necessary 'intent' for other crimes (e.g. murder, theft). The Law Commission recommended in 1996 maintaining this *'Majewski rule'*, but their 2009 report has more complex recommendations.

Corporate liability: distinguish cases where the company is vicariously liable for the crimes of others, from cases where the company is itself liable. (Note also the Corporate Manslaughter and Corporate Homicide Act 2007.)

Introduction

4.1 Neither childhood nor insanity is properly described as a 'defence', of course: it is the child's status as a child which prevents him or her being guilty of an offence. It is a key characteristic, her 'abnormal condition', which excuses her from liability. It is worth noting that, although a child or an insane person may not be blameworthy, such a person may still be 'punished' in some sense: a person not guilty by reason of insanity may still be compulsorily detained in a mental hospital, a 'criminal' child may still be subject to care proceedings. In the case of a child, should the law recognize a sliding scale of criminal responsibility (see **4.2**)? With the insane, it is the lack of autonomy in the sense of a lack of ability to make effective choices which makes D not guilty, but there is no sliding scale (except when it comes to sentencing). However, this lack of ability may be caused by:

   (i) internal causes: in which case he may be not guilty by reason of insanity (**4.9**);

   (ii) external causes: in which case he may be acquitted if he was not at fault (see automatism: **4.18**) or convicted if he was at fault (see intoxication **4.19**);

   (iii) a mixture of both external and internal causes.

This chapter also explores the effect of intoxication on liability generally. Again, not a 'defence', but a person may be so incapacitated by drink or drugs that he or she does not form the necessary intent to justify conviction. Criminal offences have largely been designed with human wrongdoers in mind so, finally in this chapter, we will look at the ways in which a company may or may not be convicted of criminal offences.

Childhood

4.2 A child under the age of 10 is *doli incapax* (i.e. incapable of committing a crime): see the CYPA 1933, s 50. She may be the subject of care proceedings, but may not be prosecuted for a crime. From the age of 10 the child may be guilty. Until the Crime and Disorder Act 1998, it was well established that until D reached the age of 14, P had to prove not only that the child had the *mens rea* for the relevant crime, but also that she knew that what she did was a wrong act and not merely an act of simple naughtiness or mischief. But this requirement was challenged both in the courts and then by Parliament. The law was unsettled after the murder of a toddler by two 11-year-olds in 1993 shook the nation, resulting in a wave of popular emotion that something should be done to instil greater respect for the law amongst children. However, the HL upheld the *doli incapax* rule, reversing a DC attempt to abolish it:

C v DPP **(1995)** D, aged 12, was seen with another boy using a crowbar to interfere with a motorcycle on a private driveway. When they saw the police, they ran away. D was convicted before the magistrates of interfering with a motor vehicle with the intention to commit theft or to take and drive away without consent, contrary to the CAA 1981, s 9(1).

DC: upheld D's conviction. The doctrine of *doli incapax* should no longer be regarded as part of the common law.

HL: reversed the DC's decision. It is still the law that a child between the ages of 10 and 14 is presumed incapable of committing a crime unless there is clear evidence that he knew that what he did was seriously wrong.

The presumption was not merely window-dressing:

***CC (a minor) v DPP* (1996)** D, aged 11 years and 11 months, at the time, and another boy, attacked a 12-year-old on his bicycle. D took a lock knife from his pocket and the other boy held it to V's throat. Before V was released, D said 'Cut his nose to make sure', referring to V bringing money to school for them the next day. Justices rejected a submission of no case to answer, finding that it was almost inconceivable that a boy of D's age would not know that it was seriously wrong to place a knife on someone's throat and demand money.

DC (Mitchell J): quashed D's convictions for offences under the Public Order Act (POA) 1986, ss 3 and 4. 'The tribunal of fact must avoid the trap of applying...the "presumption of normality". That presumption is to this effect: any normal boy of his age in society, as it is today, must have known that what he was doing was seriously wrong. Such an approach as that reverses the relevant presumption of *doli incapax*.' Very little evidence was needed to rebut the presumption of *doli incapax*, but some evidence there had to be.

4.3 During the 1970s and 1980s, there had been a great increase in the number of children who received police cautions as an alternative to being prosecuted. Why were children treated differently from adults? Partly because we do not blame them so much: a child may have acted intentionally or recklessly, but she may not have developed the ability to apply 'normal' moral standards. A child might pull the wings off a fly to see what will happen to it next, or stamp on a spider: is his behaviour as morally blameworthy as that of an adult who acts similarly? There are other, more pragmatic, reasons why children may be 'shielded' from the full force of the criminal law. 'Labelling theory' suggests that once a child is seen (and sees herself) as criminal, then she may become more criminal. Thus, it can be argued that criminal sanctions should be applied as a last resort.

However, the Government decided that the presumption should be abolished: 'to respond effectively to youth crime, we must stop making excuses for children who offend' (para. 4.1 of the White Paper, *No More Excuses* (Cm. 3809, 1997)). Section 34 of the Crime and Disorder Act 1998 provides simply that:

The rebuttable presumption of criminal law that a child aged 10 or over is incapable of committing an offence is hereby abolished.

Walker (1999) argued that this change did not abolish the presumption, but merely reversed the burden of proof: it may still be possible for a child to argue by way of defence that she did not know that what she was doing was wrong. This argument was reviewed in:

CPS v P (2007) D, aged 13, suffered many difficulties including Attention Deficit Hyperactivity Disorder (ADHD) and special education needs. In proceedings (for numerous offences) before the CC in June 2005, professional reports had agreed that he had an IQ in the lowest centile of the population, and that he did not have the capacity to participate effectively in a criminal trial. P had accepted that he was unfit to plead, and proceedings were stayed. Later in the year he was arrested for further offences and in April 2006 the District Judge (DJ) in the Youth Court stayed these proceedings. The CPS appealed by way of case stated.

DC: allowed the appeal. The DJ had erred in law. However, since it was a year since the relevant events occurred and care proceedings had since been commenced, the stay would remain in place. The fact that the CC had previously held that P was unfit to plead did not make it an abuse of process to try him for subsequent criminal acts. The issue of the child's ability to participate effectively had to be decided afresh. Acknowledging that the point was merely *obiter*, Smith LJ said that Professor Walker (in [1999] NLJ 64) 'may well be right and that s. 34 abolishes only the presumption of *doli incapax* so that the defence is still available'. She gave various reasons, based both on the grammatical interpretation of the statute and on the intention of both the Government and of Parliament:

> …it may, particularly in the case of a young child with mental health or disability problems, be thought preferable to proceed by way of civil proceedings seeking a care or supervision order under the Children Act 1989, rather than to embark on a prosecution (para. 35).

> …as the defence of *doli incapax* would be a common law defence as opposed to a statutory one, as a matter of general principle the burden should remain on the Crown to prove that the child had the requisite understanding. Moreover, the standard of proof should be the usual criminal standard' (para. 47).

Sadly this argument did not find favour with the HL:

T (2009) D, aged 12 at the time of the offences, was convicted on 12 counts of causing or inciting a child under 13 to engage in sexual activity. He had pleaded guilty after the trial judge ruled that the defence of *doli incapax* was not available to him.

HL: dismissed his appeal. When s 34 was read in isolation, its meaning was ambiguous. The appeal could not be deduced from the language of s 34 alone. The Consultation

> Paper and the White Paper that preceded the legislation had made it quite clear what was meant by the abolition of the presumption of *doli incapax*. Therefore, in using the language of s 34, Parliament intended to abolish both the presumption and the defence and, accordingly, the trial judge and the CA were correct to hold that s 34 abolished the defence of *doli incapax*.

The doctrine of *doli incapax* has been called a 'merciful concept' (Bennion (2009), at p. 770): do you think there should be a sliding scale of responsibility? Many children continue to be prosecuted (indeed, many with significant learning and mental difficulties: see *C v Sevenoaks Youth Court* (2009) for an example). Is this really appropriate? As Professor Andrew Ashworth stated, in his commentary to the decision of the ECtHR in *SC v UK* (2005) at [2005] Crim LR 132:

> …what is absolutely clear is that the Strasbourg approach is to give far greater emphasis to the principle of effective participation than the English courts have tended to do… In most other European countries it would not be possible to prosecute a child of 11, and it is no surprise that the ECHR insists on high standards for effective participation and on special arrangements if such cases do go ahead.

In 2010, the Children's Commissioner called for a raising of the age of criminal responsibility. So have many academics: see Keating (2007) and Davies and McMahon (2007).

Of course adults who use an under-age child to carry out their own crimes will be guilty of an offence themselves under the doctrine of innocent agency (see 6.6). On the other hand, if you are attacked by a child, you may use reasonable force to resist that aggression even if the child is not convicted of a crime (see self-defence, 5.33).

Mental disorder

4.4 When D's conduct is the result of mental disorder, or mental illness, he may be

   (i) unfit to plead;

   (ii) not guilty by reason of insanity;

   (iii) not guilty by reason of automatism;

   (iv) convicted of a more minor offence than that charged: thus if D is charged with murder, he may be convicted only of manslaughter if he is suffering from diminished responsibility by reason of some 'abnormality of mind' (see 8.9);

(v) convicted of the offence charged, but the mental disorder may be taken into consideration at the sentencing stage.

Unfitness to plead

4.5 Very few people are found to be unfit to plead. This is perhaps because severely mentally handicapped, ill or disordered people are diverted from the criminal justice system before they reach the stage of court proceedings. However, there has been a significant increase in the number of cases where the issue of unfitness is raised (see *Walls* (2011)). Where the prosecution does initiate proceedings, D must be 'of sufficient intellect to comprehend the course of the proceedings in the trial so as to make a proper defence, to challenge a juror to whom he might wish to object and comprehend the details of the evidence' (Alderson B in *Pritchard* (1836), where D was deaf and dumb). The test is not exactly up to date: Ds rarely get the chance to challenge jurors since the abolition of peremptory challenges in 1988, but the principle is clear: D must be able to plead, and to instruct his lawyers. He need not necessarily be capable of acting in his own best interests. Mackay (1995) argues that the test is too restrictive and should include a test of 'decisional incapacity' to cover, for example, the mentally disordered person who pleads guilty against the advice of his or her lawyer.

4.6 In practice where there is evidence that D is unfit to plead, the court first hears evidence on this issue. If he is fit to plead, then the trial proceeds. If he is not fit to plead, another court then decides if D 'did the act or made the omission charged against him as the offence' (Criminal Procedure (Insanity and Unfitness to Plead) Act 1991, as amended by s 22 of the DVCVA 2004; see also *Antoine* (2000): see 2.3). If the court is satisfied that he did what was alleged, then the court has a choice of disposals, including admission to hospital with or without a restriction order or an absolute discharge. An example is provided by:

Grant (2001) D admitted stabbing V, her boyfriend, who died from his injuries. She was charged with murder. A jury, having heard evidence from three psychiatrists, found her unfit to be tried, pursuant to the Criminal Procedure (Insanity) Act 1964, s 4(5) as amended. A second jury then found that she had committed the act charged against her as the offence, namely the stabbing, pursuant to s 4A of the

1964 Act. The judge made a hospital order together with a direction equivalent to a restriction order under the Mental Health Act (MHA) 1983, s 41 without limitation of time. D appealed against the jury's finding that she did the act charged against her, on the ground that the judge should have left the 'defences' of lack of intent and/or provocation to the jury. The judge also stated a case for the opinion of the HC asking, inter alia, whether the relevant provisions of the 1964 and 1991 Acts contravened the HRA 1998.

CA (also sitting as DC): it was clear from the decision of the HL in *Antoine* (2000) (see **2.3**) that lack of intent could not be left to the jury in proceedings under s 4A(2), since the jury need only be satisfied that D committed the *actus reus*. The procedures laid down did not fail the tests laid down under Art 5 of the ECHR for the detention of people of unsound mind. Subject to one important point of concern, the Court held that it is not unreasonable for Parliament to have decided to lay down a mandatory hospital order for someone charged with murder and found unfit to plead. The point of concern was that it might be possible for a person to be found unfit to be tried without his suffering from a mental disorder sufficiently serious to warrant detention.

The HL confirmed in *H* (2003) that the procedure for determining whether a person found unfit to plead did the act or made the omission charged against him (Criminal Procedure (Insanity) Act 1964, s 4A) was not incompatible with Art 6 of the ECHR (see **1.25**).

4.7 Until 1991, the law was extraordinarily harsh on those unfit to plead: indefinite committal to hospital was the only possible outcome. This now only applies in the case of murder, since the Criminal Procedure (Insanity and Unfitness to Plead) Act (CP(IUP)A) 1991 (and the DVCVA 2004) gave courts the discretion to choose from a wide variety of sentencing options. If D's condition improves, he may be remitted to court for trial: this appears to happen in about half of all cases: the CA in *Grant* expressed concern about the criteria which justify detention. The Court was satisfied that a mandatory hospital order was not 'arbitrary' for the purposes of Art 5(1)(e) and that the right to make an immediate application to the Mental Health Review Tribunal (MHRT) following admission to hospital ensures compliance with Art 5(4) (though this raises the thorny question about what is an acceptable delay).

4.8 In 2010 the Law Commission published a Consultation Paper on *Unfitness to Plead* in which they provisionally proposed that the current *Pritchard* test should be replaced by a new test which assesses whether D has 'decision-making capacity for trial'. The Commission ask a number of questions about appropriate procedures to be followed in these cases, and has yet to publish a final Report on the subject.

Insanity

4.9   The rules on insanity derive from the celebrated case of *M'Naghten* (1843) who, in attempting to shoot the Home Secretary, had killed his secretary. After M'Naghten's acquittal by a jury, the judges of the HL were asked to formulate rules for the guidance of juries. Despite some reluctance about answering hypothetical questions on which they had not heard argument, Tindal CJ did report that:

> …jurors ought to be told in all cases that every man is to be presumed to be sane, and to possess a sufficient degree of reason to be responsible for his crimes, until the contrary is proved to their satisfaction; and that to establish a defence on the ground of insanity, it must be clearly proved that, at the time of the committing of the act, the party accused was labouring under such a defect of reason, from disease of the mind, as not to know the nature and quality of the act he was doing; or, if he did know it, that he did not know he was doing what was wrong.

Thus D must be suffering from a defect of reason which causes him either not to know what he was doing, or not to know that what he was doing was wrong.

Windle (1952)   D was convicted of the murder of his suicidal wife. His defence had been that he was insane, and had thought it was morally right to kill her.

CCA: dismissed his appeal. The judge was right to withdraw the defence of insanity since D knew that what he was doing was contrary to law. Lord Goddard CJ: 'wrong' means contrary to law 'and does not have some vague meaning which may vary according to the opinion of different persons whether a particular act might or might not be justified.'

This definition is remarkably narrow—someone is only insane if he did not know that what he did is *legally* wrong. Should the test be a failure to realize that what he did was *morally* wrong? Does it also mean that a person who thinks that his act is morally wrong but not legally wrong, would be entitled to the defence of insanity?

Johnson (2007)   D forced his way into V's flat shouting aggressively and stabbed him four times. Two psychiatrists subsequently assessed him and agreed that he was suffering from paranoid schizophrenia at the time. They also agreed that he knew that his actions were against the law, but one said that D did not consider what he had done to be morally wrong. The judge ruled that since he knew what he was doing was against the law, the defence of insanity was not available. He was convicted of wounding with intent (OAPA 1861, s 18: see **9.2**).

CA: dismissed his appeal. It was unequivocally held in *Windle* that the meaning of 'wrong' was that it was contrary to law and did not have a vague meaning that might vary according to the opinion of different persons whether a particular act might or might not be justified.

It is encouraging to know that the Law Commission has finally returned to this difficult subject (see **4.17**).

4.10 Until the CP(IUP)A 1991, the court had no option but to impose a mandatory hospital order on someone found not guilty by reason of insanity, which of course made the defence very unattractive. The law was further amended by the DVCVA 2004, ss 24 and 25. Now if D is found to be not guilty by reason of insanity (except in murder cases, where a mandatory life sentence will be imposed), he may still be detained in a mental hospital, but the court has a variety of options: admission to hospital with or without a restriction order, a supervision order, or an absolute discharge. The burden is placed on D (on a balance of probabilities) to prove that he is insane (except that P may raise insanity if D pleads diminished responsibility to a murder charge). Given the consequences of an insanity verdict, it is perhaps odd that the burden to prove it lies on D: surely the defence raises important questions not only about D's own welfare but also about the welfare of the community and so either party (and the judge) should be able to raise it.

Disease of the mind

4.11 To qualify for the defence of insanity, the accused must be suffering from a defect of reason caused by a disease of the mind. Curiously, this is a legal question for the judge, not a medical one.

Sullivan **(1984)** D inflicted grievous bodily harm on V, a friend, during a minor epileptic seizure. When the trial judge ruled that his defence amounted to insanity, he changed his plea to guilty of assault occasioning actual bodily harm.

HL: dismissed his appeal. Lord Diplock:

The nomenclature adopted by the medical profession may change from time to time…But the meaning of the expression 'disease of the mind' as the cause of a 'defect of reason' remains unchanged for the purposes of the application of the *M'Naghten Rules*…'mind' in the *M'Naghten Rules* is used in the ordinary sense of the mental faculties of reason, memory and understanding. If the effect of a disease is to impair these faculties so severely as to have either of the consequences referred to in the latter part of the rules, it matters not whether the aetiology of the impairment is organic, as in epilepsy, or functional, as to whether the impairment itself is permanent or is transient and intermittent, provided that it subsisted at the time of the commission of the act.

Thus the HL held that a special verdict of not guilty by reason of insanity was correct where an epileptic fit brought about a temporary suspension of the mental faculties of reason, memory and understanding during which an offence was committed. Similarly, it has been held that both a person who commits an offence whilst sleepwalking (see *Burgess* (1991)) and one who suffers from arteriosclerosis—hardening of the arteries—(see *Kemp* (1957)) are rightly described as suffering from a disease of the mind. This latter case is particularly odd given that arteriosclerosis is of physical rather than mental origin.

4.12 The rules have become particularly obtuse in relation to those suffering from diabetes. Since a disease of the mind is treated as something internal to D, if the cause of the disease is external, the defence does not apply. This distinction between internal and external causes results in an extraordinary distinction: if D is suffering from hyperglycaemia (high blood sugar level) caused by his failure to take insulin, then he is suffering from a disease of the mind. If he is suffering from hypoglycaemia (low blood sugar) caused by taking insulin but without appropriate food, he does not have a disease of the mind.

Quick **(1973)** D, a diabetic and a nurse, was charged with a serious assault on a patient in his charge. He had taken his insulin, but had eaten no lunch. He had also been drinking alcohol. When the trial judge ruled that his diabetes was a 'defect of reason caused by a disease of the mind', he changed his plea to guilty.

CA: quashed his conviction since his mental condition was caused not by his diabetes but by the use of insulin. The alleged malfunctioning of his mind had therefore been caused by an external factor and not by the disease. D's defence of automatism should have been left to the jury. The court could not say with the requisite degree of confidence that the jury would have convicted him and so his conviction had to be quashed as being unsatisfactory.

Hennessy **(1989)** D, a diabetic in a hyperglycaemic state because he had not taken insulin for a few days, was convicted of taking and driving away a vehicle.

CA: D's hyperglycaemia (excessive blood sugar) was caused by the diabetes when uncorrected by the administration of insulin and was rightly a disease of the mind. He was not therefore entitled to a defence of automatism.

In such cases, the culpability of the defendants is often similar: D's insulin balance has not been controlled for a period of time, often because of the 'pressures of life' upon him. Yet as the Ontario Court of Appeal said in the Canadian case of *Rabey* (1977), 'the ordinary stresses and disappointments of life which are the common lot of mankind do not constitute an external cause'. Should a diabetic be guilty of a crime when he fails to keep a reasonable control over his diabetes? However you answer that question, the label 'insanity' is hardly appropriate.

4.13 As *Hennessy* shows, the main impact of the *M'Naghten Rules* is to restrict other defences: automatism, for example. D cannot escape conviction by relying on the defence of automatism (which results in a complete acquittal) if she falls within the *M'Naghten Rules*. In the past, some Ds chose to plead guilty to a crime rather than face the prospect of being found not guilty by reason of insanity:

Clarke (1972) D was charged with theft from a supermarket. There was evidence that she had transferred goods from the wire basket in a supermarket into her shopping basket and then left without paying. Two doctors certified that she was suffering from mild depression and that this could cause absent-mindedness in which the patient might do things she would not normally do in periods of confusion and memory lapse. The trial judge held that this constituted evidence of insanity, and so D changed her plea to guilty.

CA: quashed her conviction. Ackner J:

> The *M'Naghten Rules* relate to accused persons who by reason of a disease of the mind are deprived of the power of reasoning. They do not apply and never have applied to those who retain the power of reasoning but who in moments of confusion or absent-mindedness fail to use their powers to the full.

Oye (2013) D, aged 29 and with no previous convictions, had been discovered behaving oddly in the staff area of a cafe. When the police were called D hid in a void in the ceiling, giving nonsensical reasons for his refusal to come down, and throwing crockery at the police officers. He was arrested and detained. He tried to escape, knocking a police officer to the ground and punching another, fracturing her jaw. He fought violently, lashing out and shrieking. He was then detained in hospital, where he continued to act strangely. D said he had fought the officers in self-defence, believing them to have demonic faces and to be the agents of evil spirits against whom he needed to protect himself. D described feeling as though he had acquired supernatural powers. Medical evidence agreed that D had experienced a psychotic episode, suffering such a defect of reason that he had not known what he was doing, and/or had not appreciated that what he was doing was wrong. The trial judge made clear distinctions for the jury between insanity and self-defence and gave proper directions as to the elements of the offences charged. He emphasized that the unchallenged psychiatric evidence was that D had been insane at the time of the offences.

Nevertheless, the jury rejected the defences of insanity and self-defence. The issue on appeal was whether, if a person reacted violently to a genuine, but insanely deluded, belief that he was being attacked or threatened, and used force that was reasonable in the circumstances as he believed them to be, he was entitled to an acquittal on the basis of reasonable self-defence, which involved consideration of the meaning of the CJIA 2008, s 76 (see **5.35**).

CA: quashed his convitions for affray and OAPA 1861, s 20 (see **9.8**). It was clear, particularly from s 76(6) of the 2008 Act, that the second limb of the defence of self-defence, namely whether the nature and degree of force used had been reasonable in the circumstances, was subjective, but included an objective element by reference to reasonableness. An insane person could not set the standards of reasonableness as to the degree of force used by reference to his own insanity; the position required objective assessment. The defence of self-defence had rightly been rejected. The proper verdicts would have been one of not guilty by reason of insanity and such verdicts were substituted. As D had made a full recovery from the psychotic incident, and had been in prison for some time, a hospital order or supervision order would serve no purpose. So CA ordered an absolute discharge.

This is an unusual decision: the CA reverses a jury's decision. But it is a humane decision. D's 'insanity' generated his belief that he needed to use force.

Insanity and intoxication

4.14   ***Coley, McGhee and Harris* (2013)** C, aged 17, was a heavy cannabis user who claimed that he 'blacked out' when he attacked a neighbor with a knife. He was convicted of attempted murder. In a separate case, M took a prescription tranquiliser and a lot of alcohol, despite warnings that he should not drink. He assaulted a shopkeeper and a customer in an off-licence at 4am and was convicted of wounding with intent (see **9.4**) and actual bodily harm (see **9.15**). In a third unrelated case, H set fire to his own house whilst suffering from a psychotic episode brought on by heavy binge drinking, followed by a sudden cessation of drinking. He was charged with arson being reckless as to whether the lives of others, namely his neighbours, would be endangered (see aggravated arson, **12.6**). He accepted that he had deliberately started the fire and that he knew it was wrong, but said he had given no thought to the risk to others. The trial judge ruled that the jury had to consider H's recklessness as if he had not been drinking. After that ruling, H pleaded guilty, but appealed.

CA dismissed the appeals of C and M, but quashed H's conviction. In order to engage the law of insanity, it is not enough that there is an effect on the mind or, in the language of the *M'Naghten Rules*, a 'defect of reason'. There must also be what the law classifies as a 'disease of the mind'. Direct acute effects on the mind of intoxicants, voluntarily taken, are not so classified. Every 'defect of reason' is not a 'disease of the mind':

> …[T]here is scope for the argument that an illness caused by his own fault ought as a matter of policy to be treated in the same way as is drunkenness at the time of the offence. This would, however, represent a significant extension of *Majewski* and of the similar principle expounded in *Quick*, which likewise concerned a case where what was asserted was an acute condition (there of automatism) induced arguably by D's fault. A great many mental illnesses have their roots in culpable past misconduct of the sufferer: those attributable to many years of past drug or alcohol abuse are perhaps the most obvious, but there could be many other examples such as, perhaps, a culpable failure to follow a recommended medical regime or maybe the consequences of traumatic brain injury caused by one's own drunken driving. Whether the *Majewski* approach ought to be extended to such cases may be a topic which might be addressed in the forthcoming work of the Law Commission on loss of capacity, and it should, no doubt, be the subject of proper public debate. But in the present state of the law, *Majewski* applies to offences committed by persons who are then voluntarily intoxicated but not to those who are suffering mental illness. This D (H) was, it is clear, suffering from a condition of mental illness when he set fire to his own house. That it was not long-lasting does not mean that it was not a true illness. In our view he was entitled to have tried the question of whether, in the condition in which he was, he was actually aware of the risk which he created for his neighbours (para. 59).

Proposals for reform

4.15 The insanity defence is rarely used for two main reasons. First, it is so narrow as to be seen as irrelevant. Secondly, there is sufficient stigma attached to the label that many wish to avoid it. If you are seriously mentally handicapped or ill, you may be unfit to plead. If you are not, you will be wary of the stigma and the possible penalty attached to the 'defence'. Many states in the USA have abolished the insanity defence. Rather as the acquittal of M'Naghten caused a furore in England in 1843, so did the acquittal of Hinckley for the attempted murder of the then President of the USA, Ronald Reagan, in 1982. The state of Idaho was first to abolish the defence, and others have followed suit. In these jurisdictions even the mentally ill and the insane may be prosecuted in the normal way. If a defendant has the necessary *mens rea*, then his mental condition becomes relevant only at the sentencing stage in much the same way that other social factors may be taken into account. If his 'insanity' means that he did not have the required *mens rea*, then he is not convicted. Under such a system, D may still be committed to a secure hospital under the provisions of the relevant civil law if he is perceived to be dangerous.

4.16 However, if you prefer a solution that accepts that those who are not blameworthy should not be convicted of crimes, then there should be a defence of mental illness. The Butler Committee in 1975 recommended that the insanity defence should be replaced by a verdict of 'not guilty on evidence of mental disorder'. The DCC (1989) adopted the recommendations of the Butler Committee with some modifications. It provided both a defence of severe disorder (clause 35) and a qualified defence 'on evidence of disorder' (clause 36).

Clause 35 provided that:

(1) A mental disorder verdict shall be returned if the defendant is proved to have committed an offence but it is proved on the balance of probabilities (whether by the prosecution or by the defendant) that he was at the time suffering from severe mental illness or severe mental handicap.

(2) Subsection (1) does not apply if the court or jury is satisfied beyond reasonable doubt that the offence was not attributable to the severe mental illness or severe mental handicap.

(3) A court or jury shall not, for the purposes of a verdict under subsection (1), find that the defendant was suffering from severe mental illness or severe mental handicap unless two medical practitioners approved for the purposes of section 12 of the Mental Health Act 1983 as having special experience in the diagnosis or treatment of mental disorder have given evidence that he was so suffering.

'Severe mental illness' was defined in clause 34 as:

...a mental illness which has one or more of the following characteristics—

(a) lasting impairment of intellectual functions shown by failure of memory, orientation, comprehension and learning capacity;

(b) lasting alteration of mood of such degree as to give rise to delusion appraisal of the defendant's situation, his past or his future, or that of others, or lack of any appraisal;

(c) delusional beliefs, persecutory, jealous or grandiose;

(d) abnormal perceptions associated with the delusional misinterpretation of events;

(e) thinking so disordered as to prevent reasonable appraisal of the defendant's situation or reasonable communication with others.

'Severe mental handicap' is defined in the same clause as:

...a state of arrested or incomplete development of mind which includes severe impairment of intelligence and social functioning.

The main differences from the Butler Committee recommendations are that P or D would be able to raise the defence, and that the prosecution would be allowed to persuade the jury, if it could, that the offence was not attributable to the disorder. The Law Commission believed that this would 'improve the acceptability of the Butler Committee's generally admirable scheme' as a basis for legislation. Also controversial would be any attempt to define mental disorder: the area is a minefield for both doctors and lawyers (note the MHA 2007, which provides that a mental disorder is 'any disorder or disability of the mind').

4.17 Clause 36 would have provided a separate defence that, where evidence of mental disorder causes a jury or court to doubt whether D acted with the required fault, they should be able to bring in a qualified defence. D would be 'not guilty on evidence of mental disorder'. Whereas the defence under clause 35 would apply whether or not the disorder negated D's *mens rea*, the defence under clause 36 would apply only to those whose *mens rea* was affected by the disorder. Meanwhile, the political mood seems to be becoming increasingly intolerant: the Home Office (1999) proposed new civil powers which would allow the indefinite detention of 'dangerous' people with severe personality disorders, on the basis of the risk that they present rather than the crimes that they have committed. Prisons house many, many people who are seriously mentally ill. Meanwhile, the insanity defence has already been found to contravene Art 5 of the ECHR in Jersey (see [2001] Crim LR 560). Mackay and Reuber (2007), having looked carefully at actual cases of 'insanity', argue that the current law has no place in the 21st century.

The Law Commission is at long last exploring the subject again. In 2012, the Law Commission published a 'scoping paper' on insanity seeking to discover whether the current law causes problems in practice. Then, in 2013, they published a 'discussion paper' on both insanity and automatism, which set out provisional proposals for reform of both defences, based on lack of capacity. They made eleven provisional proposals:

(1) That the common law rules on the defence of insanity be abolished.

(2) The creation of a new statutory defence of not criminally responsible by reason of recognized medical condition.

(3) The party seeking to raise the new defence must adduce expert evidence that at the time of the alleged offence D wholly lacked the capacity:

  (i) rationally to form a judgment about the relevant conduct or circumstances;

(ii) to understand the wrongfulness of what he or she is charged with having done; or

(iii) to control his or her physical acts in relation to the relevant conduct or circumstances

as a result of a qualifying recognized medical condition.

(4) That certain conditions would not qualify, including acute intoxication or any condition which is manifested solely or principally by abnormally aggressive or seriously irresponsible behaviour.

(5) That if there is a dispute as to whether the medical condition which D claims to have had is a recognized medical condition and/or whether it is a qualifying condition, then this shall be a question of law and not one for the tribunal of fact.

(6) That if sufficient evidence is adduced on which, in the opinion of the court, a properly directed jury could reasonably conclude that the defence might apply, the defence should be left to the tribunal of fact to consider. P then bears the burden of disproving the defence beyond reasonable doubt.

(7) The jury (or magistrates) shall return a special verdict of 'not criminally responsible by reason of recognised medical condition' unless satisfied beyond reasonable doubt that the accused did not suffer a complete loss of capacity by reason of a recognized medical condition.

(8) That the special verdict of 'not criminally responsible' may only be returned where evidence on D's medical condition has been received from two or more experts, one of whom is a registered medical practitioner.

(9) That whether a person has been, or is going to be, held not criminally responsible by reason of recognized medical condition shall not affect the criminal liability of any other person.

(10) That the following disposals should be available following a special verdict of 'not criminally responsible by reason of recognised medical condition': a hospital order (with or without a restriction), a supervision order, or an absolute discharge.

(11) That in respect of a D who is under 18, the court should also have the power to make a non-penal Youth Supervision Order following a special verdict of 'not criminally responsible by reason of recognised medical condition'.

Automatism

4.18 Clearly a person should not be guilty for acts committed as a result of an involuntary movement of their body. As Wilson (2005) Crim LR 108 puts it:

> For automatism the nature of the external crisis blocks the attribution of wrongdoing to the defender since it is of a nature to inspire the belief that D's reaction may be simply a dislocated manifestation of his humanity rather than of his personal character or mental attitude (at p. 120).

Normally they will not be guilty because they had no *mens rea*. If I hit you on the nose whilst sneezing, I am not guilty of assault since I was not subjectively reckless. However, it is more usual to say in these circumstances that D is not guilty because he did not do a voluntary act.

Hill v Baxter (1958) D was charged with dangerous driving, and claimed he had no recollection of what had happened. The magistrates dismissed the action against him.

QBD: the magistrates came to the wrong decision in law. Lord Goddard CJ:

> …there may be cases where the circumstances are such that the accused could not really be said to be driving at all. Suppose he had a stroke or an epileptic fit, both instances of what may properly be called acts of God; he might well be in the driver's seat even with his hands on the wheel, but in such a state of unconsciousness that he could not be said to be driving. A blow from a stone or an attack by a swarm of bees I think introduces some conception akin to *novus actus interveniens*.

But this case fell far short of that, and the defence of automatism was not applicable. Another attempt to rely on the defence also failed:

A-G's Reference (No. 2 of 1992) (1994) D drove his lorry 700 yards along the hard shoulder of a motorway before crashing into a stationary van killing two people. D relied on expert evidence of a condition known as 'driving without awareness', a trance-like state induced by repetitive visual stimuli on flat featureless motorways. The judge left the defence of automatism to the jury, who acquitted D.

CA: the defence of automatism should not have been left to the jury since automatism depends on a total destruction of voluntary control on D's part. 'Driving without awareness' involved only partial or reduced control.

Whether automatism negates the *actus reus* or the *mens rea* of an offence can be important (see **2.3** for a discussion of *Broome v Perkins* (1987) and whether a diabetic driver should have the defence of automatism). If automatism is related simply to the *mens rea*, D's recklessness may mean that he cannot rely on it. Remember that if the automatism is caused by insanity or intoxication, D will not be able to rely on it. In 2013, the Law Commission provisionally proposed that the common law rules on the defence of automatism be abolished and that where the magistrates or jury find that D raises evidence that, at the time of the alleged offence, he or she wholly lacked the capacity to control his or her conduct, and the loss of capacity was not the result of a recognized medical condition (whether qualifying or non-qualifying), he or she should be acquitted unless P disproves this plea to the criminal standard. Do you think that this 'lack of capacity to control' defence would work better than the current rules?

Intoxication

4.19 Many offenders have been drinking alcohol or taking drugs, or both. Are you less culpable if you have been drinking, because you didn't realize the extent of your criminality? Or are you more culpable because society needs to stress that, on social policy grounds, you cannot hide behind your drunkenness in order to 'get away' with your crimes? English law reflects this dilemma by making a basic distinction between crimes of 'specific intent' and those of 'basic intent'. Crimes of specific intent are, generally speaking, those for which the required *mens rea* is intention. Here drunkenness may be used to show that D did not have the relevant intent. On the other hand, in crimes of basic intent (generally those for which the required *mens rea* is only recklessness or less) evidence of drunkenness actually supplies the necessary *mens rea*, and can never negate it.

> *DPP v Majewski* (1977) D spent a day taking a variety of drugs and drinking heavily. In the evening he was involved in a fight in a pub, and attacked both the landlord and the policeman who eventually arrested him. He was charged with assault occasioning actual bodily harm and with assaulting a police officer in the execution of his duty. His defence was that he was so intoxicated as to have no recollection at all of the events of the evening.
>
> CA and HL: affirmed his convictions. Self-induced intoxication could not provide a defence to the offences charged.

4.20 There were seven separate speeches in the HL in *Majewski*, and it is not altogether clear where the line is to be drawn between those offences for which intoxication supplies evidence of *mens rea*, and those where evidence of intoxication may negate *mens rea*. However, it is clear that evidence of drunkenness may negate the required *mens rea* in crimes such as murder which are based on intention. If I am so drunk that I think you are a dartboard and I throw darts at you with the result that you die, I will not be guilty of murder as I did not intend to kill. I will nonetheless be guilty of manslaughter, a basic intent offence.

But is it right to convict people of an offence when their fault is more closely related to getting drunk, not to the crime that they actually commit? Is the recklessness (negligence?) involved in getting drunk as deserving of blame as the recklessness required for most crimes of basic intent? Before you can be convicted of an offence of assault occasioning ABH, for example, it has to be proved that you foresaw the risk that you might frighten someone (see **9.17**). D when drunk does not foresee the risk of the result which actually occurs. As Ashworth suggests, the rule is inconsistent with the principle of contemporaneity in that it bases D's conviction on the antecedent fault of voluntarily taking intoxicants (PCL, p. 200).

Heard **(2007)** Police officers had been called to D's home, where he was found drunk and in an emotional state. He had cut himself. They took him to hospital, where he became angry, punching V, a police officer, in the stomach. D then undid his trousers, took his penis in his hand and rubbed it up and down on V's thigh. D was arrested. During interviews D stated that although he could not remember anything that had occurred, he accepted that when he was ill or intoxicated he was prone to being 'silly and start stripping'. He was charged with sexual assault, contrary to s 3 of the SOA 2003 (see **10.17**). At trial, the judge directed the jury that P had to prove that D had touched V deliberately. D submitted that since reckless touching would not suffice, the jury ought to have been directed to consider if his voluntary intoxication meant that he did not have the intention to touch V.

CA: dismissed the appeal. Not every offence could be categorized simply as one of either specific or basic intent. That might conceal the truth that different elements of it might require proof of different states of mind. This offence was an example: the different elements of the offence identified in s 3(a) to (d) did not call for proof of the same state of mind. It was of limited help to try and label the offence as one particular type of intent because the state of mind that must be proved varied with the issue. However, on the evidence available, D plainly intended to touch V with his penis. That he was drunk could have meant that he was either disinhibited and did something that he would not ordinarily have done when sober, or that he did not remember it afterwards. Neither of those matters would destroy the intentional character of his touching V. A drunken intent was still an intent and D's behaviour, both in committing the offence and his interviews afterwards, made it clear that the touching had been deliberate. The judge had been correct in his direction to the jury on intent. Following *Majewski*, it was not open to a D charged with sexual assault to contend that his voluntary intoxication prevented him from intending to touch. Historically the law of England regarded voluntary intoxication as an aggravation rather than a potential excuse and it was unlikely that Parliament had intended to change the law by permitting reliance on voluntary intoxication where it previously had not been permitted. There was no basis for construing the Act as having altered the law.

4.21 Whilst the *Majewski* 'rule' provides a workable distinction, it does create inconsistencies. The intoxicated may have a possible defence to murder or intentional wounding, but they will still be guilty of a lesser offence (manslaughter or unlawful wounding). But not all crimes of specific intent have a lesser, basic intent, offence beneath them. Thus, for example, if a drunk is charged with theft, he may not be guilty if he can show he was drunk and so did not intend to permanently deprive the owner of the goods. But there is no lesser offence of 'reckless stealing' with which he may be charged. The *Majewski* rule also means that drunkenness may lead to D's acquittal of a charge of attempt, whereas he would have been guilty had he successfully completed his attempt. Thus, whilst drunkenness is no defence to rape, it may be a defence (a way of establishing that he did not have the *mens rea*) to a charge of attempted rape.

4.22 It goes almost without saying (I hope) that if D gets drunk in order to give himself the courage to commit an offence, he has no defence (*A-G for Northern Ireland v Gallagher* (1963)). As Lord Denning said in that case:

> If a man, while sane and sober, forms an intention to kill and makes preparation for it… and then gets himself drunk so as to give himself Dutch courage to do the killing, and while drunk carries out his intention, he cannot rely on this self-induced drunkenness as a defence to a charge of murder.

Such cases are in practice rare: perhaps because the very drunk are unlikely to carry out their plans successfully.

4.23 The rules of intoxication apply equally to alcohol and to drugs. If you deliberately take a drug which makes you do irresponsible (and criminal) things, you will be convicted. However, if the effect of the drug on you was unpredictable, you may have a defence:

Hardie (1984) D took some of his ex-girlfriend's Valium to ease his misery at being asked to move out of her flat. He then started a fire in a wardrobe, and was in due course convicted of arson (and sentenced to two years' imprisonment).

CA (Parker LJ): quashed his conviction.

> If the jury came to the conclusion that as a result of the Valium, the appellant was, at the time, unable to appreciate the risks to property and persons from his actions, they should consider whether the taking of the Valium was itself reckless.

It is difficult to reconcile this case with *Caldwell* recklessness (which was then the required *mens rea* for arson: see **3.22–3.28**). However, most commentators would have said that the case to criticize was *Caldwell*. The decision in *Hardie* has the merit of confirming at least some fault element in the *Majewski* rule. However, it also forces the courts, perhaps without the benefit of medical evidence, to decide whether taking a particular drug is 'dangerous' or 'non-dangerous'.

Intoxication and mistake

4.24 Although a genuine mistake may relieve D of liability (see **5.27**), the courts have generally held that mistakes induced by drunkenness do not do so. Intoxicated people cannot rely on mistakes which they would not have made when sober. As Ashworth says, 'where the subjective rule for mistake clashes with the objective rules for intoxication, the latter takes priority' (PCL, p. 199).

> *Woods* **(1981)** D and three others raped a girl when they were drunk.
>
> CA: upheld their convictions. Self-induced intoxication is no defence to allegations of recklessness as to consent.

> *O'Grady* **(1987)** D and V, two drunk men, went to sleep in a large bed. D woke up to find his friend hitting him, so he fought back and eventually went back to sleep. In the morning he discovered that his friend was dead. He was charged with murder, but convicted of manslaughter
>
> CA (Lord Lane CJ): dismissed his appeal. 'A D is not entitled to rely, so far as self-defence is concerned, on a mistake of fact which has been induced by voluntary intoxication.'

The CA in *Hatton* (2005) held that the decision in *O'Grady* (1987), that, where D sought to establish the defence of self-defence, it was not open to him to rely on a mistake induced by voluntary intoxication, applied equally to murder and to manslaughter.

4.25 But sometimes a statute is drafted so as to provide what looks like a wider defence. The CDA 1971, s 5(2) provides that D has a lawful excuse for causing criminal damage:

> (a) if at the time of the act or acts alleged to constitute the offence he believed that the person or person whom he believed to be entitled to consent to

the destruction of or damage to the property in question had so consented, or would have so consented to it if he or they had known of the destruction or damage and its circumstances;

This section has been interpreted so as to lead to the acquittal of those whose mistaken beliefs may be caused by their own drunkenness, particularly since s 5(3) states that:

> For the purposes of this section it is immaterial whether a belief is justified or not if it is honestly held.

Jaggard v Dickinson **(1981)** D, who had been drinking, mistook V's house for that of her friend, with whom she had planned to stay. Finding the house locked and no one at home, she broke a window in order to get in. She was convicted of criminal damage.

DC (Mustill J): quashed her conviction. The defence under the CDA 1971, s 5(2)(a) was still available although D was drunk.

The court is required by s 5(3) to focus on the existence of the belief, not its intellectual soundness; and a belief can be just as much honestly held if it is induced by intoxication, as if it stems from stupidity, forgetfulness, or inattention.

4.26 The danger with this defence is that it suggests that if D sets fire to a hotel under the influence of LSD believing that he had the permission of the owner to burn it down (Glanville Williams' example at (1990) 140 NLJ 1564), he will be acquitted. Perhaps the answer is that the present law treats a mistaken belief brought about by intoxication in different ways according to whether it is categorized as negating an element of the offence or as forming part of a defence. Is this distinction appropriate, or indeed always possible to apply? The TA 1968, s 12(6) provides that a person does not commit an offence of taking a motor vehicle without authority:

> ... by anything done in the belief that he has lawful authority to do it or that he would have the owner's consent if the owner knew of his doing it and the circumstances of it.

How would you categorize this?

In other statutes, it is made clear that mistaken beliefs induced by intoxication are no excuse. Section 6(5) of the POA 1986 provides that for the purposes of the offences in the POA, ss 1–5 (see Chapter 12):

> ... a person whose awareness is impaired by intoxication shall be taken to be aware of that of which he would be aware if not intoxicated, unless he shows

either that his intoxication was not self-induced or that it was caused solely by the taking or administration of a substance in the course of medical treatment.

Proposals for reform

4.27 The Law Commission has looked at the question of drunken offenders several times. In the DCC (1989) they proposed simply to abolish the specific/basic intent distinction and to replace it with liability based on recklessness: D would be guilty of an offence which may be committed recklessly if he was intoxicated at the time. However, in 1993, the Law Commission produced a lengthy Consultation Paper (No. 127) on *Intoxication and Criminal Liability*. This looked at six different proposals for reform, preferring one of the last two:

(i) Option 5: abolish the *Majewski* approach without replacement. D's intoxication would be taken into account with any other relevant evidence in determining whether he had the mental element required for the offence. This is closer to the current Australian and New Zealand position (see the Australian case of *O'Connor* (1980)). The Canadian Supreme Court, too, stepped in this direction in *Daviault* (1994). Pointing out that 'the most vehement and cogent criticism' of the *Majewski* approach is that it substitutes proof of drunkenness for proof of the required mental element, the Supreme Court of Canada held that the mental element of voluntariness is a fundamental aspect of the crime which cannot be taken away by a judicially developed policy. Where D is incapable of forming the minimal intent required for a crime of general intent, he should have a defence akin to that of insanity or automatism.

(ii) Option 6: abolish the *Majewski* approach and introduce a new offence of criminal intoxication. This offence would have been committed by a person who, while 'deliberately intoxicated' caused the harm proscribed by any of a number of specified offences (e.g. homicide, bodily harm, rape, criminal damage).

4.28 Their Report (Law Com No. 229 (1995)) was very much more cautious, recommending simply minimal changes which would make the law more coherent and easier to apply. In a major shift of opinion, the Law Commission concluded that the *Majewski* approach operated fairly, on the whole, and without undue difficulty. On the other hand, the Australian law was seen to create its own problems, relying on juries not to acquit unworthy drunks too readily. The Law Commission recommended that where P alleges any intention, purpose, knowledge, belief, fraud, or dishonesty, evidence of intoxication should be taken into account in determining whether that allegation has been proved. For the purpose of any allegation of any other mental element of an offence (in particular, allegations of recklessness or awareness of risk), a voluntarily intoxicated defendant should be treated as having been aware of anything of which he would have been aware but for his intoxication. These proposals have the merit of dispensing with the need to distinguish between crimes of specific and of basic intent. The proposed rules, instead of applying to some offences but not to others, were so formulated as to be capable of applying in relation only to certain kinds of mental element. But they have not been adopted.

4.29 In 2009, The Law Commission published another report *Intoxication and Criminal Liability* (No. 314). At pains to stress the complexity of the topic, they start by considering five issues, which they say the current law does not satisfactorily address:

(1) the question whether D's intoxication should be classified as 'voluntary' or 'involuntary';

(2) the question whether the fault element in the definition of the offence charged is or is not one to which voluntary intoxication should be considered relevant;

(3) the question whether voluntary intoxication should be considered relevant to the defences to which D's state of mind may be relevant;

(4) the test to be applied in cases where voluntary intoxication is not relevant to the determination of D's criminal liability; and

(5) the test to be applied in cases where it is alleged that D did not perpetrate the offence charged but encouraged or assisted a perpetrator to commit it.

This leads to a number of recommendations. The main ones for our present purposes are:

- they suggest the *Majewski* rules would be simplified if the general rule was that if D is charged with having committed an offence as a perpetrator; and the fault element of the offence is not an integral fault element (e.g. because it merely requires proof of recklessness); and D was voluntarily intoxicated at the material time; then, in determining whether or not D is liable for the offence, D should be treated as having been aware at the material time of anything which D would then have been aware of but for the intoxication. D should not be able to rely on a genuine mistake of fact arising from intoxication in support of a defence to which D's state of mind is relevant;

- the following subjective fault elements should be excluded from the application of the general rule and should, therefore, always be proved:

(1) intention as to a consequence;

(2) knowledge as to something;

(3) belief as to something (where the belief is equivalent to knowledge as to something);

(4) fraud; and

(5) dishonesty;

- D should not be able to rely on a genuine mistake of fact arising from self-induced intoxication in support of a defence to which D's state of mind is relevant, regardless of the nature of the fault alleged. D's mistaken belief should be taken into account only if D would have held the same belief if D had not been intoxicated. The rule governing mistakes of fact relied on in support of a defence should apply equally to 'honest belief' provisions which state how defences should be interpreted.

It is not clear whether these recommendations are likely to be adopted by the Government. Do you think they would make a significant improvement on the current law?

Involuntary intoxication

4.30 You might have thought that if your drink is 'laced' by someone else, that is, you get drunk without realizing it, you might be excused the criminal offences that you then commit. This is not the case. Thus, you may be convicted of an offence under the RTA 1988, s 5 (driving, or being in charge of, a motor vehicle with alcohol concentration above the prescribed limit), an offence of strict liability, even though you did not know your drink had been laced (*A-G's Reference (No. 1 of 1975)* (1975)). Even where P must prove recklessness or even intent, D may still be convicted:

Kingston **(1994)** D was invited to the flat of a man who intended to blackmail him. The blackmailer had already enticed a 15-year-old boy to the flat and had given him drugs which sent him to sleep. D then sexually abused the boy, and was photographed doing so. His defence was that his coffee had been drugged by the blackmailer, causing him to lose the inhibitions which normally controlled his paedophilic tendencies.

CA: quashed his conviction. He was not guilty if, because of his involuntary intoxication, he forms an intention that he would not have formed if sober.

HL: overruled CA, upholding D's conviction. Lord Mustill said that there is no principle of English law that if no blame was attached to the accused, he did not have the *mens rea* and therefore was not guilty.

4.31 Perhaps the main argument in favour of the HL's decision is that it prevents bogus claims. There is no easy line to draw between voluntary and involuntary intoxication: if I did not realize the strength of the gin and tonics that you give me, am I involuntarily or voluntarily intoxicated if I drink them? Doubtless the HL was influenced by the fact that D admitted to being a homosexual paedophile. But is this a reason for convicting him in this particular case? Should moral judgments such as this affect only the sentence, or also criminal liability? For another viewpoint, see Sullivan (1994) who argues that 'it is not a fair test of character to remove surreptitiously a person's inhibitions and confront him with a temptation he ordinarily seeks to avoid.' He argues for a character-based defence to apply where D is in a state of unblameworthy disequilibrium and in that condition engages in untypical behaviour which is essentially the product of the exceptional circumstances prevailing at the time of the offence. The Law Commission, in their Report No. 314 (2009), recommended that

- D's state of involuntary intoxication should be taken into consideration:

    (1) in determining whether D acted with the subjective fault required for liability, regardless of the nature of the fault element; and

    (2) in any case where D relies on a mistake of fact in support of a defence to which his or her state of mind is relevant.
- There should be a non-exhaustive list of situations which would count as involuntary intoxication:

    (1) the situation where an intoxicant was administered to D without D's consent;

    (2) the situation where D took an intoxicant under duress;

    (3) the situation where D took an intoxicant which he or she reasonably believed was not an intoxicant;

    (4) the situation where D took an intoxicant for a proper medical purpose.

- D's state of intoxication should also be regarded as involuntary if, though not entirely involuntary, it was *almost* entirely involuntary.

Would this be a recipe for uncertainty? In the latest Discussion Paper, *Insanity and Automatism* (2013), the Law Commission provisionally propose that D should be treated as pleading the recognized medical condition defence and not involuntary intoxication where:

    (1) D suffered from a recognized medical condition, and

    (2) D took a properly authorized or licensed medicine or drug for the treatment of that condition, and

(3) D took the medicine or drug in accordance with a prescription, with advice given by a suitably qualified person, or in accordance with the instructions accompanying the medicine or drug in the case of over-the-counter medicines, or, if D did not take it in accordance with instructions, it was nevertheless reasonable for D to take it in the way he or she did in the circumstances, and

(4) D had no reason to believe that he or she would have an adverse reaction to that medicine which would cause him or her to act in that way, and

(5) the taking of that medicine or drug caused D totally to lack the relevant criminal capacity.

Is this any clearer than the current position?

Corporate liability

4.32 These is something odd about including the liability of corporations in a chapter on incapacitating conditions, but then there is something odd about making companies liable for crimes. As it is, partnerships, unincorporated associations, the Crown, and government agencies cannot usually be convicted of crimes. (But see *L* (2008, at 3.42) where the CA held that a prosecution for a strict liability environmental crime could be brought against a golf club, an unincorporated body, and/or against the individual members.) Most crimes seem appropriately to be addressed at human beings and not at corporate bodies, and the *mens rea* concepts in Chapter 3 apply uncomfortably to companies. The difficulties go much further than simply *mens rea* questions: can a company 'act' or 'cause' something to happen? Yet companies do cause dreadful harms, and there are a number of ways the law has evolved in order to convict a company. Thus for many years the doctrine of vicarious liability (see 3.36) has been used to convict companies of strict liability offences. A statute may also impose liability on a company specifically or by necessary implication. For example, if a statute penalizes the occupier of premises, a company which is the occupier will be as guilty as any human occupier.

4.33 Sometimes a company is not merely vicariously guilty, but is itself guilty. We deal with the offence of corporate manslaughter (created in the Corporate Manslaughter and Corporate Homicide Act 2007) in Chapter 8. Here the focus is on other offences, largely what are often known as 'regulatory offences'. The doctrine of identification means that the company itself is deemed to have *mens rea*. The law seeks to identify who is or are the 'brains' or controlling mind of the company, and then their acts can be attributed to the company, not because they are the servants of the company but because the law deems them to be the company. These principles apply more easily in the case of small companies than in the case of large ones:

Tesco Supermarkets v Nattrass (1972) A pensioner complained to an inspector of weights and measures when he was unable to find a packet of washing powder at the advertised 'lower than normal' price. D, a company, was prosecuted under the Trade Descriptions Act 1968, s 11, which provides that:

> If any person offering to supply any goods gives, by whatever means, any indication likely to be taken as an indication that the goods are being offered at a price less than that at which they are in fact being offered he shall…be guilty of an offence.

D argued that since the manager of the store had failed to check on whether there were enough boxes of soap powder, they had a defence under s 24(1) of the Act that the offence was due to the mistake of another person. The question was therefore whether the manager was 'another person'.

DC: dismissed D's appeal, holding on a theory of delegation that the manager was an embodiment of the company.

HL: allowed D's appeal. Here the board never delegated any part of their functions. They set up a chain of command, but they remained in control. The acts or omissions of shop managers were not acts of the company itself.

4.34 This is an extraordinarily narrow test. Not many people who work in Tesco could qualify as part of its 'controlling mind'. And is it not fair that since the 'profits of the crime' go to Tesco the company, so should the penalty for breaking the criminal law? Or was the HL in effect saying that it did not approve of strict liability criminal offences? Wells points out that it was a bizarre decision: the identification route to liability, which was developed as a means of finding corporations guilty beyond the regulatory sphere, being exploited to allow the company to escape liability for a trading standards offence (see (1996) 1 *Archbold News* 5).

St Regis Paper Co Ltd (2011) S, the technical manager of one of D's five plants, falsified records so as to commit a criminal offence under the Pollution Prevention and Control (England and Wales) Regulations 2000, reg 32(1)(g), which required proof of *mens rea*. The issue was whether his acts could be attributed to D, the company, so as to make it likewise guilty of the offence. At first instance, a judge had ruled, founded on Lord Hoffmann's speech in *Meridian Global Funds Management Asia Limited v The Securities Commission* (1995), that D was capable of being identified as committing the offence through the acts and state of mind of S, who, although not the directing mind and will of D, was a person who carried out management functions and in doing so was in actual control of the operations of the company in the area in question. Were it not otherwise, the judge considered, environmental regulations would be emasculated.

CA: allowed the appeal. The trial judge was wrong. Lord Hoffmann in *Meridian Global*, was not seeking to replace the traditional identification rule in *Tesco Supermarkets Limited v Nattrass* (1972), but to affirm it, while identifying a special rule of attribution, geared to the specific purposes of the statute in issue in that case. The question, therefore, was whether the judge was right to construe reg 32(1)(g) as justifying a departure from the normal rule, and the Court concluded that he was not. The regulation created a number of offences of strict liability (to which D had pleaded guilty), so there was no question that the regulations would be undermined by the application of the normal rule to those offences which did require *mens rea*. Once it was clear that the normal rule was to be applied, S was not capable in law of being a directing mind of the company, given his position in the management hierarchy. On the contrary, the directors of the company had set environmental policies which S's actions had breached. (Counsel also argued that the company could be liable on the basis of vicarious liability (see **3.36**): D having delegated responsibility for making the relevant returns to S. No: the delegation principle derived from licensee cases, where liability was imposed on a licensee for *mens rea* offences on the basis of delegation of management of the licensed premises (e.g. *Allen v Whitehead* [1931]). The principle was unlikely to be extended and certainly could not be in this case.)

4.35 Penalties for 'regulatory' offences under such statutes as the Health and Safety at Work etc. Act (HSAWA) 1974 are regularly increased, and at the same time the courts seem to be taking a firmer line in favour of corporate liability:

Tesco Stores Ltd v Brent London Borough Council (1993) D was prosecuted with selling videos to under-age children. By way of defence, they argued that their controlling officers had no means of knowing the age of the purchasers, and the knowledge of the check-out assistant was irrelevant since she could not act as the company.

CA: dismissed their appeal against conviction. Staughton LJ pointed out that it would be absurd to accept D's argument, since it would mean in effect that no large company could ever commit this offence.

British Steel plc (1994) D was prosecuted under the HSAWA 1974, s 3 which imposes a duty on employers to ensure, so far as is reasonably practicable, that others are not exposed to risk to their health and safety. D argued that because they had taken steps at a senior level to ensure safety, they should not be liable.

CA: dismissed their appeal against conviction. Since all reasonable steps had not been taken at operating level, D was guilty. The Court commented on the inadequacy of a fine of £100 imposed where a man had died.

Gateway Foodmarkets **(1996)** V, the duty manager in a store, fell though a trap-door in the lift control room and died.

CA: upheld D's conviction under the HSAWA 1974, s 2 (which imposes a duty on employers in relation to their own employees), and a fine of £10,000.

Chargot Ltd **(2008)** V, an employee of D company, had died when the dumper truck he was driving fell onto its side and buried him in a load of spoil that was being transported at the time. D was convicted for failure to comply with the duties laid down in the HSAWA 1974.

CA and HL (Lord Hope): dismissed the appeal. An employer had to ensure the health and safety at work of all its employees and had to ensure that persons not employed by it were not exposed to risks to their health and safety. 'In cases such as the present, where a person sustains injury at work, the facts will speak for themselves. Prima facie, his employer, or the person by whose undertaking he was liable to be affected, has failed to ensure his health and safety. Otherwise there would have been no accident.'

Spencer (2009) is very critical of this decision:

The practical effect of this decision is to turn an important group of offences of negligent behaviour into offences of 'situational liability'. What is punished is no longer negligent conduct in the running of your business, but the fact of being an employer or director in an organization where an industrial accident has happened; in which situation, should you find yourself, you are now liable to two years' imprisonment as well as massive fines, unless you can identify an innocent explanation and persuade the court that it is probably the truth (at p. 265).

Tangerine Confectionery Ltd, Veolia ES (UK) Ltd **(2011)** CA: dismissed appeals by two companies, and sought to give further (and lengthy!) explanations of the principles described in *Chargot*. These offences (HSAWA 1974, ss 2 and 3) are not primarily concerned with ascribing responsibility for the cause of injury. Indeed, they are primarily concerned with avoiding injury. The offences can just as well be committed when there has been no injury as when there has. The offence lies in the failure to ensure safety so far as reasonably practicable, i.e. in exposure to risk of injury, not in the doing of actual injury. Causation of the injury is not an ingredient of either offence. Lord Hope (in the passage in *Chargot* quoted earlier) was not saying that once there has been an injury then *ipso facto* there was a relevant risk:

> The context of his speech makes clear that he was saying no more than that the fact of the injury is *evidence* of the existence of the risk. Of course, it may well be very strong evidence, and this is what he was saying (Hughes LJ at para. 14).

Further reform

4.36 One way to deal with increasing concerns about 'criminal' companies is to make them subject to much stiffer punitive damages in civil courts. But whether you call corporate misbehaviour a crime or impose regulatory sanctions, or administrative fines, the problem remains: finding suitable penalties (see Jefferson (2001)). Is it time to recognize the need for different schemes and principles to apply to corporate rather than individual wrongdoing? Should 'regulatory offences' be removed from the main criminal law? The Law Commission usefully consulted on 'criminal liability in regulatory contexts' in 2010: they underline the huge growth in the number of criminal offences in recent years, many of which are rarely used. They also show how costly and uncertain criminal prosecutions are often ineffective (in terms of retribution or deterrence).

FURTHER READING

Bennion, F., 'Mens Rea and Defendants Below the Age of Discretion' [2009] Crim LR 757.

Butler Committee, *Report of the Committee on Mentally Abnormal Offenders* (Cmnd 6244, 1975).

Clarkson, C., 'Kicking Corporate Bodies and Damning their Souls' (1996) 59 MLR 557.

Davies, Z. and McMahon, W. (eds), *Debating Youth Justice: From Punishment to Problem Solving?* (Centre for Crime and Justice Studies, 2007, freely available online at <www.crimeandjustice.org.uk/publications/debating-youth-justice-punishment-problem-solving>).

Fisse, B. and Braithwaite, J., 'The Allocation of Responsibility for Corporate Crime: Individualism, Collectivism and Accountability' (1988) 11 Sydney LR 468.

Gobert, J., 'Corporate Criminality: New Crimes for the Times' [1994] Crim LR 722.

Home Office, *Managing Dangerous People With Severe Personality Disorder* (1999).

Horder, J., 'Pleading Voluntary Lack of Capacity' [1993] Camb LJ 298.

Jefferson, M., 'Corporate Criminal Liability: The Problem of Sanctions' (2001) 65 JCL 235.

Keating, H., 'Reckless Children?' [2007] Crim LR 546.

Law Commission, *Intoxication and Criminal Liability* (Report No. 314, 2009).

Law Commission, *Criminal Liability in Regulatory Contexts* (LCCP No. 195, 2010).

Law Commission, *Unfitness to Plead* (LCCP No. 197, 2010).

Law Commission, *Criminal Liability: Insanity and Automatism: A Discussion Paper* (2013).

Loughnan, A., 'Manifest Madness: Towards a New Understanding of the Insanity Defence' (2007) 70 MLR 379.

Mackay, R. D., *Mental Condition Defences in the Criminal Law* (1995).

Mackay R. D. and Mitchell B. J., 'Sleepwalking, Automatism and Insanity' [2006] Crim LR 901.

Mackay, R. D. and Reuber, M., 'Epilepsy and the Defence of Insanity' [2007] Crim LR 782.

Royal Society, 'Neuroscience and the Law' (2011) (available at <http://royalsociety. org/uploadedFiles/Royal_Society_Content/policy/projects/brain-waves/ Brain-Waves-4.pdf>).

Spencer, J. R., 'The Sexual Offences Act 2003: Child and Family Offences' [2004] Crim LR 347.

Spencer, J. R., 'Criminal Liability for Accidental Death: Back to the Middle Ages?' (2009) 68 Camb LJ 263.

Sullivan, G., 'Involuntary Intoxication and Beyond' [1994] Crim LR 272.

Sullivan, G., 'The Attribution of Culpability to Limited Companies' [1996] Camb LJ 515.

Walker, N., 'The End of an Old Song?' [1999] NLJ 64.

Wells, C., *Corporations and Criminal Responsibility* (2nd edn, 2001).

SELF-TEST QUESTIONS

1   Dee and Bee, both aged 13, are playing with a plastic gun. They point it at close range at a pensioner, Phil, and demand that he hands over his money. Phil is terrified and has a heart attack. He dies two days later. Dee and Bee maintain that they were only having fun and thought that Phil would know it was a game. Discuss Dee's liability.

2   Dee believes that fairies live in the corner of the public park, and that they must never be disturbed. When she sees Phil, a gardener, stacking flowerpots in the area where she believes the fairies live, she chases him away by throwing bricks at him. One grazes him on the arm as he flees. Discuss Dee's liability.

3   Dee, a diabetic, is charged with dangerous driving. Her defence is that her doctor has been experimenting with a new regime of insulin treatment, and she was not

sure whether in fact she had injected herself with the correct dose that morning. Medical evidence suggests that she might have been in a hypoglycaemic condition at the time the police stopped her. Discuss Dee's liability.

4   David has sex with Violet without her consent. Is he criminally liable if he had been drinking heavily and thought she was consenting? Would your advice to him be different if he had been drinking orange juice which had been laced with neat lab alcohol by his so-called friends?

5   Should companies be liable to criminal conviction?

5

General defences

SUMMARY

The chapter explores, first, the nature of a 'defence' (and the differences between justifications and excuses), and then key issues in relation to various 'defences':

Consent: there are few clear general principles on what D can consent to. If consent is available as a defence, so too is Ds mistaken belief in consent (but does this mistake have to be reasonable?). Notice the different definition in relation to sexual offences.

Duress: not available to some crimes (murder, attempted murder); also there is a lack of clarity about the degree of threats required.

Necessity: exceptionally recognized as a justification, but more usually accepted as an excuse, as 'duress of circumstances'.

Mistake: genuine (even if unreasonable) beliefs may excuse, but some mistakes must be reasonable.

Self-defence and the prevention of crime: common law defences and a statutory defence under the Criminal Law Act (CLA) 1967, s 3 co-exist. NB: the supposed 'clarification' of the CJIA 2008, s 76 (reasonable force for purposes of self-defence, etc.).

Lawful chastisement: no longer a defence?

Introduction

5.1   Chapter 4 looks at various incapacitating conditions which act in some ways as 'defences': they explain why someone is not guilty of what otherwise looks like a crime. In this chapter we explore other ways in which D may escape liability. It is difficult to generalize about the nature of defences: sometimes a defence is seen simply as a way of showing that P has not proved all the elements of the crime. Glanville Williams suggested that all the elements of a crime are divisible into *actus reus* or *mens rea* and that the *actus reus* involves absence of defence (see 2.1). Other writers prefer to argue that a crime is made up of *actus reus, mens rea,* and absence of defence. If a woman consents to sex, the man is not guilty of rape because an essential element of the crime (the absence of consent) is missing. Is the absence of consent an element in the offence or is the presence of consent a defence?

5.2 Can a clear distinction be drawn between the offence and the defence elements of a crime? Glanville Williams (1982) seemed to argue that there is no such clear distinction. He considered:

> ... two draft statutes, each of which is intended to turn assault into a statutory offence. The first draft defines an assault as an intentional or reckless attack upon a person without his consent. Non-consent is then, presumably, a definitional element of the offence. The second draft defines assault as an intentional or reckless attack upon a person, but adds the proviso or qualification that the offence is not committed where the person attacked has consented. Consent now appears to be a matter of defence ... yet the difference between the two drafts is purely verbal, a matter of convenience in expression. Is there any reason why rules of substantive law should hinge upon a draftsman's convenience?

5.3 Campbell (1987) disagreed, suggesting that there is a clear conceptual difference: offence definitions delimit that against which the law always takes there to be prima facie reason, whereas defences set out conditions under which D is to be exonerated even though the prima facie reason against his conduct subsists. It would not make sense to say 'sexual intercourse by a man with a woman is an offence. It is a defence to this offence that the woman was consenting.' Thus absence of consent to sex is part of the definition of the offence. There is no doubting that the law has traditionally adopted the distinction between offence and defences and the student would be lost without it. Just be aware of the definitional difficulties. Ashworth prefers (in PCL) to talk of 'negative fault requirements' in order to point out that such matters are generally those that P does not have to disprove unless D raises them with some credibility.

5.4 The strong arguments in favour of codifying the criminal law (see **1.30**) do not necessarily apply to defences. One should know in advance the limits of the criminal law, but not necessarily the outer limits of defences. The DCC (1989) therefore, and the Criminal Law Bill attached to Law Commission Report No. 218 (Cm 2370, 1993), preserved many existing common law rules and defences to maintain the flexibility within the operation of the law which is much valued. In this chapter we will not examine all defences, but simply give examples of the most common. There are others: for example, new life was breathed into the defence of marital coercion (to be found in the CJA 1925, s 47) by the CA in *Shortland* (1995).

Justifications and excuses

5.5 Defences can usefully be subdivided into excuses and justifications (see J. C. Smith's readable and enjoyable 1989 Hamlyn Lectures). In essence, your behaviour may be said to be excused if you are not sufficiently at fault or culpable. An excuse can be seen as a 'concession to human frailty'. Such behaviour is not necessarily approved of, simply excused as not meriting punishment. On the other hand, your behaviour is justified if it was the most appropriate course of conduct in the circumstances. This distinction is important for two main reasons:

(i) It has legal consequences: for example, excusable conduct may be resisted by a person who is threatened by it, but justifiable conduct may not be resisted. Again, if D aids and abets a person who is merely excused liability, D may still be guilty of an offence; if D was aiding and abetting someone whose behaviour was justified, he too will not be guilty of an offence.

(ii) It may colour the way we think about the defence. The difference in the moral quality of excuses and justifications may help us in devising improvements or reforms to the law. For a discussion of how the distinction can be useful when the law is in flux, see A. T. H. Smith (1978) and Padfield (1992). Keep the distinction in mind; but remain conscious of the difficulties in maintaining the distinction in borderline cases:

Shayler **(2003)** D, who worked for M15 (the Security Service) from 1991–6, was charged with offences under the Official Secrets Act 1989 (of passing on information unlawfully) and sought to raise a defence of duress or necessity.

CA (2001): necessity, or the extended form of duress, was available as a defence to crimes generally, except where expressly or impliedly excluded. But it was only available where D committed an unlawful act to avoid imminent peril of danger to life or serious injury to himself or some person for whom he was responsible. The defences of duress and necessity are part of the same defence.

HL (2003): dismissed D's appeal. Interpreting the natural and ordinary meaning of ss 1 and 4 of the Official Secrets Act (OSA) 1989, D could not rely on a defence that he believed it to be in the national or public interest to make a disclosure.

The case is interesting in order to see what the judges said about the possible defences. The CA seems to have confused two different defences, which are not essentially the same. Necessity is in some senses narrower: a justification and not an excuse; in some senses wider: it is available for murder (see *Re A* (2001), at 5.23), and not only where the threats of death or serious bodily harm overbear someone's will. The HL avoided the issue!

5.6 A defence of 'reasonable excuse' may sometimes be available. For example, s 57(1)–(2) of the Terrorism Act 2000 provides:

> **s 57** (1) A person commits an offence if he possesses an article in circumstances which give rise to a reasonable suspicion that his possession is for a purpose connected with the commission, preparation or instigation of an act of terrorism.
>
> (2) It is a defence for a person charged with an offence under this section to prove that his possession of the article was not for a purpose connected with the commission, preparation or instigation of an act of terrorism.

And s 58(1)–(3) provides:

> **s 58** (1) A person commits an offence if—
>
> (a) he collects or makes a record of information of a kind likely to be useful to a person committing or preparing an act of terrorism, or
>
> (b) he possesses a document or record containing information of that kind.
>
> (2) In this section 'record' includes a photographic or electronic record.
>
> (3) It is a defence for a person charged with an offence under this section to prove that he had a reasonable excuse for his action or possession.

R v G; R v J **(2009)** G, who was mentally ill, was awaiting trial on two counts of terrorism, one under s 5(1) of the Terrorism Act 2006 Act (see **9.34**) and the other under s 58 of the 2000 Act. P's case was that, while in custody, G collected and recorded information (including plans for making bombs and textbooks on explosives). A map of a Territorial Army Centre, plans to attack and kidnap its caretaker, and other observations on the waging of Jihad in Great Britain were recovered during cell searches. He said he just wanted to 'wind up' the prison staff because they were provoking him, and that he left the material in his cell so that it could be found. At a preparatory hearing, the judge held that G had no defence of reasonable excuse under s 58(3) but granted leave to appeal.

J was in custody awaiting trial on six counts, including offences contrary to both ss 57 and 58 of the 2000 Act. P's case was that, when arrested, he was in possession of a large quantity of digitally stored information, contained on his iPod, laptop computer, and digital disks. Much was of an extreme Islamist nature, including the electronic 'key' (a torrent file) to a large library of bomb-making and other manuals, some with an express terrorist (as opposed to simply military) purpose. He denied the offences, saying he had downloaded the documents to learn the nature of the training he would undertake were he to return to the Gambia for a military career. He was unfamiliar with the procedure for using the torrent file, was never able to open it, and was not aware of its exact content or the contents of the material to which it might afford access. In both cases, three points of law of general public importance were certified by the CA:

(a)   What are the ingredients of the offence contained in s 58(1) of the Terrorism Act 2000?

(b)   What is the scope of the defence contained in s 58(3) of the Terrorism Act 2000?

(c)   What is the relationship between s 57 and s 58 of the Terrorism Act 2000?

HL (Lord Rodger): allowed the Crown's appeals in both cases. The s 57 offence covers the possession of far more things than could ever fall within the scope of s 58. P must prove beyond reasonable doubt that the circumstances in which D possessed the article gave rise to a reasonable suspicion that his possession was for a purpose connected with the commission, preparation, or instigation of an act of terrorism. So, in contrast to s 58(1), the circumstances of D's possession form one of the crucial elements of the s 57(1) offence. It is unusual, but not unprecedented, for Parliament to create an offence of this kind, based on a reasonable suspicion as to the purpose behind D's possession: s 57(1) was presumably modelled on s 4(1) of the Explosive Substances Act 1883. Because s 57(1) covers any 'article', the section only bites on D's possession of the article in 'circumstances which give rise to a reasonable suspicion that his possession is for a purpose connected with the commission, preparation or instigation of an act of terrorism'. So, while s 57 focuses on the *circumstances of the defendant's possession* of the article, s 58 focuses on the *nature of the information* which the defendant collects, records, or possesses in a document or record. Subject to the defence in s 58(3), the circumstances in which D did these things are irrelevant. So, unless it amounts to a reasonable excuse under subs (3), his purpose in doing them is irrelevant. Nothing in the terms of s 58(1) requires P to show that D had a terrorist purpose for doing what he did. Section 57 is dealing with possessing articles *for the purpose* of terrorist acts. Section 58 is dealing with collecting or holding information that is *of a kind likely to be useful* to those involved in acts of terrorism. Section 57 includes a specific intention, s 58 does not. The CA had stated that if D proved that his purpose was not terrorism-related, the defence under s 58(3) would be made out and he would have to be acquitted, even if his purpose might infringe some other provision of the criminal or civil law. Parliament could not have intended s 58(3) to be interpreted or applied that way. A desire to wind up prison officers could on no view be a reasonable excuse for collecting the information.

This case is important, of course, as an interpretation of the Terrorism Act offences/defences. It was followed in *AY* (2010) by the CA which held that a defence of reasonable excuse advanced under s 58(3) had to be left to the jury unless it was quite plain that it was incapable of being held by any jury to be reasonable. Look at it again when you are thinking about inchoate offences (see **7.1**): these are merely 'preparatory offences', yet providing for very lengthy terms of imprisonment. Are they drawn too widely? A defence of reasonable excuse appears in other contexts:

Unah **(2011)** D appealed against her conviction for possessing a false passport, contrary to the Identity Cards Act 2006, s 25(5) (now replaced by the Identity Documents Act 2010): 'It is an offence for a person to have in his possession or under his control, without reasonable excuse … an identity document that is false.'

CA: quashed her conviction. The mere fact that a D did not know or believe that the document was false could not of itself amount to a reasonable excuse. However, that lack of knowledge or belief could be a relevant factor for a jury to consider when determining whether or not the defendant had a reasonable excuse for possessing the document.

Consent

5.7 Absence of consent is an essential element of many offences (and not a defence in the same strict sense as duress or self-defence, for example). In establishing a crime such as rape, P must exclude consent in order to establish the essential ingredients of the offence. As detailed in Chapter 10, Parliament has enacted various presumptions in relation to consent in sexual offences. But the general rule remains: if you consent to sexual intercourse then it is not rape; if I consent to you kissing me, then you have not assaulted me (as long as I am not a child or mentally disordered); if I agree to you destroying my property then you have not committed criminal damage or theft. But the law is more paternalistic than that: there are many things to which you are not permitted to consent: most obviously, death. If someone intentionally kills another, even though that other begs him to do it, the offence of murder (with its mandatory life sentence) is nonetheless committed. Whether or not euthanasia should be permitted is clearly a moral and political 'hot potato'. The issues were dramatically raised in *Airedale NHS Trust v Bland* (1993) which was discussed in the context of defining the difference between acts and omissions (**2.10**). *Bland* did not consent to his death: but might it be that the paternalistic attitude of the judiciary allowed them to decide that it was reasonable for the doctors to believe that, had he been able to, he would have consented? Do you think that the HL was correct to 'allow Bland to die'? See our discussion of euthanasia and assisted dying at **8.45**.

5.8 A defence of consent was not allowed in this manslaughter case:

> *Andrews* (2002) D caused V's death by injecting her with a prescription-only drug. V had consented to an injection of insulin for recreational purposes with the intention of experiencing a 'rush' such as that gained from amphetamine. P advanced the case on the basis that D was guilty of manslaughter as he had committed an unlawful and dangerous act that had caused death. The trial judge ruled that, on the facts, D could be found guilty of administering a prescription-only medicine when not qualified to do so in contravention of the Medicines Act 1968, s 58(2)(b) and s 67. D argued that V's consent to the injection amounted to a defence under the 1968 Act and, as such, he had committed no unlawful act and therefore could not be convicted of manslaughter.
>
> CA: dismissed the appeal. A recipient's consent provided no defence to a charge of administering a prescription-only medicine when not qualified to do so. The statutory purpose of the 1968 legislation was to restrict the distribution and use of prescription medicines and this would be seriously undermined if consent allowed an inappropriate practitioner to avoid the effect of the statute. Legislative policy indicated that the judge had been right to rule that D's actions could amount to a criminal offence and therefore D's manslaughter conviction was safe.

5.9 It is more difficult to state the law with any certainty when it comes to non-fatal injuries. Assaults and woundings must be 'unlawful'. The unlawfulness stems in most cases from the lack of consent of the victim, but the courts have had great difficulty in establishing the line between those acts/omissions to which one may consent, and those to which one may not:

> *Donovan* (1934) D beat a 17-year-old consenting girl for his own sexual gratification. He was convicted of indecent and common assault.
>
> CCA: quashed the conviction because of a misdirection by the trial judge. Swift J stated *obiter* that if an act is unlawful in the sense of being in itself a criminal act, it is plain that it cannot be rendered lawful because the person to whose detriment it is done consents to it. No person can license another to commit a crime.

This rather circular advice proved of little help:

> *A-G's Reference (No. 6 of 1980)* (1981) Two young men aged 18 and 17 quarrelled and agreed to settle their difference with a fight in the street. They were acquitted by the jury after the trial judge said that consent might be a defence if they had used only reasonable force. The issue of consent was referred for the opinion of the CA on a point of law under the CJA 1972, s 36.

CA (Lord Lane): held that consent was not a defence as it was not in the public interest that people should cause each other actual bodily harm 'for no good reason'. He said that the public/private place distinction was immaterial: it was not a function of the criminal law of assault to stop public disturbances.

Nothing which we have said is intended to cast doubt on the accepted legality of properly conducted games and sports, lawful chastisement or correction, reasonable surgical interference, dangerous exhibitions, etc. These apparent exceptions can be justified as involving the exercise of a legal right, in the case of chastisement or correction, or as needed in the public interest, in the other cases.

Lord Lane gave no advice on when the 'public interest' might provide good reason for allowing people to consent to minor harms. He lists the usually accepted categories but these are not without problems. What is reasonable surgical interference? What is a lawfully conducted game? Why is boxing lawful, when the intent of the participants is to assault each other, and a lawful game can result in devastating injuries? Tattooing too is lawful (though it is unlawful to tattoo someone under the age of 18). Is the answer here to be found in the fact that where there is seen to be an effective system of regulatory control, whether created by a licensing regime, or by the standards or ethics of a profession, or by a species of self-regulation in which Parliament has trust, the activity may be safely left to be lawful? Tattoo parlours must be licensed by local authority environmental health departments, and tattooists must use sterilized needles. But there are of course many unlicensed tattooists: is this more an area for a public health campaign than for the criminal law?

5.10 Many curious examples can be found in the case law:

Jones (1986) Schoolboys aged 14 and 15 were tossed into the air by Ds, former schoolfellows, who had waited for them outside the school. One boy suffered a broken arm, the other a ruptured spleen.

CA: quashed Ds' convictions for offences under the OAPA 1861, s 20. A genuine belief, whether or not it was reasonably held, in consent to rough and undisciplined play could be a defence where there was no intention to commit an injury.

Aitken (1992) RAF officers were convicted of inflicting GBH contrary to the OAPA 1861, s 20 after pouring white spirit over a drunk and sleeping colleague, who was wearing a fire-resistant flying suit, and then setting fire to it. He suffered 35 per cent burns.

Courts-Martial Appeal Court (CMAC): quashed their convictions. Their mistaken belief in V's consent should have been left to the jury.

> **Brown (1994)** A group of sado-masochist homosexuals inflicted pain on each other for pleasure. They pleaded guilty to offences under the OAPA 1861, ss 20 and 47 after the trial judge ruled that consent could be no defence in these circumstances.
>
> HL (by a majority of 3 to 2): dismissed their appeals. Lords Templeman, Lowry, and Jauncey were in the majority:
>
> > In principle there is a difference between violence which is incidental and violence which is inflicted for the indulgence of cruelty. The violence of sado-masochistic encounters involves the indulgence of cruelty by sadists and the degradation of victims. Such violence is injurious to the participants and unpredictably dangerous. I am not prepared to invent a defence of consent for sado-masochistic encounters which breed and glorify cruelty and result in offences under ss 47 and 20 of the 1861 Act (Lord Templeman).
>
> Lords Mustill and Slynn (dissenting) concentrated on the issue of whether the public interest required the criminalization of this behaviour and found no compelling reason for so doing.

Remember that this case was then taken to the ECtHR but the complainants failed in their claim that their right to privacy had been infringed (see **1.26**). However, compare the case with:

> **Wilson (1996)** Evidence came from V's doctor that D, her husband, had branded his initials on V's buttocks with a hot knife, at her request.
>
> CA: quashed his conviction for an offence under the OAPA 1861, s 47. There was no aggressive intent, and there was no evidence that what he did was more dangerous than tattooing. It was not in the public interest that such consensual activity between husband and wife should result in a prosecution.

> **Emmett (1999)** Evidence against D again came from V's doctor: 'high-risk' sexual activity had resulted on one occasion in haemorrhages to her eyes and bruising to her neck caused by asphyxiation, and on another in burns to her breast.
>
> CA: upheld D's conviction. Consent is no defence where the harm caused consists of more than transient or trivial injury.

Can these cases be reconciled? D's conviction in *Emmett* is upheld although he did not intend any injury. Does the case simply signify that the courts are tightening up on 'dodgy' domestic violence, even when consensual? Or would *Brown* actually be decided differently if before the SC today? Judge Murphy (2011) points out that if a D is charged today with assault occasioning actual bodily harm and sexual assault arising from the same facts, the trial judge is placed in the 'truly invidious position' of directing the jury to consider consent in relation to sexual assault (see **5.13**), but under *Brown*, they must be directed to disregard it in relation to assault occasioning actual bodily harm. He argues that judges should be 'free of the domination of *Brown*'.

5.11 The problems continue:

> **Dica (No. 1) (2004)** D was convicted of two offences of causing GBH, contrary to the OAPA 1861, s 20 (see **9.8**). P's case was that the appellant had had sexual intercourse with two women who would not have consented if they had known he was suffering from HIV. He would have argued that the women had willingly had sex with him, knowing of his condition, but did not give evidence once the judge had ruled at the end of the prosecution case that:
>
> (i)   it would be open to the jury to convict despite *Clarence* (1888, at **9.8**); and
>
> (ii)   whether or not the complainants knew of his condition, their consent was irrelevant and provided no defence.
>
> CA (Judge LJ): allowed the appeal and ordered a retrial. They agreed with the judge's first ruling:
>
>> …the reasoning which led the majority in *Clarence* to decide that the conviction under s 20 should be quashed has no continuing application … it was open to the jury to convict the appellant of the offences alleged in the indictment.
>
> If the victims were ignorant of the appellant's HIV status,
>
>> …the answer is entirely straightforward. These victims consented to sexual intercourse. Accordingly the appellant was not guilty of rape. Given the long-term nature of the relationships, if the appellant concealed the truth about his condition from them, and therefore kept them in ignorance of it, there was no reason for them to think that they were running any risk of infection, and they were not consenting to it. On this basis, there would be no consent sufficient in law to provide the appellant with a defence to the charge under s 20 (para. 39).
>
> If, on the other hand, the victims knew of the state of D's health, and consented to sexual intercourse, the issue of consent should have been considered by the jury. Whilst the consent of the victim to the deliberate infliction of serious harm does not generally provide the perpetrator with a defence, the position is different when the victim is 'simply prepared, knowingly, to run the risk—not the certainty of infection, as well as all the other risks inherent in and possible consequences of sexual intercourse' (para. 47). Judge LJ explained:
>
>> The problems of criminalising the consensual taking of risks like these include the sheer impracticality of enforcement and the haphazard nature of its impact. The process would undermine the general understanding of the community that sexual

relationships are pre-eminently private and essentially personal to the individuals involved in them (para. 51).

Barnes (2005) D appealed against his conviction for unlawfully and maliciously inflicting grievous bodily harm, contrary to the OAPA 1861, s 20 (see **9.8**). V sustained a serious leg injury as a result of a tackle by D during a football match after V kicked the ball into the opposition net. While accepting that the tackle was hard, D maintained that it was a fair challenge and that the injury caused was accidental.

CA: allowed D's appeal. The prosecution of those who inflicted injury on another in the course of a sporting event was reserved for those situations where the conduct was sufficiently grave to be properly categorized as criminal. Where injuries were sustained in the course of contact sports, such as football, public policy limited the availability of the defence of consent to situations where there had been implicit consent to what had occurred. The fact the tackle was a foul did not necessarily mean the threshold of criminal conduct had been reached; it was important for the jury to understand the distinction between going for the ball, albeit late, and 'going for' the victim.

Konzani (2005) D had unprotected consensual sex with three women without disclosing that he was HIV positive. Each V contracted the HIV virus. He was charged with inflicting GBH, contrary to the OAPA 1861, s 20 (see **9.8**). The judge directed the jury that if V's consent was to provide D with a defence, it had to be an informed and willing consent to the risk of contracting the HIV virus. 'Willingly' meant 'consciously' and involved knowing the implications of infection with the virus. He appealed against his conviction.

CA: dismissed the appeal. There was a critical distinction between taking a risk as to the various potentially adverse and possibly problematic consequences of unprotected consensual sex, and the giving of informed consent to the risk of infection with a fatal disease. For consent to the risk of contracting HIV to provide a defence, the consent had to be an informed consent. Where consent provided a defence to an offence against the person, it was generally the case that an honest belief in consent would also provide a defence. However, in the circumstances, D's honest belief had to be concomitant with the consent which provided a defence. Unless the consent would provide a defence, an honest belief in it would not assist D. On the evidence, there was nothing from which the jury could have inferred that D honestly believed that Vs had consented to that specific risk and the judge's directions could not be faulted.

Dica (No. 2) (2005) After two retrials, Dica was convicted again, and appealed again. At the second retrial, the judge held himself bound by the CA's earlier decision in this case on the issue of consent as a defence. As D's original appeal against conviction had been allowed, no application for leave to appeal to the HL had been made. D therefore sought leave to appeal so that the original decision of the CA could be reconsidered in the HL.

CA: again dismissed the appeal. Like the trial judge, the CA was also bound by its own decision in the first appeal and also by the decisions in *Barnes* and *Konzani* (earlier in this section). However, if the first appeal against conviction had been dismissed, the CA would have certified a question of law of public importance and that importance had not diminished because of the lapse of time. Permission to appeal against conviction would therefore be granted, and a question of public importance would be certified, namely, 'in what circumstances, if any, may a defendant who knows or believes he is infected with a serious sexually transmitted infection and recklessly transmits it to another through consensual sexual activity be convicted of an offence of inflicting grievous bodily harm contrary to the Offences against the Person Act 1861, s 20.' But leave to appeal to the HL was refused.

Weait (2005) argues that criminalization founded on a person's reckless non-disclosure of their positive HIV status casts the net of liability too wide and risks doing more harm than good. He suggests the non-intentional transmission of HIV is better dealt with as a public health issue. Do you agree? And what of those who transmit other diseases? Untreated syphilis can be fatal and untreated chlamydia can lead to infertility. As far as I know, no one has yet been prosecuted for recklessly transmitting these diseases.

5.12   The problem has surfaced in the law of kidnapping too:

Cort (2003) D was convicted of two counts of kidnapping and ten counts of attempted kidnapping. He falsely told women waiting at bus stops that their bus had broken down. He then offered each one a lift in his car to her destination. The majority refused his offer (the attempted kidnapping offences). However, two had accepted, one of whom changed her mind and was released from the car, the other was taken to her destination. D contended that the taking of Vs had been with their consent and, accordingly, that the requisite element of lack of consent to the offence was not present. Further, D argued that the Vs had not been mistaken as to the nature of the act in which they had engaged as they had been riding in a car to their intended destination.

CA: dismissed the appeal. D had taken Vs away by fraud and their consent had been obtained under a mistake as to the nature of that act. In kidnapping cases, where fraud was established, consent could not be relied upon. All that the women had consented to was a ride in his car which was irrelevant to the taking away by fraud which formed the basis of the offence. *Clarence* (1888) and *Linekar* (1994, see **5.13**) were considered.

Hendy-Freegard **(2007)** D was a confidence trickster whose pretence that he was an undercover agent working for M15 or Scotland Yard had enabled him to influence Vs and take control of their lives, directing them on what to do, and where to live, and fleecing them and their parents of large sums of money. In 1992, D had falsely told V1 that he was a secret agent investigating an IRA cell and that, consequently, the lives of those associated with him, V2 and V3, were in danger, and that it was necessary for them to leave their homes. This they did and D continued to have an influence over them for ten years. D was convicted of kidnapping and offences of dishonesty.

CA: quashed the conviction for kidnapping. The four ingredients of the crime of kidnapping were (i) the taking or carrying away of one person by another; (ii) by force or fraud; (iii) without the consent of the person so taken or carried away; and (iv) without lawful excuse. Causing a person, by a fraudulent misrepresentation, to move from one place to another was not enough in itself to constitute the 'taking and carrying away' that was a necessary element in the offence of kidnapping. However, the CA did accept *Cort* (2003) as authority for the proposition that 'there was probably no room for the requirement of lack of consent in the case of kidnapping where the taking and carrying away was induced by fraud':

> The consequence of the decision in *Cort* would seem to be that the mini-cab driver, who obtains a fare by falsely pretending to be an authorised taxi, will be guilty of kidnapping ... Our conclusion is that the decision in *Cort* represented an unjustified departure from established principle. It is, however, not necessary for us to consider whether we are bound to follow *Cort* for, even if it binds us, it is not determinative of the result on the facts of this case (paras 55–6).

5.13 *Consent and sexual offences* The law in relation to consent and sexual offences is just as difficult to set out clearly, despite Parliament's definition. The SOA 2003, s 74 provides simply that:

> For the purposes of this Part, a person consents if he agrees by choice, and has the freedom and capacity to make that choice.

The words 'freedom' and 'capacity' are difficult to apply in practice. Do you think that a prostitute 'consents' to have sex with a man who never intended to pay her fee (see *Linekar* (1994), where under the pre-2003 law of rape it was held that the reality of V's consent is not destroyed by D's pretence that he would pay her. Is this consistent with the reasoning in *Cort* (**5.12**))?

B **(2007)** D and V had sex in the street following their meeting outside a nightclub in the early hours of the morning. Two delivery drivers saw them and asked V if she was in need of help. V ran into the arms of one of the drivers and made a complaint of rape. D was arrested and informed the custody officer that he was HIV positive. He had not disclosed this to V prior to their having intercourse. At trial, the issue for the jury was consent and they were told of D's HIV status. He was convicted of rape.

CA: allowed D's appeal and ordered a retrial. D's failure to disclose his HIV status was not relevant to the issue of consent under the SOA 2003, s 74 (see also **10.12**) and should have been excluded from the jury: the issue for the jury was whether or not V consented to sexual intercourse, not whether she consented to intercourse with a person suffering from a sexually transmitted disease. The fact that a person had a sexually transmitted disease that was not identified to another person did not vitiate any consent that may have been given concerning sexual activity. However, D would have no defence to the harm created by the sexual activity merely by virtue of that consent, as the consent related to the sexual activity not to the disease. *Dica* (**5.12**) established that where there was consent to sexual activity there would be sufficient harm to give rise to an offence under the OAPA 1861, s 20.

Do you agree with Latham LJ who says that the issue of consent in relation to those carrying sexually transmittable diseases required.

> … *debate, not in a court of law but as a matter of public and social policy, bearing in mind all the factors that are concerned including the questions of personal autonomy in delicate personal relationships. That does not mean that we in any way dissent from the view of the Law Commission that there would appear to be good reasons for considering the extent to which it would be right to criminalise sexual activity by those with sexually transmissible diseases who do not disclose that to their partners. But the extent to which such activity should result in charges such as rape, as opposed to tailor-made charges of deception in relation to the particular sexual activity, seems to us to be a matter which is a matter properly for public debate. All we need to say is that, as a matter of law, the fact that the appellant may not have disclosed his HIV status is not a matter which could in any way be relevant to the issue of consent under section 74 in relation to the sexual activity in this case (paras 21–2).*

Bree (2007) D and V both voluntarily consumed a considerable amount of alcohol before returning to V's flat and having sex. P initially alleged that V had lacked the capacity to consent because she had been unconscious throughout most of the sexual activity but, following the evidence at trial, altered its stance to maintain that, although her ability to resist D's sexual advances had been hampered by the effects of alcohol, she still had capacity to consent and that she had made clear, so far as she could, that she did not wish to have sex. V accepted that her recollection of events was very patchy and that she did not say 'no' to intercourse; however, she maintained that she had not consented. D maintained that V had been conscious throughout the incident and that he had reasonably believed that she was consenting. D was convicted of rape.

CA (Sir Igor Judge, President, QBD): allowed the appeal.

> ...if, through drink (or for any other reason) V has temporarily lost her capacity to choose whether to have intercourse on the relevant occasion, she is not consenting, and subject to questions about D's state of mind, if intercourse takes place, this would be rape. However, where V has voluntarily consumed even substantial quantities of alcohol, but nevertheless remains capable of choosing whether or not to have intercourse, and in drink agrees to do so, this would not be rape.

> We should perhaps underline that, as a matter of practical reality, capacity to consent may evaporate well before a complainant becomes unconscious. Whether this is so or not, however, is fact specific, or more accurately, depends on the actual state of mind of the individuals involved on the particular occasion.

> Considerations like these underline the fact that it would be unrealistic to endeavour to create some kind of grid system which would enable the answer to these questions to be related to some prescribed level of alcohol consumption. Experience shows that different individuals have a greater or lesser capacity to cope with alcohol than others, and indeed the ability of a single individual to do so may vary from day to day. The practical reality is that there are some areas of human behaviour which are inapt for detailed legislative structures. In this context, provisions intended to protect women from sexual assaults might very well be conflated into a system which would provide patronising interference with the right of autonomous adults to make personal decisions for themselves.

> For these reasons, notwithstanding criticisms of the statutory provisions, in our view the 2003 Act provides a clear definition of 'consent' for the purposes of the law of rape, and by defining it with reference to 'capacity to make that choice', sufficiently addresses the issue of consent in the context of voluntary consumption of alcohol by the complainant. The problems do not arise from the legal principles. They lie with infinite circumstances of human behaviour, usually taking place in private without independent evidence, and the consequent difficulties of proving this very serious offence (paras 34–6).

In this case, although D conceded that V had been drunk, it was a fundamental part of his defence that she had been conscious throughout and had in fact consented to sexual intercourse. That critical aspect of the case had not been addressed in the summing up. The summing up was inadequate, and the appeal allowed.

R (F) v DPP (2013) V sought judicial review of the decision not to prosecute her former partner for rape. V, a mother with one child, claimed that the relationship was marred by D's abusive dominance, including in sexual ways. V did not want another child, was unable for medical reasons to take contraceptive pills and it had been agreed between them that D would use a condom or withdraw. On one occasion during sexual intercourse without a condom D told V he would not withdraw and as a result V became pregnant.

HC: quashed the decision not to prosecute. If D had decided before penetration that he would act as he allegedly had done just because he deemed V to be subservient to his control, she was deprived of choice relating to the crucial feature on which her original consent to intercourse was based. Accordingly, her consent was negated. Lord Judge made clear that:

> …we are not addressing the situation in which sexual intercourse occurs consensually when the man, intending to withdraw in accordance with his partner's wishes, or their understanding, nevertheless ejaculates prematurely, or accidentally, within rather than outside his partner's vagina. These things happen. They always have and they always will, and no offence is committed when they do. They underline why withdrawal is not a safe method of contraception. Equally we are not addressing the many fluctuating ways in which sexual relationships may develop, as couples discover and renew their own levels of understanding and tolerance, their codes of communication, express or understood, and mutual give and take, experimentation and excitement. These are intensely private matters, personal to the couple in question (para. 24).

These are difficult lines to draw. What about this:

McNally (2013) D, aged 17, led V, aged 16, to believe that she was a boy. After four visits to V's home, where sexual conduct took place, D admitted to V's mother that she was in fact a girl. V said she would never have consented to the sexual acts had she known. D originally pleaded to 6 counts of assault by penetration, but appealed against sentence (three years imprisonment) and conviction.

CA: upheld conviction (but reduced the sentence to nine months detention, suspended for two years).

> …. B was not saying that HIV status could not vitiate consent if, for example, the complainant had been positively assured that D was not HIV positive; it left the issue open As [P] contends, the argument that in *Assange (2012)* and *R. (F)* [see earlier in this section] the deceptions were as to the features of the act is not sustainable: the wearing of a condom and ejaculation are irrelevant to the definition of rape and are not 'features' of the offence and no such rationale is suggested. In the last two cases, it was alleged that V had consented on the basis of a premise that, at the time of the consent, was false (namely, in one case, that her partner would wear a condom and, in the second, that he would ejaculate outside her body). In reality, some deceptions (such as, for example, in relation to wealth) will obviously not be sufficient to vitiate consent. In our judgment. Lord Judge CJ's observation that 'the evidence relating to "choice" and the "freedom" to make any particular choice must be approached in a broad common-sense way' identifies the route through the dilemma.

> Thus while, in a physical sense, the acts of assault by penetration of the vagina are the same whether perpetrated by a male or a female, the sexual nature of the acts is, on any common sense view, different where the complainant is deliberately deceived by a defendant into believing that the latter is a male. Assuming the facts to be proved as alleged, M chose to have sexual encounters with a boy and her preference (her freedom

> to choose whether or not to have a sexual encounter with a girl) was removed by D's deception (paras 24–6).
>
> Depending on the circumstances, deception as to gender could vitiate consent. Accordingly, X's pleas were not vitiated by a fundamental mistake of law or fact.

It is also important to note that a mistaken belief in consent in sex cases must be reasonable before it affords Ds a defence: see **5.30** and **10.13**. (Another problem with the SOA 2003 is that it does not explicitly state that children under a certain age cannot consent to sexual acts. The Act singles out offences committed against those under 13 for particularly severe punishments, but clearly the Home Office envisaged that children under 16 should not be able to consent: we return to what Spencer (2004) calls 'legislative overkill' in Chapter 10.)

Reform

5.14 Not surprisingly, the Law Commission has found the analysis of consent very tricky. They published a consultation paper on *Consent and Offences against the Person in 1993* (LCCP No. 134), but instead of producing a report as a result of consultation (the usual process: see **1.31**), they felt compelled by the responses that they received to produce a fuller and longer consultation paper in 1995 on *Consent in the Criminal Law* (LCCP No. 139). In this, they provisionally proposed that consent should not be a defence for those who intentionally or recklessly cause serious disabling injury, but that consent should be a defence for those who intentionally or recklessly cause other, less serious, injuries. Is it appropriate simply to draw a line at a certain level of injury or is the issue more difficult than this? Roberts wrote a paper for the Law Commission on the philosophical foundations of the law on consent, which is included in an Appendix to LCCP No. 139, and which concludes that those who advocate criminalization from a paternalistic or moralistic perspective must overcome powerful and widely accepted liberal counter-arguments. 'The presumption in favour of individual autonomy places the burden of persuasion firmly on the shoulders of liberalism's opponents' (p. 281).

Duress

5.15 If you commit a crime only because you have been threatened with a dreadful consequence if you don't do it, you may have a defence. As we will see, the 'standard' defence is duress, but this is narrowly construed. The courts are reluctant to acknowledge necessity as a defence (see **5.21**), and so a new 'hybrid' defence of duress of circumstances has evolved in the last 20 years or so (see **5.25**). Duress is normally considered to be an excuse (see **5.5**), whereas its first cousin necessity is more properly treated as a justification. But the courts are not consistent in their use of this terminology (see **5.5**), and as we shall see, there are considerable overlaps between these three defences. Let us start with duress. Once D has introduced the defence, P has to prove beyond reasonable doubt that D was not acting under duress.

Type of threat required

5.16   The threat must be of death or serious bodily harm against D, his immediate family, or someone close to him, and is normally an imminent or immediate threat. A sliding scale of threats would perhaps be fairer, such that more minor threats might provide a defence to more minor offences, but would this create too much uncertainty?

> *Hudson and Taylor* **(1971)** Ds gave false evidence in court because they were frightened by threats that they would be beaten up if they gave evidence against W.
>
> CA: quashed their convictions for perjury as the Recorder had been wrong to instruct the jury that the threats were not sufficiently present and immediate to constitute duress. The Recorder should have left to the jury the question whether the threats had overborne Ds' will at the time when they gave evidence. Lord Parker CJ:
>
>> It is essential to the defence of duress that the threat shall be effective at the moment when the crime is committed. The threat must be a 'present' threat in the sense that it is effective to neutralise the will of the accused at the time.

> *Valderrama-Vega* **(1985)** D was arrested with 2 kg of cocaine at Gatwick Airport. He was convicted of being knowingly concerned in the fraudulent evasion of the prohibition of the importation of a controlled drug despite his defence that he had received threats that his homosexuality would be exposed, as well as death threats to his family, if he did not act as a courier.
>
> CA: dismissed his appeal. The defence of duress, which had been left fairly to the jury, should be available so long as it was reasonably possible to say that the threat of death or serious injury was a *sine qua non* of his decision to offend, though it need not be the only factor. The threats must be of death or serious injury whatever the offence.

See also *Rodger and Rose* (1997) and *Abdul-Hussain* (1998) at **5.24**.

5.17   In general, the test of duress is whether the threat was of such gravity that it might well have caused a reasonable man placed in the same position to act in the same way as D acted, and whether a sober person of reasonable firmness sharing D's characteristics would have responded to the threat as he did.

***Bowen* (1996)** D was convicted on five specimen counts of obtaining services by deception. He gave evidence that two men had threatened to petrol bomb him and his family if he did not do as instructed. Other witnesses gave evidence that he was a simple man (with an IQ of 68) who was abnormally suggestible and vulnerable.

CA (Stuart-Smith LJ): dismissed his appeal. It was not necessary to direct the jury on D's low intelligence.

The mere fact that D is more pliable, vulnerable, timid, or susceptible to threats than a normal person is not a characteristic with which it is legitimate to invest the reasonable/ordinary person for the purpose of considering the objective test.

Only if D belongs to a category of persons (probably based only on age or sex) who the jury may think less able to resist pressure than others should the judge comment on such characteristics.

Buchanan and Virgo (1999) asserted that the *Bowen* test is unworkable: there are no recognized criteria for identifying a group whose ability to withstand threats is reduced.

***Antar* (2004)** D, an 18-year-old with a mild to moderate learning disability, appealed against his conviction for conspiracy to rob. His defence was duress. The trial judge did not admit in evidence a psychological report which concluded that he had a low IQ which amounted to mental impairment and a higher than usual level of suggestibility.

CA: allowed D's appeal. The judge had erred in excluding the psychologist's evidence. It was for the jury to decide on all the evidence whether D fell into a category of persons who were less able to resist pressure than the sober person of reasonable firmness.

5.18 The courts have wisely distinguished those cases where D has voluntarily put himself in a position where he would be likely to be subject to duress, in which case the defence is not available:

***Sharp* (1987)** D, a member of a gang which he knew used loaded firearms to carry out robberies, took part in a robbery in which a sub-postmaster was shot dead. D said that he had not wanted to participate in the robbery when he knew that firearms would be used but that he was threatened that his head would be blown off if he did not.

CA (Lord Lane CJ):

> …where a person has voluntarily, and with knowledge of its nature, joined a criminal organisation or gang which he knew might bring pressure on him to commit an offence and was an active member when he was put under such pressure, he cannot avail himself of the defence of duress.

Shepherd (1987) D's defence to charges of burglary was that the organizer had threatened him with violence if he dropped out.

CA: quashed his convictions. Not every criminal conspiracy deprives its adherents of the defence of duress. It depends on the nature of the duress and whether D knew he was submitting himself to the risk of compulsion. Where there is evidence of duress, the jury should decide on the exact facts.

See also *Hasan* (2005), at **5.20**.

5.19 Duress is not available as a defence to all offences.

Howe (1987) Ds confessed to taking part in the killing of Vs, but said that they acted through fear.

HL: upheld their conviction for murder, overruling the decision in *DPP for Northern Ireland v Lynch* (1975), which had allowed the defence of duress to those who aid and abet murder. Lord Hailsham:

> I have known in my lifetime of too many acts of heroism by ordinary human beings of no more than ordinary fortitude to regard a law as either 'just or humane' which withdraws the protection of the criminal law from the innocent victim and casts the cloak of its protection upon the coward and the poltroon in the name of a 'concession to human frailty'.

This decision has been much criticized. J. C. Smith (1989) called it a 'blueprint for saintliness'. Milgate (1988) analysed seven reasons that could be found for over ruling *Lynch (1975)*, but stood each one on its head. Thus, Lord Hailsham had suggested that since Parliament had not acted on the Law Commission's recommendation (in Law Com No. 83 (1977)) that duress should be available in all cases of murder, it had clearly not accepted the report. Milgate points out that it is just as easy to argue that since Parliament had not overruled *Lynch*, it should be taken to support it. As a result of *Howe*, we now may have a duty to be a hero. A taxi driver who delivers a bomb, which blows up and kills someone, for a terrorist organization because the gang is holding his family hostage has no defence to a charge of murder: should he be allowed one? Certainly the law is now inconsistent: where do we now draw the line between those offences for which duress is available and those where it is unavailable?

> *Gotts* **(1992)** D stabbed and seriously injured his mother, after his father had threatened to kill him if he did not do so. He was convicted of attempted murder after the trial judge ruled that his defence of duress could not be left to the jury.
>
> HL: dismissed the appeal. Lord Jauncey:
>
>> The reason why duress has for so long been stated not to be available as a defence to a murder charge is that the law regards the sanctity of human life and the protection thereof as of paramount importance.

Do you agree? It may be more appropriate for lawyers to talk of a 'right to life' (a legal/moral concept) and not the 'sanctity of human life' (a theological concept). Is the right to life an absolute right? Think again about the issues raised in *Bland* (1993, **2.10** and **5.7**).

5.20 What happens if D makes a mistake about the threat he is under? Duress is only a defence if D reasonably believed in the facts which gave him good cause to fear: see *Graham* (1982, **5.30**). If D reasonably believes there is a threat, it does not matter that there is in fact no threat: see *Cairns* (1999, **5.25**). This is the objective element in the defence: the belief must be reasonable.

> *Safi* **(2003)** Ds appealed against conviction for offences of hijacking an aircraft, false imprisonment, possession of a firearm with intent, and possession of explosives. In 2000 they had hijacked a plane as it left Afghanistan and, having travelled via Tashkent, Atyubinsk, and Moscow, eventually arrived at Stansted Airport. They maintained that they were political opponents of the Taliban regime and had been at risk of capture, torture, and execution. Thus, they contended that they had acted under an imminent threat of death or serious injury. The judge had directed that in order to meet the threshold test of duress there had to be evidence that there was in fact or might in fact have been an imminent peril.
>
> CA: allowed the appeal. The correct test for establishing a defence of duress had been established in *Graham* (1982, see **5.30**) and was made up of a subjective and objective limb. Accordingly, the judge should have directed the jury to ask themselves (i) whether Ds had been compelled to act in the way they did because they reasonably believed that they faced death or serious injury and (ii) whether a reasonable person in the same circumstances would have acted in the same way. The judge had made a material misdirection in directing that there had to be a threat in fact and accordingly the convictions were unsafe.

However, there has been uncertainty as to whether D had to have anticipated pressure to commit a crime of the type charged. This may now have been resolved:

> *Hasan* **(2005)** D was convicted of aggravated burglary (see **11.30**). His defence of duress was that a drug dealer, the boyfriend of his employer, who ran an escort agency involved in prostitution and who had a reputation for violence, had threatened that he and his family would be harmed if he did not carry out the burglary. CA had quashed his conviction.

HL: allowed the Crown's appeal from the decision of the CA, and restored D's conviction. The defence of duress was excluded when as a result of D's voluntary association with others he foresaw or ought reasonably to have foreseen the risk of being subjected to any compulsion by threats of violence. The decision of the CA in *Baker* (1999) was overruled: the law of duress did not require there to have been foresight of coercion to commit crimes of the kind with which D was charged. Policy pointed towards an objective test of what D, placed as he was and knowing what he did, ought reasonably to have foreseen. The policy of the law had to be to discourage association with known criminals, and it should be slow to excuse the criminal conduct of those who did so.

So it now seems clear that duress is only available where D honestly and reasonably believed that he was under threat: compare the position with self-defence (see **5.33**). Lord Bingham, who gave the main speech, explored the history of duress as an excuse to show why he was inclined towards tightening rather than relaxing the conditions to be met before duress could be relied on. But Lady Hale (who was a Law Commissioner from 1984 to 1993), whilst also allowing the appeal, had a different analysis of the law of duress. She explored the history of the Law Commission's consistently subjective approach to the defence, pointing out that the Law Commission's proposed solution to the dangers of widening the defence was that the persuasive burden of proving duress should be placed, on a balance of probabilities, on the defence. That possibility not being open to the HL, she preferred the '*Fitzpatrick* doctrine' (see the decision of the CCA in Northern Ireland in [1977] NI 20): irrespective of whether there was a threat which he could not reasonably be expected to resist, had D so exposed himself to the risk of such threats that he cannot now rely on them as an excuse? It had to be foreseeable that duress would be used to compel the person to commit crimes of some sort. Thus while Lord Bingham, with whom the other Law Lords agreed, suggested that the defence of duress is excluded when as a result of D's voluntary association with others engaged in criminal activity, he foresaw or ought reasonably to have foreseen the risk of being subjected to any compulsion by threats of violence, for Lady Hale the defence should only be excluded when D foresaw the risk of being subjected to compulsion to commit criminal offences. Baroness Hale, who described herself as a 'reasonable but comparatively weak and fearful grandmother' (para. 73), remains attracted to the Law Commission's subjectivist approach. Do you agree?

Necessity

5.21 The status of necessity in English law has been unclear, largely because it is an area of common law where there is an absence of case law (though a statute may expressly or impliedly create a defence of necessity). You can argue that the dearth of case law suggests that necessity is not a defence; more convincing is the argument that necessity is so clearly a defence in some cases that no prosecutions are brought. Thus, if you break the speed limit to get a severely wounded person to hospital, or you burn down your neighbour's shed simply to save a row of houses from fire, you may well not be prosecuted. The normal starting point in any discussion of necessity is *Dudley and Stephens*:

***Dudley and Stephens* (1884)** After a shipwreck, four men found themselves cast adrift in an open boat. After drifting for 20 days, and having not eaten for nine days and having been without water for seven days, two of the men agreed to kill the weakest, the cabin boy. Having done so, they fed on his flesh for four days, and were then picked up by a passing ship. They believed that if they did not feed on one of themselves, they would all have died of starvation.

CCCR (Lord Coleridge CJ): upheld their conviction for murder, rejecting the defence of necessity.

5.22   It is unclear from Lord Coleridge's speech whether he was saying that it was not necessary in that case for Ds to kill the cabin boy, or whether there is simply no defence of necessity.

***Shayler* (2003)** D, charged with an offence under the OSA 1989, sought, at a pre-trial hearing, to be allowed to raise a public interest defence (of duress/necessity) at his trial. The trial judge ruled that no such defence was possible.

HL: dismissed D's appeal. Having regard to the entirety of the 1989 Act and giving s 1(1)(a), s 4(1), and s 4(3)(a) their natural and ordinary meaning, D could not rely on a defence that he believed it to be in the national or public interest to make a disclosure. Sections 1(1)(a), 4(1), and 4(3) of the 1989 Act were compatible with Art 10 of the ECHR.

The following cases may suggest that there is a general defence of necessity, except where, as in *Shayler*, expressly or impliedly excluded by statute. (See also *Jones et al* (2004) at **5.39**.)

***Bourne* (1939)** D, a well-respected surgeon, carried out an abortion on a 14-year-old girl who had become pregnant as the result of a violent rape. He was prosecuted with unlawfully procuring a miscarriage. Macnaghten J, summing up to the jury, said they should acquit if they believed that the doctor had acted in good faith for the purpose only of preserving the life of the girl. The doctor was acquitted.

***Gillick v West Norfolk and Wisbech Area Health Authority* (1985)** In judicial review proceedings, P challenged the legality of a Department of Health memorandum which advised doctors that they would not be acting unlawfully if they prescribed contraceptives to girls under 16 without parental consent so long as they were acting in good faith to protect the girl against the harmful effects of sexual intercourse.

HL: the memorandum was not unlawful. A girl under 16 does not merely by her age lack the capacity to consent. A doctor who in the exercise of his clinical judgement gave contraceptive advice and treatment to a girl under the age of 16 without her parents' consent does not commit an offence because the bona fide exercise by the doctor of his clinical judgement negated the *mens rea* which was an essential element of the offence (upheld in *R (Axon) v Secretary of State for Health* (2006)).

Re F (mental patient: sterilization) **(1990)** The mother of a 36-year-old mentally handicapped woman issued a summons seeking a declaration that the sterilization of her daughter would not be an unlawful act by reason only of the absence of the daughter's consent.

HL: accepted that the sterilization was in the woman's best interest, and granted a declaration. Conscious of the need for 'a measure to protect those from the insults of an unnecessary sterilisation' (Lord Griffiths), the House nonetheless accepted that 'a man who seizes another and forcibly drags him from the path of an oncoming vehicle, thereby saving him from injury or even death, commits no wrong' (Lord Goff).

5.23 The Law Commission has changed its mind several times about the need for a defence of necessity. More than 30 years ago, in the Law Commission Working Paper No. 55, they proposed a general defence of necessity, which would be available where D himself believed that his conduct was necessary to avoid some greater harm, and that the harm to be avoided was, judged objectively, found to be out of all proportion to that actually caused by D's conduct. However, in their 1977 Report (Law Com No. 83), they rejected this proposal, suggesting that such a defence was not required. The DCC includes a proposed defence of duress of circumstances (see **5.25**) but not a justificatory choice-of-evil type defence.

However, the CA has now clearly recognized the defence:

Re A (Children) **(2001)** A Healthcare Trust sought a declaration that it was lawful and in the best interest of conjoined ('Siamese') twins, J and M, to operate to separate them, despite the facts that one baby would be certain to die and that the parents did not consent.

CA: rejecting the parents' appeal, granted the declaration. Ward LJ reviewed medical and family law in order to ascertain the children's best interests, before going on to consider the lawfulness of the proposed action. He concluded that the babies were two separate persons, and that it was not in the best interests of the one who would die that the operation be performed. Nor should any distinction between acts and omissions be relied upon: 'It seems to me to be utterly fanciful to classify this invasive treatment as an omission in contra-distinction to an act.' He balanced the 'paramount welfare' of both children: 'The prospect of a full life for J is counterbalanced by an acceleration of certain death for M.' He went further than the other judges in suggesting that the parents and doctors had a legal duty to J to carry out the operation which would save her life:

> ...in their natural repugnance at the idea of killing M, they fail to recognise their conflicting duty to save J and they seem to exculpate themselves from, or at least fail fully to face up to the consequence of the failure to separate the twins, namely death for J. In my judgement parents who are placed on the horns of such a terrible dilemma simply have to choose the lesser of their inevitable loss. If a family at the gates of a concentration camp were told they might free one of their children but if no choice were made both would die, compassionate parents with equal love for their twins would elect to save the stronger and see the weak one destined for death pass through the gates.

He also used the example of a 6-year-old shooting all and sundry in the school play-ground to explain his reasoning, suggesting that while the boy is not acting unlawfully because of his age, killing him in self-defence of others would not be unlawful.

Brooke LJ developed a detailed analysis of the criminal law arguments, particularly in relation to the doctrine of necessity. He distinguished the defence of necessity from that of duress since:

> ...in cases of pure necessity the actor's mind is not irresistibly overborne by external pressures. The claim is that his or her conduct was not harmful because on a choice of two evils the choice of avoiding the greater harm was justified.

He concluded with Sir James Stephens' three necessary requirements for the application of the doctrine of necessity:

 (i)   the act is needed to avoid inevitable and irreparable evil;

 (ii) no more should be done than is reasonably necessary for the purpose to be achieved;

 (iii) the evil inflicted must not be disproportionate to the evil avoided.

Since 'the principles of modern family law point irresistibly to the conclusion that the interests of J must be preferred to the conflicting interests of M', Sir James Stephens' three necessary requirements were satisfied.

Walker LJ concluded that the proposed operation would be in the best interests of both twins: M's death would not be the purpose or intention of the surgery, and she would die because her body on its own is not and never has been viable.

Lord Coleridge CJ asked in *Dudley and Stephens* (1884) (**5.21**), 'Who is to be the judge of this sort of necessity? By what measure is the comparative value of lives to be measured?' The answers are not necessarily for the judiciary. According to Ward LJ, the arguments which dominated the case were the sanctity of human life and the worthwhileness of the treatment. Brooke LJ suggested that:

> ...although parts of our criminal law, as enacted by Parliament, reflect a shift away from some of the tenets of Judaeo-Christian philosophy (in particular, for example, a shift away from the Catholic Church's teaching on abortion) in favour of the views of the majority of the elected representatives of an increasingly secular (and increasingly multi-cultural) modern state, there is no evidence that this process is at work in that part of the law concerned with the protection of human life between the moment of birth and the moment of death.

Is this true? There is widespread concern about decisions taken at the end of life (euthanasia) and about the resource and ethical implications of some medical decisions. Perhaps judges should concern themselves with the right to life, but not the sanctity of human life.

5.24   The courts remain cautious about accepting necessity:

CS (2012)   D took her child, aged 10, from England to Spain in breach of a court order. The trial judge held that following *Quayle* (2005; **5.25**), there was no room for a defence of necessity or duress of circumstances to an offence under s 1 of the Child Abduction Act 1984.

CA: dismissed the appeal. The judge was right to conclude that there could not be a defence of necessity within the legislative scheme of the 1984 Act. If, contrary to their view, the defence was available, it could not apply on the facts of this case: there could be no reasonable belief that a threat was imminent nor could it be said that a person was acting reasonably and proportionately by removing the child from the jurisdiction in order to avoid the threat of serious injury.

This raises the interesting question of whether necessity should be available in a wider range of circumstances than duress, or duress of circumstances. My view is that we could do quite happily without duress of circumstances altogether (see later at **5.25**). (Duress, of course, is limited to cases where D faces a threat of imminent death or serious injury.) Note that the defence of necessity can apply to less serious crimes:

Santos v CPS (2013)   D was convicted of two offences: riding a motorcycle without insurance and without protective headgear. His defence was that the motorbike had been stolen and hotwired, and that he was merely taking it to a place of safety. The legal adviser to the magistrates took the view that since both offences were strict liability offences (see **3.40**) the defence of necessity could not be advanced.

Admin Ct: The case was remitted to a differently constituted bench with a different legal adviser for reconsideration: the CPS had acknowledged that the magistrates were wrong to exclude the defence of necessity.

The Court appears to have relied on *Martin* (1989, 5.25)—although that case is probably better thought of as a case of 'duress of circumstances', than necessity. But the principle is right: necessity is a justificatory defence, nothing to do with denying *mens rea*.

Duress of circumstances

5.25 In the late 1980s a new defence seemed to appear:

Willer **(1987)** D's car was surrounded by a group of aggressive youths, and so he mounted the pavement and drove slowly out of a narrow alleyway. The Assistant Recorder refused to leave a defence of necessity to the jury and he was convicted of reckless driving.

CA (Watkins LJ): quashed his conviction. The question whether D 'was wholly driven by force of circumstances into doing what he did and did not drive the car otherwise than under that form of compulsion' should have been left to the jury.

Conway **(1989)** Fearing for the safety of his passenger, D drove recklessly to escape from people (who turned out to be plain-clothes police officers) who he feared would make a fatal attack on his friend. No defence of necessity was left to the jury.

CA (Woolf LJ): quashed D's conviction.

> …necessity can only be a defence to a charge of reckless driving where the facts establish 'duress of circumstances', as in *Willer*, i.e. where D was constrained by circumstances to drive as he did to avoid death or serious bodily harm to himself or some other person … 'Duress of circumstances' is available only if from an objective standpoint D can be said to be acting in order to avoid a threat of death or serious injury.

Martin **(1989)** D's wife threatened suicide if he didn't drive her son to work, even though he was disqualified from driving.

CA: quashed his conviction for driving whilst disqualified. Simon Brown J:

> English law does, in extreme circumstances, recognise a defence of necessity. Most commonly this defence arises as duress, that is pressure upon the accused's will from the wrongful threats or violence of another. Equally, however, it can arise from other

objective dangers threatening the accused or others. Arising thus it is conveniently called 'duress of circumstances'.

Two questions should have been left to the jury: first, was D, or may he have been, impelled to act as he did because as a result of what he reasonably believed to be the situation, he had good reason to fear that otherwise death (including suicide) or serious physical injury would result? If so, might a sober person of reasonable firmness, sharing D's characteristics, have responded to that situation by acting as D did?

The defence is now (unfortunately) regularly discussed in the case law:

Rodger and Rose **(1997)** Two life sentence prisoners escaped from Parkhurst Prison because they felt suicidal after the Home Secretary significantly raised their tariffs (the minimum period they had to serve before their cases could be heard by the Parole Board).

CA (Sir Patrick Russell): dismissed their appeals. They did not escape because of the Home Secretary's decision, but because of their own suicidal tendencies. The defences of 'duress by necessity or duress of circumstances' are not available unless the causative feature of the commission of the offence is extraneous to the offender:

> If allowed it could amount to a licence to commit a crime dependant on the personal characteristics and vulnerability of the offender.

Abdul-Hussain **(1998)** Fugitives from Iraq hijacked an aircraft from Sudan to Stansted, and were convicted under the Aviation Security Act 1982 after the trial judge ruled that a defence of necessity or duress of circumstances could not be left to the jury, since the threat was insufficiently close or immediate.

CA (Rose LJ): allowed the appeals. The defence of duress should have been left to the jury: the imminent peril of death or serious injury to D or his dependants had to operate on his mind so as to overbear his will at the time he committed the act. The threat must be imminent, but need not be immediate. The Court stressed the need for legislation in this area:

> If Ann Frank had stolen a car to escape from Amsterdam and had been charged with theft, the tenets of English law would not, in our judgement, have denied her a defence of duress of circumstances, on the ground that she should have waited for the Gestapo's knock on the door.

Cairns **(1999)** V spread-eagled himself on D's windscreen. D, who was small and timid, did not know V and said he was intimidated by V's friend shouting from the roadside. He drove on, braking when he got to a speed hump. V fell under the car and fractured his spine, which rendered him paraplegic. D was convicted under the OAPA 1861, s 20 (see **9.8**).

CA (Mansell LJ): quashed his conviction. Where D relies on the defence of necessity or duress of circumstances, it was sufficient for him to show that he acted because he reasonably perceived a threat of serious physical injury or death; he was not required to prove that the threat was actual or real.

A novel use of the defence was tried unsuccessfully in *Quayle*:

Quayle **(2005)** Five Ds appealed against convictions for cultivation, production, importation, and possession of cannabis (and the A-G made a reference in respect of another case where the defence of medical necessity had been accepted). Some Ds, who suffered from various illnesses which caused them severe pain, grew cannabis plants at their homes for personal use. They argued that this was excusable in law since they genuinely and reasonably believed that it was necessary to avoid them suffering serious injury or pain, and that the charges against them should have been left to the jury on that basis. Two other Ds supplied cannabis to sufferers of such illnesses from a holistic centre.

CA: dismissed the appeals. Medicinal use of cannabis was not allowed, even on a doctor's prescription, except in the context of ongoing trials for medical research purposes, by the Misuse of Drugs Act 1971 or by the Misuse of Drugs Regulations 2001. Neither judges nor juries were well equipped to resolve issues as to when and how far the deliberate policy of clear legislation should give way in a particular case to countervailing individual hardship, or as to what the overall effect of such derogations would be on the whole legislative scheme. For the defence of necessity of circumstances to be potentially available, there had to be extraneous circumstances capable of objective scrutiny by judge and jury: the legal defences of duress by threats and necessity by circumstances should be confined to cases where there was an imminent danger of physical injury and pain.

Perhaps a more convincing argument for a defence of necessity in the medical context is offered by Ost (2005) who suggests that it might be available to doctors in some cases of euthanasia (see also **8.45**).

5.26 The Law Commission seems to have accepted that this defence is an excuse, close to duress. The Criminal Law Bill in Law Com No. 218 included separate definitions of duress by threats; duress of circumstances; and justifiable use of force. By clause 36(2) various common law defences would be abrogated:

(a) the defence of duress, whether by threats or of circumstances;

(b) the defence of coercion of a wife by her husband;

(c) any defence available in respect of the use of force ... but without prejudice to any distinct defence of necessity.

This seems to be a convenient way of sidestepping the problem: does or should the defence of necessity operate as a justificatory defence quite separately from the excusatory defence of duress? Clarkson argues at [2004] Crim LR 81 in favour of col-lapsing the defences of duress by threats and circumstances, necessity, and self-defence into one general defence of necessity, termed necessary action. He explores whether this could help to resolve current anomalies. Do you think such a broad defence would go against the principle of fair labelling (see **1.2**)? See also Wilson (2005). My view is that we should keep duress (an excuse, to be applied narrowly), and necessity (a justification, which may be more widely applicable: 'true' cases of necessity are difficult to find only because those who are genuinely justified are rightly not prosecuted!). Duress of circumstances (a curious hybrid) should simply be abolished.

Mistake

5.27 Some mistakes may mean that P fails to prove an essential element of the necessary guilty mind: intention or recklessness (see Chapter 3). For example, if I intention-ally throw darts at you thinking you are a shop's dummy, I am not guilty of your murder if you die from the wounds I cause you. I did not intend to kill a person. However, we are here concerned with situations when a mistake may give rise to a distinct defence. Everyone is presumed to know the law: so only mistakes of fact may give rise to a defence. Why is this? Do we have a moral obligation to know the law? Husak and von Hirsch (1993) argued that ignorance of the law should normally be excused if D's legal mistake was a reasonable one in the circumstances, and that D's punishment should be mitigated if he did not know, but should have known, of the illegality of his conduct. As the law gets ever more complicated this argument seems irresistible. However, it is not always easy to distinguish fact from law:

> *Gould* **(1968)** D was convicted of bigamy under the OAPA 1861, s 57. At the time of the second marriage he honestly believed that his first marriage had been dissolved and he had reasonable grounds for this belief. In fact the marriage had not been dissolved and his first wife was still living.
>
> CA: quashed his conviction. An honest belief on reasonable grounds was a good defence to a charge of bigamy if the consequences of that belief being true would be that an offence had not been committed.

5.28 If knowledge of a surrounding circumstance is an ingredient of an offence then an honest mistake as to that circumstance may be a defence. This mistake need not be reasonable, as long as it is genuinely held.

> *Gladstone Williams* **(1987)** D punched V because he believed that V was beating up a third party, when in fact V was arresting the third party.

CA (Lord Lane CJ): quashed his conviction.

> The reasonableness or unreasonableness of D's belief is material to the question of whether the belief was held by D at all. If the belief was in fact held, its unreasonableness, so far as guilt or innocence is concerned, is neither here nor there.

Beckford v R **(1987)** D, a police officer, was at the scene where V, an armed man, was terrorizing his family. D shot V dead after he had given himself up and after he had been disarmed. D's defence was that he honestly believed that his life was in danger. The Jamaican CA upheld his conviction for murder on the ground that his belief that he was acting in self-defence had to be reasonable, and not just honestly held.

PC (Lord Griffiths): quashed his conviction '… a man about to be attacked does not have to wait for his assailant to strike the first blow or fire the first shot; circumstances may justify a pre-emptive strike.'

These cases are cited in *B (a minor) v DPP* (2000) where, as we saw at **3.40**, the HL held that the offence under the Indecency with Children Act 1960 was not an offence of strict liability: P had to prove that D knew that, or was reckless whether, the child was under 14.

5.29 Can one always distinguish a mistaken belief from the more culpable state of mind which may arise where D has no knowledge of the surrounding circumstances because he gave the matter no thought, or forgot it? At **10.12** we will consider whether the law of rape should distinguish reckless ignorance from mistake and acknowledge a duty to think arising from D's conduct. Should D be liable for his failure (omission) to think?

5.30 As we have seen at **5.20**, the mistake may in some circumstances have to be reasonable, particularly in two areas: cases of duress and in sexual offences in relation to belief in consent: see **10.13**:

Graham **(1982)** D, a homosexual, lived in a *ménage à trois* with his wife and a man. D played a leading part in the killing of his wife, but said that he acted under duress, and that his behaviour was affected by the drink and drugs he had taken.

CA (Lord Lane CJ): upheld his conviction for murder. There is an objective element in the defence of duress: the jury must determine whether the threat was one which the D in question could not reasonably have been expected to resist.

> As a matter of public policy, it seems to us essential to limit the defence of duress by means of an objective criterion formulated in terms of reasonableness … if a mistake is to excuse what would otherwise be criminal, the mistake must be a reasonable one.

5.31 Both the courts (see *DPP v Rogers* (1997)) and the Law Commission resisted this development in the law, but it has been confirmed in *Abdul-Hussain* (1998, see **5.25**) and by the HL in *Hasan* (2005, see **5.20**). In Law Com No. 218, the Law Commission says that there was 'almost no support' for the view that D's belief must be reasonable, and it recommends that reasonableness should be a matter of evidence only. Thus, the emphasis in its recommendation is on the actor's 'knowledge or belief'. Similarly, the courts do not always seem to follow *Graham*:

> **Scarlett (1993)** D, a publican, used excessive force to eject V, a drunken man, from his pub. V died, and D was convicted of manslaughter.
>
> CA: quashed his conviction. Provided that D 'believed that the circumstances called for the degree of force used, he was not to be convicted even if his belief was unreasonable.'

But the CA has subsequently moved away from this position:

> **DPP v Armstrong-Braun (1998)** D, trying to protect great crested newts from building developments, obstructed V, who was using a mechanical digger on the site being developed. He was convicted of an assault under the CJA 1988, s 39.
>
> CA: the force used by D when accused of battery in self-defence was to be assessed in an objective sense as to whether it was reasonably necessary in the circumstances as D subjectively believed them to be. There was no necessity for an additional test requiring a subjective approach to the question of proportionality of the response.

J. C. Smith (in [1999] Crim LR 128) comments 'the law was misstated, probably inadvertently, in *Scarlett* and it is best forgotten'.

5.32 The Law Commission use *Scarlett* (in Law Com No. 218, p. 3) to illustrate the need for a codification of the criminal law. Mr Scarlett spent five months in prison before the CA quashed his conviction, a conviction which happened, it could be said, just because everyone in the case had overlooked the requirement that the reasonableness of the force used must be judged in the circumstances as D believed them to be. But was this actually the law?

Should the test vary according to the offence charged? Or according to the defence raised? Or is a more principled approach possible? Williams (2008) identifies the difficulties in developing watertight rules. For the added complexity where D makes his mistake because he is drunk: see **4.23**. And remember that, with sexual offences, a belief in consent must be genuinely held and reasonable in all the circumstances: see **5.13**.

Self-defence and the prevention of crime

5.33   These offences are usually dealt with together since they are first cousins: both are seen as justificatory defences. (See also the statutory defence of 'acting reasonably' to offences of assisting and encouraging, charged under the Serious Crime Act 2007 at **7.36**.) Self-defence (along with defence of property and defence of another) is a common law defence, which has been made more complex by the enactment of s 76 of the CJIA 2008 (see **5.35**), whereas prevention of crime is to be found in the CLA 1967, s 3:

> (1) A person may use such force as is reasonable in the circumstances in the prevention of crime, or in effecting or assisting in the lawful arrest of offenders or suspected offenders or of persons unlawfully at large.

5.34   A person may use such force as is reasonable in the circumstances for the purposes of self-defence, defence of property or of another, prevention of crime, or lawful arrest. What is reasonable is a question of fact for the jury. D is judged on what is reasonable on the facts as he believed them to be (see *Beckford* (1987), at **5.28**).

> *A-G's Reference (No. 2 of 1983)* **(1984)** D, of previously good character, made petrol bombs, intending to use them in the event of an attack on his shop by rioters in an area where serious rioting had occurred. The judge ruled that self-defence was available, and the jury acquitted.
>
> CA (Lord Lane CJ): the defence was indeed available. D had to satisfy the jury on a balance of probabilities that his object was to protect himself or his family or property against imminent apprehended attack and to do so by means which he believed were no more than reasonably necessary to meet the force used by the attackers.

> *Martin* **(2001)** D shot two burglars who had broken into his farmhouse, and was convicted of murder and wounding with intent (see OAPA 1861, s 18 at **9.2**).
>
> CA: allowed his appeal, admitting fresh medical evidence that D was suffering from a paranoid personality disorder at the time and that this was exacerbated by depression. A conviction of manslaughter on the ground of diminished responsibility was substituted. However, evidence of D's psychiatric condition was not admissible in a case of self-defence where the use of excessive force was the issue. It was what D himself believed that was important, not the scientific description of his condition. The CA certified the following point of law as being of general public importance: 'Whether expert psychiatric evidence is admissible on the issue of a D's perception of the danger he faced (in a case where he relies on self-defence).'

J. C. Smith [2002] Crim LR 136 argued that the understanding of the facts and the assessment of the danger are inseparable: if psychiatric evidence is admissible in duress (see **5.17**), why not here?

> *There is an urgent need for some rationalization of the law of necessity, private defence, duress and provocation, all of which raise questions of the relevance of D's personal characteristics but lack any consistent principle (at p. 138).*

5.35 Because of the public/media discussion about the extent of the right to act in self-defence the Government decided to legislate simply to confirm the common law: that a person who uses force is to be judged on the basis of the circumstances as he perceived them, that in the heat of the moment he will not be expected to have judged exactly what action was called for, and that a degree of latitude may be given to a person who only did what he honestly and instinctively thought was necessary. But the end result was far from simple. Section 76 of the Criminal Justice and Immigration Act 2008 (which has already been heavily amended by s 148 of the Legal Aid, Sentencing and Punishment of Offenders Act 2012, as you will spot by the subsections with A etc. in their numbering) is not straightforward:

Section 76 Reasonable force for purposes of self-defence etc.

(1) This section applies where in proceedings for an offence—

  (a) an issue arises as to whether a person charged with the offence ("D") is entitled to rely on a defence within subsection (2), and

  (b) the question arises whether the degree of force used by D against a person ("V") was reasonable in the circumstances.

(2) The defences are—

  (a) the common law defence of self-defence;

  (aa) the common law defence of defence of property; and

  (b) the defences provided by section 3(1) of the Criminal Law Act 1967 (c. 58) or section 3(1) of the Criminal Law Act (Northern Ireland) 1967 (c. 18 (N.I.)) (use of force in prevention of crime or making arrest).

(3) The question whether the degree of force used by D was reasonable in the circumstances is to be decided by reference to the circumstances as D believed them to be, and subsections (4) to (8) also apply in connection with deciding that question.

(4) If D claims to have held a particular belief as regards the existence of any circumstances—

  (a) the reasonableness or otherwise of that belief is relevant to the question whether D genuinely held it; but

(b) if it is determined that D did genuinely hold it, D is entitled to rely on it for the purposes of subsection (3), whether or not—

(i) it was mistaken, or

(ii) (if it was mistaken) the mistake was a reasonable one to have made.

(5) But subsection (4)(b) does not enable D to rely on any mistaken belief attributable to intoxication that was voluntarily induced.

(5A) In a householder case, the degree of force used by D is not to be regarded as having been reasonable in the circumstances as D believed them to be if it was grossly disproportionate in those circumstances.

(6) In a case other than a householder case, the degree of force used by D is not to be regarded as having been reasonable in the circumstances as D believed them to be if it was disproportionate in those circumstances.

(6A) In deciding the question mentioned in subsection (3), a possibility that D could have retreated is to be considered (so far as relevant) as a factor to be taken into account, rather than as giving rise to a duty to retreat.

(7) In deciding the question mentioned in subsection (3) the following considerations are to be taken into account (so far as relevant in the circumstances of the case)—

(a) that a person acting for a legitimate purpose may not be able to weigh to a nicety the exact measure of any necessary action; and

(b) that evidence of a person's having only done what the person honestly and instinctively thought was necessary for a legitimate purpose constitutes strong evidence that only reasonable action was taken by that person for that purpose.

(8) Subsections (6A) and (7) are not to be read as preventing other matters from being taken into account where they are relevant to deciding the question mentioned in subsection (3).

(8A) For the purposes of this section "a householder case" is a case where—

(a) the defence concerned is the common law defence of selfdefence,

(b) the force concerned is force used by D while in or partly in a building, or part of a building, that is a dwelling or is forces accommodation (or is both),

(c) D is not a trespasser at the time the force is used, and

(d) at that time D believed V to be in, or entering, the building or part as a trespasser.

(8B) Where—

(a) a part of a building is a dwelling where D dwells,

(b) another part of the building is a place of work for D or another person who dwells in the first part, and

(c) that other part is internally accessible from the first part, that other part, and any internal means of access between the two parts, are each treated for the purposes of subsection (8A) as a part of a building that is a dwelling.

(8C) Where—

(a) a part of a building is forces accommodation that is living or sleeping accommodation for D,

(b) another part of the building is a place of work for D or another person for whom the first part is living or sleeping accommodation, and

(c) that other part is internally accessible from the first part, that other part, and any internal means of access between the two parts, are each treated for the purposes of subsection (8A) as a part of a building that is forces accommodation.

(8D) Subsections (4) and (5) apply for the purposes of subsection (8A)(d) as they apply for the purposes of subsection (3).

(8E) The fact that a person derives title from a trespasser, or has the permission of a trespasser, does not prevent the person from being a trespasser for the purposes of subsection (8A).

(8F) In subsections (8A) to (8C)—

"building" includes a vehicle or vessel, and

"forces accommodation" means service living accommodation for the purposes of Part 3 of the Armed Forces Act 2006 by virtue of section 96(1)(a) or (b) of that Act.

(9) This section, except so far as making different provision for householder cases, is intended to clarify the operation of the existing defences mentioned in subsection (2).

(10) In this section—

(a) *"legitimate purpose"* means—

(i) the purpose of self-defence under the common law,

(ia) the purpose of defence of property under the common law, or

(ii) the prevention of crime or effecting or assisting in the lawful arrest of persons mentioned in the provisions referred to in subsection (2)(b);

(b) references to self-defence include acting in defence of another person; and

(c) references to the degree of force used are to the type and amount of force used.

This section has done little to clarify anything! In particular, s 76(7) and (8) has led to a flood of appeals. For example:

Kitchens (2011) V's ex-boyfriend objected to D moving in with V. The ex-boyfriend had, on a previous occasion, got into the flat and threatened V. When he came round again, D urged V not to let him in, and when she would not listen, he slapped her across the face. In response to a jury question, the judge stated that the ex-boyfriend was not about to commit a crime, and the possibility that he might do so was not sufficient to justify D's actions in slapping her. D was convicted of common assault.

CA: dismissed the appeal. Self-defence and the defence furnished by s 3 of the CLA 1967 were capable of extending to the use of force against an innocent third party to prevent a crime being committed by someone else.

Gross LJ cites with support the statement in *Archbold* at para. 19–39b:

> [Section 76] does indeed do nothing other than restate the common law principles in particular as to (i) a defendant being entitled to be judged on the facts as he believed them to be even if he made an unreasonable mistake, (ii) the defendant not being entitled to rely on a mistake as to the facts that was induced by his own voluntary intoxication, (iii) the reasonableness or otherwise of any claimed mistake going only to the issue of whether or not the claim was genuine, (iv) the force used having to be proportionate, (v) there being no expectation that in an emergency a person should weigh to a nicety the force required, and (vi) a person doing only what he instinctively and honestly thought was necessary being strong evidence that only reasonable force was used.

But:

> …both the common law and statutory defences have greater scope for operation where it is certain or nearly certain that a crime will be committed immediately if action is not taken' (at para. 31).

Although on the facts of this case, the conviction was quite safe, he gave two examples when self-defence might extend to the use of force against a third party:

1. A police constable bundles a passerby out of the way to get at a man he believes about to shoot with a firearm or detonate an explosive device.

2. Y seeks to give Z car keys with Z about to drive. X, believing Z to be unfit drive through drink, knocks the keys out of Y's hands and retains them.

Ashworth agrees that both these examples involve a common assault that appears justifiable, but comments that 'it is questionable whether the situation has to be so extreme. If in the first example the police constable used substantial force on the passer-by, who initially resisted the constable's attempt to push past, might not the constable's actions be a defence to assault occasioning actual bodily harm or worse?' (at [2011] Crim LR 875). (See also *Oye* (2013) on insanity and self-defence: **4.13**.)

5.36 The Protection from Harassment Act 1997, s 1(3)(a) exempts liability for a course of conduct 'pursued for the purpose of preventing or detecting crime'. The SC (in a civil case) recently decided that, to benefit from that defence, the alleged harasser has to show that he had acted rationally:

Hayes v Willoughby **(2013)** At the outset of D's campaign against V, there was a reasonable basis for D's suspicions that V was guilty of tax evasion and fraud. But once the authorities had examined the case, and decided that D's suspicions were ill-founded, D's persistence ceased to be reasonable. V sued (in civil law) for damages and for an injunction to restrain continuing harassment.

SC (by a majority of 4 to 1, Lord Reed dissenting): dismissed D's appeal. In the context of s 1(3)(a), purpose was a subjective state of mind, but a wholly subjective test was problematic. The necessary control mechanism was to be found in the concept of rationality. Rationality was not the same as reasonableness. Reasonableness was an external, objective standard applied to the outcome of a person's thoughts or intentions; the question was whether a notional hypothetically reasonable person in his position would have engaged in the relevant conduct for the purpose of preventing or detecting crime. A test of rationality, by comparison, applied a minimum objective standard to the relevant person's mental processes. It imported a requirement of good faith, a requirement that there should be some logical connection between the evidence and the ostensible reasons for the decision, and an absence of arbitrariness, of capriciousness, or of reasoning so outrageous in its defiance of logic as to be perverse.

Lord Reed dissented: Parliament could not have intended to impose a requirement that the pursuit of the course of conduct should have been rational. First, Parliament did not say so. Second, s 1(3)(a) and the similarly worded provisions elsewhere in the Act provided defences to criminal as well as civil liability; it was trite that a statute was not normally to be construed as extending criminal liability beyond the limits which Parliament itself made clear in its enactment. Third, it could not be inferred that criminal liability was intended to turn on the subtle distinction between what was unreasonable and what was irrational:

> I am not convinced that Parliament can have intended that a jury should be expected to understand and apply the sophisticated distinctions which Lord Sumption seeks to draw (para. 28).

Lord Reed is surely right?

5.37 Self-defence and prevention of crime are 'all or nothing' defences: why is there no half-way house where excessive force is used, resulting in a partial reduction, rather as murder is reduced to manslaughter in cases of provocation (see **8.14**)?

> **Clegg (1995)** D, a British soldier based in Northern Ireland, was on night patrol in 1990. A car failed to stop at a checkpoint some way down the road, and sped past D. Responding to a call to stop the car, D fired four shots at the car, and one killed the passenger. Scientific evidence suggested that the fatal shot was fired after the car had passed and was some fifty feet down the road.
>
> HL: upheld D's conviction for murder. Where a plea of self-defence to a charge of murder fails because the force used was excessive and unreasonable, D is guilty of murder not manslaughter.

Clegg was sentenced to a mandatory life sentence of murder, but despite this was released after a short time and returned to a post in the army. Perhaps better than a reform which would allow a reduction to manslaughter in such cases would be the abolition of the mandatory life sentence for murder. (In 1998 the Court of Appeal quashed Clegg's conviction and ordered a retrial on the grounds of fresh evidence. At the retrial, he was acquitted of murder, but convicted of attempting to injure the car driver. This conviction was also quashed on appeal.)

Note the new partial defence to murder of 'loss of control': see **8.15**. To what extent does this overlap with self-defence?

Unknown circumstances justifying force in self-defence

> **Dadson (1850)** D shot and wounded a fleeing poacher. The degree of force was permissible if V was a felon: he was, but D did not know this.
>
> CCCR (Pollock CB in a five-line judgment): D's conviction upheld as he was 'not justi-fied in firing at the poacher'.

5.38   This case provides the starting point for a discussion of the principle that whenever D seeks to rely on a justification or excuse, he must have known or believed in those circumstances. Some writers would argue that the principle should be limited to excuses and not to justifications, but this argument takes us back to where we started in this chapter. Not everyone accepts that the distinction in English law is useful: see the discussion of the law on mistake (see **5.27**), and J. C. Smith's Hamlyn Lectures (1989).

Section 3 and the protection of private property

> **DPP v Bayer (2003)** Ds had gone on to private farmland and had attached themselves to tractors, which were sowing genetically modified maize, with the intention of dis-rupting the sowing. They were charged with aggravated trespass, contrary to the CJPOA 1994, s 68(1) (see **12.21**). The DJ(MC) found that Ds had honestly held and genuine

beliefs about the dangers of genetically modified crops, had genuine fears about the surrounding property, had reasonable grounds for those beliefs and fears, and had acted with all good intentions and had gone no further than was absolutely necessary to try to prevent the sowing of the crops. He concluded that they had a defence at common law of 'defence of property'. The DPP appealed (by way of case stated) against their acquittal.

CA: allowed the DPP's appeal. It was a principle of common law that a person might use a proportionate degree of force to defend his property or the property of others from attack or the threat of imminent attack. Where the common law defence was raised, the court should first ask itself whether Ds were contending that they used reasonable force in order to defend property from actual or imminent damage which constituted or could constitute an unlawful or criminal act. If the answer to that question was no, then the defence was not available. If the answer was yes, the court had to go on to consider the facts as Ds honestly believed them to be and to determine objectively whether the force they used was no more than reasonable in all the circumstances, given their beliefs. The sowing of maize seed on the land was not unlawful, even if the seed might have blown on to neighbouring land, and so the 'defence of property' defence was not available on these facts.

***

Jones et al **(2006)** Ds were charged with conspiracy to cause criminal damage. They allegedly damaged equipment at a military air base that they claimed would be used for an attack on Iraq, which they maintained was part of an unlawful war. Their defences at trial, under s 3 of the CLA 1967, and of necessity, and of lawful excuse under s 5(2)(b) of the CDA 1971, were all unsuccessful.

HL: unanimously dismissed the appeals. The focus of the 1967 Act was entirely domestic. It was very unlikely that Parliament understood 'crime' in s 3 as covering crimes recognized in customary international law but not assimilated into domestic law by any statute or judicial decision. Even if the Government had committed the international law crime of aggression in preparing to make war on Iraq, this did not justify Ds' otherwise unlawful conduct. The customary international law crime against peace (or crime of aggression) was not a crime within the meaning of s 3 of the CLA 1967 or an 'offence' within the meaning of s 68(2) of the CJPOA 1994. It had not been tacitly assimilated into domestic law. Lord Bingham (at para. 30) put particular emphasis on the democratic principle that it was for Parliament to decide what constitutes a crime in domestic law, and on the 'well-established rules that the courts will be very slow to review the exercise of prerogative powers in relation to the conduct of foreign affairs and the deployment of the armed services, and very slow to adjudicate upon the rights arising out of transactions entered into between sovereign states on the plane of international law.' Lord Hoffmann went further than Lord Bingham in considering the possible defence under s 3 of the 1967 Act (see **5.33**) which he stated did not excuse a D if he uses such force as he himself thinks to be reasonable: it must actually have been reasonable.

5.39 Some of the cases considered in *Jones* will have returned to the Crown Court where further arguments on the defence of necessity and under s 5 of the CDA 1971 will no doubt have been deployed. Remember you are studying a constantly moving picture of the criminal law! Ormerod [2005] Crim LR 959 argues that although, for duress of circumstances to apply, D (or those he acts to protect) must face an imminent threat of death or serious injury, that death or serious injury need not be criminal in origin. (Thus, D might plead the defence where he steals V's car to take to safety his family when they are faced with a threat of death from a looming cloud of noxious gas that has escaped from a factory without criminal fault.) The jury, in evaluating the reasonableness of D's response must, he argues, have regard to the type of threat D faces. How can the jury assess the proportionality of D's actions in ignorance of the lawfulness of the action D is responding to? (See also Gardner (2005).) It is interesting to note that juries can sometimes be persuaded to acquit 'activists' with whom they sympathize: Greenpeace activists were acquitted in 1999 of criminal damage to GM crops, and in 2008 other activists were acquitted of criminal damage to a coal-fired power station on the basis of a 'lawful excuse'.

Lawful chastisement

5.40 There is a common law 'defence' which allows parents and people *in loco parentis* to use reasonable and moderate chastisement. But the extent of this defence has long been unclear:

A v United Kingdom **(1998)** The stepfather of A, aged 9, had been acquitted (by a jury) of assault occasioning actual bodily harm for caning him, despite the bruises which were still visible several days later.

ECtHR: there was a breach of Art 3 (prohibition of torture); the UK Government was responsible for the violation committed by the stepfather as the criminal law afforded too great a degree of latitude to a jury. The breadth of the defence of reasonable chastisement 'fails to provide adequate protection to children and should be amended'.

R v H **(2001)** A pre-trial appeal on what the judge could say to the jury in a case where lawful chastisement was raised as a defence.

CA: the defence still exists. The jury should be directed as to what constitutes reasonable chastisement: the nature of D's behaviour, the age and characteristics of the child, the physical and mental consequences for the child, the reasons given by D for his conduct were all relevant.

Teachers do not have the right to use corporal punishment:

> *R (on the application of Williamson) v Secretary of State for Education and Employment (2005)* W and his co-applicants were head teachers, teachers, and parents of certain Christian schools who maintained that corporal punishment represented part of their religious beliefs which the state was obliged to respect because of the HRA 1998. They appealed against the dismissal of their application for judicial review arguing that the Education Act 1996, s 548 as amended by the School Standards and Framework Act 1998, s 131 did not completely abolish the use of corporal punishment in independent schools. At first instance the court had held that s 548, when construed in the ordinary manner, removed the right to administer reasonable chastisement in its entirety. A belief in the administration of corporal punishment, whilst derived from the Christian convictions of the applicants, could not be regarded as a religious conviction in its own right.
>
> HL: dismissed the appeal. Article 9 of the ECHR was not engaged since neither the infliction of corporal punishment by teachers, nor support for such punishment on the part of parents, manifested a 'belief' in the sense in which it was used in the article. Section 548 did not infringe the right of parents to subject their children to corporal punishment for breaches of school discipline but, rather, removed the right to inflict such punishment from teaching staff with the consequence that parents were unable to delegate their right to inflict such punishment.

5.41 Parliament has since acted to remove the defence from parents as well:

Children Act 2004, s 58 (Reasonable punishment)

(1) In relation to any offence specified in subsection (2), battery of a child cannot be justified on the ground that it constituted reasonable punishment.

(2) The offences referred to in subsection (1) are—

 (a) an offence under section 18 or 20 of the Offences against the Person Act 1861 (wounding and causing grievous bodily harm);

 (b) an offence under section 47 of that Act (assault occasioning actual bodily harm);

 (c) an offence under section 1 of the Children and Young Persons Act 1933 (cruelty to persons under 16).

(3) Battery of a child causing actual bodily harm to the child cannot be justified in any civil proceedings on the ground that it constituted reasonable punishment.

(4) For the purposes of subsection (3) 'actual bodily harm' has the same meaning as it has for the purposes of section 47 of the Offences against the Person Act 1861.

We started this chapter by suggesting that the arguments in favour of codification of the criminal law do not necessarily apply to the outer limits of defences (see 5.4). Do you think Parliament was right to legislate here? Would you want Parliament to codify the other defences discussed in this chapter? We should mention briefly the defence of marital coercion (see s. 47 of the Criminal Justice Act 1925), which was raised unsuccessfully in the high profile trial of Vicky Pryce in 2013, when she argued that she took her husband's speeding points under the coercion of her husband. As we go to print, the Government has wisely agreed that the defence should be abolished. A defence available only to wives, it is surely obsolete: in appropriate cases, the defence of duress remains available. In other cases, if a woman is bullied to commit a crime by her partner, this should surely mitigate the sentence imposed, but not affect her criminal liability.

FURTHER READING

Buchanan, A. and Virgo, G., 'Duress and Mental Abnormality' [1999] Crim LR 517.

Campbell, K., 'Offence and Defence' in I. H. Dennis (ed.), *Criminal Law and Justice* (1987).

Clarkson, C., 'Necessary Action: A New Defence' [2004] Crim LR 81.

Elliott, C. and de Than, C., 'The Case for a Rational Reconstruction of Consent in Criminal Law' (2007) 70 MLR 225.

Gardner, S., 'Direct Action and the Defence of Necessity' [2005] Crim LR 371.

Husak, D. and von Hirsch, A., 'Culpability and Mistake of Law' in S. Shute, J. Gardner, and J. Horder (eds), *Action and Value in Criminal Law* (1993).

Milgate, M., 'Duress and the Criminal Law: Another Turn by the House of Lords' (1988) 47 Camb LJ 61.

Murphy, P., 'Flogging Live Complainants and Dead Horses: We May No Longer Need to be in Bondage to Brown' [2011] Crim LR 758.

Ost, S., 'Euthanasia and the Defence of Necessity: Advocating a More Appropriate Legal Response' [2005] Crim LR 355.

Padfield, N., 'Duress, Necessity and the Law Commission' [1992] Crim LR 778.

Smith, A. T. M., 'On Actus Reus and Mens Rea' in P. R. Glazebrook (ed.), *Reshaping the Criminal Law* (1978).

Smith, J. C., *Justification and Excuse in the Criminal Law* ('The Hamlyn Lectures') (1989).

Weait, M., 'Knowledge, Autonomy and Consent: R v Konzani' [2005] Crim LR 763.

Williams, G., 'The Theory of Excuses' [1982] Crim LR 732.

Williams, R., 'Deception, Mistake and Vitiation of the Victim's Consent' (2008) 124 LQR 132.

Wilson, W., 'The Structure of Criminal Defences' [2005] Crim LR 108.

SELF-TEST QUESTIONS

1   Dee gives Phil a passionate kiss on the neck and an affectionate bite on the ear. The bite turns septic and Phil has to have a small part of his ear amputated. Discuss Dee's criminal liability if (i) Phil was consenting and (ii) he was not consenting.

2   Dee is arrested at Heathrow Airport with a large quantity of heroin in her suitcase. Questioned by the police she admits knowing that she was bringing in a package which she suspected contained illegal materials of some sort, but the man who gave it to her told her to ask no questions or 'something bad would happen to her baby'. Discuss Dee's liability.

3   Late at night Dee, an elderly lady, was attacked by a young man who she believed to be carrying a knife. She stabbed him in the face with her umbrella, permanently blinding him in the eye. Discuss Dee's liability.

6

Accomplices

SUMMARY

A difficult area, built on theoretical uncertainties. What degree of involvement in someone else's crime merits conviction? Flexible conduct requirements (aiding, abetting, counselling, or procuring) + *mens rea* (an intention to encourage or assist + knowledge of (or recklessness as to) 'the essential matters').

The extent of joint enterprise liability: D is guilty of murder if he realizes (without agreeing to such conduct being used) that X may intentionally kill or inflict serious injury, but nevertheless continues to participate with X in the venture: is this simply a form of aiding and abetting or is a different justification needed? A confused, and confusing, area.

Accomplice liability has been seen traditionally as 'derivative liability': other justifications may be more appropriate.

Note the proposals for change in Law Com No. 305, *Participating in Crime* (2007).

Introduction

6.1 A person may be convicted of a substantive offence merely because he or she took part in a criminal activity with someone else. The Accessories and Abettors Act 1861 tidied up the procedure for indicting, trying, and punishing all those who were parties to a crime (then principals in the first degree, accessories before the fact, and so on). When the distinction between felonies and misdemeanours was abolished in 1967, the Act was amended. Section 8 now provides:

> …whosoever shall aid, abet, counsel or procure the commission of any indictable offence, whether the same be an offence at common law or by virtue of any Act passed or to be passed, shall be liable to be tried, indicted, and punished as a principal offender.

Similarly the Magistrates' Courts Act 1980, s 44 provides that a person convicted of aiding, abetting, counselling, or procuring a summary offence is guilty of the like offence. Aiding and abetting is thus not a separate offence, but simply a means of convicting someone of the main offence. If A asks B to kill C, and B does so, both A and B will be convicted of murder. So in this chapter we focus on the liability of accomplices for the crime committed by the principal: Chapter 7 looks at the specific (separate) offences which 'catch' those who help, encourage, and assist (or try to help, encourage, or assist) others to commit crimes.

6.2 Some crimes are defined such that they can only be carried out by two or more principals: see riot and affray, for example (in Chapter 12), but even here there may be secondary parties.

Jefferson **(1994)** Ds were involved in various disturbances in Bedford following an English victory in the football World Cup in 1990. They were convicted of offences of riot and violent disorder. P's case was that their presence at various of the specific disturbances during the night was sufficient evidence that they aided and abetted the violence of the night. D argued that presence denoted an onlooker and not necessarily a participant.

CA (Auld J): nothing in the POA 1986 excludes common law principles of aiding and abetting, and dismissed their appeals.

Unless Parliament specifically excludes the possibility, one can be a secondary party or accomplice to any offence, even an attempt:

Dunnington **(1984)** D stole a car in order to be the getaway driver for a failed robbery.

CA (Beldam J): upheld his conviction for aiding and abetting an attempted robbery. Where a person does an act which would amount to aiding and abetting if the offence was completed, he may be convicted of the attempt.

Principals and accessories

6.3 In this chapter, the term 'principal' (rather than an alternative term 'perpetrator') and the term 'accomplice' (to deal with the accessory or secondary party who 'aids, abets, counsels or procures') are used. Although the law suggests that the accomplice may be charged as a principal, she will normally be charged as an accomplice in order to give her clearer details of the offence of which she is accused. The maximum penalty for the accomplice is normally the same as that for the principal, though there are exceptions. For example, the Road Traffic Offenders Act 1988, s 34(5) provides that, where disqualification is mandatory for the principal offence (in cases such as driving with excess alcohol), a person convicted of aiding and abetting such an offence is liable only to discretionary disqualification.

6.4 Normally, the principal is the person who carries out the substantive crime, while the accomplice merely aids or abets. Sometimes both parties will be co-principals, for example where both Ds intend to kill and both stab V. Where one of two people is guilty of an offence, but P cannot prove which of the two did it, nor that there was any agreement between them, neither can be convicted:

> **Strudwick (1993)** M and her co-habitee, S, were jointly charged with the manslaughter of her child.
>
> CA: quashed S's conviction. His admission of some violence towards the child and his manifest lies were not sufficient evidence as to which of the Ds had struck the blows.

The important distinction between principal and accessory was recently blurred by the SC in the case of *Gnango*:

> **Gnango (2011)** V was caught in a public gun fight between B and D, who were members of rival gangs. B, who shot V dead, was aiming for D. He has not been arrested. D argued that he could not be guilty of murder as he had not aided or abetted B, and there was no common purpose or joint enterprise between them. The trial judge directed the jury that they could convict if they were sure that D was party to a joint enterprise (see **6.20–6.25**) to commit affray, and foresaw the possibility of murder. D was convicted of murder.
>
> CA (five judges, unusually): quashed the conviction. The judge's direction was wrong.
>
> SC (by a majority of 6 to 1): re-instated the murder conviction. But the judgments do not clarify the law. The main judgment was given by Lords Phillips and Judge, with whom Lord Wilson simply agrees. They uphold the murder conviction by saying that D is a 'standard' accessory: he encouraged B in his criminal act (to shoot at D) and the ordinary rules of transferred malice apply (see **3.33–3.35**). Lords Brown, Clarke, and Dyson held that D was a co-principal to murder, not an aider and abettor. Lords Philips and Judge say that this disagreement is not a 'difference of substance': whether D is correctly described as a principal or an accessory is irrelevant to his guilt (para. 62). Dissenting, Lord Kerr argues that D was not a co-principal:
>
> > If B fired at D first, it seems to me highly questionable (at least) that D's returning fire *caused* B to fire again. The first shot surely betokened an intention on the part of B to fire at and to hit D, irrespective of whether D fired back. It might be said, to borrow the words of Professor Glanville Williams, that D's firing on B made it much more likely that B

would fire again, but that is not enough to show that B was caused to fire because of D's shot. I do not consider, therefore, that D can be guilty of V's murder as a joint principal.

Since it was 'likely in the extreme' that the jury had convicted on the wrongful 'joint enterprise' basis, there would have been no occasion for them to consider whether D had the requisite intention to be found guilty on the basis of aiding and abetting. So Lord Kerr, alone, decided a conviction for murder would be unsafe.

This case raises many conceptual problems. D was surely not a principal: he did not cause V's death. Does it make any more sense to say that D aided and abetted his own murder? He could hardly be said to be encouraging it! And Lord Kerr is surely right that there is an important conceptual difference between liability as a principal and that of an accomplice: to be a principal 'each must contribute by his own act to the commission of the offence with the necessary *mens rea*'. The majority of the SC blur an important distinction!

Banfield **(2013)** Ds, mother and daughter, were convicted of the murder of V, D1's husband, although his body had not been found. There was no suggested mechanism of death, no identified day when the murder was said to have occurred, no time and no place, and no suggestion of what happened to the body. P relied on circumstantial evidence, largely evidence that V had given to police and friends of previous murder attempts on him by his wife, and of Ds' dishonesty with his money after he disappeared.

CA: quashed the murder convictions. Since P could not identify which D killed V, whether encouraged by the other or alone, the case should not have been left to the jury.

6.5 Both parties will be guilty if one is the principal and the other the accessory, even if it is not known which was which, but only as long as it can be proved that both were either principal or accomplice:

Mohan v R **(1967)** Ds both attacked V with cutlasses. It could not be proved who struck the fatal blow.

PC: upheld their convictions for murder.

Russell and Russell **(1987)** Ds, registered drug addicts in receipt of prescribed methadone, were convicted of the manslaughter of their 15-month-old daughter who died of a massive overdose of methadone.

CA: dismissed their appeals. P had to prove simply that D aided, abetted, counselled, or procured the commission of the crime by the other. Where the drug had been administered by one or both parents without any indication which one was responsible, it could be inferred that they were jointly responsible. There was evidence that in the

> past both Ds had jointly administered the drug and, in the absence of any explanation from either, the jury could infer that the administration of the drug on the day in question was a joint enterprise.

Thus both parties are guilty where it is proved that each must be liable either as principal or accessory. But that cannot always be proved. The failure of the law to 'protect' the vulnerable, particularly children, was highlighted in a report by the National Society for the Protection of Children (NSPCC) 'Which of you did it?' (2003), and by the Law Commission in their report *Children: their non-accidental death or serious injury (criminal trials)* (No. 282 (2003)). Parliament then created the offence of 'causing or allowing the death of a child or vulnerable adult': see the DVCVA 2004, s 5 (discussed (and criticized) at **8.36**).

The innocent agent

6.6 Occasionally a person may be considered as the principal even when the *actus reus* was performed by another. This is where the main actor is in fact 'innocent': perhaps she is a child, or is unaware of the crime she has been set up to commit, or she has a defence. In Glanville Williams' words, 'the physical actor is treated as a puppet, so that the guilty actor who activates him to do the mischief becomes responsible not as an accessory but as a perpetrator acting through an innocent agent' (TCL, p. 368).

> **Bourne (1952)** D was convicted of aiding and abetting his wife to commit buggery with a dog (and sentenced to eight years in prison). The evidence was that she had been terrorized into submission and had not consented.
>
> CA: upheld his conviction. The fact the wife had a defence did not mean that no offence had been committed; simply that she had no *mens rea*. Since D caused his wife to have connection with a dog, he was guilty.

> **Cogan and Leak (1976)** D compelled V, his wife, to have sex with C against her will.
>
> CA: quashed C's conviction since he believed she was consenting, but upheld D's conviction. The fact that C was acquitted did not affect the position that V had been raped.

Where D procures the *actus reus* of an offence, he may be guilty even if the principal lacks *mens rea*:

> **Millward (1994)** D instructed his employee to tow a trailer behind a tractor on a main road. Due to a defective hitch mechanism, the trailer became detached and killed V in another vehicle. The employee was acquitted of causing death by reckless driving, but D was convicted of procuring the offence.

> CA: dismissed his appeal. The *actus reus* had been taking the vehicle on the road in a defective condition. D could procure the *actus reus* of an offence irrespective of whether or not the principal offender had the necessary *mens rea*.

As J. C. Smith pointed out (at [1994] Crim LR 529), this case broke new ground, and marked a move away from the traditional idea that accomplice liability is a form of derivative liability (see also *DPP v K* (1997) and **6.26**). Clearly, the doctrine of innocent agent is a useful way of imposing liability when the person who commits the crime is not guilty. Law Commission Report No. 305 (2007) proposed a complex draft clause which they suggested would improve the law:

Using an innocent agent

(1) If a person (D) uses an innocent agent (P) to commit an offence, D is guilty of that offence.

(2) P is an innocent agent in relation to an offence if—

    (a) he does a criminal act, and

    (b) he does not commit the offence itself for one of the following reasons

        (i) he is under the age of 10,

        (ii) he has a defence of insanity, or

        (iii) he acts without the fault required for conviction,

and there is no other reason why he does not commit it.

(3) D uses P to commit an offence if—

    (a) D intends to cause a person (whether or not P) to do a criminal act in relation to the offence,

    (b) D causes P to do the criminal act, and

    (c) subsection (4) or (5) is satisfied.

(4) If a particular state of mind requires to be proved for conviction of the offence that D uses P to commit, D's state of mind must be such that, were he to do the act that he intends to cause to be done, he would do it with the state of mind required for conviction of the offence.

(5) If the offence which D uses P to commit is a no-fault offence, D must know or believe that, were a person to do the act that D intends to cause to be done, that person would do it—

    (a) the circumstances (if any), and

    (b) with the consequences (if any),

proof of which is required for conviction of the offence.

Taylor (2008) suggests that this proposal would submerge 'within an automatic fiction of innocent agency' too many cases which should more properly be dealt with as ordinary cases of secondary liability, to which we now turn. (Remember that these Law Commission proposals are very unlikely to become law in the near future.)

Actus reus

6.7 The conduct requirements are vague (and minimal): the Accessories and Abettors Act 1861 uses the words 'aid, abet, counsel or procure', and even though the statute was probably only designed to provide a procedure and not a definition, the words seem to have taken on a life of their own. For many decades, it was accepted that the particular words used in s 8 had no particular meaning. However, the position seemed to change in 1975:

> **A-G's Reference (No. 1 of 1975) (1975)** D, who had laced someone's drinks knowing that he would be driving home shortly afterwards, was indicted for aiding and abetting driving with excess alcohol.
>
> CA (Widgery CJ): D should have been convicted.
>
> > … if four words are employed here, 'aid, abet, counsel or procure', the probability is that there is a difference between each of those four words and the other three, because, if there were no such difference, then Parliament would be wasting its time in using four words where two or three would do … To procure means to produce by endeavour. You procure a thing by setting out to see that it happens, and taking the appropriate steps to produce that happening … You cannot procure an offence unless there is a causal link between what you do and the commission of an offence.

6.8 In this case, Lord Widgery accepted the pre-1861 distinction that if you were present at the substantive offence you were an aider or abettor, if you were absent you were a counsellor or procurer. But you should not spend too much time trying to distinguish these words: the courts seem to use them fairly indistinguishably. However, there may be an important distinction when we consider whether the accomplice has to communicate his objectives to the principal. Agreement is not always required: if D restrains the policeman who would have prevented P from committing the crime, without P being aware of this assistance, probably D is guilty of 'aiding'. Ormerod's Smith and Hogan (2011) sums up the position thus (at p. 192):

> … the law is probably that:
>
> (1) 'aiding' requires actual assistance but neither consensus nor causation;
>
> (2) 'abetting' and 'counselling' imply consensus but not causation;
>
> (3) 'procuring' implies causation but not consensus.

As the Law Commission put it in 1993, the distinction between aiding, abetting, counselling, and procuring 'partakes of a considerable element of over-elaboration and indeed artificiality' (LCCP No. 131, p. 21). They therefore preferred to say that the physical element here consists either of encouragement or assistance, and this wording was adopted in the 2007 Report (see **6.27**).

Liability by mere presence

6.9 Can a person be convicted as an accomplice merely for watching? If so, this would suggest liability for a failure to act, for a mere omission (see **2.5**). There will be no problem establishing liability if the accomplice had a duty to act: if the tenant of my house deliberately leaves the door unlocked for the burglar, her failure to lock the door is in breach of her duty. Normally it is held that there must be an intention to encourage, and actual encouragement, but there is a fine line here. Does your presence at an animal rights demonstration mean that you are encouraging, and intending to encourage, offences of public disorder by others?

Coney **(1882)** D watched an illegal boxing match.

CCCR (by a majority): mere voluntary presence did not necessarily render the audience guilty of aiding the illegal fight. Hawkins J: '... to constitute an aider and abettor some active steps must be taken by word, or action, with the intent to instigate the principal or principals.'

Clarkson **(1971)** Ds entered a room where soldiers were raping a woman. They watched and did nothing to stop the rape.

CMAC: quashed their conviction for aiding and abetting rape. It is not enough that the presence of the accused has given encouragement: it must be proved that he intended to give encouragement.

6.10 The problem also arises where people are living together and may well know what their friends or partners are up to:

Bland **(1987)** D was charged with unlawful possession of controlled drugs because she lived with a man who she knew dealt in drugs.

CA: quashed her conviction as there was no evidence of assistance, passive or active. There must be some positive encouragement.

6.11 As Ashworth points out, such cases illustrate 'a vivid conflict between the individuals' rights of privacy in their personal relationships and the social interest in suppressing serious crime' (PCL, p. 417). The DCC (1989) would have dealt with the problem thus:

> Clause 27(3): Assistance or encouragement includes assistance or encouragement arising from a failure by a person to take reasonable steps to exercise any authority or to discharge any duty he has to control the relevant acts of the principal in order to prevent the commission of the offence.

For Glanville Williams this was astonishingly wide: 'everyone who lets an offence happen shall be liable as though he had committed it himself' ([1990] Crim LR 780). Law Commission Report No. 305 suggests simply that 'encouraging or assisting a person to do a criminal act should include doing so by failing to take reasonable steps to discharge a duty' (at para. 3.38). Is this too vague?

Failure to exercise control

6.12 Failure to act may amount to participation where D has power to control the actions of others but fails to do so:

> ***Du Cros v Lambourne* (1907)** D, the owner of a car, was sitting in the passenger seat while a friend drove at a dangerous speed.
>
> KBD: D was guilty of aiding and abetting dangerous driving since he allowed her to drive and did not interfere in any way. He failed to exercise his power to prevent the driving.

> ***Tuck v Robson* (1970)** D, the licensee of a pub, called 'time' at 11 pm and switched off the main lights; at 11.05 he called for glasses. No consumption of alcohol was allowed after 11.10, but when the police arrived at 11.23 some customers were still drinking up. D was convicted of aiding and abetting the consumption of alcoholic drinks after hours.
>
> DC (Lord Parker CJ): dismissed his appeal. D had the legal power to get customers to leave at closing time, and was guilty.

The Law Commission in Report No. 305 says that 'it is open to question whether any general principle can be devised from these cases' (at para. 3.30) and it is clearly reluctant to impose liability on D who simply fails to prevent P from committing a crime. Is it right to place the obligations of law enforcement on car owners or pub landlords?

Mens rea

6.13 D must *intend* to do acts of assistance and be aware of their ability to assist.

***Blakely v DPP* (1991)** Ds laced P's drink with vodka, intending to inform him so that he would not be able to drive home and would have to stay the night. He left before they told him and was convicted of driving with excess alcohol (receiving an absolute discharge by way of sentence). Ds were convicted of procuring drunken driving.

DC: quashed their convictions.

> While it might now be the law that advertent recklessness to the consequence of his deliberate act of assistance might suffice to convict some, if not all, of those accused of being an accessory before the fact, it was clear that inadvertent recklessness did not. It must, at least, be shown that the accused contemplated that his act would or might bring about or assist the commission of the principal offence: he must have been prepared nevertheless to do his own act, and he must have done that act intentionally ... In relation to those accused only of procuring and perhaps also those accused only of counselling and commanding, it might be ... that it was necessary to prove that the accused intended to bring about the principal offence.

6.14 D must *know* the essential matters which constitute the offence, but the line which shows exactly how much D must know to justify punishment has proved to be extremely difficult to draw. Clearly those who knowingly help others to commit serious crimes should be guilty of an offence, but not those who do not really realize what is going on.

***Bainbridge* (1960)** The cutting equipment used in a burglary was proved to have been bought by D six weeks earlier. He said he had bought it for a friend, but admitted that he was suspicious that the equipment was going to be used for an illegal purpose, but said he did not know that it was for burglary. He was convicted of being an accessory to office-breaking.

CA (Lord Parker CJ): upheld D's conviction. While it was not enough merely to prove that D knew that some illegal venture was intended, it was not necessary to prove that he knew of the particular crime that was to be committed.

***DPP for Northern Ireland v Maxwell* (1978)** D, a member of an illegal organization in Northern Ireland, driving his own car, led a second car to a remote country pub. He then left. The men in the second car, whom D knew to be members of the organization, then threw a bomb. D was convicted as an accomplice to doing an act with intent to cause an explosion.

HL: dismissed his appeal. Lord Scarman: 'An accessory who leaves it to his principal to choose is liable, provided always the choice is made from the range of offences from which the accessory contemplates the choice will be made.'

> ***Webster* (2006)** D allowed his friend who had been drinking to drive his car. The friend drove erratically and excessively fast and V, a passenger, was thrown out of the car and killed. D was convicted of aiding and abetting the friend to cause death by dangerous driving.
>
> CA: allowed D's appeal. The trial judge's directions to the jury were defective. Moses LJ:
>
>> It is D's foresight that the principal was likely to commit the offence which must be proved and not merely that he ought to have foreseen that the principal was likely to commit the offence.

Virgo (2006) argues that since one cannot 'know' future circumstances, 'belief' would be a better test and, better still, subjective recklessness, i.e. reckless foresight of the possible commission of the substantive offence. Law Commission Report No. 305 suggests that D should have to intend that P should engage in the conduct element of the offence, not simply know or risk that he was likely to do so.

Possible defences to accomplice liability

6.15 It is not very clear whether there are specific defences available only to accomplices. The DCC (1989) suggested in clause 27 that three specific defences should be available to the accomplice:

(6) A person is not guilty of an offence as an accessory by reason of anything he does—

(a) with the purpose of preventing the commission of the offence; or

(b) with the purpose of avoiding or limiting any harmful consequences of the offence and without the purpose of furthering its commission; or

(c) because he believes that he is under an obligation to do it and without the purpose of furthering the commission of the offence.

6.16 These defences would appear to protect the accomplice from liability simply because of his worthy purpose or motive. Yet the normal rule, in line with the rules governing the liability of the principal (see **3.3**), is that a worthy motive will not excuse:

> ***National Coal Board v Gamble* (1959)** D was the NCB, whose weigh-bridge operator issued a ticket to a lorry driver certifying the lorry's weight. He told the lorry driver that he was nearly 4 tons overweight, but the lorry driver said that he would risk it.
>
> DC: upheld D's conviction for aiding and abetting the lorry driver's firm in the commission of the offence. Devlin J: '*mens rea* is a matter of intent only and does not depend on desire or motive.'

6.17 Despite this, examples of all three defences proposed in clause 27(6) can be found in the case law. First, the law enforcement defence:

> **Clarke (1984)** D's defence to burglary was that he was there simply to assist the police.
>
> CA (Macpherson J): in exceptional cases an informer's conduct which was calculated and intended to frustrate the ultimate result of a crime could amount to a defence. It was for the jury to decide if a case fell within that exceptional and rare category.

Law Commission Report No. 305 would allow a defence if D acted for the purpose of preventing the commission of either the offence that he or she was encouraging or assisting or another offence, but it would have to be 'reasonable' to act as D did in the circumstances (para. 7.16).

6.18 Secondly, where D acts with the purpose of limiting harmful consequences:

> **Gillick v West Norfolk and Wisbech Area Health Authority (1985)** A Department of Health memorandum stated that exceptionally contraceptive advice could be given to under-16s without parental consent. A mother sought a declaration that the memorandum was unlawful.
>
> HL (by a majority of 3 to 2): held that a doctor who supplies contraceptives to a girl under the age of 16, knowing that this will assist her boyfriend to have unlawful sexual intercourse with a girl under the age of 16, is not an accomplice to the boy's offence. Lord Scarman: '… the bona fide exercise by a doctor of his clinical judgement must be a complete negation of *mens rea*.'

Look at the dissenting judgments of Lord Brandon and Lord Templeman: even if aiding the unlawful sexual intercourse is not the doctor's purpose or desire, if he knows it will result, does he not intend it? (See also **5.25**.) The decision of the majority was upheld in *R (Axon) v Secretary of State for Health* (2006), where Silber J confirmed that the decision in *Gillick* (1985) does not infringe parental rights under Art 8 of the ECHR (see **1.25**). Law Commission Report No. 305 suggests a defence where D acts for the purpose of preventing or limiting the occurrence of harm: but it would have to be 'reasonable' to act as D did in the circumstances (para. 7.16).

6.19 The third possible defence is D's belief in his legal obligation. If I have been looking after your knife for you, and you ask for it back telling me that you intend to stick it into your mother (which you then do), do I (and should I) have a defence to aiding and abetting murder when I say that I believed that I had no option but to give you what was, after all, your own property? The answer in English law today is unclear. Law Commission Report No. 305 does not seem to propose such a defence.

Joint enterprise/common purpose

6.20 Where two or more people agree to carry out a common purpose or joint enterprise, the secondary party or accomplice may be liable for crimes committed in carrying out that purpose, even unforeseen consequences. It is not necessary for P to show that the accomplice intended the crime: it is enough that he should have foreseen the event as a real possibility. If the principal by mistake kills the wrong person or carries out the intended purpose by an unexpected method, then the accomplice is still guilty. There has been much theoretical debate as to whether this is a separate form of secondary liability (as Simester (2006) and Sullivan (2008) suggest), or simply part of the general law on accomplices (as Buxton (2009) argues). Simester (2006) presents a clear argument that they are different: D's responsibility in joint enterprise cases results from his collusion ('a discrete and independent wrong') with the principal, and not simply from the foresight of what the principal might do.

6.21 From the case law, it is clear that liability of the secondary party when the principal intentionally deviates from the agreed course of conduct turns on knowing that there was a possible risk that the principal might commit the offence. At one time there had been some suggestion that the accomplice should only be liable if he knew that the eventual outcome was 'probable' (see *Jubb and Rigby* (1984)), but the courts have preferred the 'possible' consequence test of *Chan Wing-Siu* (1985): a test which required P to prove that D knew that the crime was a probable consequence was seen as unduly restrictive.

> *Slack* (1989) Ds were two robbers, one of whom killed an elderly widow. D2 said that although he knew his mate had a knife, he thought he would only use it to frighten people. They were both convicted of murder.
>
> CA (Lord Lane): dismissed D2's appeal. For D2 to be guilty, he must be proved to have lent himself to a criminal enterprise involving the infliction, if necessary, of serious harm or death, or to have had an express or tacit understanding with D1 that such harm or death should, if necessary, be inflicted.

> *Hyde, Sussex and Collins* (1990) Ds attacked V outside a pub, and he died of a heavy kick to the head. D1 and D2 said there was no joint enterprise, and that the fatal blow was struck by the third. D3 said that there was no joint attack, and that he had not caused the blow.

CA (Lord Lane CJ): dismissed all their appeals.

> If B realizes (without agreeing to such conduct being used) that A may kill or intentionally inflict serious injury, but nevertheless continues to participate with A in the venture, that will amount to a sufficient mental element for B to be guilty of murder if A, with the requisite intent, kills in the course of the venture.

Powell and Daniels; English (1997) D1 and D2 and another went to buy cannabis from V, a small-time drug dealer. One of them shot V dead on his doorstep. D1 and D2 were convicted of murder as secondary parties, although it was not established who fired the shot. In the other case, E agreed with another man to attack V, a policeman, with wooden posts. The other then produced a knife and stabbed V dead.

HL: dismissed D1 and D2's appeals; E's appeal was allowed. Lord Hutton:

> … participation in a joint criminal enterprise with foresight or contemplation of an act as a possible incident of that enterprise is sufficient to impose criminal liability for that act carried out by another participant in the enterprise.

There will no longer be scope for argument over 'tacit agreements': the test is one of foresight. D must contemplate death:

> … as a possible incident of the joint venture, unless the risk was so remote that the jury take the view that the secondary party genuinely dismissed it as altogether negligible.

Lord Steyn and Lord Mustill examined the principles behind liability and exhorted Parliament to reform the law of homicide and the law of punishment for homicide. As Lord Mustill says, criminal law reform may not be a popular choice, 'but surely it is justice which counts'.

After *Powell*, a string of appeals on this topic were heard in the Court of Appeal (*Uddin* (1999), *Roberts and Day* (2001), *Amies, Ryder, Kite and Ellis* (2003), *O'Flaherty, Ryan and Toussaint* (2004), *A-G's Reference (No. 3 of 2004)* (2005)), turning, as ever, on whether the judge had correctly summed up the law on this difficult subject.

6.22 The doctrine of 'joint enterprise' was then revisited by the HL in:

Rahman (2008) V died from two deep knife wounds but it was not clear which of a group of Ds (armed with baseball bats and metal bars) had stabbed him. There was no evidence that these Ds inflicted the fatal injuries; the participant who did probably escaped arrest. The four Ds were all convicted of murder. The question posed for the HL was:

> If in the course of a joint enterprise to inflict unlawful violence the principal party kills with an intention to kill which was unknown to and unforeseen by a secondary party, is the principal's intention relevant, (i) to whether the killing was within the scope of a

common purpose to which the secondary party was an accessory? (ii) to whether the principal's act was fundamentally different from the act or acts which the secondary party foresaw as part of the joint enterprise?

HL: unanimously dismissed the appeals. But the judges give very different reasons: Ormerod at [2008] Crim LR 981 calls the decision 'disappointing in terms of its failure to develop or clarify the law significantly'. Lord Bingham concluded that:

> The decision of the House in *English* did not lay down a new rule of accessory liability or exoneration. Its significance lies in the emphasis it laid (a) on the overriding importance in this context of what the particular D subjectively foresaw, and (b) on the nature of the acts or behaviour said to be a radical departure from what was intended or foreseen. The greater the difference between the acts or behaviour in question and the purpose of the enterprise, the more ready a jury may be to infer that the particular D did not foresee what the other participant would do (para. 16).

He said there were two strong reasons for answering the questions in the negative (and his approach was supported by Lord Rodger). First, the practical argument:

> Given the fluid, fast-moving course of events in incidents such as that which culminated in the killing of [V], incidents which are unhappily not rare, it must often be very hard for jurors to make a reliable assessment of what a particular D foresaw as likely or possible acts on the part of his associates. It would be even harder, and would border on speculation, to judge what a particular D foresaw as the intention with which his associates might perform such acts. It is safer to focus on the D's foresight of what an associate might do, an issue to which knowledge of the associate's possession of an obviously lethal weapon such as a gun or a knife would usually be very relevant (para. 24).

The second reason was more theoretical:

> To rule that an undisclosed and unforeseen intention to kill on the part of the primary offender may take a killing outside the scope of a common purpose to cause really serious injury, calling for a distinction irrelevant in the case of the primary offender, is in my view to subvert the rationale which underlies our law of murder (para. 25).

Lord Bingham did not agree with the majority, who doubted the decision in *Gamble* [1989] NI 268, which he considered to be consistent with authority.

Lord Brown concluded that the first certified question was 'misconceived', unconvinced by the value of the term 'common purpose' and declined to answer it. But he too answered the second part in the negative. He said that he had 'some difficulty' with *Gamble* (at para. 67) and suggested a restatement of the *Hyde* principle (see **6.21**):

> If B realises (without agreeing to such conduct being used) that A may kill or intentionally inflict serious injury, but nevertheless continues to participate with A in the venture, that will amount to a sufficient mental element for B to be guilty of murder if A, with the requisite intent, kills in the course of the venture *unless (i) A suddenly produces and uses a weapon of which B knows nothing and which is more lethal than any weapon which B contemplates that A or any other participant may be carrying and (ii) for that reason A's act*

is to be regarded as fundamentally different from anything foreseen by B. (The italicized words are designed to reflect the *English* qualification (para. 68).)

Lord Scott and Lord Neuberger both explicitly agreed with this interpretation. Lord Scott added that he thought that the relative culpability of accomplices was better dealt with at the point of sentencing.

Do you agree? Would it be better to leave it to sentencing law to measure the relative moral culpability of those involved in gang violence? It is difficult to do this at the moment given the rigid rules surrounding the mandatory life sentence for all those convicted of murder.

Whilst these speeches reveal detailed reading of the case law, their Lordships were not moved by academic comments or calls for reform: for example, Virgo's argument at (2006) 6 *Archbold News* 6, for a test for accomplice liability of subjective reckless foresight of the possible commission of the substantive offence.

6.23 The appeals keep coming (of course): not least, perhaps, because accomplices don't perceive themselves to be murderers and certainly don't welcome a mandatory life sentence.

Badza **(2009)** D1 and D2 were convicted of murder. The fatal stabbing had happened soon after they got off a late night bus. P's case was that, if D2 did not do the stabbing, he was guilty of murder because he had participated in a joint enterprise. There was evidence of a discussion between the two Ds concerning a knife at the bus stop before they had got on the bus; of an aggressive argument between D2 and V on the bus; of V pursuing D2 off the bus; and of a fight between D2 and V. There was no evidence that D2 solicited help from D1, but evidence that D1 then came forward and did the stabbing. P accepted that the preponderance of the evidence pointed to D1 as the stabber.

CA: dismissed D2's appeal. The Court (Sir Anthony May, President of the QBD) summarized the decision of the HL in *Rahman* (2008) thus:

> The HL held that the judge's direction had been correct. It was held that, where the principal committed an unlawful killing with the requisite intent for murder, a secondary party would be liable for murder on the basis of his foresight of what the principal might do, rather than his foresight of the intention with which the principal's act might be performed. Knowledge of the principal's possession of an obviously lethal weapon would usually be very relevant to the secondary party's foresight of what the principal might do (para. 30).

Applying this to the facts of this case, the Court concluded that:

> An essential question in the present case therefore was whether [D2] knew that [D1] was in possession of an obviously lethal weapon, and whether he engaged in a common

> enterprise with [D1] foreseeing that [D1] might use the knife aggressively. The Crown would say that the common enterprise was a late night outing together which, as [D2] must have foreseen, might result in their participation in violence during which [D1], if he had not passed the knife to [D2], might use the knife aggressively with the requisite intent for murder (para. 32).

This case is a good illustration of the harshness and artificiality of the current rules on 'joint enterprise'. Surely, it would be preferable if the jury were told to focus, not on the 'joint' enterprise, but simply on the *mens rea* (recklessness rather than mere foresight?) of each party, as Virgo (2006) argues. See also *Yemoh* (2009); *Mendez* (2010), and now the important but difficult decision of the SC in *Gnango* (2011, discussed more fully at 6.4). Importantly, for our present purposes, Lord Kerr (dissenting) agreed with Lord Phillips and Lord Judge that 'joint enterprise' liability, what Lord Kerr called 'this form of parasitic accessory liability' was not a basis on which the jury could convict on those facts. That is some small comfort in a very difficult area of law! It is surely time simply to reject the language and concept of 'joint enterprise'.

6.24 It is worth underlining that it does not matter for 'joint enterprise' liability whether or not D is present at the scene of the crime:

Rook **(1993)** Three men agreed to kill a taxi driver's wife for £20,000. D took a leading part in planning the murder, but said he did not plan to go through with it. He believed, wrongly, that if he did not turn up at the scene of the crime, his colleagues would not go ahead without him. However, they did.

CA (Lloyd LJ): upheld D's conviction for murder. It was no defence for a secondary party to say that he did not intend the victim to be killed if he contemplated or foresaw the killing as a real or serious risk. His absence on the day of the murder did not amount to unequivocal communication of his withdrawal from the agreement to murder.

So the law here is very wide: the principal is liable if he intends to kill or do GBH, but the accomplice is liable as long as he foresees that P *might* cause GBH with intent.

Jogee **(2013)** D1 and D2 were drunk and had been taking cocaine. They had visited V's girlfriend's home. Both left, but later D1 returned. V's girlfriend rang D2 and asked him to take D1 away. He did. But they both then returned. D1 entered the house and stabbed V, killing him. D2 remained outside, but had been shouting and encouraging D1. Both were convicted of murder.

CA: dismissed D2's appeal. There is no principled basis on which the reasoning in *Rahman* (2008) should be applied only to cases of participation and not to cases of encouragement. Indeed, the distinction between the two is, to say the least, permeable:

Encouragement is a form of participation; that is why it is enough to convict a secondary party. The *actus reus* of the secondary party's crime is lending support to the primary actor, whether by active participation or encouragement or both. The mental element, the *mens rea*, of the secondary party's crime is an appreciation that the primary actor might inflict grievous bodily harm and a willingness to lend his support notwithstanding (Laws LJ, para. 23).

6.25 What happens if the principal commits a different and less serious offence than that agreed?

Howe **(1987)** Ds confessed to taking part in the killing of Vs, but said that they acted through fear.

HL: upheld their conviction for murder. The decision withdrew the defence of duress from those accused of aiding and abetting murder (see **5.19**) but it is also important as the HL overruled the decision in *Richards* (1974), which had held that the accomplice who was not present at the scene could not be convicted of a more serious crime than the actual perpetrator.

Thus, where a person procures or incites another to commit murder, but that other person is convicted only of manslaughter, the incitor/procurer may still be convicted of murder.

Derivative liability

6.26 The traditional justification for accomplice liability is simply that D's liability 'derives' from that of the principal. J. C. Smith (1997) distinguished basic accessory liability (D is liable for the commission by P of crime X which D intentionally assists or encourages P to commit) from parasitic accessory liability (D is liable not because he intentionally assisted or encouraged P, but merely because he foresaw that P would commit crime X). Yet this causes many problems: why should someone be guilty just because someone else is? Kadish (1985) preferred to say that liability is 'dependent', rather than derivative (see **6.27**). If liability is derivative, the decision in *Howe* (see **6.25**) is curious. However, perhaps *Howe* says little more than that those who aid and abet criminals should not get away with it. An alternative route to liability would be to extend the doctrine of innocent agency. If you send a child into the house to steal for you, you are guilty as a principal acting through an innocent agent. Thus in *Cogan and Leak* (1976, **6.5**) it could be argued that the husband should have been guilty, not of being an accomplice, but as the principal. Or that someone who secretly laces someone's soft drinks with alcohol should be guilty of drunken driving as a principal, not as an accomplice.

There remain the linguistic complaints that Leak did not actually rape his wife, and that the drink spiker might not even be able to drive. Another theory to justify liability might base liability on what the accomplice set out to do. Thus J. C. Smith (1997) justifies accomplice liability in murder cases by emphasizing the difference between recklessness whether death be caused (which is sufficient for manslaughter but not murder) and recklessness whether murder be committed. The accomplice's recklessness must extend to the principal's *mens rea* for murder (on which see **8.5**). As Wilson (2008) puts it, 'the common law treats the accessory as if he had committed the wrong himself for both practical and moral reasons' (at p. 3). The practical reasons are evidential and procedural, the moral ones suggest that there is often little difference between the responsibility of principal and accessory for the outcome. As Wilson puts it, 'secondary liability allows a degree of flexibility in setting the parameters of accountability for criminal wrongdoing' (p. 4). Do you agree?

Reform

6.27 Let us now turn to the Law Commission. Their quite recent Report No. 305 (2007) is very much less radical than the proposals on which they consulted 14 years earlier (see LCCP No. 131 (1993)). They then proposed that the division between aiding and abetting and incitement (see **7.27**) should be abandoned and that all the matters addressed by 'those two institutions' should be replaced by a single set of rules. They started from first principles, identifying the conflicting demands of, on the one hand, the need to provide an efficient and clearly defined means of controlling those who involve themselves in the commission of crime by others; and, on the other hand, the need to formulate such rules in terms that do not impede or threaten legitimate social activities. They adopted Kadish's analysis:

> Two kinds of action render the secondary party liable for the criminal actions of the primary party: intentionally influencing the decision of the primary party to commit a crime, and intentionally helping the principal actor commit the crime, where the helping actions themselves constitute no part of the actions prohibited by the definition of the crime (at (1985) 73 California Law Review 342).

Kadish explained (at p. 405) that these are the only two forms of affecting the conduct of the principal which are consistent with the notion of the principal having freely chosen to act as he did. This led the Law Commission to propose the abolition of the current rules on complicity, by extending the law of inchoate offences (see Chapter 7) and by creating two new offences: assisting crime and encouraging crime. As we see in Chapter 7, offences of intentionally encouraging or assisting an offence, and encouraging or assisting an offence believing it will be committed, have now been created. But this is the place to consider why the Law Commission is no longer committed to a new crime of assisting crime.

A rejected proposal: assisting crime

6.28 The Law Commission in LCCP No. 131 of 1993 proposed that:

(1) A person commits the offence of assisting crime if he

    (a) knows or believes that another ('the principal') is doing or causing to be done, or will do or cause to be done, acts that do or will involve the commission of an offence by the principal; and

    (b) knows or believes that the principal, in so acting, does or will do so with the fault required for the offence in question; and

    (c) does any act that he knows or believes assists or will assist the principal in committing that offence.

(2) Assistance includes giving the principal advice as to [how to] commit the offence, or as to how to avoid detection or apprehension before or during the commission of the offence.

(3) A person does not assist the commission of an offence for the purposes of this section if all that he does is to fail to prevent or impede the commission of that offence.

(4) 'Offence' in sub-paragraphs (a)–(c) of sub-section (1) above means the breach of a specified prohibition laid down by statute or the common law; but, provided the defendant knows or believes sufficient facts to show that such a breach is taking place or will take place, he need not know the time, place or other details of the offence.

(5) A person also commits an offence under this section if he knows or believes that the principal intends to commit one of a number of offences and does any act that he knows or believes will assist the principal in committing whichever of those offences the principal in fact intends.

6.29 The Law Commission (1993) emphasized that they had not reached a final decision as to how the *mens rea* of the offence should be expressed. This was a problem: they suggested two possible formulations (the first of which is included in the proposal at 6.28):

- that the assister knows or believes that the principal crime is being or will be committed; or

- that the assister's purpose is that the principal crime should be committed.

Their uncertainty arose from their concern that the ambit of the criminal law should not be too wide. If the offence would be committed whether or not the principal offence occurs, only requiring knowledge or belief is perhaps too wide. The reach of the criminal law is spread too far if it brings within it those who have not committed a substantive crime themselves and who, while prepared to assist those who do commit such crimes, do so not to promote those crimes but for other motives. For example, if a generous host believes that her guest is going to drive home in his car, but continues to ply him with drink to an extent which puts him over the statutory limit, should she be guilty of a crime if in the event he does not drive home, and she never wanted him to anyhow? Or should someone who sells oxyacetylene cutting equipment, believing that the purchaser intends to use it to commit a burglary, but whose personal interest is only in his own profit, be guilty of an offence where the purchaser does not commit the burglary, either because he is arrested at the scene of the crime, or because he thinks better of it, or because he never intended to do so? The 'knowledge or belief' test also raises the *Gillick* (1985) problem (see **6.18**): we have already considered whether a doctor who prescribes contraceptives to a 15-year-old in order to minimize the risk of pregnancy should be guilty of an offence. One of the attractions of the 'purpose' definition is that it excludes the need for such vague defences as 'limiting harmful consequences'.

6.30 However, if the mental element is limited to purpose, this excludes those who may well be seen to be culpable: the regular supplier of goods or of transport who knows that they are to be used for criminal purpose, but is merely interested in making a profit on the sale; or suppliers, such as the supplier of oxyacetylene equipment mentioned earlier, who may well positively prefer the completed crime not to take place, so long as they obtain payment, since that may make their part in the affair less likely to be detected. Is there a midway point between purpose and belief? For example, if a test of intention was adopted, the courts might well evolve a *Nedrick*-type (see **3.10**) test of intent: 'If the jury are satisfied that at the material time D recognized that his act would be virtually certain to assist the principal, then that is a fact from which they may find it easy to infer that he intended to assist the principal, even though he may not have had any desire to achieve that result.' In cases where a consequence is foreseen as virtually certain, then intention may be inferred. This test would provide a narrower test of culpability than that of mere knowledge or belief, but would not be as exclusive as the purpose test.

6.31 Perhaps it is not surprising that it took 14 years for the Law Commission to formulate a Report, following this consultation! In 2007 (Report No. 305), they reject the proposal to abolish secondary liability for two main reasons: (i) D would sometimes be insufficiently condemned and labelled if she were to be convicted 'merely' of assisting or encouraging the commission of the principal offence (especially if she was the instigator) and (ii) because secondary liability has a 'forensic' advantage especially where it is impossible for P to prove the precise role of the various parties (see paras **1.38–1.40**; see also Wilson (2008)). What the Law Commission propose now is simply an updated version of the Accessories and Abettors Act 1861 and a statute (they published a draft Participating in Crime Bill) which would deal with secondary liability in two ways:

(i)   D would be liable, provided he or she satisfies the requisite fault element, for an offence that P commits with D's encouragement or assistance.

(ii) D would be liable, provided he or she satisfies the requisite fault element, for any offences committed pursuant to a joint criminal venture.

6.32   The latest draft Bill provides:

LIABILITY FOR OFFENCES COMMITTED OR ACTS DONE BY OTHERS

Ways in which a person may become liable

1 *Assisting or encouraging an offence*

(1)   Where a person (P) has committed an offence, another person (D) is also guilty of the offence if

(a)   D did an act with the intention that one or more of a number of other acts,

(b)   would be done by another person,

(c)   P's criminal act was one of those acts,

(d)   D's behaviour assisted or encouraged P to do his criminal act, and

(e)   subsection (2) or (3) is satisfied.

(2)   This subsection is satisfied if D believed that a person doing the act would commit the offence.

(3)   This subsection is satisfied if D's state of mind was such that had he done the act he would have committed the offence.

2 *Participating in a joint criminal venture*

(1)   This section applies where two or more persons participate in a joint criminal venture.

(2)   If one of them (P) commits an offence, another participant (D) is also guilty of the offence if P's criminal act falls within the scope of the venture.

(3)   The existence or scope of a joint criminal venture may be inferred from the conduct of the participants (whether or not there is an express agreement).

      (4) D does not escape liability under this section for an offence committed by P at a time when D is a participant in the venture merely because D is at that time

         (a) absent,

         (b) against the venture being carried out, or

         (c) indifferent as to whether it is carried out.

Clause 1 is perhaps uncontroversial, but clause 2 is so vague as to be unsettling. Sullivan (2008), perhaps somewhat hopefully, called it a 'signifier of change' rather than a clear statement of the content of change. This writer thinks the present law on joint ventures, uncertain as it is, is less uncertain than what is proposed. Probably the proposals will come to nothing: students must struggle on with the current copious case law to understand the breadth of liability of accomplices in criminal law today.

Concealing offences

6.33 A person who helps a person after the main crime may be guilty, not simply as an accomplice, but of himself or herself committing a substantive offence. A person who, knowing or believing that another person is guilty of an offence for which a person may be sentenced to five years' or more imprisonment, does 'any act with intent to impede his apprehension or prosecution' is guilty of an offence under the CLA 1967, s 4. Similarly, anyone who accepts money (or other bargain) in return for withholding information about such an offence will be guilty of an offence under the CLA 1967, s 5. A person who lies in court under oath may be guilty of the serious offence of perjury, and someone who intentionally interferes with the due administration of justice in court may be guilty of a criminal contempt of court.

FURTHER READING

Buxton, R., 'Joint Enterprise' [2009] Crim LR 233.

Giles, M., 'Complicity: The Problems of Joint Enterprise' [1990] Crim LR 383.

Kadish, S., 'Complicity, Cause and Blame: A Study in the Interpretation of Doctrine' (1985) 73 *California Law Review* 324.

Law Commission, *Assisting and Encouraging Crime* (Consultation Paper No. 131, 1993).

Law Commission, *Participating in Crime* (Report No. 305, 2007).

Simester, A., 'The Mental Element in Complicity' (2006) 122 LQR 578.

Smith, J. C., 'Criminal Liability of Accessories: Law and Reform' (1997) 113 LQR 453.

Smith, K. J. M., *A Modern Treatise on the Law of Criminal Complicity* (1991).

Sullivan, G. R., 'Participating in Crime: Law Com No. 305—Joint Criminal Ventures' [2008] Crim LR 19.

Taylor, R., 'Procuring, Causation, Innocent Agency and the Law Commission' [2008] Crim LR 32.

Virgo, G., 'Making Sense of Accessorial Liability' (2006) 6 *Archbold News* 6.

Wilson, W., 'A Rational Scheme of Liability for Participating in Crime' [2008] Crim LR 3.

SELF-TEST QUESTIONS

1   Discuss the liability of the participants in the following events:

   (i)   Dee and Acka agree to beat up Phil in order to teach him a lesson for his own brutish behaviour in the past. Unknown to Acka, however, Dee has decided to kill Phil if she gets the chance. When they find Phil, Acka knocks him to the ground, and Dee kills Phil with a knife that Acka did not know that Dee was carrying.

   (ii) Dee invites Phil to a party. Although she knows that he plans to drive home, she plies him with wine all evening. When he says he ought not to have any more she laughingly assures him that the police never stop people in her area. He eventually drives home, is stopped by the police, and is subsequently convicted of drunken driving.

   (iii) Dee, Bee, and Fee decide to burgle an old lady's house. Bee remains outside to be a lookout, but soon gets bored and goes off to the pub. When Dee and Fee find a box of jewellery, Dee decides to kill Phyllis, the old lady, so that she can't give any information on the burglars to the police. Fee looks on without attempting to stop Dee, who stabs Phyllis with a bread knife she finds in the kitchen. Phyllis dies.

2   Do you think that the Law Commission's proposals in Consultation Paper No. 131 (1993) offered an improvement in the current law on secondary liability? How do their proposals in Report No. 305 (2007) differ?

7 Inchoate offences

SUMMARY

Many crimes are defined in an inchoate form; here we focus on specific offences:

Attempt: since the CAA 1981, liability for attempts is purely statutory. D must perform a 'more than merely preparatory' act with the intention that the crime be committed. Too vague, leaving too much to the jury?

Conspiracy: mostly governed by the CLA 1977, but common law offences survive uncomfortably alongside. There must be an agreement to commit the crime; but some debate surrounds mental element (*Anderson; Siracusa; Saik*).

Incitement: common law abolished in Serious Crime Act 2007; now statutory offences: **intentionally encouraging or assisting an offence**; encouraging or assisting an offence believing it will be committed.

Problems:

  (i) inconsistencies and overlaps between the various offences;

 (ii) breadth of liability;

(iii) more reform on its way.

Introduction

7.1 The criminal law needs to be able to punish those who fail to complete their crimes, but how far back should liability extend? Merely having the idea that you might rob a bank is surely too far removed from the completed offence to justify punishment. The 'inchoate' offences cover various areas where English law penalizes offences which have not been completed. The *Oxford Reference Dictionary* defines inchoate as 'just begun or undeveloped'. The crime proper has just begun. How far must D have gone before he becomes guilty of an offence? Many offences are really inchoate in nature: possession offences, or those defined in terms of doing an act 'with intent to ....' (e.g. burglary, fraud, or perjury). It is also the case in some of the many new offences related to terrorism (see **5.5** and **9.34**). Look at s 5 of the Terrorism Act 2006:

s 5 Preparation of terrorist acts

(1) A person commits an offence if, with the intention of—

(a) committing acts of terrorism, or

(b) assisting another to commit such acts,

he engages in any conduct in preparation for giving effect to his intention.

(2) It is irrelevant for the purposes of subsection (1) whether the intention and preparations relate to one or more particular acts of terrorism, acts of terrorism of a particular description or acts of terrorism generally.

(3) A person guilty of an offence under this section shall be liable, on conviction on indictment, to imprisonment for life.

This is a sweepingly wide offence, with a maximum sentence of life imprisonment!

In this chapter we focus on the law on attempt, conspiracy, incitement, and the new offences of encouraging or assisting crime. These offences overlap and produce numerous difficulties for both student and practising lawyer. **Table 7.1** seeks to explain these curiosities. Why are so many boxes on the table marked unlikely or inappropriate? Sometimes it is difficult to know the answer. If no one has been prosecuted, convicted, and then appealed, we are unlikely to have guidance from the CA.

7.2 What harm is the law seeking to prevent in the case of inchoate offences: that which would have been done had D been successful, or the potential harm which D (or other Ds) might commit if the law did not seek to deter unsuccessful criminals? The law in this area illustrates the tension which exists in criminal law between harm-based liability and intention-based liability. Ashworth (1987, at p. 7), lays out these tensions clearly:

> Those of us who accept both the proposition that intentions are more important than outcomes in determining criminal liability and the proposition that the reach of the criminal law should be kept to the minimum have a great deal more thinking to do.

Another tension is created by the courts' struggle to adapt unsuitable offences in order to convict those who are in reality simply guilty of 'trying to help others commit a crime': see *Anderson* (1986, at **7.19**). To remedy this, in 1987 J. R. Spencer proposed a new offence of facilitation. This proposal led (indirectly and many years later!) to the new broad offences of the Serious Crime Act 2007, discussed

To attempt	To conspire	To aid, abet, counsel or procure	To intend to encourage/ assist	To believe to encourage/ assist	
An attempt	Inappropriate/ unlikely	Abolished: CAA 1981, s 1(4)(a)	No offence: CAA 1981, s 1(4)(b)	Yes	Yes
A conspiracy	Inappropriate/ unlikely	Inappropriate/ unlikely	No offence: Hollinshead (1985); Kenning (2008)	Yes	Inappropriate/ unlikely
Aid, abet, counsel or procure	Offence: Dunnington (1984)	Offence	No offence	Yes	Yes
Intend to encourage/assist	Inappropriate/ unlikely	Inappropriate/ unlikely	Yes	Yes	Yes
Believe to encourage/ assist	No offence: SCA 2007, s 49(5)	No offence: SCA 2007, s 49(5)	Yes	Yes	No offence: SCA 2007, s 49(5)

Table 7.1 The relationship between inchoate offences and accessorial liability

This is a chart created by Professor Graham Virgo, whose permission to reproduce it is very gratefully acknowledged.

at **7.34–7.38**. Although these offences have been in force since 1 October 2008, we still have little appellate case law: it may be that the new law is so complex that it is not being used very much. Or that the law is so broad that few are advised to appeal their conviction!

Jurisdictional issues

7.3 The common law position was that where there had been an agreement to carry out a crime abroad, the agreement even if made in England could not be enforced unless the implementation of the agreement would necessarily have involved the commission of an offence in England. However, widespread concern that there should be more international cooperation in law enforcement has led to many statutory amendments in this area. Thus the CJA 1993, s 5 made it an offence in certain circumstances to conspire, attempt, or incite offences of dishonesty and blackmail even where the substantive offence would not itself be triable in this country; the Sexual Offences (Conspiracy and Incitement) Act 1996 made it an offence to conspire to commit certain sexual acts against children abroad; the Criminal Justice (Terrorism and Conspiracy) Act 1998, s 5 added a s 1A to the Criminal Law Act 1977 (see **7.16**) making it an offence to conspire to commit an offence abroad. The Anti-Terrorism, Crime and Security Act 2001 gives courts in this country jurisdiction over crimes of bribery committed by UK nationals and UK incorporated bodies overseas; the SOA 2003 has its own jurisdictional rules. The Serious Crime Act 2007 has complex rules on prosecutions when either D or the encouraged crime is outside the jurisdiction. Of course, international cooperation in investigations, and improved extradition laws, are as important in reducing crime as allowing prosecutions in the UK of crimes only loosely connected with this country. These cases often provide difficult sentencing dilemmas: for reasons of consistency, should the English court sentence on the basis of domestic law, or the foreign country's sentencing law? (See *Patel* (2009) for an example.)

Attempt

7.4 This is perhaps the most straightforward of the inchoate offences, since it is closest to the completed offence. Ashworth (PCL, p. 439) distinguishes completed attempts (you have done everything you set out to do: fired the gun, or smuggled the goods you think are drugs into the country) from incomplete attempts (you are arrested before you fire the gun or before you enter the bank that you plan to rob), since it is easier to justify punishing the former than the latter. However,

English law punishes both. Common law attempt was replaced by a statutory offence in the CAA 1981, s 1:

s 1 (1) If, with intent to commit an offence to which this section applies, a person does an act which is more than merely preparatory to the commission of the offence, he is guilty of attempting to commit the offence ...

(2) A person may be guilty of attempting to commit an offence to which this section applies even though the facts are such that the commission of the offence is impossible.

(3) In any case where—

(a) apart from this subsection a person's intention would not be regarded as having amounted to an intent to commit an offence: but

(b) if the facts of the case had been as he believed them to be, his intention would be so regarded, then, for the purposes of subsection (1) above,

he shall be regarded as having had an intent to commit that offence.

Actus reus

7.5 D must have carried out acts 'more than merely preparatory' to the commission of the offence. What does this mean? First, the word 'act' suggests that an omission cannot constitute an attempt. Would it not be an attempted murder if a mother deliberately withheld food from her child intending the child to die? More careful drafting might have avoided this problem which has not yet been faced by the courts. The DCC (1989) would have defined the word 'act' in this context to include 'an omission only where the offence intended is capable of being committed by an omission' (see clause 49(3)). This is the approach adopted in Consultation Paper, No. 183 (2007), at paras 18.83–18.88.

7.6 Secondly, the test for when an act is 'more than merely preparatory' is not explained. Section 4(3) of the CAA 1981 leaves the jury with a wide, largely uncontrolled, discretion:

Where, in proceedings against a person for the offence under section 1 above, there is evidence sufficient in law to support a finding that he did an act falling within subsection (1) of that section, the question whether or not his act fell within that subsection is a question of fact.

The old common law tests were more restrictive: for example, the *Eagleton* (1855) test was that D must have done the last act towards the commission of the offence proper. Other tests included whether D had 'burnt his boats' or 'crossed the Rubicon'. Clearly a balance needs to be struck between the social interest in preventing harm at an early stage and, at the same time, upholding individual liberties. The police need to be able to arrest, for example, the bank robber outside the bank and not only once he has taken aim and fired at the cashier. Yet if he is arrested too soon we will not necessarily know whether he really intended to rob the bank. Consider whether you think that the five cases discussed draw the line appropriately:

Boyle and Boyle **(1986)** Ds damaged a door with a view to breaking in and burgling.

CA: upheld their conviction for attempted burglary, holding that whatever test was applied they were clearly guilty. (However, under the pre-1981 law it seems unlikely that they would have been guilty: they had not 'burnt their boats' or 'crossed the Rubicon'.)

Gullefer **(1990)** D distracted dogs in a greyhound race hoping that a 'no-race' would be declared and that he would get his £18 bet back.

CA (Lord Taylor CJ): quashed his conviction for attempted theft. When he jumped on to the track he was not attempting to steal £18, but was still at the stage of preparation. 'It seems to us that the words of the Act of 1981 seek to steer a mid-way course', i.e. the statute provided a compromise between a preparatory act and the last act before the commission of the substantive crime.

Jones **(1990)** D bought a gun, shortened the barrel, got into the back of V's car, and pointed the gun at him. The gun was loaded, but the safety catch had not been removed.

CA (Lord Taylor CJ): upheld D's conviction for attempted murder. Courts should look at the natural meaning of the words of the section and should not attempt to adapt old common law tests.

Campbell **(1991)** D was charged with attempting to rob a sub-post office. He had been seen earlier by police lurking in the vicinity wearing a crash helmet and sunglasses. He returned a short while later. He was without the sunglasses but he was found to be carrying an imitation gun, and also a threatening note, which he intended to pass over to the cashier as part of a demand for money. He was arrested within a yard of the entrance. He admitted his intention to rob. However, he appealed against the conviction on the ground that the judge should have ruled that there was no case to go to the jury that he had attempted to rob the post office.

CA: allowed appeal. Watkins LJ:

> In order to effect the robbery it is equally beyond dispute it would have been quite impossible unless obviously he had entered the post office, gone to the counter and

made some kind of hostile act—directed, of course, at whoever was behind the counter and in a position to hand him money. A number of acts remained undone and the series of acts which he had already performed—namely, making his way from his home where he commenced to ride his motor cycle on a journey to a place near a post office, dismounting from the cycle, walking towards the post office door—were clearly acts which were, in the judgment of this court, indicative of mere preparation even if he was still of a mind to rob the post office, of the commission that is of the offence of robbery. If a person, in circumstances such as this, has not even gained the place where he could be in a position to carry out the offence, it is extremely unlikely that it could ever be said that he had performed an act which would properly be said to be an attempt. (at p. 355)

Mason v DPP (2009) D reported to the police that, whilst opening his car door with the intention of driving home, he had been robbed of his car at knifepoint. At the police station, he was breathalysed and the alcohol level in his breath was found to be almost twice the legal limit. At interview, D admitted his intention to get into his car and drive it home knowing that he was possibly over the legal limit for alcohol. He was convicted (in a magistrates' court) of attempting to drive a motor vehicle whilst under the influence of excess alcohol. He then appealed by way of case stated against his conviction.

DC: allowed the appeal. Whether a given set of facts were capable of amounting to an attempt to commit an offence, rather than merely a preparatory act, was a question of law. D could not be said to have embarked on the 'crime proper' until he did something that was part of the actual process of putting the car in motion, such as turning on the engine; starting to open the car door was not capable of being so. D's acts were not capable of being characterized as more than merely preparatory.

In *DPP v Moore* (2010), Toulson LJ says that courts should use their common sense, though

> I find particularly helpful the first and last sentences of paragraph 14.5 [of Conspiracy and Attempts (LCCP No. 183, 2007)]:
>
> > To elaborate further, preparatory conduct by D which is sufficiently close to the final act to be properly regarded as part of the execution of D's plan can be an attempt ... In other words, it covers the steps immediately preceding the final act necessary to effect D's plan and bring about the commission of the intended offence.

7.7 Clearly there is a very fine line here, and the Law Commission were keen to limit the role of the fact-finder. K. J. M. Smith (1991), too, argued that *Gullefer* (1990) and *Jones* (1990) offer the lower courts inadequate guidance. Over 40 years ago, Glazebrook went further, suggesting in a challenging article (1969) that it was neither necessary nor desirable to have a law of attempted crime at all. Thus he argued that since the key issue in rape should not be whether D succeeded in penetrating his victim, but whether he assaulted her with sexual intent, the crime should be redefined to emphasize this. However, this argument falls foul of the 'fair labelling' principle (**1.2**): people understand that rape means non-consensual sex. To widen the definition would be inappropriate. There are also evidential dangers in taking too subjective a position, since guilty intent should not start to overshadow guilty conduct. We do not necessarily want to punish those who have criminal thoughts, but do not carry them out. This uncertainty perhaps explains s 4(3), which gives (rightly or wrongly!) such a wide role to the jury.

Mens rea

7.8 D must intend to complete the crime. The criminal law is not so wide as to impose liability on those who merely take risks, nearly committing crimes. Intention here does not necessarily mean purpose. James LJ's statement in *Mohan* (1976, see **3.8**), that what is needed is proof of 'a decision to bring about [the offence], no matter whether the accused desired that consequence of his act or not', was applied in *Pearman* (1985), where the CA held that the word 'intent' in s 1 has the same meaning as at common law.

> ***Walker and Hayles* (1989)** Having threatened to kill V, Ds dropped him from a third floor balcony.
>
> CA. upheld their conviction for attempted murder. Lloyd LJ confirmed that normally there is no need in attempt for a direction on inferred intention.

7.9 What if the substantive crime involves *mens rea* both in relation to the prohibited act and in relation to the circumstances surrounding the act? One view is that the section requires intent with regard to every element of the offence. However, this is clearly not the current position:

> ***Khan* (1990)** D was convicted of attempted rape, after the judge summed up to the jury that recklessness as to the woman's consent was sufficient to constitute the offence.
>
> CA (Russell LJ): dismissed his appeal.
>
> > The intent of the defendant is precisely the same in rape and in attempted rape and the *mens rea* is identical, namely an intention to have intercourse plus a knowledge of, or recklessness as to the woman's absence of consent.

This reasoning presumably also applies to other offences such as burglary or fraud. Thus to be convicted of an attempted fraud (**11.46**), D must intend to make a gain or loss, but only know that the representation is or might be untrue or misleading. In *Khan*, the CA drew a distinction between consequences (which must be intended) and circumstances (which need not be). But the distinction is not really clear: the consequence of rape could be defined as sex with a woman who is not consenting. Why is consent merely a circumstance? (See Glanville Williams (1991).) The reasoning in *Khan* was extended in:

A-G's Reference (No. 3 of 1992) (1994) Ds threw a petrol bomb, which smashed into a wall, towards Vs. No one was hurt. The question referred to the CA was whether D could be convicted of attempting to commit aggravated criminal damage, contrary to s 1(2) of the CDA 1971 (see **12.6**), when he was merely being reckless as to whether life was endangered.

CA (Schiemann J): it was enough for the Crown to establish a specific intent to cause damage by fire and that D was reckless as to whether life would be endangered.

This decision can be criticized for leading in the direction of a general law of reckless attempts, for which the law does not and should not provide. Do you think it is the appropriate solution?

Impossibility

7.10   There are numerous reasons why a crime might fail. You might fail to kill me because you are a bad shot, or because you are using a useless gun, or because I am already dead. Whether or not you should be guilty of attempted murder in these cases is subject to enormous debate, best explored through two cases:

Anderton v Ryan (1985) D admitted to the police that she believed that she was handling a stolen video player, although there was no evidence that it was in fact stolen.

HL (by a 4 to 1 majority; note Lord Edmund Davies' dissent): quashed her conviction for attempting to handle stolen goods. Lord Bridge distinguished the person who acts 'in a criminal way with a specific intent to commit a particular crime which he erroneously believes to be, but which is not, in fact, possible', who is guilty under s 1(3), from the person who does objectively innocent acts where 'the action is throughout innocent and the actor has done everything he intended to do'. This latter person, the HL concluded, is not guilty.

Glanville Williams (1986) wrote a 50-page diatribe against the decision, which explored the criticisms of it shared by many academics. He summarizes his analysis as an:

> ... *account of how the judges invented a rule based upon conceptual misunderstanding; of their determination to use the English language so strangely that they spoke what*

by normal criteria would be termed untruths; of their invincible ignorance of the mess they made of the law; and of their immobility on the subject, carried to the extent of subverting an Act of Parliament designed to put them straight (at p. 33).

7.11 It was perhaps not surprising that the HL soon caved in, in the face of such an onslaught:

> **Shivpuri (1987)** D, who admitted to customs officers that he thought he was smuggling illegal drugs, was convicted of attempting to be knowingly concerned in dealing with a controlled drug, namely heroin, although it was proved that the material he was smuggling was in fact harmless.
>
> HL (expressly overruling their decision in *Anderton v Ryan*): upheld his conviction. Lord Bridge acknowledged his gratitude to Glanville Williams, saying that he was unable to extract from his own speech in *Anderton v Ryan*, or from that of Lord Roskill, a clear and coherent principle.

The HL is normally reluctant to overrule their previous decisions, given 'the especial need for certainty as to the criminal law' (*Practice Note (Judicial Precedent)* [1966] 3 All ER 77; but see also *Howe* (1987) discussed at **5.19**). Were they right to do so here, or has the law now gone too far in punishing impossible attempts? It can be argued that *Shivpuri* represents subjectivism gone mad: if you take your own umbrella from my house, believing that it is mine, you are now guilty of attempted theft. Are you being charged with attempted theft of my umbrella (I don't have one: so clearly nonsense) or attempted theft of your own umbrella (also clearly nonsense)? Society needs protection from would-be drug smugglers such as *Shivpuri*, but the case raises both pragmatic and moral questions. Is it necessary to imprison such a person for a number of years for a crime he failed to commit? The fact that he was caught by customs officers may serve as a greater deterrent than any court sentence: he now knows that customs officers do catch people, and that if he is caught again, he will be sent to prison. Is it just to imprison someone for their mistaken belief? The law is close to punishing thought crime. If Shivpuri had denied all knowledge of any drugs to the customs officers, he could not have been convicted of any crime.

7.12 A more recent example of the application of *Shivpuri* is S:

> **S (2005)** D, aged 14 at the time, had allegedly intended his 15-year-old girlfriend, V, to kill herself and encouraged her to jump from a jetty on to rocks below. She gave evidence that she had no intention of committing suicide or of jumping but had been pushed to the edge of the jetty and encouraged by D. She was rescued by passers-by. D was convicted of attempting to aid, abet, counsel, or procure another to commit suicide, and appealed, primarily on the ground that the trial judge had failed to direct

the jury that it was necessary that D should have known or at least believed that V was intending or contemplating suicide.

CA: dismissed the appeal. The jury's attention was properly directed to D's intention and no one else's. Whilst an offence of aiding and abetting suicide would be impossible where the other had no intention to commit suicide, for an offence of attempt the possibility of suicide was enough. It was no defence that the crime would have been impossible. In many circumstances it could be implicit that D had a belief in the other person's intention or contemplation of suicide but in certain circumstances such a belief could fade into nothing if D aided and abetted any person at all, even where one who would never contemplate suicide was persuaded to do so.

> The fact that [the] intention to aid and abet the suicide, or attempted suicide, of another would be impossible in circumstances where that another had no intention herself to commit suicide, or even attempt to commit suicide, merely means that on the facts of such a case the attempt would merely be the attempt of an impossibility. But it is clear from *Shivpuri* (1987) that it is no impediment to the offence of an attempted crime that the actual crime would have been impossible on the facts of the case, such as attempting to pick an empty pocket or attempting to handle goods which have not been stolen, or attempting to murder not a person but a bolster in a bed. So, at pages 19 to 20 of Lord Bridge of Harwich's speech in *Shivpuri* the critical ingredients of an attempted crime under section 1 of the 1981 Act are focused on as being D's intent, and, with that intent, the doing of an act more than merely preparatory to the commission of the offence (Rix LJ at para. 40).

(Whilst suicide is not a crime, aiding and abetting it, and now encouraging and assisting it, is: see **7.39**.) Another example of an 'impossible attempt' is *Jones* (2007, see **10.21**), where D was convicted of attempting to commit an offence under s 8 of the SOA 2003, where he believed he was inciting a 12-year-old to have sex with him although she was in fact an undercover police officer.

7.13 What happens where someone uses impossible means? If you attempt to kill your enemy by sticking pins into a wax model of her, should you be guilty of attempted murder? French law would say no, since there is no 'real' connection between the act done and that sought to be achieved. The answer to the problem is not entirely clear in English law, even after *Shivpuri*. The HL may have abolished the need to distinguish different categories of impossibility, but now we have to rely on a wide police discretion not to prosecute certain people, those who they deem to be harmless.

Conspiracy

7.14 Why is it necessary to have a law of conspiracy? Once the parties have gone far enough, all conspirators can be charged as accomplices to an attempt (see *Dunnington* (1984), at **6.2**). Surprisingly, too, D may still be charged with a conspiracy even if the substantive offence has been completed: the conspiracy may be easier to prove, and the rules of evidence more relaxed. Thus following the decision of the HL in *Preddy* (1996), that those who commit mortgage frauds could not be guilty of theft or obtaining property by deception in that they did not intend to deprive the owner of the cheque permanently of it (see **11.37**), prosecutors may have fallen back again on conspiracy to defraud as an alternative route to conviction. Ashworth (PCL, pp. 455–9) discusses the 'double-life' of conspiracy, partly as an inchoate offence and partly as a quasi-substantive offence. Thus while the rationale for inchoate offences, including conspiracy, is often early prevention of crime, prosecutors may choose to prosecute someone for conspiracy simply because this is seen as a fuller and better description of their criminal course of conduct. See also Harding's argument for an offence of 'belonging', in the sense of supportive participation in a criminal group, in [2005] Crim LR 690.

7.15 Common law conspiracies were largely abolished by the CLA 1977, s 5(1). A common law conspiracy was wider than simply an agreement to commit a crime, including such offences as conspiracy to defraud, corrupt public morals, or outrage public decency. Unfortunately, largely due to the uncertainties surrounding fraud at that time, the Act did not abolish these, which has created many subsequent problems: we return to this at **7.22**.

Statutory conspiracy

7.16 The CLA 1977, s 1 provides:

> **s 1** (1) Subject to the following provisions of this part of this Act, if a person agrees with any other person or persons that a course of conduct shall be pursued which, if the agreement is carried out in accordance with their intentions, either—
>
> > (a) will necessarily amount to or involve the commission of any offence or offences by one or more parties to the agreement, or
> >
> > (b) would do so but for the existence of facts which render the commission of the offence or any offences impossible,
>
> he is guilty of conspiracy to commit the offence or offences in question…
>
> (2) Where liability for any offence may be incurred without knowledge on the part of the person committing it of any particular fact or circumstance necessary for the commission of the offence, a person shall nevertheless not be guilty of conspiracy to commit that offence by virtue of subsection (1) above unless he and at least one other party to the agreement intend or know that the fact or circumstance shall or will exist at the time when the conduct constituting the offence is to take place.

Actus reus

7.17 There must be an agreement, which may involve minimal or no conduct, between at least two people. Unlike in many other countries (France and USA, for example), there is no need for some act in pursuance of the agreement; the agreement itself is deemed sufficiently culpable to come within the criminal law. As O'Connor LJ said in *Siracusa* (1989), 'the essence of the crime of conspiracy is the agreement'. Other conspirators need not be identified, nor need all the parties know about each other. A person who conspires only with a child under ten does not commit a conspiracy, nor do a husband and wife who conspire only with each other.

7.18 The use of the word 'necessarily' in s 1(1)(a) might suggest that a conditional agreement might not amount to a conspiracy. However, if two burglars agree to kill if they get caught, then this conditional agreement constitutes conspiracy to murder:

> *Jackson* (1985) Ds agreed to shoot V, their friend, in the leg if he was convicted of burglary, as they believed he would then get a more lenient sentence.
>
> CA: upheld their conviction for conspiracy to pervert the course of justice.

Ashworth calls the word 'necessarily' in the section an 'unduly concrete term' (PCL, at p. 454), and the enactment of clause 48 of the DCC would avoid its use:

> (1) A person is guilty of conspiracy to commit an offence or offences if—
>
>   (a) he agrees with another or others that an act or acts shall be done which, if done, will involve the commission of the offence or offences by one or more of the parties to the agreement; and
>
>   (b) he and at least one other party to the agreement intend that the offence or offences shall be committed.

Mens rea

7.19 According to s 1, D must intend that the crime be carried out, but this has caused difficulties:

> *Anderson* (1986) D agreed to supply diamond cutting wire to help a prisoner escape. He did it for money, with no intention to help the prisoner escape: indeed he thought that the plan was doomed to failure.
>
> HL: upheld his conviction for conspiracy to effect the escape. Lord Bridge:

> The necessary *mens rea* of the crime is, in my opinion, established if, and only if, it is shown that the accused when he entered into the agreement, intended to play some part in the agreed course of conduct in furtherance of the criminal purpose which the agreed course of conduct was intended to achieve. Nothing less will suffice; nothing more is required.

If A asks B, who agrees, to kill C, then A and B should be guilty of conspiracy but does Lord Bridge's definition cause a difficulty where A does not agree to play some part in the agreed course of conduct? In *Anderson*, D did not really intend to help the prisoner escape but he surely merited punishment. This case was one of those raised by Spencer (1987) when he proposed a new offence of facilitation. It would seem that Anderson's culpability lay in his knowingly helping other criminals, rather than in his role in the possible escape. O'Connor LJ in *Siracusa* (1989) tried to unravel the confusion:

> We think it obvious that Lord Bridge cannot have been intending that the organiser of a crime who recruited others to carry it out would not himself be guilty of conspiracy unless it be proved that he intended to play some active part himself thereafter ... Consent, that is the agreement or adherence to the agreement, can be inferred if it is proved that he knew what was going on and the intention to participate in the furtherance of the criminal purpose is also established by his failure to stop the unlawful activity.

7.20 It would perhaps have been more logical if Anderson had been charged with aiding and abetting a conspiracy. What of the person who is taking part in order to help the police? At **3.3** we discussed the distinction between intent and motive: a good motive does not necessarily negate *mens rea*:

Yip Chiu-Cheung v R (1994) D was charged with conspiring with a US drugs enforcement officer who had agreed to act as his courier. D argued there was no conspiracy since the officer did not have the *mens rea* for the offence, since his motive was simply to entrap D.

PC (Lord Griffiths): the officer did intend to commit the crime. '[T]he fact that ... the authorities would not prosecute the undercover agent does not mean that he did not intend to commit the crime.' D was therefore rightly convicted of conspiracy.

7.21 Section 1(2) also provides that the conspirator will not be guilty of an offence unless he 'intends or knows' certain facts: would 'believes' be clearer in this context?

Ali (2005) Ds, convicted in two separate trials, appealed against their convictions for conspiracy to contravene the Drug Trafficking Act 1994, s 49(2), contrary to the CLA 1977, s 1, and D4 further appealed against his conviction for conspiracy to contravene the CJA 1988, s 93C(2). The two trials were the second and third trials arising out of a complex Customs investigation. It was alleged that D1, D2, and D3 had concealed, disguised, or removed from the jurisdiction banknotes knowing or having reasonable grounds to suspect that in whole or in part they represented another person's proceeds of drug trafficking and that D4 had conspired with others to conceal banknotes knowing or having reasonable grounds to suspect that, in whole or in part, they represented another person's proceeds of drug trafficking or other criminal conduct. In summing up, the judges told the jury to convict a D only if they found that he knew or suspected that at least part of the money he was dealing with was another person's proceeds of drug trafficking.

CA: allowed the appeals. The substantive offences under s 49(2) and s 93C(2) required proof that a D was in fact dealing with the proceeds of drug trafficking or other criminal conduct. It was not enough that a D had reasonable grounds to suspect that the property was the proceeds of drug trafficking or other criminal conduct (applying the decision of the HL in *Montila* (2004)). A jury could therefore only convict of conspiracy if D knew that he was dealing with the proceeds of drug trafficking or other criminal conduct. The fact that the property was the proceeds of drug trafficking or other criminal conduct was a fact upon which s 1(2) of the 1977 Act bit: the jury should not have been directed to convict if D only suspected that at least part of the money he was dealing with was another person's proceeds of drug trafficking.

This case is one of a large number in the area of conspiracy to money launder. The problem is with the wording of the CLA 1977, s 1(2) (see **7.15** earlier). How can D 'intend' or 'know' a future circumstance will exist? The question reached the HL in 2006:

Saik (2006) D was charged with 'conspiracy to convert the proceeds of drug trafficking and/or criminal conduct contrary to s 1(1) of the CLA 1977'. The essence of P's case was that D and others:

> ... conspired together ... to convert ... banknotes, for the purpose of assisting another to avoid prosecution for ... a criminal offence ..., knowing or having reasonable grounds to suspect that such property ... represented another person's proceeds of ... criminal conduct. D pleaded guilty on the basis of laundering money which he suspected was the proceeds of crime.

CA dismissed his appeal but certified two points of law:

1. Can a D be convicted of a statutory conspiracy to contravene s 93C(2) of the CJA 1988 if he enters into an agreement to convert property in respect of which he had reasonable grounds to suspect and did in fact suspect but did not actually know was the proceeds of crime?

2. Is the objective requirement that a D can be convicted of an offence under s 93C(2) of the CJA 1988 if he had reasonable grounds to suspect that the property converted etc. was the proceeds of crime (without having actual knowledge or suspicion) incompatible with the subjective requirement that the activity of the D must be for the specified purpose of assisting another to avoid prosecution for a criminal offence or avoiding the making or enforcement of a confiscation order?

HL unanimously allowed the appeal. We focus on the first question. The majority said clearly, no, D must know that the property was the proceeds of crime (but Baroness Hale, as we shall see, gave a different answer to this first question):

…where the property has *not* been identified when the conspiracy agreement is reached, the prosecution must prove the conspirator *intended* that the property would be the proceeds of criminal conduct (Lord Nicholls, at para. 23).

The phrase 'intend or know' in section 1(2) is a provision of general application to all conspiracies. In this context the word 'know' should be interpreted strictly and not watered down. In this context knowledge means true belief. Whether it covers wilful blindness is not an issue arising on this appeal (Lord Nicholls, at para. 26).

Lord Hope agreed, including a wide review of the academic literature.

Baroness Hale sought to draw a discernible dividing line between conditional intention and recklessness. Using an analogy with rape, she pointed out that:

It is important to distinguish between what happens when the substantive offence is committed—when the men have intercourse with the woman whether or not she consents—and what happens when they agree to do so. When they agree, they have thought about the possibility that she may not consent. They have agreed that they will go ahead *even if at the time when they go ahead they know that she is not consenting.* If so, that will not be recklessness; that will be intent to rape. Hence they are guilty of conspiracy to rape (para. 99).

She would therefore have answered the first certified question: 'yes, provided that he intended to put the agreement into effect even if the property was in fact the proceeds of crime.'

This decision to limit the potential scope of conspiracy should be welcomed: conspiracy is an inchoate offence which should not be drawn too widely. As Lord Brown points out, conspiracy is the 'prosecutor's darling' (para. 123) which may be seen as evidentially easier to prove than a completed offence. But it is important that prosecutors understand why, in order to keep the breadth of the law on inchoate offences within proper bounds, the *mens rea* requirements of conspiracy may be more demanding than those for the substantive offence. We return to this at the end of the chapter when looking at the Law Commission's latest proposals for reform.

Impossibility

7.22 At common law, the fact that the substantive crime was impossible could be a defence to a charge of conspiracy:

***DPP v Nock* (1978)** Ds agreed to produce cocaine from a specific powder which in fact could never yield cocaine.

HL: quashed their conviction for conspiracy. Impossibility was a defence.

However, now re-read s 1(1)(b) (inserted by the CAA 1981, s 5) which makes it clear that impossibility is no longer a defence to a statutory conspiracy. Today statutory conspiracies to do impossible things will be treated in the same way as attempts to do impossible things (see **7.11**). Equally, a conspiracy to aid and abet an offence is a legal impossibility: *Hollinshead* (1985).

***Kenning* (2008)** D1 and D2 owned a shop selling hydroponic equipment, cannabis seeds, and cannabis-related literature, and D3 occasionally worked there. Producers of cannabis on whose premises equipment from the shop had been found had already been prosecuted. The police made two undercover visits to the shop. On the first the undercover officer discussed with D1 and D2 the equipment needed to grow plants in his loft, and D1 stated that he could provide anti-detection foil. On the second visit, the officer told D3 that he wanted to grow plants to make money. Both D1 and D3 referred to anti-detection measures and advised on yield for the first crop. The items purchased from the shop could have been used lawfully to grow other plants. Ds were charged with conspiracy to aid and abet the production of cannabis, and were convicted.

CA: quashed the conviction. There could be no conviction for aiding and abetting, counselling, or procuring an offence unless the *actus reus* of the substantive offence was shown to have occurred. It was possible for people to agree to aid and abet an offence that they intended or expected would be committed by a person who was not a party to that agreement, but it was hard to conceive that such an agreement would constitute statutory conspiracy contrary to s 1(1) of the 1977 Act.

Ormerod explains this well (at [2009] Crim LR 37):

The offence of conspiracy under s.1 of the Criminal Law Act 1977 requires D1 and D2 to reach an agreement that will involve 'a course of conduct' amounting to or involving 'the commission of an offence'. If 'course of conduct' is interpreted to mean no more than that D1 and D2 sell the equipment to P (the grower or as here the undercover officer posing as a grower) it seems clear that they are not guilty.

Selling the equipment is not an offence, and s.1 of the 1977 Act requires proof that D1 and D2 have agreed on a course of conduct which will necessarily amount to or involve the commission of an offence. If 'course of conduct' is construed more broadly to include P's use of the equipment in growing the cannabis there is still no offence. The agreement must be as to 'the commission of any offence by one or more of the parties to the agreement'. P (the grower) is not a party to the agreement.

Common law conspiracies today

7.23 Confusion over the status of common law conspiracies continues. The CLA 1977, s 5 provides that:

> **s 5** (1) Subject to the following provisions of this section, the offence of conspiracy at common law is hereby abolished.
>
> (2) Subsection (1) above shall not affect the offence of conspiracy at common law so far as relates to conspiracy to defraud.
>
> (3) Subsection (1) above shall not affect the offence of conspiracy at common law if and in so far as it may be committed by entering into an agreement to engage in conduct which—
>
>   (a) tends to corrupt public morals or outrages public decency; but
>
>   (b) would not amount to or involve the commission of an offence if carried out by a single person otherwise than in pursuance of an agreement …

Conspiracy to defraud

7.24 If the parties agree to commit an offence under the Fraud Act 2006, for example, a statutory conspiracy may be charged. But the prosecution may instead charge D with a common law conspiracy. The HL's decision in *Ayres* (1984), that the common law and the statutory offence were mutually exclusive, resulted in many Ds having their convictions quashed simply because they had been wrongly charged with the common law offence. Two years later, the CLRC was therefore asked to review the restriction on the use of a charge of conspiracy to defraud in the light of *Ayres*, and to consider whether these restrictions could be removed without causing injustice. Their Report (18th Report (1986)), which was a model of clarity and good essay-writing style, concluded that the simplest solution to the problem was also the most satisfactory: the full ambit of conspiracy to defraud should be restored. This was achieved in the CJA 1987, s 12.

7.25 For there to be a common law conspiracy to defraud, D must be dishonest. Yet his motive need not be to commit economic loss:

> ***Wai Yu-tsang v R (1992)*** D, the chief accountant of a bank, was convicted of conspiring with others to defraud the bank and its existing and potential shareholders, creditors, and depositors. He said that he had concealed the dishonouring of certain cheques in the bank's accounts on the managing director's instructions and in order to prevent a further run on the bank. He believed he was acting in the bank's best interests.
>
> PC (Lord Goff): upheld his conviction. It is enough that the conspirators have dishonestly agreed to bring about a state of affairs which they realize will or may deceive V into so acting, or failing to act, that he will suffer an economic loss or his economic interests will be put at risk. The mere fact that D did not wish his victim to suffer harm will not itself prevent the agreement from constituting a conspiracy to defraud.

There continues to be no shortage of complex prosecutions for conspiracy to defraud (doubtless because prosecutors perceive the advantages of not being bound by complex statutory offences: see the difficulties in proving, for example, a statutory conspiracy to launder money in *Ali* (2005), see **7.21**) but the common law continues to cause many difficulties, too.

> ***K (2005)*** Ds were alleged to have induced investors to put money into a company by making false representations that the company owned the rights to a product which it would develop and market. Most of the investors' money in fact had gone to Ds. The company had never acquired the rights in the product and it had been wound up. P argued that the company had been a hollow shell with no assets and that Ds had defrauded the investors either by selling shares to them or by participating in the company with knowledge of its fraudulent purpose. D was convicted of conspiracy to defraud. He argued that the judge should have directed the jury to convict only if they were satisfied that he had been both a party to the conspiracy to defraud the shareholders and unanimous that he had been a party to an agreement to make at least one of the specific representations set out in the particulars to the indictment.
>
> CA: dismissed the appeal. When conspirators agreed to make dishonest representations about a company to induce investors to buy shares, that was sufficient to constitute a certain agreement, and it was not necessary for the conspirators to agree more specifically on the misrepresentations that were to be made. It was the agreement to defraud that was the essential ingredient of the offence. Although it was established law that a jury could not convict unless unanimous on each ingredient of the offence, the precise nature of the representations made did not constitute ingredients of the offence of conspiracy to defraud. The particulars had been given only to provide

reasonable information as to the nature of the charge and as to the principal matters upon which P would invite the jury to infer that there was an agreement to defraud, and that D was party to it. The particulars did not purport to define the agreement.

Ormerod points out in [2005] Crim LR 301, citing an earlier commentary of Professor Sir John Smith, 'the excessive breadth of the offence of conspiracy to defraud and the fact that its breadth allows P to succeed where the jury is "satisfied in a general way that the appellants were a dishonest lot, up to no good".' The Government's recognition in their 2004 consultation on fraud that there is no need for a 'fall back' common law offence was very welcome. However, the Government rejected the recommendation: see the discussion of the Fraud Act 2006 (at **11.40**). Common law conspiracy to defraud lives on. (The fact that the offence is so very broad sometimes makes it difficult to draw up the indictment properly, but that is a question of criminal procedure, not substantive law: see *GG Ltd* (2008).)

Mehta (2012) The indictment contained a single count alleging that D, D2, and 'others unknown' had conspired to defraud a bank. This covered 17 alleged fraudulent loan applications made by different applicants. D had introduced all of them to the bank and had received a fee from them. D2 was employed by the bank and processed the applications. P's case was that the principal conspirators were D and D2, and that another person (X), who made one of the applications and also introduced applicants to D, became a party to the conspiracy. X separately pleaded guilty to four counts of fraud. He was referred to in P's case against D and D2 but was not identified on the indictment. No dishonest role was attributed to any individual other than D, D2, or X. The judge directed the jury that if it acquitted D2 it could still convict D, but only if sure that he had made 'a necessary agreement with a person or persons other than [D2]'. D2 was acquitted, and D was convicted.

CA: dismissed D's appeal. No principle of law prevented the jury from convicting D on the basis that they were sure that he conspired with X to defraud the bank by making false loan applications. The authorities establish the following propositions:

1. A conspiracy requires that the parties to it have a common unlawful purpose or design.

2. A common design means a shared design. It is not the same as similar but separate designs.

3. In criminal law (as in civil law) there may be an umbrella agreement pursuant to which the parties enter into further agreements which may include parties who are not parties to the umbrella agreement. So, A and B may enter into an umbrella agreement pursuant to which they enter into a further agreement between A, B, and C, and a further agreement between A, B, and D, and so on. In that example, C and D will not be conspirators with each other.

But here the jury must have been satisfied that the agreement between D and X, which was limited in scope to the transactions in which X was involved, fell within the language of the indictment and within the case advanced by P.

Conspiracy to corrupt public morals or outrage public decency

Shaw v DPP (1962)   D published a Ladies' Directory, offering the names, addresses, and telephone numbers of prostitutes. His intent was to help prostitutes ply their trade after the SOA 1959 had made it more difficult for them to solicit on the street (see 10.31).

HL: upheld his conviction for conspiring to corrupt public morals. A conspiracy to corrupt public morals was a common law offence and there was evidence fit to be left to the jury.

> There is in [the] court a residual power, where no statute has yet intervened to supersede the common law, to superintend those offences which are prejudicial to the public welfare (Viscount Simonds).

Knuller v DPP (1973)   Ds all took part in the publication of a magazine which included advertisements by homosexuals for partners.

HL: upheld their conviction for conspiring to corrupt public morals, relying on *Shaw*. Parliament alone would be the proper authority to overrule such an authority.

7.26   Is the CAA 1981, s 5(3), which preserves common law conspiracies to corrupt public morals or outrage public decency, really necessary? The CA in both *Gibson* (1990) and *Hamilton* (2007) (see 1.24) have confirmed that the offence of outraging public decency still exists, and therefore a conspiracy to outrage public decency can be charged as a statutory conspiracy, under the CLA 1977. What behaviour could be left open for the common law conspiracy? It is surely time to abolish the common law version of the offence.

Common law conspiracy and impossibility

7.27   The decision in *DPP v Nock* (1978), that impossibility could be a defence to (common law) conspiracy, has survived the insertion of s 1(1)(b) into the CLA 1977 by the CAA 1981 (see 7.21) since this section applies only to statutory conspiracies (see 7.31).

Incitement

7.28 Incitement as a common law offence has been abolished by s 59 of the Serious Crime Act 2007, although there are a number of specific statutory offences of incitement which remain, such as s 4 of the OAPA 1861 (incitement to murder), s 8 of the SOA 2003 (causing or inciting a child under 13 to engage in sexual activity), and s 26 of that Act (inciting a child family member to engage in sexual activity). We will look at the pre-Serious Crime Act 2007 law not only because it will continue to apply for years to come as the police may uncover old offences but also because it may be a useful guide to the new law. But tread carefully!

Actus reus

7.29 D must have encouraged or persuaded someone to commit an offence. If that other person commits the crime, then D is liable for that crime as an accessory (see Chapter 6). If D communicates his encouragement, the incitement is complete, even if it has no influence: the incitement need have no effect. There must be an element of persuasion or encouragement: just offering to supply someone with equipment for a burglary which they already intend to commit would not constitute incitement.

> *Most* (1881) D wrote an article in a newspaper advocating the assassination of the crowned heads of Europe.
>
> QBD: upheld his conviction. An endeavour to persuade or to encourage is nevertheless an endeavour to persuade or an encouragement even if D did not personally address those people whom his encouragement reaches.

An interesting question under the old law of incitement was whether the incitement had to come to the attention of the incitee. If the encouragement (e.g. in the form of a letter) was intercepted, then D was probably guilty only of attempted incitement. *Most* was followed in *Jones* (2007, see **10.21**), where it was held that the criminality of the offence defined in s 8 of the SOA 2003 was the incitement of children under the age of 13 to engage in sexual activity, and it did not matter whether or not it was directed at a particular child, or whether a particular child could be identified.

Mens rea

7.30 For old-style common law incitement, D had to intend that the crime be committed, and to know the circumstances of the act which made it an offence. The person incited did not need to have the *mens rea*, but D had to believe that they would commit the crime.

***Invicta Plastics Ltd v Clare* (1975)** D, a company, advertised in magazines a device which would give car drivers advance warning of a police radar speed trap.

QBD: upheld their conviction for inciting others to use unlicensed apparatus for wireless telegraphy contrary to the Wireless Telegraphy Act 1949, s 1(1).

Ds were not charged with incitement to speed since it would be difficult to prove this, and were simply charged with inciting people to have a radio without a licence. As Spencer (1987) pointed out, this is an artificial decision, stretching the ambit of incitement to include incitements to people in general too far. It was one of the cases which made Spencer decide to recommend a more specific offence of 'facilitation'.

Impossibility

7.31 Remember that if D knows that the person incited does not have the *mens rea* for the full offence, this person will be an innocent agent and D will be the principal offender if the full offence is committed (see **6.6**). If the act incited or encouraged would not constitute a crime, there will be no incitement: see *Taaffe* (1984) at **3.14**. Where the person incited was the person protected by the criminal offence in question, then D could not be guilty since the victim would not be committing an offence:

***Whitehouse* (1977)** D's daughter, aged 15, refused to have sex with him. He was convicted of incitement to commit incest.

CA (Scarman LJ): allowed his appeal. Had he had sex with her, he would have committed incest, but he had not therefore there was no crime. Therefore he could not be guilty of incitement to commit incest.

As a result of this case, the CLA 1977, s 54 introduced an offence for a man to invite a girl aged under 16 who is his daughter, granddaughter, or sister to have sex with him. This was repealed in the SOA 2003, but the general principle of *Whitehouse* remains good: at common law, the incitor is not liable if the person incited cannot commit the crime in question. It is not always easy to see how this applies now in sexual offences, since the broad definitions suggest 'victims' may also be 'offenders': see Chapter 10. The Serious Crime Act 2007 deals with the problem by providing (in s 51) that in the case of a 'protective offence' (one which exists wholly or partly to protect a particular category of person), a person who falls within that category cannot be convicted of a statutory offence under the Act as long as he is or would have been the victim of that offence.

7.32 If the incitement encouraged someone to commit a crime using inadequate means, D's liability depended on whether D knew that the means were inadequate. If the crime was impossible whatever means were used, D would not be guilty of incitement.

Fitzmaurice **(1983)** D was asked by his father to find someone to rob a woman on her way to the bank. In fact, the robbery was a fiction invented by the father who hoped to create a situation in which he could claim a reward.

CA (Neil LJ): upheld D's conviction of incitement to commit robbery. The element of persuasion was satisfied by a 'suggestion, proposal or request accompanied by an implied promise of reward'. The old common law decision on conspiracy, *DPP v Nock* (1978, see **7.22**), applies to incitement, and impossibility could render an incitement lawful. Here, however, the future robbery was possible, so D was rightly convicted.

7.33 Thus impossibility could be a defence to incitement at common law (as well as to common law conspiracy): it was important to assess the possibility at the time of the incitement, not at the time of the further offence.

Encouraging and assisting crime

7.34 As we have seen, the common law crime of incitement punished actions far removed from the completed offence, and had been stretched in extraordinary ways to compensate for the limitations of the law on accessory liability. We saw at **6.27** that in 1993 the Law Commission proposed and consulted on new offences of assisting and of encouraging crime, and that it was more than a decade before they produced their Report on *Inchoate Liability for Assisting and Encouraging Crime* (Law Com No. 300, Cm. 6878 (2006)). This was swiftly enacted, in the Serious Crime Act 2007, which replaces the common law offence of incitement with three new offences. The provisions were brought into force on 1 October 2008.

Intentionally encouraging or assisting an offence

7.35 Section 44 provides:

s 44 (1) A person commits an offence if—

(a) he does an act capable of encouraging or assisting the commission of an offence; and

(b) he intends to encourage or assist its commission.

(2) But he is not to be taken to have intended to encourage or assist the commission of an offence merely because such encouragement or assistance was a foreseeable consequence of his act.

This is a very broad offence, and will presumably lead to much litigation: what is an act which is 'capable of encouraging' an offence? D must believe that his act will encourage or assist: s 47(2) makes clear that 'if it is alleged under s 44(1)(b) that a person (D) intended to encourage or assist the commission of an offence, it is sufficient to prove that he intended to encourage or assist the doing of an act which would amount to the commission of that offence'. But mere foresight is not enough. So far, however, the cases have been sentencing appeals (including the notorious case, where the CA upheld a sentence of four years' imprisonment imposed on a man who had pleaded guilty to an offence of 'intentionally encouraging or assisting the commission of an offence' by setting up a Facebook webpage to encourage a riot (which he later cancelled and said had been a joke): *Blackshaw* (2011).

Encouraging or assisting an offence believing it will be committed

7.36 Section 45 provides:

A person commits an offence if—

(a) he does an act capable of encouraging or assisting the commission of an offence; and

(b) he believes—

  (i) that the offence will be committed; and

  (ii) that his act will encourage or assist its commission.

This too is a very broad offence. The *mens rea* is belief. Section 47, on 'proving an offence', shows just how wide the new offences are designed to be:

s 47 (1) Sections 44, 45 and 46 are to be read in accordance with this section.

(2) If it is alleged under section 44(1)(b) that a person (D) intended to encourage or assist the commission of an offence, it is sufficient to prove that he intended to encourage or assist the doing of an act which would amount to the commission of that offence.

(3) If it is alleged under s 45(b) that a person (D) believed that an offence would be committed and that his act would encourage or assist its commission, it is sufficient to prove that he believed—

  (a) that an act would be done which would amount to the commission of that offence; and

  (b) that his act would encourage or assist the doing of that act.

(4) If it is alleged under section 46(1)(b) that a person (D) believed that one or more of a number of offences would be committed and that his act would encourage or assist the commission of one or more of them, it is sufficient to prove that he believed—

    (a) that one or more of a number of acts would be done which would amount to the commission of one or more of those offences; and

    (b) that his act would encourage or assist the doing of one or more of those acts.

(5) In proving for the purposes of this section whether an act is one which, if done, would amount to the commission of an offence—

    (a) if the offence is one requiring proof of fault, it must be proved that—

        (i) D believed that, were the act to be done, it would be done with that fault;

        (ii) D was reckless as to whether or not it would be done with that fault; or

        (iii) D's state of mind was such that, were he to do it, it would be done with that fault; and

    (b) if the offence is one requiring proof of particular circumstances or consequences (or both), it must be proved that—

        (i) D believed that, were the act to be done, it would be done in those circumstances or with those consequences; or

        (ii) D was reckless as to whether or not it would be done in those circumstances or with those consequences.

(6) For the purposes of subsection (5)(a)(iii), D is to be assumed to be able to do the act in question.

(7) In the case of an offence under section 44—

    (a) subsection (5)(b)(i) is to be read as if the reference to 'D believed' were a reference to 'D intended or believed'; but

    (b) D is not to be taken to have intended that an act would be done in particular circumstances or with particular consequences merely because its being done in those circumstances or with those consequences was a foreseeable consequence of his act of encouragement or assistance.

(8) Reference in this section to the doing of an act includes reference to—

    (a) a failure to act;

    (b) the continuation of an act that has already begun;

    (c) an attempt to do an act (except an act amounting to the commission of the offence of attempting to commit another offence).

Thus, for example, it is sufficient for D to believe that the offence (or one or more of the offences) will be committed if certain conditions are met (s 49(7)): he is liable even if the commission of the offence is conditional.

Encouraging or assisting offences believing one or more will be committed

7.37 Section 46 provides:

> **s 46** (1) A person commits an offence if—
>
> > (a) he does an act capable of encouraging or assisting the commission of one or more of a number of offences; and
> >
> > (b) he believes—
> >
> > > (i) that one or more of those offences will be committed (but has no belief as to which); and
> > >
> > > (ii) that his act will encourage or assist the commission of one or more of them.
> >
> (2) It is immaterial for the purposes of subsection (1)(b)(ii) whether the person has any belief as to which offence will be encouraged or assisted.
>
> (3) If a person is charged with an offence under subsection (1)—
>
> > (a) the indictment must specify the offences alleged to be the 'number of offences' mentioned in paragraph (a) of that subsection; but
> >
> > (b) nothing in paragraph (a) requires all the offences potentially comprised in that number to be specified.

Whilst offences under s 44 or 45 are triable in the same way as the anticipated offence, an offence under s 46 is triable only on indictment (see s 55(2)). It is another broad offence: here it is immaterial whether the actor has any belief as to which offence will be encouraged or assisted. Sections 47(3) and 49(7) apply here too. It was intended as a 'backstop', when ss 44 or 45 won't 'work'. The case of *Sadique* (2013) has now been to the CA twice: first as an appeal from a preparatory hearing and then again after conviction:

> *Sadique and Hussain* **(2011)** P alleged that the Ds were concerned with a national business supplying chemical cutting agents direct to drug dealers and to regional distributors of cutting agents, and that the supply of the cutting agents was capable of assisting one or more offences of supplying/being concerned in the supply of class A or class B controlled drugs and that the Ds believed that one or more of those offences would be committed and that their act would assist in the commission of one

or more of them. The Ds argued at a preparatory hearing that s 46 was incompatible with Art 7 of the ECHR (see **1.25**) in that it was too vague and uncertain and that the trial on that count should therefore be stayed as an abuse of process. They argued that it was not 'possible to arrive at a workable and intelligible interpretation of' s 46. The judge ruled against that submission.

CA (Hooper LJ): dismissed their appeals. Section 46 should only be used when P alleges that D's act is capable of encouraging or assisting more than one offence. If P wishes to allege that D's act was capable of encouraging or assisting the commission of offences X, Y, and Z, those three offences must be identified in the indictment (or count).

> Section 46 should only be used, and needs only to be used, when it may be that D, at the time of doing the act, believes that one or more of *either* offence X, *or* offence Y, *or* offence Z will be committed, but has no belief as to which one or ones of the three will be committed. To take an example. D gives E a gun. Giving E a gun is, we shall assume, capable of encouraging or assisting the commission of offences X, Y, and Z and the prosecution specify those three offences in the indictment. If D, at the time of giving the gun, believes that one or more of offences X, Y, and Z will be committed but has no belief as to which will be committed, s 46 should be used. The Law Commission Report reveals that s 46 is thought to be necessary because of a belief that if, in these circumstances, D is charged with three s 45 offences, one in relation to X, one in relation to Y, and one in relation to Z, D would have to be acquitted of each s 45 offence if he believed that one of the three offences would be committed but he did not know which one (para. 40).

P must identify which offences D's act was capable of encouraging and assisting and upon which it wished to rely.

Sadique (2013) At the trial, D1 was convicted and D2 acquitted. D1 appealed. CA (Lord Judge, LCJ) dismissed the appeal. The Act created three distinct offences and had to be interpreted to give effect to their creation. The purpose of the legislation might have been achieved in a less tortuous fashion but it was not open to the court to set one or other of the offences aside. None took priority over the other two. Section 46 reflected practical reality. Its purpose was 'to provide for the relatively common case where a D contemplated that one of a variety of offences might be committed as a result of his or her encouragement' (see Virgo (2013)). The ingredients of the s 46 offence and the ancillary provisions, particularly ss 58(4)–(7), underlined that an indictment charging a s 46 offence by reference to one or more offences was permissible, and covered the precise situation for which the legislation provided. Before D1 could be convicted, the jury had had to be satisfied that (a) he was involved in the supply of relevant chemicals and (b) that, if misused criminally, the chemicals were capable of misuse by others to commit offences of supplying or being concerned in the supply of, or being in possession with intent to supply, class A and/or class B drugs. None of that would be criminal unless it was also proved that (c) at the time of supply of the chemicals, D1 believed that what he was doing would encourage or assist the commission of one or more drug-related offences, and (d) that he also believed that that was the purpose for which the chemicals would be used by those to whom he supplied them. At the earlier hearing in the case, the purpose of which had been to resolve certain procedural issues, the CA had analysed the ingredients of a s 46 offence, but the foundation for that analysis was flawed, obiter, and therefore not binding on this court. It was an essential ingredient of the s 46 offence that D had to believe that one or more offences would be committed. The effect of the words in s 46(1)(b)(i) 'but has no belief as to which' underlined that the offence was directed to precisely the situation where, notwithstanding that D was unable to identify which of one or more specific offences would be committed, he nevertheless believed that one or more would be committed.

What a complexity! The first CA (Hooper LJ) seemed to be requiring a complicated number of counts, in order to make it clearer what the D is charged with—but wasn't he likely to be acquitted of all if P couldn't prove which offence precisely he was encouraging or assisting? The decision in the second appeal makes things slightly easier (see Stark (2013) and Virgo (2013)), but there is still a confusing overlap between s 45 and s 46, and prosecutors are still very confused as to how to draw up incitements.

7.38 Section 50 provides a defence to all three offences of 'acting reasonably':

s 50 (1) A person is not guilty of an offence under this Part if he proves—

(a) that he knew certain circumstances existed; and

(b) that it was reasonable for him to act as he did in those circumstances.

(2) A person is not guilty of an offence under this Part if he proves—

(a) that he believed certain circumstances to exist;

(b) that his belief was reasonable; and

(c) that it was reasonable for him to act as he did in the circumstances as he believed them to be.

(3) Factors to be considered in determining whether it was reasonable for a person to act as he did include—

(a) the seriousness of the anticipated offence (or, in the case of an offence under section 46, the offences specified in the indictment);

(b) any purpose for which he claims to have been acting;

(c) any authority by which he claims to have been acting.

How does this fit with, for example, the defence of prevention of crime, under s 3 of the CLA 1967 (see 5.33)? It presumably includes the defence of prevention of crime and goes very much further.

Further proposals for reform

7.39 The Law Commission has continued to work in this area: first, they produced a Consultation Paper (No. 183 (2007)), on *Conspiracy and Attempts*. On conspiracy, they proposed that a person who agrees to commit an offence ('a principal offence') should in general be guilty of conspiracy if he was reckless as to the possible existence of a circumstance element of the principal offence. An example they give is that a person who agrees to 'launder' money commits conspiracy if he suspects that the money might be the proceeds of criminal conduct even if he does not know or intend that it is. This is of course a very different test to that laid down in *Saik* (2006) (see 7.21). On attempt, they proposed that s 1(1) of the CAA 1981 should be repealed and replaced by two separate inchoate offences, both of which would require an intention to commit the relevant substantive offence:

(1) *an offence of criminal attempt, limited to last acts needed to commit the intended offence; and*

(2) *an offence of criminal preparation, limited to acts of preparation which are properly to be regarded as part of the execution of the plan to commit the intended offence.*

Their final Report No. 318 (2009) recommends on conspiracy that:

> ...it should be possible to charge conspiracy when conspirators deliberately take a risk that they will engage in criminal activity (e.g. where they agree to handle large amounts of cash, realising that the cash might be the proceeds of crime). Clearly, this would be a broadening of the current law. They conclude that the Saik test needs amending, not least because it is inconsistent with the fault requirements respecting circumstance elements in the offences of encouraging or assisting crime [see 7.34]. If D is charged with encouraging or assisting crime, he or she need only be proved to have been reckless with regard to whether or not the circumstance element would exist at the time that the substantive offence was to be committed. The Law Commission see no reason why the fault element with regard to circumstance elements should necessarily be much more stringent for conspiracy than it is for encouraging or assisting crime. [I would suggest that the existing Saik test is better: see my comments at 7.21.]
>
> The rule that prevents married couples from being charged with conspiring to commit a crime should be abolished.

A new defence of reasonableness to a charge of conspiracy should be introduced (available, for example, to an undercover police officer entering into a conspiracy in order at a later point to expose the other participants).

On attempt, the principal change they recommend is that it should be possible to charge a person (D) with attempted murder if D endeavoured to kill someone (V) by not doing what he or she was legally required to do in relation to V. Thus, if a father or mother (D) decided to kill their child (V) by not providing the child with food, and had gone some way towards achieving that objective, it would be possible to charge D with the attempted murder of V by starvation.

Encouraging or assisting suicide

7.40 Suicide itself ceased to be a crime in the Suicide Act 1961, but s 2 made clear that a person who aids, abets, counsels, or procures the suicide of another or an attempt by another to commit suicide, should be liable on conviction on indictment to 14 years' imprisonment.

McShane **(1977)** D encouraged her mother to commit suicide so that she could inherit her money. She was convicted of attempting to counsel or procure her mother's suicide, contrary to the Suicide Act 1961, s 2 and with attempting to cause to be taken by her mother a destructive or noxious thing so as to endanger life, contrary to the OAPA 1861, s 23.

CA (Orr LJ): dismissed her appeal. The Court went so far as to say that no consent can render a dangerous act innocent, but that statement is too broad (see **5.6**).

Pretty v DPP **(2001)** P, who was terminally ill, wanted reassurance from the DPP that if her husband helped her to die he would not be prosecuted. She challenged the DPP's refusal to undertake not to give his consent to a prosecution of P's husband for aiding, abetting, counselling, or procuring her suicide contrary to the Suicide Act 1961, s 2(1).

HL: dismissed P's appeal from the DC. P's rights under Arts 2, 3, and 8 of the ECHR were not contravened. Whilst the DPP may make policy statements, as a rule a decision of the DPP was not amenable to judicial review where there was no dishonesty or *mala fides*.

ECtHR (2002): unanimously declared her application inadmissible. Article 2 extends to a right to live, not a right to die. The ECtHR differed from the HL in holding that Art 8 was engaged, but it did not assist P as the provisions of the Suicide Act did not amount to a disproportionate interference with her rights: the ECtHR leaves a 'margin of appreciation' to individual states.

(See also *S* (2005), at **7.12**), where the CA upheld the conviction of a boy for attempting to aid, abet, counsel, or procure another to commit suicide.)

R (Purdy) v DPP (2009) P sought a clarification from the DPP of the policy grounds on which he makes decisions whether to consent to a prosecution under s 2(1) of the Suicide Act 1961.

HL: unanimously allowed her appeal, requiring the DPP:

> …to promulgate an offence-specific policy identifying the facts and circumstances which he will take into account in deciding, in a case such as that which Ms Purdy's case exemplifies, whether or not to consent to a prosecution under section 2(1) of the 1961 Act (Lord Hope, para. 56).

It was 'plain' when the judgment in *Pretty v United Kingdom* (2002) is read as a whole:

> …that the Strasbourg court did find that Mrs. Pretty's rights under article 8(1) [see **1.25**] were engaged. It said so in terms in the first sentence of para. 87, where it referred in a footnote to its discussion of the issue in paras 61 to 67. That sentence removes any doubt that the words used in para. 67 might give rise to … even if there was a doubt as to whether article 8(1) was engaged in Mrs. Pretty's case, the same cannot be said in the case of Ms Purdy. It seems to me that her situation is addressed directly by what the Strasbourg court said in para. 65 of its judgment...
>
> I would therefore depart from the decision in *R (Pretty) v Director of Public Prosecutions (Secretary of State for the Home Department Intervening)* [2002] 1 AC 800 and hold that the right to respect for private life in article 8(1) is engaged in this case (Lord Hope, paras 38–9).

The law has to be accessible and foreseeable. The Director's own analysis shows that, in a highly unusual and extremely sensitive case of this kind, the Code offers almost no guidance at all. The question whether a prosecution is in the public interest can only be answered by bringing into account factors that are not mentioned there (Lord Hope, para. 53).

Baroness Hale was more specific:

> If it is the Convention which is leading us to ask the Director for greater clarity, a relevant question must be in what circumstances the law is justified in interfering with a genuinely autonomous choice (at para. 69).

Lord Hope and Lord Phillips queried whether s 2(1) of the 1961 Act covered acts done in England which aid and abet a suicide which is to be assisted in another jurisdiction where such acts are lawful. Lord Hope concluded that it did, whereas Lord Phillips' provisional conclusion was that:

> …section 1 does not apply to suicide committed outside England and Wales. If that falls to be treated as murder, so that assisting it is also murder, it would seem to follow that if a British subject accompanies a relative, who is also a British subject, to Switzerland

> and assists in Switzerland the relative to commit suicide with help from Dignitas, that
> person will under English law commit the crime of murder and will be subject to the
> jurisdiction of the courts of England and Wales in relation to that offence. It must be a
> moot point whether, in respect of acts of assistance that take place in this jurisdiction
> in relation to suicide that takes place in Switzerland, section 2(1) applies so as to reduce
> the offence from murder to one under section 2(1). Logically it seems to me that it
> should not, but plainly considerations of legislative policy would weigh the other way
> (paras 12–13).

As a result, the DPP adopted new guidelines on prosecuting policy: see <www.cps.gov.uk/publications/prosecution/assisted_suicide_policy.html>. But that will not be the end of the matter! Nobles and Schiff (2010) provocatively ask whether the case signals a legal right to civil disobedience.

7.41   Meanwhile, s 59 of the Coroners and Justice Act 2009 has created a new inchoate offence of encouraging and assisting suicide, replacing the original s 2 of the Suicide Act 1961 with the following complex provision:

(1)   A person ('D') commits an offence if—

   (a)   D does an act capable of encouraging or assisting the suicide or attempted suicide of another person, and

   (b)   D's act was intended to encourage or assist suicide or an attempt at suicide.

(1A)   The person referred to in subsection (1)(a) need not be a specific person (or class of persons) known to, or identified by, D.

(1B)   D may commit an offence under this section whether or not a suicide, or an attempt at suicide, occurs.

(1C)   An offence under this section is triable on indictment and a person convicted of such an offence is liable to imprisonment for a term not exceeding 14 years.

The provision gets yet more complex, as s 59 provides that after s 2 there shall be inserted:

2A Acts capable of encouraging or assisting

(1)   If D arranges for a person ('D2') to do an act that is capable of encouraging or assisting the suicide or attempted suicide of another person and D2 does that act, D is also to be treated for the purposes of this Act as having done it.

(2)   Where the facts are such that an act is not capable of encouraging or assisting suicide or attempted suicide, for the purposes of this Act it is to be treated as so capable if the act would have been so capable had the facts been as D believed them to be at the time of the act or had subsequent events happened in the manner D believed they would happen (or both).

(3) A reference in this Act to a person ('P') doing an act that is capable of encouraging the suicide or attempted suicide of another person includes a reference to P doing so by threatening another person or otherwise putting pressure on another person to commit or attempt suicide.

2B Course of conduct

A reference in this Act to an act includes a reference to a course of conduct, and a reference to doing an act is to be read accordingly.

7.42 This new offence came into force on 1 February 2010. Why did Parliament consider it to be necessary? Section 1 of the CAA 1981 (see **7.4**) already makes it an offence to attempt to aid, abet, counsel, or procure the suicide or attempted suicide of another person (the attempt offence). So s 59 replaces the substantive and attempt offences with a single offence, supposedly to simplify and modernize the law. The person committing the new offence need not know, or even be able to identify, the other person. Thus, the author of a website promoting suicide who intends that one or more of his or her readers will commit or attempt to commit suicide is guilty of an offence, even though he or she may never know the identity of those who access the website. The offence applies whether or not a person commits or attempts suicide. Clearly, there is widespread confusion at the moment as to whether and, if so, to what extent the law should recognize either euthanasia, or an offence of 'mercy' killing or a partial defence of 'mercy' or consensual killing. But that is a different issue (see **8.45**) and is no excuse for such complicated new legislation!

FURTHER READING

Ashworth, A., 'Defining Criminal Offences Without Harm' in P. Smith (ed.), *Criminal Law Essays* (1987).

Glazebrook, P.,'Should We Have a Law of Attempted Crime?' (1969) 85 LQR 27.

Harding, C, 'The Offence of Belonging: Capturing Participation in Organised Crime' [2005] Crim LR 690.

Law Commission, *Assisting and Encouraging Crime* (LCCP No. 131, 1993).

Law Commission, *Inchoate Liability for Assisting and Encouraging Crime* (Report No. 300, 2006).

Law Commission, *Conspiracy and Attempts* (LCCP No. 183, 2007).

Law Commission, *Participating in Crime* (Report No. 305, 2007).

Law Commission, *Conspiracy and Attempts* (Law Com No. 318, 2009).

Nobles, R. and Schiff, D., 'Disobedience to Law—Debbie Purdy's Case' (2010) MLR 295.

Ormerod, D. and Fortson, R., 'Serious Crime Act 2007: The Part 2 Offences' [2009] Crim LR 389.

Smith, K. J. M., 'Proximity in Attempt: Lord Lane's "Midway Course"' [1991] Crim LR 576.

Spencer, J. R. 'Trying to Help Another Commit a Crime' in P. Smith (ed.), *Criminal Law Essays* (1987).

Stark, F., ' Encouraging or Assisting Clarity?' (2013) 72 Camb LJ 497.

Sullivan, G. R., 'Inchoate Liability for Encouraging Crime' [2006] Crim LR 1047.

Virgo, G., '*R v Sadique*: Making Sense of s. 46 of the SCA 2007' (2013) 7 *Archbold Review* 4.

Williams, G., 'The Lords and Impossible Attempts, or Quis Custodiet Ipsos Custodes?' (1986) 45 Camb LJ 33.

Williams, G., 'Wrong Turning on the Law of Attempt' [1991] Crim LR 416.

SELF-TEST QUESTIONS

1   In the pub one night, Dee tells Andy the barman that she wishes Phil was dead. She then telephones Phil and threatens to kill him within the next month. She writes to Bob offering him £5,000 to kill Phil and posts the letter. Bob receives the letter and agrees to kill Phil. He finds him apparently asleep in the park and shoots him at close range through the head. Unknown to either Dee or Bob, Phil had already been dead for three hours at the time he was shot. Explore all the possible inchoate offences to be found in this sorry tale.

2   Dee tells Bob that she would like him to blackmail Phil for her and that if he is not prepared to help, she would like him to find someone else who is prepared to do so. Discuss Dee's liability.

3   Dee decides to rob a bank. She tells Fee her plans and asks for her help, saying that they can then share the proceeds. Fee tells her that she will help but, in fact, Fee tells the police of the plan. Dee is arrested the next day. Discuss Dee's liability.

4   Dee offers to drive a getaway car for Carla whom she believes to be planning a burglary. The police learn of the offer and Dee is arrested. Carla denies that she planned a burglary. What crimes (if any) has Dee committed?

8 Homicide

SUMMARY

Murder: killing with the intention to kill or to cause GBH. The main problems lie in defining (not inferring) intent.

Voluntary manslaughter: specific partial defences, each of which causes difficulties in interpretation:

s 2 HA 1957 (as amended by s 52 of the C&JA 2009): 'diminished responsibility'. extremely vague test of abnormality.

s 54 C&JA 2009: 'loss of control' (replaces provocation, s 3 HA 1957). First CA ruling, *Clinton* (2012), confirmed complexity!

s 4 HA 1957: suicide pact: is this necessary?

Involuntary manslaughter: note the overlap between 'constructive manslaughter' (D does an intentional, unlawful, and dangerous act which causes death), reckless manslaughter, and the re-emerged gross negligence manslaughter (vague: what is the duty of care?). Causation issues. All too broad?

Frequent proposals for reform: Law Com No. 237 (1996) *Legislating the Criminal Code: Involuntary Manslaughter*; LCCP No. 173 (2003) *Partial Defences to Murder* (followed by their Report No. 290, 2004), LCCP No. 177 (2005) *A New Homicide Act for England and Wales?*; Law Com No. 304 (2006) *Murder, Manslaughter and Infanticide*: first degree and second degree murder ... Eventually led to the Coroners and Justice Act 2009 reforms, but they are different to the Law Com proposals.

8.1 Homicide is the word used to describe any unlawful killing of a human being. The most common homicide offences in English law are murder and manslaughter, but there are others: for example, infanticide, child destruction, causing death by dangerous or careless driving. The difference between murder and manslaughter is vital since anyone convicted of murder is subject to a mandatory life sentence of imprisonment (until 1965 the death penalty was imposed for murder). Even though it is rare for a mandatory life sentence prisoner to serve the rest of his or her life in prison, the trial judge may impose a 'whole life' tariff. Lifers, even if released, remain on licence and liable to recall for the rest of their lives, if their behaviour causes their probation officer concern (i.e. you do not have to commit a fresh offence to be recalled to prison). The complex sentencing framework was radically altered in the CJA 2003, and lies outside the scope of this book. But it is important to note that in the case of those convicted of manslaughter, the sentencing judge may impose any sentence, from life to a non-custodial penalty (and that the Law Commission proposed in 2006 a distinction between first degree and second degree murder in part in order to limit the impact of the mandatory life sentence).

8.2   The arguments concerning the various elements of the law of murder and manslaughter in England are thus often clouded by the existence of the mandatory life sentence for all murderers. If you were starting from scratch, or if the mandatory life sentence were abolished, would you distinguish between varying degrees of culpable homicide? There is a world of difference between the person who deliberately kills someone in cold blood, and the person who causes death by his gross negligence. Despite the sentencing differences, there are good arguments based on fair labelling (see 1.2) that the more heinous killings should be distinguished from other, less culpable, killings. If we accept that there should be different categories of culpable homicide, does English law draw the line in appropriate places? It is astonishing that the borderlines between murder and manslaughter, and between manslaughter and no criminal liability, remain so unclear. Confusion may also be created by the terminology: many of the terms used (voluntary and involuntary manslaughter, malice aforethought) have little meaning in ordinary modern English. The need for an updated law is evident and this chapter makes frequent reference to recent Law Commission reports. But, disappointingly, recent reforms have focused on the partial defences, not on the overall structure.

Murder

Actus reus

8.3   The *actus reus* of both murder and manslaughter is the killing of a person. Thus, any act which shortens life may amount to murder. Students should re-read 2.12, etc., where the problems of causation were explored: for example, it is important to remember that the *de minimis* rule means that D's act must be a substantial cause of the victim's death. Note the interpretation of a 'person': any child born alive is a person, but a foetus is not.

> *A-G's Reference (No. 3 of 1994)* (1997) D stabbed his girlfriend whom he knew to be pregnant. The girlfriend recovered, but V, her baby, was born prematurely as a

result of the wound and died after 120 days. The trial judge held that D could not be convicted of murder or manslaughter and ordered D's acquittal.

HL: D was rightly acquitted of murder; malice could not be transferred twice (see **3.33**). A foetus cannot be treated as part of the mother but as a unique organism. Murder could not be committed where unlawful injury was deliberately inflicted on the mother where the child was subsequently born alive and enjoyed an existence independent of its mother before it died, even though the injuries inflicted *in utero* contributed substantially to the death. However, liability for manslaughter could be established: (see **8.25**). Lord Mustill announces towards the beginning of his speech that:

> …the law of homicide is permeated by anomaly, fiction, misnomer and obsolete reasoning.

This speech is well worth reading as a thorough, and highly critical, review of the historical development of the offences of murder and manslaughter.

Year and a day rule

8.4 Until 1996, D's conduct had to cause death within a year and a day. This rule made good sense in days gone by when any longer period could have raised questions about whether it really was D's act which caused V's death. However, the rule came under increasing criticism, especially as modern medicine and life-support machines meant that a murderer could avoid liability simply because of lengthy medical attempts to save someone's life. In 1995 both the House of Commons' Select Committee on Home Affairs and the Law Commission produced papers recommending the abolition of the rule, and this Parliament did in the Law Reform (Abolition of the Year and a Day Rule) Act 1996. The Act does provide a safeguard against prosecutions long after the event: the consent of the A-G is needed for proceedings against a person for a 'fatal offence' if either the injury alleged to have caused the death was sustained more than three years before the death occurred, or the person to be prosecuted has previously been convicted of an offence committed in circumstances alleged to be connected with the death.

Mens rea

8.5 The *mens rea* of murder is 'malice aforethought'. Perhaps surprisingly, this has long been interpreted to include not only an intention to kill, but also an intention to cause grievous bodily harm (GBH). The meaning of intention was discussed at **3.2**. After the Homicide Act (HA) 1957, s 1 had abolished constructive malice, there was some doubt as to whether in future an intention merely to cause GBH would be enough to constitute murder, but the following case removed all doubt:

***Vickers* (1957)**   D broke into the cellar of a shop with intent to steal. When disturbed by V, a woman of 73, he kicked and punched her. She died of the injuries she sustained.

CCA: upheld D's murder conviction. Section 1 did not abolish implied malice, i.e. the implication of malice aforethought from a voluntary act inflicting GBH and causing death. As Lord Goddard CJ said:

> Murder is, of course, killing with malice aforethought, but 'malice aforethought' is a term of art. It has always been defined in English law as, either an express intention to kill, as could be inferred when a person, having uttered threats against another, produced a lethal weapon and used it on a victim, or implied, where, by a voluntary act, the accused intended to cause grievous bodily harm he cannot say that he only intended to cause a certain degree of harm. It is called *malum in se* in the old cases and he must take the consequences. If he intends to inflict grievous bodily harm and that person dies, that has always been held in English law, and was at the time this Act was passed, sufficient to imply the malice aforethought which is a necessary constituent of murder.

8.6   In practical terms this decision is useful: it is often difficult to prove that D intended to kill, but if he shows such disregard for human life that he beats someone up sufficiently badly to kill them, most people are happy to say he is a murderer. But it does raise a question of principle: if D merely intends GBH and V happens unfortunately to die, is this not more appropriately described as manslaughter? Merely doing an act with the knowledge that it is highly probable that death or serious bodily harm will result is not enough to constitute the *mens rea* of murder. However, if the jury accept that D had such knowledge, it is open to them to infer that he had the required intent: see the discussion of *Moloney, Hancock and Shankland, Nedrick, and Woollin* at **3.9–3.11**. Lord Mustill said in *A-G's Reference (No. 3 of 1994)* (1997, see **8.3**) that the GBH rule:

> ...is an outcropping of old law from which the surrounding strata of rationalisations have weathered away. It survives but exemplifies no principle which can be applied to a new situation.

Possible reform

8.7   Clause 54 of the DCC (1989) proposed that:

(1) A person is guilty of murder if he causes the death of another—

    (a) intending to cause death

    (b) intending to cause serious personal harm and being aware that he may cause death, unless section 56 (diminished responsibility), 58 (provocation), 59 (use of excessive force) or 64 (infanticide) applies.

This proposal would have modified the present law in various respects. First, an intention to cause serious personal harm would only constitute a sufficient fault for murder if D was also aware that he might cause death. This would rarely pose an evidential problem in practice and might have been a useful narrowing of the definition. Secondly, the definition of intention in the DCC is wider than that presently used in the definition of murder (see 3.10). Under *Nedrick* (1986) and *Woollin* (1999) the jury may infer intent if they believe that D knew that death was virtually certain to result from his act. Under the DCC (clause 18(b)(i)), as we saw at 3.11, D *intends* to kill if he is aware that death will occur in the normal course of events. Does this accord with your understanding of the word? It is also worth noting that the DCC talked of 'causing death': this is wide enough to include deaths caused by omissions (see 2.6). We come later to the Law Commission's Consultation Paper No. 177 (2005) and their Report No. 304 (2006), which suggested 'first degree' and 'second degree' murder: see 8.46. But the Law Commission changed their minds about where to draw the line between the two (and the line between second degree murder and manslaughter). So the distinction between murder and manslaughter will remain for the time being: and murder remains intentionally causing death or GBH.

Voluntary manslaughter

8.8 The HA 1957 introduced three 'partial defences' to murder. Thus where a person intentionally killed someone but whilst under diminished responsibility, or loss of control, or in furtherance of a suicide pact, that person could only be convicted of manslaughter. Thus the term 'voluntary manslaughter' means an offence which would be murder but for the existence of a 'partial defence' (and so serves to avoid the mandatory life sentence for murder). Major changes were enacted in the Coroners and Justice Act (C&JA) 2009, which came into force on 4 October 2010.

Diminished responsibility

8.9 The original HA 1957, s 2 provided:

(1) Where a person kills or is a party to a killing of another, he shall not be convicted of murder if he was suffering from such abnormality of mind (whether arising from a condition of arrested or retarded development of

mind or any inherent causes or induced by disease or injury) as substantially impaired his mental responsibility for his acts and omissions in doing or being a party to the killing.

(2) On a charge of murder, it shall be for the defence to prove that the person charged is by virtue of this section not liable to be convicted of murder.

(3) A person who but for this section would be liable, whether as principal or as accessory, to be convicted of murder shall be liable instead to be convicted of manslaughter.

(4) The fact that one party to a killing is by virtue of this section not liable to be convicted of murder shall not affect the question whether the killing amounted to murder in the case of any other party to it.

Section 52 of the C&JA 2009 now provides:

s 52 (1) In section 2 of the Homicide Act 1957 for subsection (1) substitute—

'(1) A person ('D') who kills or is a party to the killing of another is not to be convicted of murder if D was suffering from an abnormality of mental functioning which—

(a) arose from a recognised medical condition,

(b) substantially impaired D's ability to do one or more of the things mentioned in subsection (1A), and

(c) provides an explanation for D's acts and omissions in doing or being a party to the killing.

(1A) Those things are—

(a) to understand the nature of D's conduct;

(b) to form a rational judgment;

(c) to exercise self-control.

(1B) For the purposes of subsection (1)(c), an abnormality of mental functioning provides an explanation for D's conduct if it causes, or is a significant contributory factor in causing, D to carry out that conduct.'

8.10 Clearly the definition of the original HA was remarkably loose: what is an 'abnormality of mind' which substantially impairs mental responsibility? Is an 'abnormality of mental functioning' arising from a 'recognised medical condition' any clearer? Clearly, if D is insane within the meaning of the *M'Naghten Rules* (see **4.9**), then she will be acquitted. Maybe the law is rightly vague? Griew (1988) argued that the original s 2 was so badly worded that it could be made to work and to work better than its framers intended. The fact that s 2 encourages role confusion between judge, jury, and psychiatrists is both its main advantage and its main disadvantage.

It may sometimes work well in practice as a means of avoiding a mandatory life sentence for those who juries decide do not deserve it. But does the defence hand power to juries, or to the psychiatrists whose evidence they receive? The Lane Committee (1989), in arguing against a mandatory life sentence for murder, concluded that the medical profession stretch s 2 out of motives of humanity. The Law Commission in Consultation Paper No. 177 (2005) pointed out that if all the partial defences were abolished, defence teams would no longer have to choose between incompatible defences, and diminished responsibility could be available for consideration on conviction, as a sentencing matter. (It is also worth noting that the CA in *Foye* (2013) confirmed that the new law maintains the reverse burden of proof, in that it is up to D to prove on the balance of probabilities that he was in a state of diminished responsibility at the time of the killing.)

Diminished responsibility and intoxication

8.11 Some of the biggest problems in practice arise where the person who suffers from an 'abnormality of mental functioning' is also drunk when they commit their crime. Where D has taken drugs or alcohol, the jury must disregard this unless alcoholism can be proved as a recognized medical condition. Asking a jury to ignore causes of abnormality which fall outside s 2 can give them a pretty impossible task:

> *Tandy* (1989) D, an alcoholic, strangled her 11-year-old daughter after discovering that the girl was suffering sexual abuse at the hands of D's boyfriend. D had that day drunk most of a bottle of vodka.
>
> CA (Watkins LJ): upheld her conviction for murder. Faced with a conflict of medical evidence on whether alcoholism is a disease of the mind and whether D's drinking was 'voluntary' or not, Watkins LJ decided that the real question was whether her abnormality of mind was a direct result of her alcoholism or a result of the fact that she was drunk on vodka. Where D had simply not resisted the impulse to drink, she could not rely on the defence of diminished responsibility.

8.12 Would this case be decided in the same way today? By dismissing her appeal, the CA was upholding the mandatory life sentence on Mrs Tandy (who shortly afterwards committed suicide in prison). There were a number of difficult cases under the old s 2 (see *Dietschmann* (2003), for example) but the law now appears to be more straighforward:

> *Dowds* (2012) D, a college lecturer with no previous convictions, was a heavy drinker. He had been drinking heavily when he had an argument with V, his partner, and killed her. He had inflicted 60 knife wounds. Nearly two days later, he phoned the police to report V's death. At the beginning of the trial, the judge ruled that voluntary

and temporary drunkenness could not found the defence of diminished responsibility under the Homicide Act 1957, s 2. So, diminished responsibility was not left to the jury. The jury found that D had intended serious harm and rejected the partial defence of loss of control. He was convicted of murder. D argued on appeal that acute intoxication was acknowledged as a 'recognised medical condition' by virtue of its classification in the International Statistical Classification of Diseases and Related Health Problems (ICD), and that as he was suffering from it when he killed V and it could well have affected the functions listed in s 2(1A) of the 1957 Act, diminished responsibility should have been left to the jury.

CA: dismissed the appeal. D's argument bypassed the clear general law against which the amendment to s 2 of the 1957 Act was enacted. The s 2 amendment had not disturbed the exception which prevented D from relying on voluntary drunkenness, save upon the limited question of whether specific intent had been formed (referring to *Wood* (2008) and *Majewski* (1977): see **4.19**. Had Parliament intended to alter the law, it would have made its intention explicitly clear. Such an intention could not be inferred from the adoption of the new formulation of the expression 'recognised medical condition', as the origins of that had been clearly explained by the Law Commission and they explicitly did not include writing the terms of the ICD or the Diagnostic and Statistical Manual into the legislation. Those terms were demonstrably unsuited to that purpose. It was possible that there might be genuine mental conditions, which were not D's fault and well recognized by doctors, which although temporary might be within the ambit of the 1957 Act. The re-formulation of the statutory conditions for diminished responsibility had not been intended to reverse the well-established rule that voluntary acute intoxication was not capable of being relied upon to found diminished responsibility. The presence of a recognized medical condition was a necessary, but not always sufficient, condition to raise the defence.

This case was only concerned with intoxication which is (a) voluntary and (b) uncomplicated by any alcoholism or dependence. We will have to wait and see if the decision in *Tandy* (1989) is subsequently overruled.

Loss of control

8.13 The HA 1957, s 3 (now repealed) provided a second partial defence, known as provocation, which reduced murder to manslaughter:

Where on a charge of murder there is evidence on which the jury can find that the person charged was provoked (whether by things done or by things said or by both together) to lose his self-control, the question whether the provocation was enough to make a reasonable man do as he did shall be left to be determined by the jury; and in determining that question the jury shall take into account everything both done and said according to the effect which, in their opinion, it would have on the reasonable man.

This defence was subject to huge criticisms and a wide variety of proposed reforms. The first concern was whether the criminal law, in excusing loss of self-control, was legitimizing violent responses. Or whether the courts, in interpreting this loss of control narrowly, were discriminating against victims of domestic violence who killed their husbands—did they really lose control? (*Thornton* (1992) and (1995) and Padfield (1996)). Secondly, the 'reasonable man' test proved very difficult to apply in practice. What were the relevant characteristics of the 'reasonable man' against whom D should be measured? There were many contradictory cases, and dramatically the PC in *A-G for Jersey v Holley* (2005) had appeared to overrule the HL in *Smith* (2000).

8.14 But all that is history. Before exploring the new statutory provision, let's look at some Law Commission proposals which led to the changes. They faced a conundrum: was it possible to define a partial defence of provocation which removed 'the evaluative free for all' of the current law and which did not appear as a charter for domestic violence? In their Provisional Conclusions on LCCP No. 173 (2004), concluding that the law of provocation was 'most unsatisfactory', the Law Commission had suggested that the trigger should be gross provocation ('words or conduct which caused the defendant to have a justifiable sense of being seriously wronged') or fear of serious violence, or a combination of both. There should also be an objective test: the defence should only be available if a person of ordinary temperament might have reacted in a similar way. Unfortunately they did not focus attention on the unfairness of the mandatory life sentence: it is in large measure the rigid sentencing framework which has led to the current uncertainties. But when, in 2005, the Government announced a review of the law of murder, they said it should 'take account of the continued existence of the mandatory life sentence for murder'.

The Law Commission stuck to this brief and Consultation Paper No. 177 merely proposed that the principles recommended in LCCP No. 173 should govern the defence. They proposed 'first degree' and 'second degree' murder: the partial defence of provocation would reduce 'first degree' murder to 'second degree' murder, not to manslaughter. But this is not what the Government then adopted. They have 'cherry picked' from the Law Commission's recommendations (see Miles (2009) for a feisty critique).

8.15 The new partial defence of 'loss of control' is to be found in s 54 of the C&JA 2009. You should note that, whereas the old s 3 defence merely supplemented the existing common law, the new law abolished both the common law and the old s 3 (see s 56 of the C&JA 2009). Section 54 provides:

s 54 Partial defence to murder: loss of control

(1) Where a person ('D') kills or is a party to the killing of another ('V'), D is not to be convicted of murder if—

    (a) D's acts and omissions in doing or being a party to the killing resulted from D's loss of self-control,

    (b) the loss of self-control had a qualifying trigger, and

    (c) a person of D's sex and age, with a normal degree of tolerance and self-restraint and in the circumstances of D, might have reacted in the same or in a similar way to D.

(2) For the purposes of subsection (1)(a), it does not matter whether or not the loss of control was sudden.

(3) In subsection (1)(c) the reference to 'the circumstances of D' is a reference to all of D's circumstances other than those whose only relevance to D's conduct is that they bear on D's general capacity for tolerance or self-restraint.

(4) Subsection (1) does not apply if, in doing or being a party to the killing, D acted in a considered desire for revenge.

(5) On a charge of murder, if sufficient evidence is adduced to raise an issue with respect to the defence under subsection (1), the jury must assume that the defence is satisfied unless the prosecution proves beyond reasonable doubt that it is not.

(6) For the purposes of subsection (5), sufficient evidence is adduced to raise an issue with respect to the defence if evidence is adduced on which, in the opinion of the trial judge, a jury, properly directed, could reasonably conclude that the defence might apply.

(7) A person who, but for this section, would be liable to be convicted of murder is liable instead to be convicted of manslaughter.

(8) The fact that one party to a killing is by virtue of this section not liable to be convicted of murder does not affect the question whether the killing amounted to murder in the case of any other party to it.

As we will see, it is not clear that this law is any better than the old!

8.16 This new partial defence is made up of three components, all of which must be proved:

    (i) D must have lost self-control;

(ii) because of a qualifying trigger; and

(iii) a person of D's sex and age, with a normal degree of tolerance and self-restraint and in the circumstances of D, might have reacted in the same or in a similar way to D.

8.17 Section 54 makes clear that the loss of control need not be sudden, but D must not have 'acted in a considered desire for revenge'. D must have lost control because of one of the 'qualifying triggers' outlined in s 55. D's loss of self-control must be attributable to either, or a combination of both:

- D's fear of serious violence from V against D or another identified person; or

- a thing or things done or said (or both) which—

  (a) constituted circumstances of an extremely grave character, and

  (b) caused D to have a justifiable sense of being seriously wronged.

To make matters more complex: see s 55(6) of the C&JA 2009:

In determining whether a loss of self-control had a qualifying trigger—

(a) D's fear of serious violence is to be disregarded to the extent that it was caused by a thing which D incited to be done or said for the purpose of providing an excuse to use violence;

(b) a sense of being seriously wronged by a thing done or said is not justifiable if D incited the thing to be done or said for the purpose of providing an excuse to use violence;

(c) the fact that a thing done or said constituted sexual infidelity is to be disregarded.

The interpretation of these new tests (the meaning of a 'justifiable sense of being seriously wronged' and of 'sexual infidelity', for example) is now challenging the CA:

Clinton; Parker; Evans **(2012)** The appeal involved three separate cases in which husbands had killed their wives, and sought to raise the defence of 'loss of control'. In C's case, the trial judge had not left 'loss of control' to the jury, in large measure because he held that the V's 'sexual infidelity' could not constitute a qualifying trigger.

CA (Lord Judge): quashed C's conviction and ordered a retrial (the other two appeals were dismissed). He identified the three statutory components of the 'loss of control' defence, but concluded that they cannot be viewed out of context:

...to seek to compartmentalise sexual infidelity and exclude it when it is integral to the facts as a whole is not only much more difficult, but is unrealistic and carries with it the potential for injustice. In the examples we have given earlier in this judgment, we do not see how any sensible evaluation of the gravity of the circumstances or their impact on D could be made if the jury, having, in accordance with the legislation, heard the evidence, were then to be directed to excise from their evaluation of the qualifying trigger the matters said to constitute sexual infidelity, and to put them into distinct compartments to be disregarded. In our judgment, where sexual infidelity is integral to and forms an essential part of the context in which to make a just evaluation whether a qualifying trigger properly falls within the ambit of subsections 55(3) and (4), the prohibition in section 55(6)(c) does not operate to exclude it (para. 39).

The Court is gently critical of the legislation:

Unfortunately there are aspects of the legislation which, to put it with appropriate deference, are likely to produce surprising results (para. 2).

This is certainly true when it comes to sexual infidelity: as Stark (2012) argues, in reality it is often very difficult to know whether V's sexual infidelity is a context for D's loss of control, or the 'cause' of it. Wake (2013), to my mind, is convincing in arguing that:

... it seems perverse to continue to allow the defence for all sudden provocations other than those that touch on intimate relationships including marriage. This is unrealistic and reflects an extreme ideological, individualistic view of marriage and of personal sexual relationship (at p. 512).

Dawes (2013)   Three separate appeals were heard together. In the first two cases, the trial judges had refused to leave the defence of loss of control to the jury. In the third, the defence had been left to the jury: D said he used force on V because he was in fear of serious violence from V and that V had made hurtful remarks about someone which were immensely provocative to D. The jury asked for clarification on whether they could look to conduct and events prior to the incident in assessing the 'qualifying trigger'. The trial judge directed that they should consider things said, and/or done, both on the day of the incident and in the period beforehand. D argued that the judge should have said more.

CA dismissed all three appeals. The LCJ said:

...the circumstances in which the qualifying triggers will arise is much more limited than the equivalent provisions in the former provocation defence. The result is that some of the more absurd trivia which nevertheless required the judge to leave the provocation defence to the jury will no longer fall within the ambit of the qualifying triggers defined in the new defence. This is unsurprising. For the individual with normal capacity of self-restraint and tolerance, unless the circumstances are extremely grave, normal irritation, and even serious anger do not often cross the threshold into loss of control.

The presence, or otherwise, of a qualifying trigger is not defined or decided by D and any assertions he may make in evidence, or any account given in the investigative process. S.55(3) directly engages D's fear of serious violence. As we have explained, in this type of case s.55(4) will almost inevitably arise for consideration. Unless D has a sense of being *seriously* wronged s.55(4) has no application. Even if it does, there are two distinctive further requirements. The circumstances must be *extremely* grave and the defendant's sense of being seriously wronged by them must be *justifiable*. In our judgment these matters require objective assessment by the judge at the end of the evidence and, if the defence is left, by the jury considering their verdict (paras 60–1).

Loss of control and other defences

8.18   Whilst the courts are wise to try to limit the scope of this partial defence, the question remains: why should there be a partial defence for those who lose control? There is already a defence of self-defence, which allows for complete acquital when applicable (see **5.33–5.37**). D's advisers are often in something of a quandary. If they raise a defence of self-defence, for example, which would result in an acquittal, it will be difficult for them to argue at the same time that D lost control. The two defences may run counter to each other. In such a case, the judge should sometimes himself put the partial defence to the jury, even if the defence did not raise it. Lord Judge, the LCJ, explained the relationship between these two defences in *Dawes* in this way:

> The circumstances in which D, who has lost control of himself, will nevertheless be able to argue that he used reasonable force in response to the violence he feared, or to which he was subjected, are likely to be limited. But even if D may have lost his self-control, provided his violent response in self-defence was not unreasonable in the circumstances, he would be entitled to rely on self defence as a complete defence. S.55(3) is focussed on D's fear of serious violence. We underline the distinction between the terms of the qualifying trigger in the context of loss of control with self-defence, which is concerned with the threat of violence in any form. Obviously, if D genuinely fears serious violence then, in the context of self-defence, his own response may legitimately be more extreme. Weighing these considerations, it is likely that in the forensic process those acting for D will advance self-defence as a complete answer to the murder charge, and on occasions, make little or nothing of D's response in the context of the loss of control defence. As we have already indicated, the decision taken on forensic grounds (whether the judge believes it to be wise or not) is not binding on the judge and, provided the statutory conditions obtain, loss of control should be left to the jury. Almost always, we suggest, the practical course, if the defence is to be left, is to leave it for the consideration of the jury after it has rejected self-defence (para. 59).

For a discussion of the effect of mistaken beliefs, see **4.24** and **5.27**. Note in particular that the CA in *Hatton* (2005) held that the decision in *O'Grady* (1987, see **4.24**) applies equally to murder as to manslaughter: if D relies on self-defence, he cannot rely on a mistake induced by voluntary intoxication. The CA has been very clear that the normal rules on intoxication apply to this new partial defence:

Asmelash **(2013)** D and V lived in the same house and often used to drink together. D stabbed V in the chest, penetrating his heart and lung. Both were intoxicated at the time of the killing. D gave evidence that V had been aggressive and physically abusive towards him, and that he had swung out at him with a knife because he was frightened. V had made him so angry that he could not control himself. The trial judge directed the jury to consider whether they were sure that a person of D's sex and age with a normal degree of tolerance and self-restraint and in the same circumstances, but unaffected by alcohol, would not have reacted in the same or similar way. D argued that the fact that he was drunk at the material time was one of his 'circumstances' that had to be considered in accordance with s 54(1)(c): he should not be precluded from advancing the partial defence of loss of control simply because he happened to be intoxicated.

CA: dismissed his appeal. LCJ:

> We can find nothing in the 'loss of control' defence to suggest that Parliament intended, somehow, that the normal rules which apply to voluntary intoxication should not apply. If that had been the intention of Parliament, it would have been spelled out in unequivocal language. Moreover, faced with the compelling reasoning of this court in *Dowds* [2012, **8.12**] in the context of diminished responsibility, it is inconceivable that different criteria should govern the approach to the issue of voluntary drunkenness, depending on whether the partial defence under consideration is diminished responsibility or loss of control. Indeed, given that in a fair proportion of cases, both defences are canvassed before the jury, the potential for uncertainty and confusion which would follow the necessarily very different directions on the issue of intoxication depending on which partial defence was under consideration, does not bear contemplation.

> …[this] does not mean that D who has been drinking is deprived of any possible loss of control defence … If a sober individual in D's circumstances, with normal levels of tolerance and self-restraint might have behaved in the same way as D confronted by the relevant qualifying trigger, he would not be deprived of the loss of control defence just because he was not sober (paras 24–5).

Suicide pacts

8.19 The Homicide Act 1957, s 4 provides that:

(1) It shall be manslaughter, and shall not be murder, for a person acting in pursuance of a suicide pact between him and another to kill the other or to be a party to the other being killed by a third person.

(2) Where it is shown that a person charged with the murder of another killed the other or was a party to his being killed, it shall be for the defence to prove that the person charged was acting in pursuance of a suicide pact between him and the other.

(3) For the purposes of this section 'suicide pact' means a common agreement between two or more persons having for its object the death of all of them, whether or not each is to take his own life, but nothing done by a person who enters into a suicide pact shall be treated as done by him in pursuance of the pact unless it is done while he has the settled intention of dying in pursuance of the pact.

8.20 As detailed in Chapter 7, suicide itself ceased to be a crime in the Suicide Act 1961, but s 2 made clear that a person who aids, abets, counsels, or procures the suicide of another or an attempt by another to commit suicide, should be liable on conviction on indictment to 14 years' imprisonment. The C&JA 2009 repealed this, substituting a new inchoate offence of encouraging and assisting suicide (see **7.40**). Clearly, there is widespread confusion at the moment as to whether and, if so, to what extent the law should recognize either euthanasia, or an offence of 'mercy' killing or a partial defence of 'mercy' or consensual killing, and this may be an area in need of further reform (see **8.45**). Note that s 4 puts the burden firmly on D to prove that he killed in pursuance of the suicide pact: see *A-G's Reference (No. 1 of 2004) (2004)*.

Involuntary manslaughter

8.21 Those guilty of manslaughter by reason of diminished responsibility or provocation intended to kill: hence it is voluntary manslaughter. We now turn to those who did not intend to kill: involuntary means simply that they did not have an intent to kill. In recent years it has generally been accepted that someone may be convicted of involuntary manslaughter by a variety of routes: constructive manslaughter, reckless manslaughter, gross negligence manslaughter, and now the new corporate manslaughter. Often the facts may allow the prosecution to follow more than one of these routes. But the categories are by no means clear-cut, and this area of the law is riddled with confusion. Partly the problem is that manslaughter is just too wide, encompassing both the 'nearly murders' and the unfortunate 'one punch' which resulted in death (see Mitchell and Mackay (2011) for a rare study of a number of case files). This is another depressing area of the criminal law, one in desperate need of a statutory simplification. This commentator, as we shall see, would prefer to abolish constructive liability and to make manslaughter a crime based simply on (subjective) recklessness.

Constructive manslaughter

8.22 Where D causes death by an intentional, unlawful, and dangerous act, she is guilty of manslaughter. There must be an act: failure to act would appear to be insufficient.

> *Lowe* **(1973)** D, of low intelligence, suggested to his partner that she should take their baby to the doctor. Despite saying that she had done so, she did not, as she was frightened that the baby would be taken into care by the local authority. The baby died of dehydration.
>
> CA: whilst D could be convicted of wilful neglect, contrary to the CYPA 1933, s 1(1), his conviction for manslaughter was quashed.
>
>> We think that there is a clear distinction between an act of omission and an act of commission likely to cause harm … if I strike a child in a manner likely to cause harm it is right that, if the child dies, I may be charged with manslaughter. If however, I omit to do something with the result that it suffers injury to health which results in its death, we think that a charge of manslaughter should not be the inevitable consequence, even if the omission is deliberate. (per Phillimore LJ)

This distinction between acts and omissions is surely untenable (see also **2.5**). In any case, a father has a duty to care for his child. Glazebrook (at [2003] Crim LR 541) calls the decision 'irredeemably irrational and confused'. See the new offence of 'causing the death of a child or vulnerable adult' at **8.36**.

8.23 The act must also be unlawful in itself:

> *Jennings* **(1990)** D had been drinking heavily. He armed himself with a sheath knife to protect himself from X, who he believed was looking for him. V, his brother, was killed trying to restrain him. He was convicted of constructive manslaughter after the trial judge had directed the jury that he had no defence except on the question whether a bystander would have realized that some injury was inevitable from the unlawful act being committed by D.
>
> CA (Lord Lane CJ): allowed the appeal. A knife is not an offensive weapon per se. Therefore walking down a walkway with a knife in hand is not an unlawful act which could have constituted the 'unlawful act' for this purpose.

See also *Dias* (2001) *Rogers* (2003), and *Kennedy (No. 2)* (2005) (discussed at **2.21** and **2.22**) and *Andrews* (2002) (discussed at **5.8**) for the particular problems associated with constructive manslaughter when assisting others to take illegal drugs.

Note that *Andrews* shows that a strict liability offence can constitute the 'unlawful' act necessary for this form of manslaughter.

8.24 Whether or not an act is dangerous depends on whether it is likely to do physical harm:

Church **(1966)** D was taunted by V about his impotence. He knocked her out, panicked, and dumped her body in a river, where she drowned. He was convicted of manslaughter.

CCA (Edmund Davies LJ): applying *Meli v R* (1954, see **2.8**), the series of acts which culminated in her death were sufficient to constitute manslaughter.

> The unlawful act must be such as all sober and reasonable people would inevitably recognise must subject the other person to, at least, the risk of some harm resulting therefrom, albeit not serious harm.

DPP v Newbury **(1977)** Three teenage Ds dropped a paving stone on to a passing train. It landed on the cab and killed the guard. The point of law certified to be of general public importance was, 'Can a D be properly convicted of manslaughter, when his mind was not affected by drink or drugs, if he did not foresee that his act might cause harm to another?'

HL: upheld their convictions for manslaughter. Lord Salmon affirmed the objective test that it is not necessary to prove that D knew that the act was unlawful or dangerous, merely whether sober and reasonable people would realize its danger.

Dawson **(1985)** Three Ds robbed a petrol station at night, carrying a replica gun and pickaxe handle. Shortly afterwards V, the garage attendant, died of a heart attack. The trial judge told the jury that it was sufficient to convict them of manslaughter as the unlawful act was likely to cause emotional or physical disturbance.

CA (Watkins LJ): quashed their convictions. The harm referred to in *Church* (1966) must be physical harm. (See also **2.14** for discussion of this case.)

Goodfellow **(1986)** D wished to be rehoused, so he set fire to his council house. This caused the death of his wife, his girlfriend, and his child. He was convicted of both manslaughter and arson.

CA (Lord Lane CJ): upheld his conviction. There is no requirement that the act be directed at V. The questions for the jury were: (i) was the act intentional? (ii) was it unlawful? (iii) was it an act which any reasonable person would realize was bound to subject some other human being to the risk of physical harm, albeit not necessarily serious harm? (iv) was that act the cause of death?

Ball (1989) D stored live and blank cartridges together, but thought he was firing a blank at V. V died.

CA: upheld his conviction for manslaughter. In manslaughter arising from an unlawful and dangerous act, D's state of mind is only relevant to establish: (i) that the act was committed intentionally, and (ii) that it was an unlawful act. Once (i) and (ii) were established, the question whether the act was dangerous was to be judged not by D's appreciation, but by that of the sober and reasonable man. At this stage, D's intention, foresight, or knowledge are irrelevant.

Carey, Foster and Coyle (2006) Ds had spent the afternoon drinking alcohol. They met another group of girls and were verbally abusive and threatening to them. They then punched V and another of her group, but two boys intervened and V's group ran off. V collapsed and died later that night. The medical evidence showed that she had a severely diseased heart, which had been unknown to doctors and her family, and that she might not have died if she had not been running. Ds were convicted of manslaughter.

CA: quashed the convictions. The only act committed against V that was dangerous was the assault; however, the physical harm resulting from the assault did not cause Vs death.

> In the present case, the only dangerous act in the relevant sense was the assault by D on V. A punch to the face is a dangerous unlawful act. If V had fallen against a hard surface and suffered an injury from which she had died, D would have been guilty of manslaughter on a straightforward application of *Church* principles. But in the circumstances of this case, V's death was not caused by injuries that were a foreseeable result of the assault in the sense that the risk of such injuries would have been recognised by a sober or reasonable person having the knowledge that the appellants had ... The slight injuries caused by the assault cannot be said to have been a cause of her death. That is why the judge did not direct the jury that it was necessary for them to be sure that the physical harm actually inflicted was a cause of her death before they could convict of manslaughter. It follows from the fact that (a) the only dangerous act perpetrated on V (D's punch) did not cause her death, and (b) the other acts and threats of violence used in the course of the affray were not dangerous in the relevant sense as against V, that none of the appellants was guilty of manslaughter (Dyson LJ at paras 46–7).

M (2012) Ds, brothers, had been involved in a fight with a doorman, V. V suffered from an undiagnosed renal artery aneurysm and died shortly afterwards. They were charged with manslaughter (and affray). The trial judge ruled that it was not open to the jury to convict them of manslaughter as they would have to be satisfied that V died as a result of the sort of physical harm that any reasonable and sober person would inevitably realize the act in question risked causing.

CA (LCJ): allowed P's appeal. There was evidence from which a properly directed jury could conclude that a sober and reasonable bystander would have recognized that he was at sufficient risk of harm for the purposes of the offence of involuntary manslaughter. There was no requirement that D should foresee any specific harm, or that the bystander should recognize the precise sort of harm that ensued. (At a later retrial, P dropped the manslaughter charge as there was no medical evidence that Ds' actions caused the aneurysm; they pleaded guilty to affray and were sentenced to 11 and 14 months' imprisonment. In 2014 the CA reduced these sentences to 4 and 6 months' imprisonment.)

This case nicely illustrates the conundrum which Ashworth identified at [2013] Crim LR 335:

> ...a deeper conflict between those who argue that the category of unlawful act manslaughter places too much significance on the 'bad luck' that a relatively minor crime which would not normally endanger life had the effect of taking life on this occasion, and those who argue that the fact that death was caused by a wrongful act should be marked by conviction of a homicide offence and a significant sentence.

Is it time that the CA took a lead in narrowing liability for manslaughter?

8.25 Why is it that someone should be guilty of manslaughter simply because they intentionally did another unlawful and dangerous act? The essence of their culpability should surely lie in the fact that they must have (should have?) foreseen the risk that V would die. That is liability based on recklessness, not simply constructing liability for a more serious crime from a less serious intentional one.

A-G's Reference (No. 3 of 1994) (1997) D stabbed his girlfriend whom he knew to be pregnant. The girlfriend recovered, but V, her baby, was born prematurely as a result of the wound and died after 120 days. The trial judge held that D could not be convicted of murder or manslaughter and ordered D's acquittal.

HL: D was rightly acquitted of murder (see **3.33** and **8.3**). However, since D intended to stab the mother and that was an unlawful and dangerous act, it followed that the requisite *mens rea* was established and although the child was a foetus at the time, on public policy grounds she was to be regarded as coming within that *mens rea* when she was a living person. Lord Hope:

> ...it is clear from the authorities that, although D must be proved to have intended to do what he did, it is not necessary to prove that he knew that his act was likely to injure the person who died as a result of it.

***Dhaliwal* (2006)** After V committed suicide it became clear that D, her husband, had subjected her to physical and psychological abuse. The trial judge held that there was no basis on which a jury could convict him of manslaughter.

CA: dismissed P's appeal against this terminating ruling. V's psychological condition (not an identifiable psychiatric illness) did not amount to actual or grievous bodily harm (following *Chan-Fook* (1994) and *Ireland (1998)* (see **9.16**)), and so the judge was right that there was no ground for a conviction for manslaughter.

Horder and McGowan (2006) argue that if Dhaliwal had been charged not with unlawful act manslaughter (i.e. by the infliction of grievous bodily harm) but with gross negligence manslaughter (see **8.29**), the prosecution would have been more likely to succeed. Do you agree? The Law Commission, in Report No. 237 (1996), (rightly in the opinion of this writer) recommended the abolition of unlawful act manslaughter in its present form. But the Home Office proposed, in *Reforming the Law of Manslaughter* (2000), simply a narrowing of the definition:

> A person by his or her conduct who causes the death of another, intending to cause injury or being reckless as to whether some injury is caused; where the conduct causing or intending to cause the injury constituted an offence.

This, at least, focuses on whether D intended or was reckless whether he caused injury. But does it go far enough? If the 'usual' *mens rea* for manslaughter is recklessness or gross negligence (see **8.26**), why should there be an alternative definition of killing another person either 'through a criminal act intended to cause injury' or 'through a criminal act in the awareness that it involved a serious risk of causing some injury' ('criminal act manslaughter'), the definition proposed by the Law Commission in their Report No. 304 (2006)? But, sadly, constructive liability lives on!

Reckless/gross negligence manslaughter

8.26 For many years it was accepted that someone whose 'gross negligence' caused death was guilty of manslaughter.

***Bateman* (1925)** CCA (Lord Hewart):

> ...the facts must be such that, in the opinion of the jury, the negligence of the accused went beyond a mere matter of compensation between subjects and showed such disregard for the life and safety of others as to amount to a crime against the State and conduct deserving of punishment.

Andrews v DPP **(1937)** Lord Atkin:

> Simple lack of care as will constitute civil liability is insufficient ... Probably of all the epithets that can be applied 'reckless' most nearly covers the case ... but it is probably not all-embracing, for 'reckless' suggests an indifference to risk, whereas the accused may have appreciated the risk and intended to avoid it and yet shown such a high degree of negligence in the means adopted to avoid as would justify a conviction.

8.27   Concern about the interpretation of gross negligence led the courts to accept that the concept of 'recklessness' as developed by the HL in *Metropolitan Police Commissioner v Caldwell* (1982) and *Lawrence* (1982) (see **3.22** and **3.23**) might be a better way of expressing the degree of culpability necessary to justify a conviction for manslaughter:

Seymour **(1983)** After an argument with his girlfriend, there was an accident between D's lorry and her car. He proceeded to crush his girlfriend between the two vehicles. He was convicted of manslaughter.

HL: dismissed his appeal. Lord Roskill: the new test of recklessness developed in *Caldwell* (1982) and *Lawrence* (1982) should be applied throughout the criminal law:

> It is appropriate also to point out that in order to constitute the offence of manslaughter the risk of death being caused by the manner of D's driving must be very high.

Kong Cheuk Kwan v R **(1985)** Two hydrofoils collided on a clear sunny day. Two passengers were killed, and D, who was in command of one of the hydrofoils, was convicted of manslaughter.

PC: allowed the appeal. Lord Roskill confirmed that it was no longer useful to refer to negligence or to the *Bateman* test:

> ...the model direction suggested in *Lawrence*, and held in *Seymour* to be equally applicable in cases of motor manslaughter, requires first, proof that the vehicle was in fact being driven in such a manner as to create an obvious and serious risk of causing physical injury to another and second, that D so drove either without having given any thought to the possibility of there being such a risk or having recognised that there was such a risk nevertheless took it.

8.28   By 1989, it seemed that the problems were fast disappearing: Lord Lane CJ was able in *Goodfellow* (see **8.24**) to point out that D in that case could equally well have been convicted of reckless manslaughter. He laid down one simple test which should be laid before the jury:

> *Has the accused acted in such a way as to create an obvious and serious risk of causing physical harm and, having recognised that there was some risk involved, ... gone on to take it?*

8.29 However, in 1995, in an about-turn, the HL rejected the application of *Caldwell/ Lawrence* to manslaughter, returning to the older test of gross negligence:

Adomako **(1995)** D, an anaesthetist, failed to notice that the tube from a ventilator had become disconnected during an operation and the patient died.

HL (Lord Mackay): rejected D's appeal against his conviction for manslaughter.

> The ordinary principles of the law of negligence apply to ascertain whether or not the D has been in breach of a duty of care towards the victim who has died. If such a breach of duty is established the next question is whether that breach of duty caused the death of the victim. If so, the jury must go on to consider whether that breach of duty should be characterised as gross negligence and therefore as a crime. This will depend on the seriousness of the breach of duty ... in all the circumstances in which the D was placed. The jury will have to consider whether the extent to which the D's conduct departed from the proper standard of care incumbent upon him involving as it must have done a risk of death, ... was such that it should be judged criminal.

Lord Mackay did not rule out the use of the word 'reckless' in directions to juries. He appeared keen that the definition should not be too precise:

> ... the essence of the matter, which is supremely a jury question, is whether having regard to the risk of death involved, the conduct of the defendant is so bad in all the circumstances as to amount in their judgement to a criminal act or omission.

8.30 *Adomako* has now been applied in very many cases (including the high-profile case of *Wacker* (2002), where 58 Chinese illegal immigrants died in a Dutch lorry driver's container). See also:

Ruffell **(2003)** V had injected heroin at D's house and had become unwell. D made attempts to revive him that night, but early the following morning V was still unwell and D put him outside the house and left him. V was later found dead, the cause of death being identified as hypothermia and opiate intoxication.

CA: upheld conviction for manslaughter. It was open to the jury to find that D had *assumed* a duty of care towards V.

Misra **(2004)** Ds were senior house officers involved in V's post-operative care. V, who had had surgery to repair a tendon, became infected with *staphylococcus aureus*. The condition was untreated, and a gradual build-up of poison within his body culminated in toxic shock syndrome, from which he died. Ds were convicted of manslaughter, and appealed primarily on the ground that manslaughter by gross negligence was an offence which lacked certainty and contravened Art 7 of the ECHR.

CA: dismissed the appeals. The ingredients of the offence had been clearly defined, and the principles outlined in *Adomako* involved no uncertainty. The hypothetical citizen, seeking to know his position, would be advised that, assuming he owed a duty of care to V, which he had negligently broken, and that death had resulted, he would be liable to conviction for manslaughter if, on the available evidence, the jury were satisfied that his negligence was gross. A doctor would be told that grossly negligent treatment which exposed a patient to the risk of death, and caused it, would constitute manslaughter. There was no uncertainty such as to offend against Art 7. The Court rejected the suggestion that the jury must determine the degree of grossness (fact) by determining whether it was criminal (law):

> ...the decision whether the conduct was criminal is described [in *Adomako*] not as 'the' test, but as 'a' test as to how far the conduct in question must depart from accepted standards to be 'characterised as criminal'. On proper analysis, therefore, the jury is not deciding whether the particular D ought to be convicted on some unprincipled basis. The question for the jury is not whether the D's negligence was gross, and whether, additionally, it was a crime, but whether his behaviour was grossly negligent and consequently criminal. This is not a question of law, but one of fact, for decision in the individual case (Judge LJ at para. 62).

As Ormerod points out (at [2005] Crim LR 237), the most perplexing aspect of this judgment is that it does not meet the criticisms that the test is circular, nor that the test requires the jury to determine the scope of the criminal law. There is still no clear advice for doctors on what might constitute 'gross negligence'. But the Court did provide welcome clarification that only a risk of death (not serious injury) will be sufficient for gross negligence manslaughter (at para. 52). As a matter of policy, the CPS did not prosecute for anything less (at para. 50).

8.31 The law remains extraordinarily difficult to define with any certainty. The Law Commission (in Law Com Report No. 237) said this about Lord Mackay's test:

> The first problem ... is that it is circular: the jury must be directed to convict D of a crime if they think his conduct was 'criminal'. In effect, this leaves a question of law to the jury, and, because juries do not give reasons for their decisions, it is impossible to tell what criteria will be applied in an individual case ... Other problems arise out of the Lord Chancellor's use of the terminology of 'duty of care' and 'negligence', and his linkage of the civil and criminal law in his speech. The meanings of these words are not entirely clear in a criminal law context (paras 3.9–3.10).

For a useful analysis of the case law, see Herring and Palser (2007) who concluded that there is indeed considerable uncertainty as to the appropriate test, with directions given to juries varying significantly in approach. Gross negligence was also the test applied in *Evans* (2009, see 2.9). There the CA was clear that the duty necessary to found gross negligence manslaughter was not confined to cases of a familial or professional relationship between D and V: when D creates or contributes to the creation of a state of affairs which she knew, or ought reasonably to have known, had become life-threatening, a consequent duty on her to act by taking reasonable steps to save the other's life normally arises. Would you prefer to say that D in *Evans* is guilty because she was *reckless* in failing to act to save her sister's life, or are you content with the concept of *gross negligence* in this area?

Reform

8.32 Clause 55 of the DCC (1989) included an offence of reckless manslaughter and this remained the recommendation of Law Commission (Report No. 237 (1996)). Their draft Bill included a clause which provided:

> (1) A person who by his conduct causes the death of another is guilty of reckless killing if—
>
> (a) he is aware of a risk that his conduct will cause death or serious injury; and
>
> (b) it is unreasonable for him to take that risk having regard to the circumstances as he knows or believes them to be.

This offence would clearly be based on a test of subjective recklessness. They also recommended the abolition of unlawful act manslaughter in its present form, and a new offence of killing by gross carelessness:

> (1) A person who by his conduct causes the death of another is guilty of killing by gross carelessness if—
>
> (a) a risk that his conduct will cause death or serious injury would be obvious to a reasonable person in his position;
>
> (b) he is capable of appreciating that risk at the material time; and
>
> (c) either—
>
> (i) his conduct falls far below what can reasonably be expected of him in the circumstances; or
>
> (ii) he intends by his conduct to cause some injury or is aware of, and unreasonably takes, the risk that it may do so.

They gave the example of a climbing instructor who takes a group of inexperienced climbers out with inadequate equipment in bad weather. Would it be easy for a jury to apply the test of whether D's conduct fell *far* below what could reasonably be expected of him? Do you think this additional offence is necessary?

8.33 The Home Office then published its proposals for reform in 2000. It accepted the Law Commission's proposals in respect of the offences of reckless killing and killing by gross carelessness, but proposed a third offence of manslaughter, where the intention was only to cause some injury and the resulting death was unforeseeable. The question here is whether people should be punished for what they could not have foreseen, what the Law Commission call the 'lottery effect'. In Consultation Paper No. 177 (2005) the Law Commission (confusingly?) argued that 'recklessness falling short of reckless indifference can really be regarded as a kind of gross negligence' (para. 3.182) and that:

> …making the difference between 'second degree murder' and manslaughter turn on the distinction between reckless indifference and gross negligence gives effect to the ladder principle, according to which there should be clear and robust differences between offences of different degrees of gravity (para. 3.183).

But their final Report No. 304 (2006) accepted that these gradations were too unclear: see 8.46. The issue seems to have left the agenda (apart from where the offence involves driving offences: see 8.37).

Corporate manslaughter

8.34 Debate on the question of whether a company could or should be guilty of manslaughter developed after this high-profile case:

> **P & O European Ferries (Dover) Ltd (1990)** A ferry, the *Herald of Free Enterprise*, sank in 1987 and 192 passengers died. The cause of the 'accident' was not only the negligence of a junior member of the ship's crew but also an irresponsible attitude to safety throughout by D, the company which owned the ferry. D was indicted on four counts of manslaughter, but sought to have the indictment quashed.
>
> CA: where a corporation, through the controlling mind of one of its agents, does an act which fulfils the prerequisites of manslaughter, it is properly indictable for the crime of manslaughter.

The end of that particular story was that the trial judge directed the jury to return a not guilty verdict, in part because of the management's evidence that they had not been aware of the dangers. Charges against the junior staff were also dropped. The first company to be convicted of manslaughter in this country was a small company, OLL Ltd, which caused the death of school children canoeists in Dorset in 1994.

8.35 The Law Commission in 1996 (see Law Com No. 237) recommended a separate offence of corporate manslaughter. Draft Bills were published in 2000 and in 2005, and the Home Affairs and Work and Pensions Committees of the House of Commons published a joint report (HC540–1) in 2005, saying that there was 'a strong need' for a statutory offence that shifted the basis of liability for corporate manslaughter away from the requirement of identifying a 'directing mind' of a guilty company. Interestingly, they suggested that the Government should remove the civil law concept of a duty of care in negligence from the Bill: 'it is surplus to requirements and adds unnecessary legal complication to the Bill. We also believe it is inappropriate to adopt a civil law concept as the basis for a criminal offence.' This was not accepted. The offence of corporate manslaughter was created in the Corporate Manslaughter and Corporate Homicide Act 2007 (corporate homicide is the name given to the offence in Scotland):

1 The offence

(1) An organisation to which this section applies is guilty of an offence if the way in which its activities are managed or organised—

   (a) causes a person's death, and

   (b) amounts to a gross breach of a relevant duty of care owed by the organisation to the deceased.

(2) The organisations to which this section applies are—

   (a) a corporation;

   (b) a department or other body listed in Schedule 1;

   (c) a police force;

   (d) a partnership, or a trade union or employers' association, that is an employer.

(3) An organisation is guilty of an offence under this section only if the way in which its activities are managed or organised by its senior management is a substantial element in the breach referred to in subsection (1).

(4) For the purposes of this Act—

   (a) 'relevant duty of care' has the meaning given by section 2, read with sections 3 to 7;

   (b) a breach of a duty of care by an organisation is a 'gross' breach if the conduct alleged to amount to a breach of that duty falls far below what can reasonably be expected of the organisation in the circumstances;

   (c) 'senior management', in relation to an organisation, means the persons who play significant roles in—

      (i) the making of decisions about how the whole or a substantial part of its activities are to be managed or organised, or

      (ii) the actual managing or organising of the whole or a substantial part of those activities.

The definitional elements of this offence are vague: whether or not management failure is a 'substantial element' is a question of fact for the jury to determine: do you think the Act provides a workable test? There is no liability for aiding and abetting this offence: individuals and companies are probably still more likely to be prosecuted for health and safety offences (Wright (2007) and see **4.35**). The provisions were brought into force in April 2008. The first conviction under the Act was in:

Cotswold Geotechnical (Holdings) Ltd (2011)   V, an employee of D, was taking soil samples in a pit when the walls collapsed and he was trapped and died. P dropped charges against D's sole director who was terminally ill at the time of the trial, and unfit to give evidence. D was convicted of corporate manslaughter.

CA: dismissed the appeal (based mainly on evidential issues). The reality is that there was no proper safe system of work in relation to V entering into unsupported pits.

The company, faced with a hefty fine, has since (unsurprisingly?) gone into liquidation. It is worth considering the discussion in **4.33** on corporate liability more generally, before you conclude whether this new offence is a useful addition to the statute book.

Causing or allowing the death of a child or vulnerable adult

8.36   Note the discussion at **6.4** of the background to the new offence of causing or allowing the death of a child or vulnerable adult. Section 5 of the DVCVA 2004 (as amended by the DVCVA (Amendment) Act 2012) provides:

s 5 (1) A person ('D') is guilty of an offence if—

(a) a child or vulnerable adult ('V') dies or suffers serious physical harm as a result of the unlawful act of a person who—

(i) was a member of the same household as V, and

(ii) had frequent contact with him,

(b) D was such a person at the time of that act,

(c) at that time there was a significant risk of serious physical harm being caused to V by the unlawful act of such a person, and

(d) either D was the person whose act caused the death or serious physical harm or–

(i) D was, or ought to have been, aware of the risk mentioned in paragraph (c),

(ii) D failed to take such steps as he could reasonably have been expected to take to protect V from the risk, and

(iii) the act occurred in circumstances of the kind that D foresaw or ought to have foreseen.

(2) The prosecution does not have to prove whether it is the first alternative in subsection (1)(d) or the second (sub-paragraphs (i) to (iii)) that applies.

(3) If D was not the mother or father of V—

(a) D may not be charged with an offence under this section if he was under the age of 16 at the time of the act that caused the death or serious physical harm;

(b) for the purposes of subsection (1)(d)(ii) D could not have been expected to take any such step as is referred to there before attaining that age.

(4) For the purposes of this section—

(a) a person is to be regarded as a "member" of a particular household, even if he does not live in that household, if he visits it so often and for such periods of time that it is reasonable to regard him as a member of it;

(b) where V lived in different households at different times, *'the same house-hold as V'* refers to the household in which V was living at the time of the act that caused the death or serious physical harm.

(5) For the purposes of this section an "unlawful" act is one that—

(a) constitutes an offence, or

(b) would constitute an offence but for being the act of—

(i) a person under the age of ten, or

(ii) a person entitled to rely on a defence of insanity.

Paragraph (b) does not apply to an act of D.

(6) In this section—

"act" includes a course of conduct and also includes omission;

"child" means a person under the age of 16;

"serious" harm means harm that amounts to grievous bodily harm for the purposes of the Offences against the Person Act 1861 (c. 100);

"vulnerable adult" means a person aged 16 or over whose ability to protect himself from violence, abuse or neglect is significantly impaired through physical or mental disability or illness, through old age or otherwise.

(7) A person guilty of an offence under this section of causing or allowing a person's death is liable on conviction on indictment to imprisonment for a term not exceeding 14 years or to a fine, or to both.

(8) A person guilty of an offence under this section of causing or allowing a person to suffer serious physical harm is liable on conviction on indictment to imprisonment for a term not exceeding 10 years or to a fine, or to both.

Stephens and Mujuru (2007) D1 and D2 lived together. D1 was convicted of murder and D2 of causing or allowing the death of V, her 4-month-old baby.

CA: dismissed D2's appeal. The interpretation of the words 'significant risk' under the 2004 Act was one of fact for the jury to decide. The trial judge had erred in defining 'significant' to mean 'more than minimal' and it should have been given its ordinary meaning, applying *Brutus v Cozens* (1973) (see **12.18**). However, there was considerable evidence that D2 knew that D1 had broken V's arm, or had good reason to think that he might have done so, and that D2 was, or ought to have been, aware that there was a significant risk that D1 might deliberately harm V again. On such findings, the jury could have gone on to find that, by leaving V with D1, D2 failed to take such steps as she could reasonably have been expected to take to protect V. It was not a borderline case with regard to the nature and magnitude of risk to V. Therefore, even by directing the jury that 'significant' meant more than minimal, there was no real danger that the jury had convicted D2 when they would not otherwise have done so, and the conviction was safe.

Herring (2007) is very critical of this (and several other) prosecutions of this offence, arguing that the law should focus on seeking to protect mothers and children from violent men, rather than punishing women who are themselves the victims of violence. Clearly Parliament intended that it should be a lesser offence than manslaughter (it has a maximum sentence of 14 years). See also:

Khan (2009) V, aged 19 and a recent immigrant to this country, was beaten to death by her husband who was convicted of murder. Four other Ds, her mother-in-law/aunt, her sisters-in-law/cousins, and her brother-in-law, who all lived in the same household, were convicted of 'allowing her death'.

CA (Lord Judge CJ): dismissed their appeals. The s 5 offence was based on a positive duty on members of the same household to protect children or vulnerable adults whose ability to protect themselves from violence, abuse, or neglect was significantly impaired. The LCJ gives a thorough review of the ingredients of the offence. The state of vulnerability could be short or temporary. Even when membership of the same household was established, frequent contact between D and V was required. If contact was frequent, D would still be entitled to be acquitted unless the criteria in s 5(1)(d)(i) and s 5(1)(d)(iii) were also established. These applied when D was aware of the risk of serious physical harm, or ought to have been aware of it, and foresaw, or ought to have foreseen, the occurrence of the unlawful act or course of conduct which resulted in death. Even if the necessary level of awareness and foresight were established,

D could not be convicted unless he failed to take the steps which could reasonably have been expected. The judge had sufficiently linked the violence on the night V died with the earlier violent occasions in the context of the risk of serious physical harm of which the jury had to be satisfied.

Causing death by dangerous driving (and other driving offences)

8.37 In 1956 Parliament introduced a new offence of causing death by reckless driving, largely, it seems, because juries were reluctant to convict bad drivers of manslaughter. But the threshold of culpability was reduced from reckless to dangerous driving by the RTA 1988, s 1:

> A person who causes the death of another person by driving a mechanically propelled vehicle dangerously on a road or other public place is guilty of an offence.

Dangerous driving is defined in s 2A of the Act objectively: a person is to be regarded as driving dangerously if (a) the way he drives falls far below what would be expected of a competent and careful driver, and (b) it would be obvious to a competent and careful driver that driving in that way would be dangerous. This avoids the problems discussed earlier in relation to the meaning of 'recklessness' in manslaughter. The maximum sentence is ten years' imprisonment and/or a fine. Of course, in a particularly serious case of death caused by dangerous driving, P may still charge D with manslaughter, which brings with it the possibility of a much higher sentence. In any case, it may be that juries would no longer have any compunction about convicting very bad drivers of manslaughter, and that a separate homicide offence for those who kill with cars is not really necessary. But Parliament has moved in the other direction: the Road Safety Act 2006 created two new offences:

(i)   Section 20 inserted a new s 2B into the RTA 1988, creating the offence of 'causing death by careless, or inconsiderate, driving':

> 2B A person who causes the death of another person by driving a mechanically propelled vehicle on a road or other public place without due care and attention, or without reasonable consideration for other persons using the road or place, is guilty of an offence.

This offence is punishable by up to five years' imprisonment.

(ii) Section 21 inserts a new s 3ZB after s 3ZA of the RTA 1988, creating the offence of 'causing death by driving: unlicensed, disqualified or uninsured drivers':

3ZB A person is guilty of an offence under this section if he causes the death of another person by driving a motor vehicle on a road and, at the time when he is driving, the circumstances are such that he is committing an offence under—

(a) s. 87(1) of this Act (driving otherwise than in accordance with a licence),

(b) s. 103(1)(b) of this Act (driving while disqualified), or

(c) s. 143 of this Act (using motor vehicle while uninsured or unsecured against third party risks).

This offence is punishable by a maximum of two years' imprisonment.

Both offences should cause you to ask several questions:

- Do we need such a proliferation of specific road traffic offences?
- If they are needed, are they appropriately defined?
- If they are needed, is the insertion of more and more new offences into an old Act with such odd numbering the right way to do it?
- Does someone who causes death by driving only carelessly (as opposed to dangerously) deserve up to five years' imprisonment? The offence under s 20 has been much criticized: is it fair to impose the stigma of this serious offence on someone who was simply momentarily careless? (See Hirst (2008) and the SC's decision in *Hughes* (2013) **2.26**.)

Offences against the foetus

8.38 Child destruction is an offence defined in the Infant Life (Preservation) Act 1929, s 1:

s 1 (1) …any person who, with intent to destroy the life of a child capable of being born alive, by any wilful act causes a child to die before it has an existence independent of its mother, shall be guilty of an offence …

(2) For the purposes of this Act, evidence that a woman had at any material time been pregnant for a period of 28 weeks or more shall be prima facie proof that she was at that time pregnant of a child capable of being born alive.

8.39 Despite the statutory presumption that a foetus over 28 weeks old is capable of being born alive, P may still attempt to prove that a younger foetus was capable of being born alive:

C v S (1988) A civil case in which a man sought an injunction to prevent the abortion of a foetus between 18 and 21 weeks old.

CA (Sir John Donaldson MR): if the foetus had reached the normal stage of development, it would be incapable of ever breathing, and so it was not capable of being born alive. There was therefore no need to decide whether the putative father had a right to be heard, and the mother could obtain an abortion.

Rance v Mid-Downs Health Authority **(1991)** Another civil case where a mother unsuccessfully sued for damages for the hospital authority's negligence in not picking up the abnormalities in her foetus, seen on a scan when the foetus was 26 weeks old. The mother, who would have had the foetus aborted, had now given up her career to care for her severely handicapped child.

DC (Brooke J): a foetus of 26 or 27 weeks' gestation, who could breathe unaided for a short period, was capable of being born alive. Therefore the mother's claim that she lost the right to an abortion failed.

8.40 An alternative offence is administering drugs or using instruments to procure abortion, contrary to the OAPA 1861, s 58:

> Every woman, being with child, who, with intent to procure her own miscarriage, shall unlawfully administer to herself any poison or other noxious thing, or shall unlawfully use any instrument or other means whatsoever with the like intent, and whosoever, with intent to procure the miscarriage of any woman, whether she be or be not with child, shall unlawfully administer to her or cause to be taken by her any poison or other noxious thing, or shall unlawfully use any instrument or other means whatsoever with the like intent, shall be guilty [of an offence].

This carries a maximum penalty of life imprisonment. This offence is discussed in detail by Munby J in *R (Smeaton) v Secretary of State for Health* (2002) when he refused an application for judicial review of the legality of the 'morning after pill'.

8.41 Since the Abortion Act 1967 was passed, certain abortions have been lawful. Significant changes were introduced by the Human Fertilisation and Embryology Act 1990 (and other subsequent legislation), such that the Abortion Act 1967, s 1 now reads:

> A person shall not be guilty of an offence under the law relating to abortion when a pregnancy is terminated by a registered medical practitioner if two registered practitioners are of the opinion, formed in good faith—
>
> (a) that the pregnancy has not exceeded its 24th week and that the continuance of the pregnancy would involve risk, greater than if the pregnancy was terminated, of injury to the physical or mental health of the pregnant woman or any existing children of her family; or

(b) that the termination is necessary to prevent grave permanent injury to the physical or mental health of the pregnant woman; or

(c) that the continuance of the pregnancy would involve risk to the life of the pregnant woman, greater than if the pregnancy were terminated; or

(d) that there is a substantial risk that if the child were born it would suffer from such physical or mental abnormalities as to be seriously handicapped.

Thus a pregnancy may be terminated lawfully up to 24 weeks if the continuance of the pregnancy would involve risk, greater than if the pregnancy was terminated, of injury to the physical or mental health of the pregnant woman or any existing children of her family. Abortions may be lawful for a longer period of time to prevent grave injury to the mother (see *Jepson v Chief Constable of West Mercia* (2003) and also *British Pregnancy Advisory Service v Secretary of State for Health* (2011)).

Infanticide

8.42 Introduced in 1922, this offence is now governed by the Infanticide Act 1938, s 1, which was amended by the C&JA 2009, s 57. It now reads (with the minor amendments italicized):

(1) Where a woman by any wilful act or omission causes the death of her child being a child under the age of 12 months, but at the time of the act or omission the balance of her mind was disturbed by reason of her not having fully recovered from the effect of giving birth to the child or by reason of the effect of lactation consequent upon the birth of the child, then, *if* the circumstances were that but for this Act the offence would have amounted to murder *or manslaughter*, she shall be guilty of [an offence], to wit of infanticide, and may for such offence be dealt with and punished as if she had been guilty of the offence of manslaughter of the child.

8.43 There is little justification for this offence, especially not drafted as it is, except that it avoids the mandatory life sentence for murder. It is in effect a defence to murder (and now manslaughter): a mother who kills her baby will be guilty only of infanticide (a form of manslaughter?). The CLRC (1980) suggested widening it to include situations where the woman's mind is disturbed 'by reason of circumstances' consequent upon the birth, in order to include the social and financial stresses that may follow the birth of a child. Women who kill their children seem often not to be blamed as severely as are men: in *Sainsbury* (1989) the CA looked at the statistics which showed that in the 59 cases of infanticide dealt with between 1979 and 1988, not one had resulted in a custodial sentence. There had been 52 probation/supervision orders, and six hospital orders, one of which was restricted.

***Kai-Whitewind* (2005)** D was convicted of the murder of V, her 3-month-old baby, whom it was alleged was conceived as the result of a rape.

CA: dismissed the appeal. But they also called for the offence of infanticide to be included in the Law Commission's then current review:

> The public interest requires that the problems arising from and connected to the offence of infanticide should be included in any review. We shall highlight two particular areas of concern. The first is whether, as a matter of substantive law, infanticide should extend to circumstances subsequent to the birth, but connected with it, such as the stresses imposed on a mother by the absence of natural bonding with her baby: in short, whether the current definition of infanticide reflects modern thinking. The second problem arises when the mother who has in fact killed her infant is unable to admit it. This may be because she is too unwell to do so, or too emotionally disturbed by what she has in fact done, or too deeply troubled by the consequences of an admission of guilt on her ability to care for any surviving children. When this happens, it is sometimes difficult to produce psychiatric evidence relating to the balance of the mother's mind. Yet, of itself, it does not automatically follow from denial that the balance of her mind was not disturbed: in some cases it may indeed help to confirm that it was.

> The law relating to infanticide is unsatisfactory and outdated. The appeal in this sad case demonstrates the need for a thorough re-examination (per Judge LJ, at paras 139–40).

Ms Kai-Whitewind is serving a mandatory life sentence, with a minimum term of 12 years before the Parole Board will consider her possible release. The Law Commission in Consultation Paper No. 177 (2005) recommended that the offence/ defence of infanticide should be retained but that the Infanticide Act 1938, s 1 should be amended to delete any reference to the 'effect of lactation consequent upon the birth of a child' and to substitute two years for 12 months (the relevant age of the child). However, the final Report (2006) recommended that the offence should be retained without amendment. The main reason against subsuming the offence within the offence/partial defence of diminished responsibility seems (disappointingly) to be because they recommend that diminished responsibility should be 'up-tariffed' to second degree murder and infanticide should be manslaughter. That confirms this writer's view that second degree murder was not a good idea!

8.44 The changes introduced by the C&JA 2009 were provoked by the case of *Gore*:

***Gore* (2007)** In 1996, D had concealed her pregnancy, given birth unassisted, and several hours later had abandoned the baby, V, in sand dunes. A post-mortem showed that the baby had lived for at least several minutes. At her trial at that time, D pleaded guilty to infanticide despite being advised that she might have a defence. She was sentenced to a probation order. She did not appeal, and died in 2003. Her parents referred the case to the CCRC which referred the case to the CA on the grounds that the particular indictment had been too narrowly drafted, and that the Act should be narrowly construed, so that a woman might only be guilty of infanticide if all the ingredients of murder were proved, particularly an intention to kill or cause really serious bodily harm.

CA: dismissed the appeal. However narrowly or broadly defined the *mens rea* for infanticide should be, D had rejected the possibility of a defence on the ground of her mental state. In any event, the particulars were not defective. The Act made no mention of an intention to kill and the particulars followed the words of s 1. There was no requirement that all the ingredients of murder be proved before a D could be convicted under s 1. Parliament had intended to create an offence of infanticide which covered situations much wider than offences that would otherwise be murder. The *mens rea* for infanticide was contained explicitly in the first few words of the section, namely P had to prove that D acted or omitted to act wilfully.

Ashworth is somewhat critical of this decision:

> ...*there seems to be an element of strain in the court's reasoning. The possibility of reducing manslaughter to infanticide has not been canvassed in the leading textbooks, and it might be thought rather late, some 70 years after the 1938 Act, to give it this expansive meaning (at [2009] Crim LR 388).*

Parliament has now made it clear, though, that the offence can apply if the circumstances were such that, but for the Infanticide Act 1938, the offence would have amounted to murder or manslaughter.

Mercy killings/euthanasia

8.45 English law has not yet developed a defence or partial defence on these grounds. Controversy surrounds the issue: in the Netherlands and Switzerland, for example, assisted deaths may be permitted in certain circumstances. In the UK, too, of course, doctors often assist a dying patient to die by increasing the doses of pain-relieving drugs which also accelerate death, but the courts seem to have accepted the doctrine of 'double effect': as long as the doctor intends to relieve pain, the courts are not concerned that he also knowingly hastens death. But a doctor (or loving friend) who helps someone to die remains liable to a mandatory life sentence for murder. A 'slippery slope' of uncertainty has been created by the courts' decisions in such cases as *Bland* (1987, see **2.10**). Is this an area which is best left vague, or should Parliament legislate to clarify the boundaries of what is and what is not legal? Those who wish to explore this subject further might like to read the debates in Parliament on Lord Joffe's Assisted Dying for the Terminally Ill Bill 2005, yet another attempt to legislate in this area, which was doomed to failure for lack of Government support. For the moment, there is insufficient political consensus on the subject of euthanasia to permit even limited legalization.

Homicide reform: the way forward?

8.46   **Table 8.1** summarizes the proposals for reform in the Law Commission's Consultation Paper No. 177 (2005) and their Report No. 304 (2006). But remember that the Law Commission was not invited to review the mandatory life sentence for murder, which may explain its proposals: the introduction of second degree murder was a way to limit the scope of the murders which result in a mandatory life sentence. But would this be a good reason for making the law more complicated, or is it time to accept that the mandatory sentence should simply be abolished? Clearly most murderers would continue to receive a life sentence even if it was not mandatory. But change is unlikely in the near future.

Causing death . . .		
Current law	Proposed structure in Consultation Paper No. 177 (2005)	Recommended structure in Report No. 304 (2006)
MURDER	FIRST TIER MURDER	FIRST DEGREE MURDER
. . . with an intention to kill	. . . with an intention to kill	. . . with an intention to cause
. . . with an intention to do serious harm		. . . with an intention to kill
		. . . with an intention to cause serious injury whilst being aware of a serious risk of causing death

Causing death . . .		
Current law	Proposed structure in Consultation Paper No. 177 (2005)	Recommended structure in Report No. 304 (2006)
MANSLAUGHTER (voluntary) . . . with an intention to kill, but with provocation/loss of control . . . with an intention to kill, but with diminished responsibility . . . with an intention to kill, in pursuance of a suicide pact . . . with an intention to do serious harm, but with provocation . . . with an intention to do serious harm, but with diminished responsibility	SECOND TIER MURDER . . . with an intention to do serious harm . . . with an intention to kill, but with (reformulated) provocation . . . with an intention to kill, but with (reformulated) diminished responsibility (incorporating what was previously killing in pursuance of a suicide pact)	SECOND DEGREE MURDER . . . with an intention to do serious injury . . . with an intention to cause some injury, or the fear of some injury or a risk of some injury whilst being aware of a serious risk of causing death
(involuntary) . . . with foresight of an unjustifiable risk of death or serious harm, where the risk is in fact unjustifiable (but may in fact be greater than that perceived) (reckless manslaughter) . . . by gross negligence as to the risk of death . . . by committing a criminal and dangerous act	. . . with an intention to kill, but under duress . . . with reckless indifference as to causing death MANSLAUGHTER . . . by gross negligence as to the risk of death . . . by committing a criminal act, intending to cause harm, or being reckless as to causing harm	. . . with the fault element for first degree murder, but with a partial defence— either (reformulated) provocation, (reformulated) diminished responsibility or in pursuance of a suicide pact MANSLAUGHTER . . . by gross negligence as to the risk of death . . . by a criminal act that the defendant intends to cause some injury or is aware involves a serious risk of causing some injury

(Continued)

Causing death . . .		
Current law	Proposed structure in Consultation Paper No. 177 (2005)	Recommended structure in Report No. 304 (2006)
OTHER SPECIFIC HOMICIDE OFFENCES	OTHER SPECIFIC HOMICIDE OFFENCES	OTHER SPECIFIC HOMICIDE OFFENCES
e.g. infanticide; causing death by dangerous driving	e.g. infanticide; causing death by dangerous driving	e.g. infanticide; causing death by dangerous driving

Table 8.1 How the homicide offences are structured
Source: *LCCP No. 177 (2005) and Report No. 304 (2006).*

FURTHER READING

Ashworth, A., 'The Doctrine of Provocation' (1976) 35 Camb LJ 292.

Ashworth, A., 'Principles, Pragmatism and the Law Commission's Recommendations on Homicide Law Reform' [2007] Crim LR 333.

Ashworth, A. and Mitchell, B. (eds), *Rethinking English Homicide Law* (2000).

Committee on the Penalty for Homicide (Lane Committee), *Report* (1993).

Edwards, S., 'Descent into Murder: Provocation's Stricture—the Prognosis for Women Who Kill Men Who Abuse Them' (2007) 71 JCL 342.

Gardner, J. and Macklem, T., 'Provocation and Pluralism' (2001) 64 MLR 815.

Griew, E., 'The Future of Diminished Responsibility' [1988] Crim LR 75.

Herring, J., 'Familial Homicide, Failure to Protect and Domestic Violence: Who's the Victim?' [2007] Crim LR 923.

Herring, J. and Palser, E., 'The Duty of Care in Gross Negligence Manslaughter' [2007] Crim LR 24.

Hirst, M., 'Causing Death by Driving and Other Offences: A Question of Balance' [2008] Crim LR 339.

Home Office, *Reforming the Law of Involuntary Manslaughter: The Government's Proposals* (2000).

Horder, J. and McGowan, L., 'Manslaughter by Causing Another's Suicide' [2006] Crim LR 1035.

Law Commission, *Legislating the Code: Involuntary Manslaughter* (Law Com Report No. 237, 1996).

Law Commission, *Partial Defences to Murder* (LCCP No. 173, 2003).

Law Commission, *A New Homicide Act for England and Wales?* (LCCP No. 177, 2005).

Law Commission, *Murder, Manslaughter and Infanticide* (Law Com Report No. 304, 2006).

Mackay, R. D., 'The Coroners and Justice Act 2009—Partial Defences to Murder (2) The New Diminished Responsibility Plea' [2010] Crim LR 290.

Mackay, R. D. and Mitchell, B., 'Provoking Diminished Responsibility' [2003] Crim LR 745.

Miles, J., 'The Coroners and Justice Act 2009: A "Dog's Breakfast" of Homicide Reform' (2009) 10 *Archbold News* 6.

Mitchell, B. and Mackay, R. D., 'Investigating Involuntary Manslaughter: An Empirical Study of 127 Cases' [2011] OJLS 165.

Norrie, A., 'The Coroners and Justice Act 2009—Partial Defences to Murder (1) Loss of Control' [2010] Crim LR 275.

Padfield, N., 'Manslaughter: the Dilemma Facing the Law Reformer' (1995) 59 *Journal of Criminal Law* 291.

Padfield, N., 'Why does Provocation Diminish Culpability?' (1996) 55 Camb LJ 420.

Stark, F., 'Killing the Unfaithful' (2012) 71 Camb LJ 260.

Taylor, R., 'The Nature of "Partial Defences" and the Coherence of (Second Degree) Murder' [2007] Crim LR 345.

Wake, N., 'Political Rhetoric or Principled Reform of Loss of Control? Anglo-Australian Perspectives on the Exclusionary Conduct Model' [2013] *Journal of Criminal Law* 512.

Williams, G., 'The Mens Rea of Murder—Leave It Alone' (1989) LQR 387.

Withey, C., 'Loss of Control, Loss of Opportunity?' [2011] Crim LR 263.

Wright, F. B., 'Criminal Liability of Directors and Senior Managers for Deaths at Work' [2007] Crim LR 949.

SELF-TEST QUESTIONS

1   Dee decides to punish Phil for breaking off their relationship. She tampers with the clutch and accelerator in his car hoping to make the car unusable. However, the car starts normally but the clutch suddenly gives out when he is doing 65 mph on a busy motorway. Phil is killed in the resulting crash. Discuss Dee's liability.

2   In the course of an argument, Phil shouts at Dee that she is excessively ugly. She picks up a beer glass and smashes it into his face and neck. He suffers

severe bleeding, and is taken to hospital. He is given an overdose of painkillers by Florence, an inexperienced nurse, and dies. Discuss the liability of Dee and Florence.

3   Dee, suffering from post-natal depression, after the birth of her second child, suffocates to death her 3-year-old son. She tells the police that she believed she had the best interest of the boy in mind, since he was severely handicapped and she couldn't believe that he faced a happy future. Discuss Dee's liability.

Crimes of non-fatal violence

SUMMARY

Still governed in the main by the piecemeal OAPA 1861, these offences contain many inconsistencies:

- s 18: wounding or *causing* grievous bodily harm with intent;
- s 20: reckless *infliction* of grievous bodily harm or wounding;
- s 47: reckless assault *occasioning* actual bodily harm;
- assault and battery now governed by CJA 1988, s 39.

Particular problems:

(i) *actus reus*: the use of the different words (causes, inflicts, assaults) makes it difficult to interpret the offences as a hierarchical ladder;

(ii) *mens rea*: recklessness is subjectively applied, but the debate continues as to the extent of the harm that D must risk: *Parmenter/Savage*.

The chapter also deals briefly with many other offences: threats, harassment, administering poison, treason, terrorism, and torture, etc.

Many proposals for reform: note in particular the DCC (1989) followed by Law Com No. 218 (1993) *Legislating the Criminal Code: Offences against the Person and General Principles*.

Introduction

9.1 Confusion in this area arises largely because the source of the majority of offences of violence remains an 1861 statute, which was never intended to be a neat codification but merely a consolidation of earlier statutes. It is worth reading the whole statute: although many offences are rarely charged, it is a fascinating source of information on how far language (and society) have and haven't shifted in the last 150 years (including offences such as placing wood, etc. on a railway with intent to endanger passengers; obstructing a clergyman or other minister in the discharge of his duties; making gunpowder to commit offences). In this chapter, we concentrate only on a few of the major offences. As Lord Mustill said in *Mandair* (1994, see **9.5**) the unsystematic language of the 1861 Act is a constant source of difficulty. Codifying this area has been a major concern of the Law Commission in recent years. Once it realized that it was unlikely to succeed in getting the DCC (see **1.31**) passed through Parliament in one dose, it concentrated on this area as being most in need of reform. In this chapter we will look in parallel at the law as it is, and the proposals for reform. If you accept that there should be some attempt to grade different offences of violence, on what would you base these gradations? If your emphasis is on the degree of harm, would it be the harm actually caused or the harm threatened or the harm intended? Look again at **1.8** before starting this chapter.

9.2 Lord Mustill points out in *Mandair* (1994, see **9.5**):

> …the reappearance of s 20 before your Lordships' House barely two years after it was minutely examined in Savage; DPP v Parmenter (1992) demonstrates once again that this unsatisfactory statute is long overdue for repeal and replaced by legislation which is soundly based in logic and expressed in language which everyone can understand.

This point is echoed in Law Com No. 218 (1993) para. 12.34, where the Law Commission stated that:

> The interests both of justice and social protection would be much better served by a law that was
>   (i) clearly and briefly stated;
> (ii) based on the injury intended or contemplated by the accused, and not on what he happened to cause; and
> (iii) governed by clear distinctions, expressed in modern and comprehensible language, between serious and less serious cases.

They therefore proposed three new offences:

>   (i) intentionally causing serious injury—maximum sentence life
> (ii) recklessly causing serious injury—five years
> (iii) intentionally or recklessly causing injury—three years

The meaning of recklessly would be *Cunningham*-type subjective recklessness (see **9.14**). The Law Commission has no doubt that this should involve a test in terms of awareness of risk of injury of the type that occurred, and not one based on the results of conduct which D neither intended nor foresaw. This requires only 'a fairly low level of awareness of risk, rather than prolonged reflection and deliberate decision-making'. Nor does it require D to have foreseen all the details of what occurred, but 'merely to have been conscious of a danger of injury of that sort occurring' (see para. 14.12 of the Report). Compare this with the definitions of 'reckless' offered in their Consultation Paper No. 177 (2005) on a reformed Homicide Act (see **8.46**).

9.3 Students may like to ponder whether they prefer the concept of 'personal harm' proposed in the DCC or 'injury'. The Law Commission's 1993 proposals suggested injury, defined in clause 18:

(a) physical injury, including pain, unconsciousness, or any other impairment of a person's physical condition, or

(b) impairment of a person's mental health.

This seems both very wide, and somewhat narrow. For example, does it include mental anguish? And would it include liability for the transmission of diseases? Should the word serious be defined or left up to the common sense of juries? The Law Commission accepted that, however the offences are defined, a lot will be left up to the courts to interpret. Difficulties in reaching agreement on drafting should not be allowed to divert attention from the basic need: any new Code is likely to be a vast improvement on the OAPA 1861. Finally, it should be remembered that many of the problems in this area concern the applicability of defences (particularly self-defence and consent): see Chapter 5. And sadly, reform is not imminent!

Grievous bodily harm with intent (intentional serious violence)

9.4 The most serious non-fatal offence of violence is that specified in the OAPA, s 18:

> Whosoever shall unlawfully and maliciously by any means whatsoever wound or cause any grievous bodily harm to any person with intent to do some grievous bodily harm to any person, or with intent to resist or prevent the lawful apprehension or detainer of any person, shall be guilty of [an offence], and being convicted thereof shall be liable to [imprisonment] for life.

Immediately one is struck by the outmoded language. What is meant by wounding or causing grievous bodily harm? This has long been interpreted as serious bodily harm:

***Bollom* (2003)** D was convicted of causing GBH on a 17-month-old child.

CA: allowed the appeal, substituting a conviction for ABH (s 47: see **9.15**). Fulford J:

> In deciding whether injuries are grievous, an assessment has to be made of, amongst other things, the effect of the harm on the particular individual. We have no doubt that in determining the gravity of these injuries, it was necessary to consider them in their real context.

This means that the injuries should be assessed in relation to the particular V. And what of 'wounding'? 'If the skin is broken, and there was a bleeding, that is a wound' (per Lord Lyndhurst CB in *Moriarty v Brooks* (1834)). Thus even a minor cut may be a wound. Yet this is the most serious offence of violence. Wounding is included in the definition for historical reasons: a hundred years ago a minor wound was more likely to lead to serious consequences than it might today. The courts have gone a small way towards limiting the scope of the definition:

> ***C (a minor) v Eisenhower* (1984)** V was hit by an air-gun pellet near his eye, which caused blood vessels in his eye to rupture. D was convicted of an offence (under s 20: see **9.8**).
>
> CA: quashed his conviction. 'Wound' means a breaking of the whole skin: the rupture of internal blood vessels in the eye was insufficient to constitute wounding.

The DCC (1989) and Law Com No. 218 (1993) omit any reference to wounding: a serious wound would constitute serious injury, and a minor wound would constitute injury.

Cause

9.5 Another key word in the OAPA 1861, s 18 is 'cause', which has a wider meaning than the word 'inflict' used in s 20 (see **9.8**). Someone may cause a result in many ways beyond inflicting it. I cause you injury if I fail to warn you of a danger I have created: do I thereby 'inflict' injury on you? I cause you injury if I leave a bucket balanced on the door which falls on your head when you push open the door: do I 'inflict' your injuries? In the OAPA 1861, the more serious the offence, the wider the definition of the *actus reus*. This has caused particular problems where D is charged with an offence under s 18, but the jury wish to bring in a lesser verdict, under s 20, since by the CJA 1967, s 6(3) the jury may only bring a verdict of guilty to a lesser offence than that charged if the allegations on the indictment 'amount to or include (expressly or by necessary implication)' an allegation of another offence. There have been many difficult appeals, for example:

> ***Mandair* (1994)** D was alleged to have thrown sulphuric acid in the face of V, his wife, when in a bad temper. His defence was that he was nowhere near the scene of the accident when the acid somehow splashed into V's face. D was charged with

causing GBH with intent, contrary to the OAPA 1861, s 18. Since there was doubt as to whether he intended to inflict the serious injury suffered by V, the trial judge left to the jury the option of returning the lesser verdict of 'causing grievous bodily harm, contrary to s 20'.

CA: quashed his conviction on the ground that 'causing grievous bodily harm' was an offence unknown to law, but

HL: restored his conviction. Lord Mackay (delivering the main speech) held that although it is better, where it is proposed that the jury should consider an alternative verdict on a lesser count, to add a new count to the indictment, an oral direction could suffice. Here it was clear that the jury's verdict of 'causing grievous bodily harm contrary to s 20' could only mean causing GBH contrary to s 20 in that what D did consisted of inflicting GBH on another person. Lord Mustill dissented on this last point, stating that the case was

> ...concerned not with a mere technicality but rather with the important principle that a defendant can be punished for a statutory offence only if he has been properly convicted of that offence.

Whilst the decision of the majority of the HL in *Mandair* may be satisfactory in the result, it is equally unsatisfactory that the HL needed to deal with such questions. This case alone shows the importance of updating the OAPA.

Mens rea

9.6 An offence under s 18 involves proof of one of the ulterior intents specified: an intent to wound, to do GBH, or to resist or to prevent the lawful arrest of any person. For the appropriate meaning of the word 'intent', see **3.13**. If D's sole intent is to resist arrest, it seems odd to convict him of an offence subject to a maximum of life imprisonment. Don't forget that the inclusion of the word 'unlawful' in both s 18 and s 20 (see **9.8**) should remind you that there may be defences available to D which make his act lawful (see **5.7** on consent).

Reform

9.7 Clause 2 of the draft Criminal Law Bill in Law Com No. 218 (1993) provided:

(1) A person is guilty of an offence if he intentionally causes serious injury to another.

(2) An offence under this section is committed notwithstanding that the injury occurs outside England and Wales if the act causing injury is done in England and Wales.

The Law Commission explain their 'general policy' grounds for clause 2(2) by way of an example: if someone in London posts a letter bomb to Paris that causes serious injury when it is opened there, English courts should have jurisdiction. The provision may become more important now that the courts recognize injury caused by telephone calls: see *Ireland* (1997) at **9.16**.

Inflicting grievous bodily harm or wounding (reckless serious violence)

9.8 Next down the ladder of seriousness is the OAPA 1861, s 20:

> Whosoever shall unlawfully and maliciously wound or inflict any grievous bodily harm upon any other person, either with or without any weapon or instrument, shall be guilty of [an offence], and being convicted thereof shall be liable to [imprisonment for not more than five years].

Again, the wording of this section has led to many difficulties. First, the word 'inflicting' GBH. There has long been an argument as to whether indirect actions can constitute an infliction, or whether a direct 'assault' was needed. Compare the approach taken by two nineteenth-century courts:

Martin (1881) D extinguished the lights of the Theatre Royal in Leeds and bolted the door. In the resulting panic, several people were injured. He was convicted of an offence under the OAPA 1861, s 20.

CCCR (Lord Coleridge CJ): in a very brief judgment, dismissed the appeal. D was not legally represented, and the LCJ made it very clear that he had no time for the appeal, holding that D did inflict GBH on those injured in the panic.

Clarence (1888) D, knowing that he had gonorrhoea, had sexual intercourse with his wife, and infected her. He was convicted of offences under both s 20 and s 47 of the OAPA 1861.

CCCR (composed of 13 judges who reached a majority decision of 9 to 4): allowed his appeal under both sections. Whilst it is difficult, because of the number of judgments (all very brief!), to identify the *ratio decidendi* of this decision, Wills J seems to sum it up well: where there was no assault, there was no infliction of harm.

9.9 This last case, unsatisfactory as it seems to be, continued to cause problems, but was perhaps (perhaps only—it still sometimes raises its head in the context of consent in sexual offences) finally laid to rest in

> ***Ireland; Burstow (1997)*** I made repeated silent phone calls at night to three women who suffered psychiatric illness, and appealed against his conviction for offences under the OAPA 1861, s 47 (see **9.16**). B conducted an eight-month campaign of harassment against one woman, which included silent and abusive phone calls and sending her a menacing note. D was convicted of inflicting GBH, contrary to s 20.
>
> HL: dismissed both appeals. The words 'bodily harm' were capable of covering recognized psychiatric illnesses. An offence of inflicting GBH could be committed even though no physical violence was applied directly or indirectly to the body of the victim. Lord Steyn:
>
>> The criminal law has moved on in the light of a developing understanding of the link between the body and psychiatric injury. In my judgement *Clarence* no longer assists.

The *actus reus* of assault is normally construed to mean the victim is caused fear (see **9.23**). Is it right to say that where someone was not assaulted (i.e. if they consented to the act in question because D lied to them, or perhaps if they did not know that it was happening at all), there could be no offence under the OAPA 1861, s 20? There have been numerous appeals, often on the grounds that a jury brought in a lesser verdict than that charged, and sometimes on the basis of incorrect wording. However, as we saw in **9.5** the HL has now decided in *Mandair* (1994) that these 'technical' problems can safely be ignored. Even before that, the HL in *Metropolitan Police Commissioner v Wilson* (1983, see **9.18**) had decided that there can be an infliction of GBH without an assault being committed, but the reasoning of the HL was not clear. Common sense, of course, suggests that someone who causes/inflicts GBH should be guilty whether or not the victim is frightened. Perhaps the HL have resolved the difficulties by their decision in *Ireland* (1997)? Note that in *Dhaliwal* (2006, **8.75**) the CA held that psychological abuse did not constitute GBH. The breadth of GBH is illustrated in

> ***Bain (2005)*** D committed a number of driving offences whilst evading the police, and V, a passenger in his car, had been seriously injured when he had crashed.
>
> CA: there is nothing wrong in principle with charging a driver with both dangerous driving and inflicting GBH, contrary to s 20, when both charges arose out of the same incident of dangerous driving (though the sentences should be concurrent, not consecutive).

Mens rea

9.10 This too has proved problematic. D must have acted 'maliciously'. It has long been accepted that this means that D must have acted recklessly, but reckless as to what: about whether some harm was caused or whether GBH was caused? And must he himself have been aware of the risk that he was taking?

***Mowatt* (1968)** D or his mate stole £5 from V's pocket. When V seized him, D hit out, allegedly in self-defence. D punched V, pulled him up from the ground, and continued to punch him until he was nearly unconscious. He was charged with robbery and under s 18 of the OAPA. He was convicted of larceny (abolished in 1968, and replaced by theft: see **11.2**) and under s 20.

CA (Diplock LJ): dismissed his appeal. In an offence charged under s 18, the word 'maliciously' adds nothing to the definition of the offence. Within s 20, the word has the meaning applied in *Cunningham* (1957, see **3.18**): D must foresee some physical harm, though not necessarily harm of the gravity charged. It would generally not be necessary to give juries specific guidance on the meaning of the word 'reckless'.

9.11 Is this test fair? Why should D be liable for the consequences of his act unless he foresaw a consequence falling into the same legal category as that which actually occurred? Glanville Williams argued that this test 'distorts the accepted meaning of statutory malice' (TCL, p. 190) and believed that D should only be guilty if he foresaw the *actus reus* of the offence charged, not that of a lesser offence. The issue has continued to confuse:

***Sullivan* (1980)** D, who had been drinking, drove his car down a narrow road, mounting the pavement in order to frighten pedestrians, one of whom was badly injured. Charged with offences under ss 18 and 20, he was convicted of an offence under s 20.

CA (Lord Lane LJ): before a person can be convicted of an offence under s 20 it must be proved that he was aware that the probable consequences of his voluntary act would be to cause some injury to his victim—an intention to frighten is not enough.

9.12 This case marked what Glanville Williams called a minor success for the subjective approach, but the introduction of an objective test of recklessness for some offences after *Caldwell* led to increased confusion. There was even some suggestion that an objective test of recklessness might apply to this offence (see *DPP v K* (1990)) but this decision was overruled in *Spratt* (1991).

9.13 In the summer of 1990 two other cases (*Savage* and *Parmenter*) reached the CA on the question of what D must be aware that he is risking before he can be convicted under s 20, but the courts gave different answers. The issue was resolved by the HL in:

***Savage; DPP v Parmenter* (1992)** D1 threw beer over another woman in a busy pub. The glass slipped from her hand and V suffered cuts. She was convicted of an offence under s 20 (but the CA substituted a conviction under s 47). In a separate case,

D2 injured his 3-month-old son, but said that his inexperience with babies meant that he did not realize that what he was doing would hurt the baby. He was convicted of an offence under s 20 (but the CA quashed his conviction).

HL (Lord Ackner): dismissed D1's appeal, and allowed P's appeal in D2's case. While acknowledging that Glanville Williams and J. C. Smith in their textbooks and in articles and commentaries argue that a person should not be criminally liable for consequences of his conduct unless he foresaw a consequence falling into the same legal category as that set out in the indictment, such a general principle runs contrary to the decision in *Roberts* (1971, see **9.17**), which in Lord Ackner's opinion was correct:

> ...it is quite unnecessary that D should either have intended or have foreseen that his unlawful act might cause physical harm of the gravity described in s 20 ... it is enough that he should have foreseen that some physical harm to some person, albeit of a minor character, might result.

Note also the important cases of *Konzani* (2005) and *Dica* (2005) on the issue of consent and s 20 (see **5.11**).

Reform

9.14 In Law Com No. 218 (1993), the Law Commission recommended simply that 'a person is guilty of an offence if he recklessly causes serious injury to another'. This involves a test in terms of awareness of risk of injury of the type that occurred. (See **9.33**.)

Assault occasioning actual bodily harm (causing some injury)

9.15 The next offence in the hierarchy (and again one that can be tried in either the MC or CC) is found in the OAPA, s 47:

> Whosoever shall be convicted of any assault occasioning actual bodily harm shall be liable ... to [imprisonment for five years].

The maximum penalty for this offence is the same as that under s 20. In reality, however, the sentences imposed are likely to be much lower than for offences under s 20.

9.16 What constitutes ABH?

Miller (1954)   D was charged with raping V, his wife, and with actual bodily harm. V had filed for divorce, but the hearing had been adjourned for D to attend.

Lynskey J (the trial judge; there was no appeal) stated that ABH includes 'any hurt or injury calculated to interfere with the health or comfort' of the victim. This included hysterical and nervous conditions. Since a divorce petition has no effect in law, he could not, as the law then was, be guilty of rape (but see now *R v R* (1992, at **10.9** and also see **10.12**). He was guilty of an offence of ABH.

Chan-Fook (1994)   D aggressively questioned V, whom he suspected of stealing his fiancée's engagement ring. D then dragged V to a second floor room, and locked him in. V, fearing that D would return, escaped through a window and was injured when he fell to the ground. D was convicted of an offence under s 47 on the basis of the psychological harm that V had suffered.

CA (Hobhouse LJ): quashed his conviction. The phrase 'actual bodily harm' may include psychiatric injury, but it does not include mere emotions such as fear or distress or panic nor does it include, as such, states of mind that are not themselves evidence of some identifiable clinical condition. Here there was no evidence to be left to the jury in support of allegations of any psychiatric injury.

Ireland (1997) (see **9.9**)   D made repeated silent phone calls to women who suffered psychiatric harm as a result. He was convicted of offences under s 47.

HL: dismissed his appeal. A silent telephone call can constitute an assault occasioning ABH: V may fear the *possibility* of immediate personal violence.

T v DPP (2003)   D was a member of a group of youths in a park. V was punched in the eye by one of the group and then chased. He fell to the ground, saw D coming towards him, covered his head with his arms and was kicked. He momentarily lost consciousness. Although V had suffered a bloody nose and swelling round his eye, it could not be proved that either of those harms was caused by D's kick rather than by the earlier punch by an unidentified youth. D was charged with assault occasioning ABH contrary to s 47. The justices found him guilty. He appealed by way of case stated, submitting that a momentary loss of consciousness could not be ABH because it was, by definition, merely transient and although an injury did not need to be permanent it had to be more than merely transient or trifling.

QBD: dismissed the appeal. The words 'actual bodily harm' were not defined in the 1861 Act and there was no reason why they should have been as they were everyday words. The word 'harm' was a synonym for injury and the word 'actual' indicated that the injury should not be so trivial as to be wholly insignificant. It could not be doubted that the loss of consciousness as suffered by V in the present case fell within the meaning of the word 'harm'. It involved an injurious impairment to his sensory functions. What was excluded from the definition of ABH was harm that was 'transient and trifling', not 'transient or trifling'. Accordingly, on the plain words of the section, the justices had been entitled to find that the assault carried out by D had occasioned ABH.

Note that in *DPP v Smith* (2006) the DC held that the cutting off of V's hair without consent could amount to ABH.

Mens rea

9.17 The *mens rea* of ABH is again a test of subjective recklessness:

> *Roberts* **(1971)** D assaulted V, a passenger in his car, by trying to take her coat off. In fear, she jumped out of the car, and was injured.
>
> CA (Stephenson LJ): the *mens rea* of actual bodily harm was the *mens rea* of assault only. Once that was satisfied, there was simply an objective test of whether D's action had caused the injury, i.e. whether it was the natural consequence of the assault.

Thus, since an intention to frighten is enough, Glanville Williams argues that 'at the most, the crime becomes one of half *mens rea*' (TCL, p. 192). As detailed at 9.33, the Law Commission would change this.

Can a person tried for an offence under s 20 be convicted of an offence under s 47?

9.18 This is a particular problem because of the unclear wording of the OAPA. Clearly s 47 was not designed simply as a lesser version of s 20. Yet it would be a procedural headache if D could only be convicted of an offence under s 47 if it had been specified on the indictment. The difficulty is that the word 'inflict' in s 20 does not necessarily imply an assault, but an assault is clearly necessary for a conviction under s 47. Section 6(3) of the CLA 1967 makes clear that where a person is tried on indictment for any offence except treason or murder, and the jury find him not guilty of the offence charged, the jury may find him guilty of another offence where 'the allegations in the indictment amount to or include (expressly or by implication)' an allegation of the other offence. The HL faced this problem head-on in:

> *Metropolitan Police Comr v Wilson; Jenkins* **(1983)** W had been charged with an offence under s 20, but was convicted under s 47; J had been charged with burglary, but was convicted under s 47.

HL (Lord Roskill): applying s 6(3), a conviction under s 47 was possible. 'Inflict' does not imply assault, but it is narrower than 'cause' because it includes only the direct application of force. The HL followed the Australian case of *Salisbury* (1976) in deciding that there can be an infliction of GBH without an assault, but that a conviction under s 47 was possible if the facts were sufficient to prove an assault. This can only be determined on examination of the facts of each particular case at the time of trial. Lord Roskill noted the danger that D might be convicted of a charge not fully investigated at trial, but said that it was up to the trial judge to guard against this.

9.19 Whilst this may make good practical sense, it again highlights the difficulties involved in trying to make a neat ladder of offences out of a statute which was not so designed (see also the discussion of *Mandair* (1994), at **9.5**).

Common assault and battery

9.20 Section 39 of the CJA 1988 replaced s 42 of the OAPA 1861:

Common assault and battery shall be summary offences and a person guilty of either of them shall be liable to a fine not exceeding level 5 on the standard scale, to imprisonment for a term not exceeding six months, or to both.

The difficulties here are often created by the sloppy use (even by the judiciary) of the two terms assault and battery.

Battery

9.21 A battery involves the direct application of force, such as punching, spitting, or merely touching. It is often said that the touching must be both unlawful and hostile. In *Wilson v Pringle* (1987), a civil case in which one schoolboy sued another for injuries caused when they were mucking around in the corridor at school, the CA held that the element of hostility in a battery must be a question of fact. However, in *Re F (mental patient: sterilisation)* (1990, at **5.22**) Lord Goff doubted whether there was a requirement that the touching be hostile. It is yet another example of an unhelpful and outdated word clouding the interpretation of the criminal law.

9.22 The *mens rea* of battery is an intention to apply unlawful force, or subjective recklessness as to whether such force will be applied.

Venna (1976) D was involved in a fight in the street and kicked V, a police officer, whose hand was fractured. He was convicted of ABH and threatening behaviour.

CA (James LJ): dismissed D's appeal. The element of *mens rea* in battery is satisfied by proof that D either intentionally or recklessly applied force to the person of another.

It is hardly surprising that the CA rejected the argument that battery could only be committed intentionally; otherwise it would be easier to prove the more serious offence of s 20 than the offence of battery.

Assault

9.23 A common assault (sometimes known as a psychic, as opposed to a physical, assault), on the other hand, is the intentional or reckless causing of an apprehension of immediate unlawful personal violence (i.e. a battery). The essence of the offence is that the victim fears the direct application of force: no touching is necessary. Even though it must be fear of immediate violence, someone may apprehend the application of force through a closed window (*Smith v Chief Superintendent of Woking Police Station* (1983)).

Can words alone constitute an assault?

9.24 Words coupled with actions clearly constitute an assault. It would be odd if it were impossible to assault someone in a dark alley at night, or impossible to assault a blind person. Yet there are uncertainties here: largely perhaps because there are few prosecutions for such minor offences. Words alone can negative an assault:

Turbervell v Savadge (1669) P put his hand on his sword and said, 'If it were not assize-time, I would not take such language from you.'

KBD: held that there was no assault. P's declaration was that he would not assault him, and it requires both the intention and the act to make an assault.

Since *Ireland* (1997, see **9.9** and **9.16**) it has been clear that even silent telephone calls may constitute an assault.

9.25 Even modern statutes cause their fair share of confusion: it has been held that to charge assault and battery contrary to s 39 in the same count is bad for duplicity (*DPP v Taylor* (1992)). Nor can a person charged with an offence under s 47 be convicted of the summary offence of common assault unless it was specified as a separate count on the indictment (*Mearns* (1991)). As was pointed out in **1.15**, the work of a criminal law practitioner is often made more complicated by procedural and evidential issues rather than by questions of substantive law.

Reform

9.26 Clause 6 of Law Com No. 218 (1993) states that:

(1) A person is guilty of the offence of assault if—

(a) he intentionally or recklessly applies force to or causes an impact on the body of another—

(i) without the consent of the other, or

(ii) where the act is intended or likely to cause injury, with or without the consent of the other; or

(b) he intentionally or recklessly, without the consent of the other, causes the other to believe that any such force or impact is imminent.

(2) No such offence is committed if the force or impact, not being intended or likely to cause injury, is in the circumstances such as is generally acceptable in the ordinary conduct of daily life and the defendant does not know or believe that it is in fact unacceptable to the other person.

This would abolish battery as a separate offence. Both modes of assault are therefore expressed in the same offence. But are both actually necessary? Since most assaults (in the clause 6(1)(b) sense) will be attempted assaults (in the clause 6(1)(a) sense), do we still need an offence of assault (in the clause 6(1)(b) sense)? The answer to this may depend on whether the proposed offence is triable only summarily, since generally it is not an offence to attempt to commit an offence which is triable only summarily (CAA 1981, s 1(4): see 7.4).

Threats

9.27 An assault has to involve fear of immediate force. The law does not protect against future threats. The only form of non-immediate threat that is an offence at present is provided by the OAPA 1861, s 16 (as substituted in Sch 12 to the Criminal Law Act 1977):

A person who without lawful excuse makes to another a threat, intending that that other would fear it would be carried out, to kill that other or a third person shall be guilty of an offence and liable on conviction on indictment to imprisonment for a term not exceeding 10 years.

A recent uncontroversial example is provided by *Marchese* (2008). It is the person to whom the threat is made who must be frightened that it will be carried out:

Tait (1990) D made threats to a five-months pregnant woman stating, 'I will come back and get your baby', by which she understood him to mean to kill her unborn baby. He was convicted of an offence under OAPA 1861, s 16.

CA (Mustill LJ): quashed his conviction. A threat to kill a foetus by bringing about a miscarriage does not constitute an offence under s 16. The foetus was not 'another person' distinct from its mother.

9.28 Most people would suggest that Tait's behaviour should be a criminal offence. But which? Perhaps he could have been prosecuted under the Public Order Act 1986, s 5, but we shall critically examine the use of this statute in cases of domestic violence at **12.20**. Another solution would be to widen the existing offence to include threats other than those to kill. The DCC (1989), which generally set out to enact current law, proposed a significant change in this area. Clause 65 states that:

> A person is guilty of an offence if he makes to another a threat to cause the death of, or serious personal harm to, that other or a third person, intending that other to believe that it will be carried out.

Not only would implementation extend the scope of the offence to serious personal harm; it also replaces the word 'fear' with 'believe'.

Protection from harassment

9.29 The Protection from Harassment Act 1997 created a novel approach to deal with those who harass others. Sections 2 and 4 create offences of harassment. Under s 2, a person who commits a course of conduct which amounts to harassment of another commits an offence. And under s 4:

> A person whose course of conduct causes another to fear, on at least two occasions, that violence will be used against him is guilty of an offence if he knows or ought to know that his course of conduct will cause the other so to fear on each of those occasions.

There is a wealth of case law. For example:

Widdows (2011) D had been involved in a volatile relationship with V. During the time in which they had lived together they had separated on many occasions, usually being reunited after a short period. D was charged with the s 4 offence along with two counts of the rape, of which he was acquitted.

CA: allowed his appeal against his conviction for s 4. The emphasis in the judge's summing up was not on what amounted to harassment but what amounted to assault. Further direction was required as to what could be a course of conduct amounting to harassment. A description of a number of acts of violence spread over nine months during a close and affectionate relationship did not satisfy the course of conduct requirement, or the requirement that it was conduct amounting to harassment.

There are three statutory defences to these offences: prevention of crime (on which see **5.35**), lawful excuse, or that the pursuit of the course of conduct was reasonable (for the offence under s 4, the conduct must be reasonable for the protection of himself or another or for the protection of property).

Haque **(2011)** D and V, his brother, were in a dispute over the care of their disabled sister. P alleged that D had been responsible for sending two letters, two emails, and a number of text messages venting his anger, causing V to fear that violence would be used against him. D said that V was not put in fear of violence and had lied when he said he was. D relied on the statutory defence that his course of conduct was reasonable and that he was acting to protect his sister. D was convicted of an offence under s 4.

CA: dismissed his appeal. But for the decisions in *Curtis* (2010) and *Widdows* (2011), the court have taken the view that the s 4(1) offence was a free-standing offence and did not require proof of harassment. But *Curtis* and *Widdows* had to be followed. P had to prove (i) that the course of conduct was targeted at an individual; (ii) that the conduct must have been calculated to produce alarm or distress. The jury here had not been directed that they had to be sure D intended to alarm V or cause him distress. But the conviction was safe: it was inconceivable that the jury, given their other conclusions, would not have been sure that D intended to alarm or distress V in order to achieve his stated objective of protecting his sister; (iii) the conduct must have been oppressive and unreasonable. But it is not for the P to show that it is unreasonable: s 1(3) provides that D has to show that his conduct was reasonable (see paras 69–73).

9.30 Under s 3, civil courts can make non-harassment injunctions, and under s 3(6) breach of such an injunction is a criminal offence punishable with up to five years' imprisonment. As well as anti-harassment laws, there are specific (but grossly inadequate?) civil remedies for domestic violence. The DVCVA 2004 criminalized the breach of non-molestation orders imposed under the Family Law Act 1996, s 1 and extended the availability of restraining orders under the Protection from Harassment Act 1997, s 12. (A not untypical case is provided by *Forsythe* (2009).)

Administering poison

9.31 The original OAPA 1861 contained many surprisingly specific offences (see **9.1**), many of which have now been repealed. Two of those which seem somewhat archaic are still regularly enforced. First, s 23:

> Whosoever shall unlawfully and maliciously administer to or cause to be administered to be taken by any other person any poison or other destructive or noxious thing, so as thereby to endanger the life of such person, or so as thereby to inflict upon such person any grievous bodily harm, shall be guilty of an offence.

See also s 24:

> Whosoever shall unlawfully and maliciously administer to or cause to be administered to or taken by any other person any poison or other destructive or noxious thing, with intent to injure, aggrieve, or annoy any such person, shall be guilty of [an offence].

The maximum penalty for an offence under s 23 is ten years' imprisonment, for an offence under s 24, five years. Section 23 penalizes those who endanger life or inflict GBH by poisoning; s 24 requires no such consequence, but there must be an intent to injure.

Administer

9.32 Something can be administered directly or indirectly, and administration may even consist of causing the victim to administer the substance to himself. *Cunningham* (1957; still the basic case on subjective recklessness: see **3.18**) was a case under s 23 where D 'administered' gas by breaking off the gas meter and allowing escaping gas to fill the next-door house.

> *Gillard* (1988) D bought CS gas to attack the doorman of a wine bar. He appealed from his conviction for 'conspiracy to cause to be administered a noxious thing ... on the ground that administer does not encompass spraying CS gas'.
>
> CA: upheld his conviction. Administer was an ordinary word which should be left to the jury. There was no need to postulate entry into the body: bringing a noxious thing into contact with the body, directly or indirectly, was enough.

Would assault be a more appropriate charge in the case of someone who sprays CS gas at someone else? Do we need this extra offence? Note its use as the basis for the unsuccessful attempt to prosecute for manslaughter the drug addict who hands V a syringe of heroin: *Kennedy (No. 2)* (2007): see **2.22**.

Reform

9.33 There is considerable doubt as to the *mens rea* for an offence under s 23; for s 24, there is clearly a need for an ulterior intent. The Law Commission (in Law Com No. 218, 1993) agree with the CLRC, *Offences against the Person* (Cmnd 7844, 1980) that conduct of the type penalized in s 23 is anyhow covered by their proposed offence of intentionally or recklessly causing serious injury, but they nonetheless propose a variation on the s 24 offence:

> (1) A person is guilty of an offence if, knowing that the other does not consent to what is done, he intentionally or recklessly administers to or causes to be taken by another a substance which he knows to be capable of interfering substantially with the other's bodily functions.
>
> (2) For the purposes of this section a substance capable of inducing unconsciousness or sleep is capable of interfering substantially with bodily functions.

This would replace the current need to prove an 'intent to injure, aggrieve or annoy' with a need to prove simply knowledge that what D administers was capable of interfering with V's bodily functions. Is this offence necessary or, again, will all serious cases coming within the clause be covered by intentionally or recklessly causing injury (or attempting to do so)?

Treason and terrorism

9.34 A student textbook which seeks to introduce the general principles of the criminal law may not be the place to discuss at length offences against the Crown and the Government. But it would be equally wrong to ignore the proliferation of recent offences related to terrorism. Treason has been an offence since before the Treason Act 1351, which limited it to

> …when a man doth compass or imagine the death of our lord the King, or of our lady his Queen or of their eldest son and heir; or if a man do violate the King's companion, or the King's eldest daughter unmarried, or the wife of the King's eldest son and heir; or if a man do levy war against our lord the King in his realm, or be adherent to the King's enemies in his realm, giving to them aid and comfort in the realm, or elsewhere, and thereof be probably attainted of open deed by the people of their condition: … and if a man slea the chancellor, treasurer, or the King's justices of the one bench or the other, justices in eyre, or justices of assise, and all other justices assigned to hear and determine, being in their places, doing their offices: and it is to be understood, that in the cases above rehearsed, that ought to be judged treason which extends to our lord the King, and his royal majesty.

Students should be aware of the many offences created by a host of Terrorism Acts. First, the Terrorism Act 2000 (an offence to belong or profess to belong to a proscribed organization and to fundraise or support such organizations), then the Anti-Terrorism, Crime and Security Act 2001 (offences to use noxious substances to cause harm and intimidate and to hoax involving noxious substances or things), and the Prevention of Terrorism Act 2005 (offences to breach control orders). The Terrorism Act 2006, s 5 (preparation of terrorist acts) is discussed at 7.1, but that Act also had other new offences including the offence of encouragement of terrorism (s 1); an offence of inciting the commission of acts of terrorism outside the UK (s 59); an offence relating to bookshops and other disseminators of terrorist publications; an offence of the preparation of terrorist acts; further terrorist training offences; offences relating to radioactive material or devices, and nuclear facilities, and amends the penalty for certain offences relating to nuclear material. Now we also have the Counter-Terrorism Act 2008 (which amends the definition of terrorism in s 1 of the Terrorism Act 2000, and other terrorism legislation, by inserting a reference to a racial cause (s 75) and creates a new offence of eliciting, publishing, or communicating information relating to members of the armed forces which is likely to be of use to terrorists, and amends the offence of failing to disclose information about a suspected terrorist offence). Many of the highly publicized challenges to these new laws have focused on procedural and evidential issues, but students may like to consider the extent to which the 'war' on terrorism can be won (or helped) simply by creating new and specific offences which overlap the existing criminal armoury. The complexity of this legislation also goes against the basic approach that is advocated in Chapter 1, for the law to be, in particular, accessible and comprehensible (see 1.31).

Slavery, servitude, and forced or compulsory labour

9.35 The C&JA 2009 adds a new offence to the statute book, which came into force on 6 April 2010:

s 71 Slavery, servitude and forced or compulsory labour

(1) A person (D) commits an offence if—

    (a) D holds another person in slavery or servitude and the circumstances are such that D knows or ought to know that the person is so held, or

    (b) D requires another person to perform forced or compulsory labour and the circumstances are such that D knows or ought to know that the person is being required to perform such labour.

A person guilty of an offence under this section is liable on conviction on indictment, to imprisonment for a term not exceeding 14 years or a fine, or both. It is mentioned here simply to remind readers that the OAPA 1861 is far from a complete code of offences against the person, and indeed it supplements the existing offence of trafficking people for exploitation, contrary to s 4(1) and (5) of the Asylum and Immigration (Treatment of Claimants) Act 2004 on which there is already a significant case law (see *SK* (2011)).

Torture, genocide, and other crimes 'against humanity'

9.36   Indeed, there are many more 'international law' crimes. The role of the International Criminal Court, which tries only those accused of the gravest crimes: genocide, crimes against humanity, and war crimes, is clearly outside the scope of this book (and in any case, should perhaps feature in Chapter 8?). However, it is certainly worth a mention in order to raise questions about the relationship between international and domestic law. The International Criminal Court is governed by the Rome Statute, which entered into force on 1 July 2002 after ratification by 60 countries (see the International Criminal Court Act 2001). It is a permanent, treaty-based, international criminal court established to help end impunity for the perpetrators of the most serious crimes of concern to the international community. It is not part of the United Nations system and has its seat at The Hague in the Netherlands. It does not act if a case is investigated or prosecuted by a national justice system unless the national proceedings are not genuine, for example if formal proceedings were undertaken solely to shield a person from criminal responsibility. So domestic law has created crimes of genocide, etc.:

Section 51 of the International Criminal Court Act 2001 provides:

(1) It is an offence against the law of England and Wales for a person to commit genocide, a crime against humanity or a war crime.

(2) This section applies to acts committed—

(a) in England or Wales, or

(b) outside the United Kingdom by a United Kingdom national, a United Kingdom resident or a person subject to UK service jurisdiction.

It is also an offence to engage in 'conduct ancillary to' genocide, etc. committed outside England and Wales. Even before that, s 134 of the CJA 1988 added an offence of torture to English law. This was to implement the Convention on Torture adopted by the UN in 1984. How does this fit in within the existing framework of offences against the person?

s 134 Torture

(1) A public official or person acting in an official capacity, whatever his nationality, commits the offence of torture if in the UK or elsewhere he intentionally inflicts severe pain or suffering on another in the performance or purported performance of his official duties.

(2) A person not falling within subsection (1) above commits the offence of torture, whatever his nationality, if—

    (a) in the UK or elsewhere he intentionally inflicts severe pain or suffering on another at the instigation or with the consent or acquiescence—

      (i) of a public official; or

      (ii) of a person acting in an official capacity; and

    (b) the official or other person is performing or purporting to perform his official duties when he instigates the commission of the offence or consents to or acquiesces in it.

(3) It is immaterial whether the pain or suffering is physical or mental and whether it is caused by an act or omission.

9.37 Section 134(4) gives a defence of 'lawful authority, justification or excuse for that conduct'. The maximum penalty is life imprisonment. The Law Commission propose to reproduce this offence within their codification of non-fatal offences against the person since it belongs more appropriately there rather than tucked away in a CJA. (The issue of torture has, of course, been much discussed in litigation: the HL held in *A v Home Secretary* (2005) that evidence obtained by torture could not be used as evidence, and in *Jones v Ministry of the Interior of the Kingdom of Saudi Arabia* (2006) that claimants could not seek damages in the UK for the results of tortures allegedly inflicted on them in Saudi Arabia.) But there has been only one successful prosecution for torture under s 134:

Zardad (2007) D, now resident in the UK, was a former commander during the Afghan Civil War between 1992 and 1996, who had his main base at a former Russian military compound. P alleged that hostage-taking and torture occurred at checkpoints controlled by D and with D's full knowledge, approval, and in some instances his direct involvement. There was evidence that those who passed through the checkpoints were often taken from their vehicles at gunpoint, beaten and kicked, and detained in a bunker for days and weeks where they would be further beaten with guns, sticks, and electric cables. D denied the allegations but was convicted of conspiracy to commit torture and conspiracy to take hostages (and sentenced to 20 years' imprisonment).

> CA: dismissed D's appeal (the appeal turned on questions regarding the admissibility of evidence).

The question for us to consider (briefly!) is whether the UK should have jurisdiction to prosecute suspects found in the UK, whether or not they are British citizens or residents, and the crime was committed abroad. Clearly, the general trend is to expand liability domestically in order to stop serious criminals being able to avoid prosecution (see s 70 of the C&JA 2009, for example): should extradition to the 'scene of the crime' be preferred to prosecution in the UK? Or is that immoral and/or unrealistic? (See also **7.3**, but this subject is probably outside your criminal law syllabus: go carefully!)

Racially or religiously aggravated offences

9.38 Offences against the person are frequently aggravated by racial or religious hostility. Should this result in prosecution for a different and more serious offence, or simply lead to an increased sentence? The Crime and Disorder Act 1998 introduced four new offences of racially aggravated assaults. The meaning of racially aggravated is explained in s 28: P must prove, beyond reasonable doubt, either:

(a) the existence of racial hostility at or around the time the offence was committed, or

(b) that the offence was motivated by racial hostility.

The four new offences of racially aggravated assaults are all found in s 29:

- racially aggravated wounding;
- racially aggravated grievous bodily harm;
- racially aggravated actual bodily harm;
- racially aggravated common assault.

These offences do not make illegal what was previously legal, but simply make the existing offences under the OAPA 1861 more serious. Section 30 deals with racially or religiously aggravated criminal damage; s 31 with racially or religiously aggravated public order offences; and s 32 with racially or religiously aggravated harassment etc. Sentencers have long given increased sentences for offences which involve racism, and this is nowadays required by statutes (see ss 145 and 146 CJA 2003). Malik (1999) suggested that it is a mistake to overestimate the role that the criminal law has in addressing the consequences of racism. Section 29 was extended by the Anti-Terrorism, Crime and Security Act 2001 to include religiously aggravated assaults. Do you agree with Baroness Hale's arguments below?

White (2001) D admitted calling a bus conductress an African bitch. He was convicted under the Crime and Disorder Act 1998, s 31.

CA: dismissed appeal. The language of the statute should be given a non-technical meaning. In ordinary speech 'African' was used to describe a racial group. There was no basis in law for the proposition that a person could not show hostility to another person based on that person's membership of the same racial group.

Rogers (2007) D argued with three Spanish women, calling them 'bloody foreigners' and telling them to 'go back to your own country'. He was convicted of using racially aggravated abusive or insulting words or behaviour with intent to cause fear or provoke violence, contrary to the Crime and Disorder Act 1998, s 31 (and sentenced to a community punishment order for 80 hours). The appeal turned on the meaning of 'racial group' in s 28(4).

HL: unanimously dismissed his appeal. Baroness Hale gave the only speech. The definition of a racial group in s 28(4) clearly went beyond groups defined by their colour, race, or ethnic origin. It encompassed both nationality (including citizenship) and national origins. That was quite deliberate. Further, the statute intended a broad, non-technical approach, rather than a construction which invited nice distinctions. That flexible, non-technical approach made sense, not only as a matter of language, but also in policy terms. The mischiefs attacked by the aggravated versions of the relevant offences were racism and xenophobia. Their essence was the denial of equal respect and dignity to people who were seen as 'other'. That was more deeply hurtful, damaging, and disrespectful to Vs than the simple versions of the offences. It was also more damaging to the community as a whole, by denying acceptance to members of certain groups, not for their own sake, but for the sake of something they could do nothing about. Fine distinctions would bring the law into disrepute. There was also an advantage to D, she suggested, in differentiating between the basic and the aggravated offence. The fact-finders, whether a jury or magistrates, have then to decide whether the offence was indeed racially or religiously aggravated. If they decide that it was not, then D should be sentenced on that basis.

SH (2010) D, arguing with a Nigerian Jobcentre employee, threatened to stab him and invited him outside, calling him a 'black monkey'. The trial judge withdrew a count of causing racially aggravated fear or provocation of violence from the jury on the ground that, in light of the history of animosity between the parties, the jury could not say that D had been motivated by hostility to members of a particular racial group (as opposed to being motivated by anger or personal dislike).

CA: P's appeal was allowed and a re-trial was ordered. It was difficult to see how it could be suggested that repeated angry references to a Nigerian national as a 'monkey' did not generate a prima facie case of an outward manifestation of racial hostility. Whether such repeated references constituted a demonstration of hostility based on race or mere vulgar abuse unconnected with hostility based on race was eminently a matter of fact for the jury to consider on all the evidence.

Do you agree that racially aggravated crimes should form the basis of separate offences, since they reflect the 'qualitatively distinct order of gravity' involved when racial hostility is shown? If so, think about (as does Ormerod at [2007] Crim LR 580) sexual orientation and disability hate crime under s 146 of the CJA 2003, which did not create any new offences, but imposed a duty upon courts to increase the sentence for any offence aggravated by hostility based on V's disability (or presumed disability) or sexual orientation. Which approach makes more sense to you?

FURTHER READING

Alldridge, P., 'Threats Offences—A Case for Reform' [1994] Crim LR 176.

Bronitt, S., 'Spreading Disease and the Criminal Law' [1994] Crim LR 21.

Gardner, J., 'Rationality and the Rule of Law in Offences against the Person' (1994) 53 Camb LJ 502.

Hare, I., 'Legislating Against Hate—The Legal Response to Bias Crimes' (1997) 17 OJLS 415.

Home Office, *Violence: Reforming the Offences against the Person Act 1861* (1998).

Horder, J., 'Reconsidering Psychic Assault' [1998] Crim LR 392.

Law Commission, *Legislating the Criminal Code: Offences against the Person and General Principles* (Law Com No. 218, 1993).

Malik, M., 'Racist Crime: Racially Aggravated Offences in the Crime and Disorder Act 1998, Part II' (1999) 62 MLR 409.

Weait, M., 'Knowledge, Autonomy and Consent: *R v Konzani*' [2005] Crim LR 763.

SELF-TEST QUESTIONS

1   In a drunken fight, Dee stabs Phil in the hand with her penknife. She told the police she thought the knife was so blunt that it could only cause a tiny scratch. Unfortunately she almost severs his finger and he has to undergo a series of operations. Discuss Dee's liability.

2   Dee deliberately hits Phil on the head with a wooden spoon, but she does not foresee any harm resulting to him. Surprised, he slips and fractures his skull. What offence(s) has Dee committed?

3   After a filthy row, Dee locks Phil in an upstairs room, telling him that he can 'wait there while I go and get something that will really sort you out'. Phil tries to escape through the window but falls and breaks both his legs. Dee says that she had no intention of injuring Phil but had merely wanted to frighten him. Discuss.

4   Dee fires her gun wildly into the air at night in a public park not thinking about the risks involved. She tells the police later that she was sure that no one normally wanders through the park at night. Phil is badly wounded in the chest. Discuss Dee's liability.

5   Dee points a toy pistol at Phil, who does not realize the gun is a toy and is very frightened. He is a weapons expert and therefore should have known that it was a toy. Discuss Dee's liability.

10 Sexual offences

SUMMARY

Problems of perception and definition: what is a sexual offence? NB: the SOA 2003: a major overhaul.

Rape: intentional penile penetration of the vagina, anus, or mouth. The main problem here is proving V did not consent and that D did not reasonably believe that V consented. NB: new presumptions on consent (ss 75 and 76). Other problems are often evidential: the word of one person against another. Why is the conviction rate so low?

Other offences discussed:

- assault by penetration;
- sexual assault (both words with tricky definitions);
- causing sexual activity.

NB also: child sex offences: strict liability: G (2008); familial child sex offences; offences against people with mental disorders, offences connected with prostitution, bigamy, … and many (too many?) more. Broad inchoate offences.

Introduction

10.1 There are a wide variety of offences which can be loosely classified as sexual:

- rape;
- offences related to prostitution such as soliciting and kerb-crawling;
- indecent photographs of children;
- bigamy;
- sexual intercourse with a girl under 16;

- sexual activity with a child;

- exposure.

What do these offences have in common? Clearly they have a sexual element. Some sexual offences are offences whether or not the parties consent (child sex offences; prostitution-related offences), whilst the essence of others (e.g. rape) is that one party was not consenting. By concentrating on the sexual element of an offence, one might be ignoring other, more important, elements in it. Many crimes, especially those of violence, may include sexual elements. For example, in the sado-masochism case of *Brown* (1994, see 1.7), although the Ds were tried for offences under the OAPA 1861, ss 20 and 47, it is clear from the speeches in the HL that their Lordships found it difficult to draw a line between the 'sexual' and the 'violent'. Lord Templeman in his majority speech said that 'In my opinion sado-masochism is not only concerned with sex. Sado-masochism is also concerned with violence.' Lord Mustill opens his dissenting speech with 'My Lords, this is a case about the criminal law of violence. In my opinion, it should be a case about the criminal law of private sexual relations, if anything at all.' Thus the majority say this is about sex and violence, so Ds are guilty; the minority say the activity is primarily about sex and should not be prosecuted as offences of violence. Can a distinction between sex and violence be usefully maintained?

10.2 Look at rape: why do we classify it as a sexual offence and not as a crime of violence? There is a danger that in labelling it 'simply' as a sexual offence, we dilute the seriousness of the offence. In Canada, the Criminal Code was radically overhauled in 1982: the offences of indecent assault and rape were replaced by the offences of sexual assault and aggravated sexual assault. Look at these three reasons given by the Law Reform Commission of Canada in 1978 for abolishing rape:

  (i) The predominant legal and behavioural characteristic of rape is not for the offender its sexual but rather its aggressive aspect, its violation of the physical integrity of the human person.

  (ii) The use of the word 'rape' attaches a profound moral stigma to the victims and expresses an essentially irrational folklore about them.

  (iii) All acts of penetration, vaginal, oral, or anal, and all acts of sexual aggression regardless of form, should come within the same scope of legal sanction.

In England, there have been few calls to abolish the term 'rape': it is an offence well understood and abhorred by the public. But some of the Canadian arguments are strong. At the end of the day, whether a 'rapist' is convicted of rape in England or of aggravated sexual assault in Canada, he is likely to be subject to a lengthy custodial sentence. Does the label matter (see 1.2)?

10.3 Chapter 1 looks briefly at the relationship between law and morals (see 1.5). It seems to have become accepted that the law should not concern itself too much with people's private morality. Yet this causes major difficulties: people are probably in greater need of protection from violence and sexual attack in the privacy of their own home than they are on the street. The family home is often portrayed as a haven of peace; personal safety campaigns concentrate on safety in open places. Yet it is vital to 'open up' sexual offences to allow victims of 'private' sexual offences to gain better protection from the law. Read again the second Canadian argument for abolishing rape: victims of rape may be unfairly stigmatized. Is this really an argument for abolishing the offence, or simply for improving the procedural safeguards for victims?

10.4 The law in England was subject to a massive reform, in the SOA 2003, which was brought into force on 1 May 2004. It was built on several major reviews. First, the Home Office produced a huge two-volume *Review of Sexual Offences: Setting the Boundaries* in 2000. The Report's first 'guiding principle' was that a judgment of what is right and wrong in sexual relationships should be based on an assessment of the harm done to the individual, and through the individual to society as a whole. See 7.2, for a discussion of the tension which exists in criminal law between harm-based liability and intention-based liability. Do you think that the Home Office got it right? The Report's other 'guiding principle' was that the criminal law should not intrude unnecessarily into the private lives of adults. How far does this principle help? Of course the criminal law should not intrude unnecessarily into the private lives of adults or children, but the difficulty with this guiding principle is in deciding when intrusion into private life becomes 'necessary'. Nobody's right to autonomy in their private life is absolute: a more useful guiding principle might have been based on the balancing of competing rights. But even this will not help in difficult cases where the law provides that consent is irrelevant: incest or consensual physical injuries arising from sexual activities, for example. Here another guiding principle is needed. Lacey comments that the Report has an 'over-optimistic attitude to both the symbolic, denunciatory/educative and the instrumental, protective/deterrent impact of substantial criminal law' [2001] Crim LR 3, at p. 13.

10.5 There followed a *Review of Part 1 of the Sex Offenders Act 1997* (Home Office (2001)). The SOA 1997 imposed notification requirements on convicted sex offenders, and this review was concerned with the perceived need to strengthen public protection against sex offenders. The White Paper *Protecting the Public: Strengthening Protection against Sex Offenders and Reforming the Law on Sexual Offences* (Cm. 5668, 2002) led to the publication of the Bill which in turn became the SOA 2003. We are mostly concerned in this chapter with the substantive offences in Part 1 of the Act. But readers should note the equally important Part 2, which further strengthens notification requirements and introduces new orders such as sexual offences prevention orders, foreign travel orders, and risk of sexual harm orders. These may be imposed on those convicted of a huge array of offences, not only of sexual offences (see Schedules 3 and 5 to the Act). Does the Act achieve a suitable balance between the need to protect and reassure the public and the rights of the offender, whose life and reputation can be hugely affected by the imposition of one of these orders?

10.6 One problem which was not anticipated was that which arises when it is difficult to establish whether the offence occurred before or after 1 May 2004, the day the new law came into force. The Government failed to provide any transitional arrangements to cover cases where V could not say whether the events in question happened before or after 1 May 2004, and this caused a significant problem in practice (see *C (also known as A) (Prosecutor's Appeal)* (2006) for an example). This gap has now been plugged by the Violent Crime Reduction Act 2006, s 55, which provides that:

> **s 55 Continuity of sexual offences law**
>
> (1) This section applies where, in any proceedings—
>
> > (a) a person ('the defendant') is charged in respect of the same conduct both with an offence under the Sexual Offences Act 2003 ('the 2003 Act offence') and with an offence specified in subsection (2) ('the pre-commencement offence');
> >
> > (b) the only thing preventing the defendant from being found guilty of the 2003 Act offence is the fact that it has not been proved beyond a reasonable doubt that the time when the conduct took place was after the coming into force of the enactment providing for the offence, and
> >
> > (c) the only thing preventing the defendant from being found guilty of the pre-commencement offence is the fact that it has not been proved beyond a reasonable doubt that that time was before the coming into force of the repeal of the enactment providing for the offence ...
>
> (3) For the purpose of determining the guilt of the defendant it shall be conclusively presumed that the time when the conduct took place was—
>
> > (a) if the maximum penalty for the pre-commencement offence is less than the maximum penalty for the 2003 Act offence, a time before the coming into force of the repeal of the enactment providing for the pre-commencement offence; and
> >
> > (b) in any other case, a time after the coming into force of the enactment providing for the 2003 Act offence.

(4) In subsection (3) the reference, in relation an offence, to the maximum penalty is a reference to the maximum penalty by way of imprisonment or other detention that could be imposed on the defendant on conviction of the offence in the proceedings in question.

(5) A reference in this section to an offence under the Sexual Offences Act 2003 (c. 42) or to an offence specified in subsection (2) includes a reference to—

(a) inciting the commission of that offence;

(b) conspiracy to commit that offence; and

(c) attempting to commit that offence; …

10.7 Many of the difficulties in this area are procedural and evidential: if there are only two people present, how does one balance the presumption of innocence with the need to protect the public from dangerous offenders? Rape remains one of the most under-enforced crimes, with a low conviction rate. The fundamental principle of autonomy was highlighted in **1.2**, yet, as Lacey, Wells, and Quick (2010) point out, the principle is a loose one and it pulls in two directions: 'Bodily autonomy can demand protection in two senses: first, protection of one's own choices, and second, protection against interference by others' (at p. 457). Although most Ds in sexual cases are male, many writers have pointed out that while the law formally penalizes men, the reality is often that it seems to reinforce male domination over women: women giving evidence in rape trials, for example, often end up feeling more defiled, more guilty than does D himself. Parliament therefore attempted in the Youth Justice and Criminal Evidence Act 1999 to create more protection for vulnerable witnesses, but at a cost for those defending themselves (see Munday (2009), Stern (2010)).

Rape

10.8 Rape is defined in the SOA 2003, s 1:

A person (A) commits an offence if—

(a) he intentionally penetrates the vagina, anus or mouth of another person (B) with his penis,

(b) B does not consent to the penetration, and

(c) A does not reasonably believe that B consents.

The maximum sentence is life imprisonment, though sentences vary enormously. The definition of rape has been expanded over the years: for example, before 1994 only vaginal intercourse constituted rape, but the CJPOA 1994 extended the definition to include anal rape, and therefore male rape. Now it also includes penetration of the mouth. It is still an offence which can only be committed by men (though a woman may be convicted of aiding and abetting rape (see **6.3**)).

10.9 'Domestic violence' has long been treated insufficiently seriously. Thus, until 1992 husbands could not be convicted of raping their wives. This was because, in the words of Sir Matthew Hale in 1736:

> ...the husband cannot be held guilty of a rape committed by himself upon his lawful wife, for by their mutual matrimonial consent and contract the wife hath given herself up in this kind unto her husband which she cannot retract.

Finally, times were acknowledged to have changed:

> **R (1992)** D and his wife, V, separated, and agreed to seek a divorce. Three weeks later D forced his way into V's parents' home, where she was now living, and attempted to rape her. He pleaded guilty after a ruling from the judge that a husband could be guilty after a wife had clearly revoked her consent to sex, and he was sentenced to three years' imprisonment.
>
> HL (Lord Keith): dismissed his appeal. 'Section 1(1) of the SOA 1976 presents no obstacle to this House declaring that in modern times the supposed marital exception in rape forms no part of the law in England.'

10.10 This case was very controversial, not because many people wanted to argue that a husband should be immune from a rape prosecution, but because the HL was accused of usurping the role of Parliament. The CLRC (15th Report, on sexual offences (Cmnd 9213, 1984)) had recommended against the extension of rape to husbands who had ceased cohabitation for the rather dubious reason of the difficulty in defining 'cohabitation'. As we saw at **1.26**, R took his case unsuccessfully to the ECtHR. At last Parliament acted, and the CJPOA 1994 statement of the law made clear that any man may be convicted of the rape of any woman (or man). Many of the controversies have now switched to the sentencing of rapists as courts struggle to find the 'appropriate' length of sentence in cases where the parties knew each other at the time of the rape, and to the need to protect V from aggressive cross-examination in court. On some occasions 'date rape' or 'marital rape' may be seen as less serious than 'stranger rape'; on others it will be seen as more serious because of the breach of trust involved. Perhaps too the time has come when the law should penalize any person who has non-consensual intercourse, and not merely men.

Actus reus: penetration

10.11 The pre-2003 law defined rape as non-consensual 'sexual intercourse'. As the SOA 1956, s 44 (now repealed) made clear, the slightest degree of penetration was all that was required:

> Where, on the trial of any offence under this Act, it is necessary to prove sexual intercourse (whether natural or unnatural) it shall not be necessary to prove the completion of the intercourse by the emission of seed, but the intercourse shall be deemed complete on proof of penetration only.

The SOA 2003, s 79(2) provides that 'penetration is a continuing act from entry to withdrawal'. Thus, if at any stage during the intercourse the other party withdraws his or her consent, the act becomes rape. Lord Scarman made it clear in the PC in *Kaitamaki v R* (1985) that although the act of rape was complete upon penetration, it was a continuing act only ending with withdrawal. If a man realizes that his partner is not consenting half-way through the act, he may still be guilty of rape. Does this mean that this is a case of rape by omission? Do the ordinary rules covering liability for omissions apply (see **2.7**)?

Mens rea

10.12 The fault element in rape is intentional sexual intercourse combined with an absence of consent or an absence of a reasonable belief in consent (what would have been discussed in the context of 'recklessness' as to the other's consent before the SOA 2003). Many of the difficulties in this area concern the issue of consent.

Absence of consent

10.13 Difficulties often arise when D argues that he mistakenly believed that V was consenting. What if a man genuinely believes that the other person is consenting? Or if he makes an unreasonable (but genuine) mistake? After a controversial decision of the HL in *DPP v Morgan* (1976), Parliament enacted the SOA 1976, s 1(2), which provided:

> It is hereby declared that if at a trial for a rape offence the jury has to consider whether a man believed that a woman or man was consenting to sexual intercourse, the presence or absence of reasonable grounds for such a belief is a matter to which the jury is to have regard, in conjunction with any other relevant matters, in considering whether he so believed.

Thus even an unreasonable but genuine belief would then result in an acquittal. This is no longer the law. In *Consent in Sex Offences* (2002) the Law Commission recommended that the law should be strengthened by requiring judges to give juries additional directions:

(i) that the jury should, in addressing the issue of the defendant's asserted belief in consent, have regard to whether the defendant availed himself of any opportunity to ascertain whether the victim consented; and

(ii) that, if his asserted belief in consent was caused solely by reason of his voluntarily intoxicated state then his failure to appreciate that she (he) might not consent is no defence.

The Law Commission defined consent as 'a subsisting, free and genuine agreement in question'. But the SOA 2003 goes further. Section 74 states:

> For the purposes of this Part, a person consents if he agrees by choice, and has the freedom and capacity to make that choice.

These terms have already resulted in some interesting appeals: what is choice? or freedom, for example? Clearly submission is not the same as consent, not even 'willing submission' (see *Kirk* (2008)). See **5.13** for the cases of *Linekar* (1995), *B* (2007), and *Bree* (2007).

B **(2013)** D was convicted of raping and assaulting his partner, V. There was expert medical evidence that D had been suffering from a mental disorder, probably paranoid schizophrenia, at the time of the offences, but that he had had the capacity to know what he was doing and that it was wrong. The expert said that the acts of intercourse might have been motivated by D's delusional beliefs that he had sexual healing powers, but that any such delusions did not extend to a belief that V had consented. On the rape counts, the judge directed the jury that they should ignore D's mental illness when asking whether any belief that he might have had in V's consent had been reasonable.

CA: upheld the convictions. There was clearly a proper basis for the jury's finding that V had not consented to sexual intercourse. But, importantly, Hughes LJ continued:

> If, however, we are wrong about that, and D's delusional beliefs could have led him to believe that his partner consented when she did not, we take the clear view that such delusional beliefs cannot in law render reasonable a belief that his partner was consenting when in fact she was not. The Act does not ask whether it was reasonable (in the sense of being understandable or not his fault) for D to suffer from the mental condition which he did. Normally no doubt, absent at least fault such as self-induced intoxication by drink or drugs, the answer to that in the case of acute illness such as this D seems to have suffered will be that it is reasonable. What the answer would be if the condition were an anti-social, borderline or psychopathic personality disorder may be more problematic. But the Act asks a different question: whether the belief in consent

was a reasonable one. A delusional belief in consent, if entertained, would be by definition irrational and thus unreasonable, not reasonable. If such delusional beliefs were capable of being described as reasonable, then the more irrational the belief of D the better would be its prospects of being held reasonable... Both the common law and statute law are well used to a rule which judges a D by his subjective state of mind. So, for example, in a case where self defence is at issue, D is to be judged according to the facts as he genuinely believed them to be, whether his belief was reasonable or not, at least unless it was attributable to voluntary intoxication. Criminal damage ... is not committed if D honestly believes he had (or would have had) the consent of the owner of the property damaged to do what he did, even if that belief was unreasonable. But the decisive indication as to the law of rape is, we think, that the SOA 2003 deliberately departs from this model. It deliberately does not make genuine belief in consent enough. The belief must not only be genuinely held; it must also be reasonable in all the circumstances. This was a conscious departure from the former law (paras 35–7).

Evidential presumptions about consent

10.14   Parliament made P's job easier (perhaps) by enacting some presumptions about consent. First, some rebuttable presumptions (in s 75):

s 75   (1)   If in proceedings for an offence to which this section applies it is proved—

(a)   that the defendant did the relevant act,

(b)   that any of the circumstances specified in subsection (2) existed, and

(c)   that the defendant knew that those circumstances existed,

the complainant is to be taken not to have consented to the relevant act unless sufficient evidence is adduced to raise an issue as to whether he consented, and the defendant is to be taken not to have reasonably believed that the complainant consented unless sufficient evidence is adduced to raise an issue as to whether he reasonably believed it.

(2)   The circumstances are that—

(a)   any person was, at the time of the relevant act or immediately before it began, using violence against the complainant or causing the complainant to fear that immediate violence would be used against him;

(b)   any person was, at the time of the relevant act or immediately before it began, causing the complainant to fear that violence was being used, or that immediate violence would be used, against another person;

(c)   the complainant was, and the defendant was not, unlawfully detained at the time of the relevant act;

(d)   the complainant was asleep or otherwise unconscious at the time of the relevant act;

(e) because of the complainant's physical disability, the complainant would not have been able at the time of the relevant act to communicate to the defendant whether the complainant consented;

(f) any person had administered to or caused to be taken by the complainant, without the complainant's consent, a substance which, having regard to when it was administered or taken, was capable of causing or enabling the complainant to be stupefied or overpowered at the time of the relevant act.

(3) In subsection (2)(a) and (b), the reference to the time immediately before the relevant act began is, in the case of an act which is one of a continuous series of sexual activities, a reference to the time immediately before the first sexual activity began.

Read this list carefully. Does it include the right 'innocent' victims, where the burden is put on D to prove his innocence? As Temkin and Ashworth (2004) put it, the Government has 'invested with great moral symbolism' the protection of these victims. What of V who gets raped when she was voluntarily drunk? Or perhaps you think any reversal of the burden of proof is wrong: why should it be for D to provide evidence of his innocence, that V was consenting? In other contexts, the courts have been reluctant to accept 'reverse burdens' of proof (see **8.9** for another example: diminished responsibility). The reverse burden here is purely evidential—D has only to 'adduce evidence sufficient to raise an issue' as to consent or his belief in it. But P still has to prove the lack of consent.

Ciccarelli (2011) After a party, D had tried to initiate sex with V. The only issue was whether he might reasonably have believed that she was consenting. D had gone into V's room and, while she was sleeping, had kissed her and had touched her with his penis. At that point she had woken up and immediately told him to leave. He did. He claimed that earlier in the evening she had tried to kiss him and, on that basis, he believed that she would consent to sex. The trial judge held that there was no evidence on the basis of which D could argue that he had reasonably believed V to be consenting. He then pleaded guilty to sexual assault.

CA: dismissed D's appeal. Before the question of a D's reasonable belief in V's consent could be left to the jury, some evidence beyond the fanciful or speculative had to be adduced to support the reasonableness of that belief. D and V were essentially strangers and he had made no attempt to wake her before touching her sexually. Taking D's case at its highest, the basis of the reasonableness of his belief in her consent was the single advance that she had, on his account, made to him earlier in the evening. Effectively, he was arguing that his mere belief that V was consenting, whether that belief was reasonable or not, was sufficient to enable the matter to be left to the jury. That was not, however, what s 75 provided. There had to be some evidence that D's belief was reasonable before the matter could be left to the jury.

Mba (2012) D allegedly punched V, dragged her to his bedroom where he bound her hands and feet with tape, held a knife to her, and vaginally, and orally, raped her. V suffered extensive bruising to her face, cuts to the inside of her mouth, and lost a tooth. At trial D asserted that V had consented to being tied up and to vaginal and oral sex; he denied prodding her with a knife or repeatedly punching her. The trial judge told the jury that P's case was that, at the time or immediately before D penetrated V's vagina, D was using violence against her or was causing her to fear that violence would be used and that he knew that. He directed the jury that if they were sure that that was the case, they had to find that V did not consent to the act of penetration. D argued that there was evidence for the jury to consider whether, at the point of penetration, M reasonably believed that V was consenting to intercourse, and that his conviction for rape was unsafe. He appealed against his convictions for rape and for causing GBH with intent.

CA dismissed the appeal. The judge's directions came perilously close to a direction to the jury to convict if they found that the facts gave rise to the evidential presumption in s 75, without leaving to them a consideration of the evidence upon which the defence raised the issue of consent. Nevertheless, notwithstanding that failure, M's conviction was clearly safe. The jury convicted D unanimously of causing GBH with intent upon V on the facts which also underlay the indictment for rape. The judge's directions on the grievous bodily harm offence could not be criticized. It was clear that the jury were satisfied that D had inflicted upon V such violence as clearly negated any question of consent on her part, or reasonable belief in her consent on his part. V's evidence on that issue was stark, with or without evidential presumptions, and was amply sufficient to compel a guilty verdict on the rape charge.

Conclusive presumptions about consent

10.15 Two situations give rise to an irrebuttable presumption of absence of consent

s 76 (1) If in proceedings for an offence to which this section applies it is proved that the defendant did the relevant act and that any of the circumstances specified in subsection (2) existed, it is to be conclusively presumed—

(a) that the complainant did not consent to the relevant act, and

(b) that the defendant did not believe that the complainant consented to the relevant act.

(2) The circumstances are that—

(a) the defendant intentionally deceived the complainant as to the nature or purpose of the relevant act;

(b) the defendant intentionally induced the complainant to consent to the relevant act by impersonating a person known personally to the complainant.

This was already the law: if D gained consent through force, or fraud, or fear, the consent was invalid. One would hope there are few people in the UK today who do not understand the 'nature or purpose' of the sexual act; and it must be exceptionally rare that someone will have sex with someone believing they are someone else (despite cases such as *Elbekkay* (1994) and *Collins* (1973)). So the conclusive presumptions may be less controversial in practice than the rebuttable presumptions.

Jheeta (2007) V met D in college and in the course of time a sexual relationship began. V then started to receive text messages and phone calls threatening to kill or kidnap her. The messages were in fact from D but he continued to purport to reassure her that he would protect her. When V decided to go to the police, D said he would do so for her, and he then sent her regular text messages from fictitious police officers. This continued for several years. Whenever she sought to end the relationship, she would receive text messages from supposed police officers, telling her that D had tried to kill himself and that she should do her duty and take care of him. V was told that she should sleep with him, and that she would be liable to a fine if she did not. She received about 50 such demands over a four-year period. On each occasion she complied with them and had intercourse with D in a hotel room. She said that but for the messages from the fictitious police officers, she would not have done so. She eventually reported the facts to the (real) police. After a discussion between counsel and the trial judge on the implications of s 76 of the SOA 2003, D pleaded guilty to two counts of procuring sexual intercourse by false pretences, contrary to s 3 of the SOA 1956, four counts of rape, contrary to s 1 of the 2003 Act, and one of blackmail. D argued on appeal that there was no deception operating on V's mind about the nature or purpose of the act and that the guilty plea had been tendered after legal advice which did not accurately reflect the statutory provisions.

CA (Sir Igor Judge, President of the QBD): upheld the convictions. Section 76 had 'wide application to effectively every incident of sexual touching' (para. 22) and required the 'most stringent scrutiny': 'the ambit of s 76 is limited to the "act" to which it is said to apply' (paras 23–4). The Court noted the rarity of occasions when the conclusive presumptions will apply, identifying *Linekar* (1995) (**5.13**) as an example of their limited role: where a man has sex with a prostitute by fraud and the prostitute was 'undeceived about either the nature or the purpose of the act, that is intercourse' (para. 27), the presumptions have no application.

> In our judgment the conclusive presumption in s 76 (2)(a) had no application, and counsel ... were wrong to advise on the basis that it did. However that is not an end of the matter. We are being asked to examine the safety of convictions for rape where D pleaded guilty. He did so on the basis of plea which accepted the accuracy of his admissions in interview with the police, and in particular did not question his unequivocal admission that there were occasions when sexual intercourse took place when V was not truly consenting. This is entirely consistent with his acknowledgement that he persuaded V

> to have intercourse with him more frequently than otherwise, and the persuasion took the form of the pressures imposed on her by the complicated and unpleasant scheme which he had fabricated. This was not a free choice, or consent for the purposes of the Act. In these circumstances we entertain no reservations that on some occasions at least V was not consenting to intercourse for the purposes of s 74, and that D was perfectly well aware of it. His guilty plea reflected these undisputed facts (paras 28–9).

Thus the CA was sure that this V on some occasions at least had no free choice and was not consenting. But the same would seem to be true of the prostitute who would never have consented to sex with a man if she knew he had no intention of paying her, or indeed V in *B* (2006), discussed at **5.13**: where D's conviction for rape was quashed and a re-trial ordered in part because the fact that he had not disclosed a sexually transmitted disease did not vitiate any consent that may have been given concerning sexual activity. One would have hoped, as Leigh (2007) pointed out, that it is an 'outmoded view' that it is only appreciation of the barest physical nature of the act and the willingness to perform it that counts for consent.

Devonald (2008) V was a 16-year-old boy who had been in a relationship with D's daughter. The relationship had broken down and D sought to teach V a lesson by deliberately embarrassing him. He pretended to be a young woman and began to correspond with V over the internet, persuading him to masturbate in front of a web-cam. D was convicted of an offence of causing a person to engage in sexual activity without consent (contrary to SOA 2003, s 4: see **10.20**), having changed his plea to guilty following a ruling by the judge. The issue was whether V had consented to masturbate. D submitted that s 76(2)(a) dealt with deception as to the act itself rather than as to the surrounding circumstances, and that V had well understood that the act in which he had engaged was a sexual one.

CA: refused the application to appeal. V had not 'consented': it was open to a jury to conclude that V had been deceived as to the purpose of the masturbation. It was difficult to see how the jury could have concluded otherwise than that V had been deceived into believing that he was indulging in sexual acts with, and for the sexual gratification of, a young woman with whom he was having an online relationship. D had over-focused on the phrase 'nature of the act' in s 76(2)(a) of the Act. While the 'nature' of the act to which V consented was undoubtedly sexual, the concept of 'purpose' in s 76 'encompasses rather more than the specific purpose of sexual gratification by the defendant in the act of masturbation'.

Linekar (1995) (see **5.13**) is distinguished because there the purpose of 'the act' was consensual sexual intercourse between V and D. The fact that agreement was obtained by the promise of money (or any other blandishment) merely identifies a secondary motive for that agreement (para. 7).

Miles (2008) points out that *Devonald* suggests that:

> ...*wherever D's true view of the relevant act's purpose (whether sexual or non-sexual) is unknown to V—in the context of s 76, because he has intentionally induced V's participation on the basis of some other ostensible purpose—the latter's consent is vitiated. This may be the right approach. Whether Vs wrongly think they are participating in a sexual act or a non-sexual act, their sexual autonomy—their right to decide whether to engage in sexual conduct (or not)— is compromised by either type of mistake. But this justification would take us quickly towards accepting any sort of 'but for' mistake as a vitiating mistake, a position that is surely too broad.*

See also Williams (2008).

Assault by penetration

10.16 There has long been debate as to whether 'rape' should extend to non-consensual oral sex, or to the D who violently inserts a bottle or broomstick into V's vagina with sexual intent. The CLRC (1980) had concluded that it would be undesirable that the definition of such a serious offence should become out of step with popular understanding. As we saw at **10.2**, Canada renamed the offence 'aggravated sexual assault' partly because it was felt that the definition of the offence was too narrow. Parliament remedied the situation in England and Wales in the SOA 2003 by widening the definition of rape to include non-consensual oral sex (see **10.8**), and by creating a new offence of assault by penetration in s 2(1):

> **s 2** (1) A person (A) commits an offence if—
>
>   (a) he intentionally penetrates the vagina or anus of another person (B) with a part of his body or anything else,
>
>   (b) the penetration is sexual,
>
>   (c) B does not consent to the penetration, and
>
>   (d) A does not reasonably believe that B consents.
>
>   (2) Whether a belief is reasonable is to be determined having regard to all the circumstances, including any steps A has taken to ascertain whether B consents.

The *mens rea* is intentional penetration and an absence of reasonable belief in consent. Note that ss 75 and 76 also apply to this offence (for s 2(3): see **10.14** and **10.15**). A person guilty of this offence is liable to imprisonment for life.

'Sexual'

10.17 Penetration may be by anything, from a finger to a broom handle. But the penetration must be 'sexual', which is defined in s 78:

> **s 78** For the purposes of this Part (except section 71), penetration, touching or any other activity is sexual if a reasonable person would consider that—
>
> (a) whatever its circumstances or any person's purpose in relation to it, it is because of its nature sexual, or
>
> (b) because of its nature it may be sexual and because of its circumstances or the purpose of any person in relation to it (or both) it is sexual.

This is a complicated definition: take the example of a doctor who conducts a gynaecological examination: is this sexual? He puts his fingers in a women's vagina: is this assault by penetration? What if it is an unnecessary gynaecological examination carried out by a doctor for fun, though V doesn't realize this? It is worth noting that the only offence to which this definition of 'sexual' does not apply is s 71 (sexual activity in a public lavatory), where an activity is to be considered sexual if a reasonable person would, in all the circumstances, but regardless of any person's purpose, consider it to be sexual. Why do you think this test was not applied to all the other offences?

H (2005) D approached V as she went to post a letter late in the evening. He asked her if she wanted a 'shag', and then grabbed at a pocket on her tracksuit bottoms. She escaped. D was convicted of sexual assault.

CA: dismissed D's appeal. Touching for the purposes of an offence contrary to s 3 included the touching of an individual's clothing. Where touching was not automatically by its nature 'sexual', the judge should ask the jury to determine whether touching was 'sexual' by answering in the affirmative two questions: (i) whether the jury, as 12 reasonable persons, considered that the touching could be sexual; (ii) whether the jury, as 12 reasonable persons, and in all the circumstances of the case, considered that the purpose of the touching had in fact been sexual.

This was the first appeal under the new Act, and it is not clear where it leaves the old case law: see **10.18**.

Sexual assault

10.18 Under the pre-SOA 2003 law, sexual assaults were called 'indecent assaults'. Assaults on women and on men were dealt with by different sections of the SOA 1956. Until

1985, there was a higher maximum penalty for assaults on men, presumably because Parliament in 1956 had felt that it was more 'unnatural' and therefore 'worse' for a man indecently to assault a man. The main difficulties, though, were in distinguishing indecent assaults from 'ordinary' OAPA assaults (see **9.20**). The test was primarily objective: if the circumstances of the assault were incapable of being regarded as indecent, the assault did not become indecent simply because of D's secret motive:

George **(1956)** D attempted to remove a girl's shoe as it gave him sexual gratification.

Streatfield J: here there was no indecency. An assault only becomes indecent if it is accompanied by circumstances of indecency towards the V.

Court **(1988)** D spanked a 12-year-old girl in the shop where he worked 12 times outside her shorts. He pleaded guilty to assault, but not to indecent assault. He admitted that he had a buttock fetish, but this was a secret motive. He was convicted of indecent assault.

HL (by a majority of 4 to 1): dismissed D's appeal. Evidence of D's secret motive was admissible. Lord Ackner distinguished three types of case: first, where the conduct would not be considered indecent by any right-minded observer, there could be no conviction whatever on D's motivation; secondly, where every right-minded observer would consider the behaviour indecent, whatever D's actual motivation, it would be an indecent assault. Thirdly, if the right-minded individual would be unsure, the court should look at D's motive: if that was indecent, the offence would be made out.

Note Lord Goff's dissent: he argued that if P could not establish that the assault was objectively indecent, they should not be allowed to justify the case by calling evidence of a secret indecent intention.

The SOA 2003, s 3 replaced the offence of indecent assault with one of sexual assault:

s 3 (1) A person (A) commits an offence if—

    (a) he intentionally touches another person (B),

    (b) the touching is sexual,

    (c) B does not consent to the touching, and

    (d) A does not reasonably believe that B consents.

  (2) Whether a belief is reasonable is to be determined having regard to all the circumstances, including any steps A has taken to ascertain whether B consents.

'Sexual' is defined in s 78 (read s 78 and *H* (2005) at **10.17** again). How would *George* and *Court* be decided today?

10.19 The *mens rea* is an intent to touch plus an absence of reasonable belief in consent. Remember that a drunken intent is still an intent: *Heard* (2007, at **4.20**). Again, ss 75 and 76 (see **10.13** and **10.14**) apply to offences under this section, and the definition of 'sexual' in s 78 applies (see **10.17**). The other key word here is 'touching'. There is some help with this in s 79(8): touching 'includes touching (with any part of the body, with anything else, through anything and in particular includes touching amounting to penetration.' The Sentencing Advisory Panel in their consultation paper on sentencing under this Act (2003) identified 13 levels of seriousness within the definition of 'sexual touching': from penetration at the most serious to 'using one's clothed genital organs to stroke, rub, press or touch any other areas of someone else's body, such as the face, neck, back or thighs ("frottage", for example).' Unsurprisingly the Sentencing Guidelines Council's Definitive Guideline on the Sexual Offences Act 2003 was less precise. But the point is an important one: is this offence too widely drawn? Is it too inclusive? A person guilty of sexual assault is liable, on summary conviction, to imprisonment for a term not exceeding six months or a fine not exceeding the statutory maximum or both; on conviction on indictment, to imprisonment for a term not exceeding ten years.

Causing sexual activity without consent

10.20 Section 4 creates a new offence:

> **s 4** (1) A person (A) commits an offence if—
>
>   (a) he intentionally causes another person (B) to engage in an activity,
>
>   (b) the activity is sexual,
>
>   (c) B does not consent to engaging in the activity, and
>
>   (d) A does not reasonably believe that B consents.
>
> (2) Whether a belief is reasonable is to be determined having regard to all the circumstances, including any steps A has taken to ascertain whether B consents.

See what is said about 'causing' in Chapter 2 at **2.12**. This broad offence is designed to penalize those who compel others to do sexual acts against their will. There is, of course, a big overlap with aiding, abetting, counselling, or procuring (see **6.3**) rape or sexual assault, but this offence ensures that D is guilty of an offence even if the principal is not guilty (because he has a defence, for example). Sections 75 and 76 (see **10.13** and **10.14**) apply once again to offences under this section, and the definition of 'sexual' in s 78 applies (see **10.17**). If the activity caused involved penetration of B's anus or vagina, penetration of B's mouth with a person's penis, penetration of a person's anus or vagina with a part of B's body or by B with anything else, or penetration of a person's mouth with B's penis, the maximum penalty is life imprisonment. Otherwise D is liable, on summary conviction, to imprisonment for a term not exceeding six months or to a fine not exceeding the statutory maximum or both; or on conviction on indictment, to imprisonment for a term not exceeding ten years. Most of the reported cases under s 4 are appeals against sentence, not conviction: but see *Devonald* (2008) at **10.15**.

Child sex offences

10.21 The four offences we have so far described are repeated (in similar but not identical terms) in ss 5–8, but in relation to children under 13 years of age. Thus, there are specific offences of rape of a child under 13 (s 5), assault of a child under 13 by penetration (s 6), sexual assault of a child under 13 (s 7), and causing or inciting a child under 13 to engage in sexual activity (s 8). Neither consent nor belief in consent are defences. Nor will a belief that the child is over 13 be a defence. Spencer (2004) questions whether these offences are in fact necessary given the offences in ss 9 and 10. He also argues that since ss 9 and 10 (see *G* (2008)) impose strict liability, there is a 'plausible argument' that for ss 5–8 which are in principle more serious, D is only guilty where he acted with *mens rea*. But now see:

> **G (2008)** D, who was 15 years old at the time of the offence, pleaded guilty to rape of a child under 13 years of age, contrary to the SOA 2003, s 5, on the basis that he had believed that V was 15.
>
> HL: dismissed D's appeal. On its natural meaning, s 5 created an offence even if D reasonably believed that the child was 13 or over. The section was not incompatible with Art 6 of the ECHR (see **1.25**) and accordingly there was no requirement to 'read it down'. Article 6 was concerned with procedural fairness not with the substantive content of the criminal law. The majority (Lord Hoffmann, Baroness Hale of Richmond, and Lord Mance) held that it was compatible with a child's rights under Art 8 to convict him of rape contrary to s 5 in circumstances where the agreed basis of plea established that his offence fell properly within the ambit of s 13. (Section 13 provides lower penalties for those under 18 who commit offences under ss 9–12, sexual activity with a child. Lords Hope and Carswell dissented on this issue, concluding that G's conviction of rape under s 5 was disproportionate and incompatible with his rights under Art 8.)

So, a majority were in favour of upholding the conviction. Baroness Hale stressed in 'characteristically vivid terms' the importance of the s 5 offence to the protection of underage girls (see Buxton (2009) who chooses this case to illustrate the impact that the personalities of individual judges can have on judicial decisions). Do you think it is 'fair' to convict this boy of rape, when P accepts that the 12-year-old was consenting? Miles (2008) points out that the dissenting judges, Lords Hope and Carswell, were clearly influenced by Scots law's generally different, welfare-focused treatment of child offenders via the children's hearings system. For them, not only were D's Art 8 rights engaged, but P's persistence with the serious charge under s 5 rather than s 13 in a case of 'mutual' sexual conduct between children constituted a disproportionate interference with those rights.

The following case on s 8 is mentioned in Chapter 7 in the context of the law on impossible attempts (**7.12**) and on incitement (**7.29**):

Jones **(2007)** A journalist saw graffiti on a toilet door on a train seeking girls of 8 to 13 years old for sex, offering payment and leaving a contact number. She telephoned the number, and then received several text messages from D, which requested confirmation of her age and whether she was prepared to perform oral sex. The journalist contacted the police who began an undercover operation. An undercover officer posing as a 12-year-old girl exchanged several texts with D which clarified her age and arrangements for a meeting. D sent the officer text messages of an explicit nature including various sexual acts that he expected he would be able to perform on her. D arranged to meet the officer and was arrested. He was charged with and convicted of a number of offences, including attempting to incite a child under 13 years old into penetrative sexual activity (s 8 of the Act).

CA: dismissed his appeal. The criminality of the offence was the incitement of children under the age of 13 to engage in sexual activity, and it did not matter if it was directed at a particular child (see *Most* (1880–81) at **7.29**). D had the objective of inciting a particular child to engage in penetrative sexual activity, his intention was to evade the prohibition of the law, and his acts were more than merely preparatory to the commission of the offence (see *Shivpuri* (1987) and **7.12**). The police did not behave improperly in choosing the age of 12. It was D who had asked the officer for her age, and he therefore believed that he was inciting penetrative sexual activity with a child under 13. The graffiti on the train was evidence that D directed his activities to 8 to 13-year-olds.

10.22 The Act contains a long list of child sex offences: sexual activity with a child (s 9), causing or inciting a child to engage in sexual activity (s 10), engaging in sexual activity in the presence of a child (s 11), causing a child to watch a sexual act (s 12), arranging or facilitating commission of a child sex offence (s 14), meeting a child following sexual grooming (s 15). Where a child under 18 commits any of the offences under ss 9–12 (which all have maximum sentences of ten or 14 years) the maximum sentence is five years (s 13).

Abdullahi **(2006)** V, a 13-year-old boy, who had been at D's home visiting D's younger brother, had been plied with alcohol, exposed to pornography, and then subjected to indecent touching by D. The judge directed the jury that they had to be satisfied that D did what he did when intentionally causing V to look at the images for the purpose of obtaining sexual gratification, either by enjoying watching V looking at the images or with a view to looking at V in the mood to provide sexual gratification to himself later. D was convicted of offences under s 9 and s 12. He submitted that the judge's direction was too wide as it went beyond reference to immediate sexual gratification, incorporating an element of future gratification.

CA: dismissed the appeal. There was nothing in the language of s 12 of the Act to suggest that there was a temporal restriction to the sexual gratification and that it had to be contemporaneous or synchronized with the display of images. Provided that it was for the corrupt purpose of obtaining sexual gratification, the offence could take many forms.

Similar offences are aggravated when they are committed in breach of trust (ss 16–19), building on the provisions of the already repealed provisions of the Sexual Offences (Amendment) Act 2000. It is beyond the scope of this book to deal with each in detail but it is important to note that the offences are complex and overlapping. Is this a case of 'legislative overkill'? See Spencer (2004), who suggests that the Act 'will eventually make indictable offenders of the whole population' (at p. 354). The Act appears to prohibit all forms of sexual behaviour between consenting children: for example, two 15-year-olds kissing are in theory liable to five years' imprisonment! Where does this leave the rights of children under the Human Rights Act 1998, particularly Art 8 (see 1.25)?

Incest (familial sexual offences)

10.23 The law of incest (previously found in the SOA 1956, s 10) was repealed by the SOA 2003. Instead we now have complicated offences of familial child sex offences (ss 25–29) and sex with an adult relative (ss 64 and 65). Let us explore the reasoning behind criminalizing consensual sex within the family. If it was simply a question of enforcing a moral belief that incest was wrong, this raises the same issues which led the Wolfenden Committee (see 1.5) to recommend the de-criminalization of adult consensual homosexuality. It is sometimes argued that it is not simply a question of morality, but that there are also more practical reasons for criminalizing it: the risk of handicapped babies. But if this were the true reason, would it also be an argument for saying that it should be a criminal offence for haemophiliacs or those who are HIV positive to have sex?

10.24 The DCC, back in 1989, recommended various modifications to the existing law:

   (i) That the offence should extend to adoptive as well as to blood relationships between father and daughter and mother and son. Extending liability beyond blood relationships shows the rationale is not seen to be the public health issue raised above. And, as we shall see, the law now extends well beyond vaginal sex.

(ii) That it should cease to be an offence for a brother and sister to have intercourse where they have both reached the age of 21. This controversial recommendation received more coverage in the popular press than any other at the time that the DCC was published. Yet the argument of the Law Commission is that the logic of the Wolfenden Committee (see 1.5) which resulted in the legalization of homosexuality should also prevent the law inquiring into the bedrooms of other consenting adults. Unsurprisingly, the Government has not followed this advice.

(iii) That daughters, granddaughters, and sons under the age of 21 should be exempt from liability.

The DCC also included a separate offence of 'aggravated incest'. The Law Commission argued that if it was agreed that incest by a man with a girl under the age of 13 should carry a higher penalty, this would require a separate offence. It is for this reason that we now have the separate offences. But the Government in 2003 did not de-criminalize. In fact, the law is now much wider than it was before.

Sex with an adult relative

10.25 Section 64 makes it a crime for someone over the age of 16 to intentionally penetrate another person's vagina or anus with a part of his body or anything else, or penetrate another person's mouth with his penis, where the penetration is sexual and the other person is aged 18 or over, and they are related as parent, grandparent, child, grandchild, brother, sister, half-brother, half-sister, uncle, aunt, nephew, or niece. The maximum sentence is two years' imprisonment.

10.26 Section 65 makes it an offence with similar punishment to consent to be so penetrated. Where, in either offence, it is proved that D was related to the other person in any of those ways, it is to be taken that D knew or could reasonably have been expected to know that he was related in that way unless sufficient evidence is adduced to raise an issue as to whether he knew or could reasonably have been expected to know that he was.

10.27 Spencer (2004) calls these offences both needless and unjust, and challenges anyone to describe a case in which they think it would be proper to prosecute a D whose sexual activity did not amount to at least one other serious criminal offence.

Sexual activity with a child family member

10.28   Whilst incest with a child is clearly a very serious offence, this is of course already covered by the law of rape (see **10.8**) and rape of a child under 13 (see **10.21**). The offence under s 25 is very much wider. A person commits an offence if he intentionally touches another person to whom he is related (within the very wide definition of s 27), the touching is sexual (see **10.17**), he knows or could reasonably be expected to know that his relation to V falls within s 27, and V is either under 13, or under 18 (where there is a defence if D reasonably believes that V is 18 or over). If it is proved that V was under 18, D is to be taken not to have reasonably believed that that person was 18 or over 'unless sufficient evidence is adduced to raise an issue as to whether he reasonably believed it' (s 25(2)). Similarly, if it is proved that D's relation to V falls within s 27, it is to be taken that D 'knew or could reasonably have been expected to know that his relation to the other person was of that description unless sufficient evidence is adduced to raise an issue as to whether he knew or could reasonably have been expected to know that it was' (s 25(3)). The proscribed relationships are parent, grandparent, brother, sister, half-brother, half-sister, aunt or uncle, or foster parent or where they 'live or have lived in the same household', etc.

Offences against persons with a mental disorder

10.29   Children are not the only category of vulnerable people whom the new law seeks to protect. There are hugely complex provisions seeking to protect those with mental disorders from sexual abuse. But there is a problem here: in protecting the vulnerable, should the law make those who are not able to communicate their choices unable to enjoy sexual activities lawfully? Sections 30–3 contain four offences where V suffers from a mental disorder which impedes their choice (where the mental disorder means he or she is 'unable to refuse'): sexual activity with a person with a mental disorder impeding choice; causing or inciting a person with a mental disorder impeding choice to engage in sexual activity; engaging in a sexual activity in the presence of a person with a mental disorder impeding choice; causing a person with a mental disorder impeding choice to watch a sexual act. Thus, s 30 of the SOA 2003 provides:

Sexual activity with a person with a mental disorder impending choice

(1)   a person (A) commits an offence if—

    (a)   he intentionally touches another person (B),

    (b)   the touching is sexual,

(c) B is unable to refuse because of or for a reason related to a mental disorder, and

(d) A knows or could reasonably be expected to know that B has a mental disorder and that because of it or for a reason related to it B is likely to be unable to refuse.

(2) B is unable to refuse if—

(a) he lacks the capacity to choose whether to agree to the touching (whether because he lacks sufficient understanding of the nature or reasonably fore-seeable consequences of what is being done, or for any other reason), or

(b) he is unable to communicate such a choice to A.

There are then four offences (ss 34–8) which cover the situation where V is mentally disordered and where the activity is caused by 'threats or deception or inducement', and another four (ss 39–41) where D is in a relationship as a carer. These provisions obviously overlap with the earlier provisions: do we need specific offences of this sort, or could the 'general' law of sexual offences be applied in cases involving mentally ill people, simply with increased sentences to reflect V's vulnerability?

C (2009) V was a woman with an established diagnosis of schizo-affective disorder, an emotionally unstable personality disorder, an IQ of less than 75, and a history of harmful use of alcohol. She met D1 and D2, took crack with them, and engaged in sexual activity with them. D1 appealed his conviction for an offence under s 30 of the SOA 2003.

CA: allowed the appeal on the ground that V's 'irrational fear' due to her mental disorder could not be equated with a lack of capacity to choose, and there was no evidence that she was physically unable to communicate any choice that she had made. The questions certified by the CA were summarized as:

Whether the decision of the CA ... has unduly limited the scope of s 30(1) of the SOA beyond that which Parliament intended. Specifically

(a) in holding that a lack of capacity to choose cannot be person or situation specific;

(b) in holding that an irrational fear that prevents the exercise of choice cannot be equated with a lack of capacity to choose;

(c) in holding that to fall within s 30(2)(b) a complainant must be physically unable to communicate by reason of his mental disorder.

HL: unanimously allowed the appeal (i.e. re-instated the conviction), answering the questions in the affirmative. According to Baroness Hale, with whom the others agreed, the CA had been 'unduly influenced by the views of Munby J. in another context':

The 2003 Act puts the matter beyond doubt. Provided that the inability to refuse is 'because of or for a reason related to a mental disorder' (s 30(1)(c)), and the other ingredients of the offence are made out, the perpetrator is guilty. The words 'for any other reason' are clearly capable of encompassing a wide range of circumstances in which a person's mental disorder may rob them of the ability to make an autonomous choice, even though they may have sufficient understanding of the information relevant to making it. These could include the kind of compulsion which drives a person with anorexia to refuse food, the delusions which drive a person with schizophrenia to believe that she must do something, or the phobia (or irrational fear) which drives a person to refuse a life-saving injection … (para. 25).

As Baroness Hale points out, V's fears may have been all too rational. Why was it not prosecuted as rape? Section 30 may be easier to prove: P has only to prove V's inability to refuse rather than V's actual lack of consent. The *mens rea* for rape is that D does not reasonably believe that V consents (s 1(1)(c)). 'This puts a greater burden of restraint upon people who know or ought to know that a person's mental disorder is likely to affect her ability to choose', as Baroness Hale puts it (at para. 32). She suggests that three offences might have been left to the jury as alternatives thus enabling the judge to distinguish them from one another and to relate them to the evidence:

- a lack of consent arising from the lack of either the freedom or the capacity to make that choice (rape);
- a lack of capacity to make that choice arising from or related to a mental disorder (s 30);
- a choice procured by threats, inducement, or deception of a person with a mental disorder (s 34).

Would this work? It would need a very clear direction on unanimity: what if some of the jury decided that the complainant had the capacity to consent, but did not do so, and others that she took part in the sexual activity in circumstances where she lacked, as a result of her mental disorder, the capacity to choose whether to agree to it? Perhaps it boils down to asking whether the CPS or the jury should decide the appropriate charge!

Preparatory offences

10.30 The SOA 2003 also creates three new preparatory offences which again may be seen to widen the existing law considerably: administering a substance with the intention of stupefying or overpowering someone so as to enable any person to engage in sexual activity that involves them (s 61), committing an offence with intent to commit a sexual offence (s 62), and trespass with intent to commit a sexual offence (s 63). These are important examples of the new crimes allowing the prosecution of offenders before they have completed their criminal activities: and they are being used (the appeal cases mostly raise sentencing issues, not questions of substantive law: see for example *H* (2011) on s 63). How do these offences fit in with the existing inchoate offences discussed in Chapter 7?

Offences connected with prostitution

10.31 It is not illegal to be a prostitute in this country, but many activities connected with prostitution are criminal. Thus, the SOA 1956 specified an offence (for a man) of living on the earnings of prostitution (s 30), an offence of keeping a brothel (s 33), an offence of knowingly allowing premises to be used for purposes of prostitution (s 36). The SOA 1959 was largely concerned with criminalizing soliciting by prostitutes. The SOA 1967 then added new offences such as an offence (for a man or woman) to live on the earnings of a male prostitute (s 5), and also extended the definition of a brothel to include premises people resort to for the purpose of 'lewd homosexual practices'. The SOA 1985 concentrated on further criminalizing various offences connected with soliciting. Thus, s 1 proscribes kerb-crawling:

> **s 1** (1) A man commits an offence if he solicits a woman (or different women) for the purpose of prostitution—
>
> > (a) from a motor vehicle while it is in a street or public place; or
> >
> > (b) in a street or public place while in the immediate vicinity of a vehicle that he has just got out of or off,
>
> persistently or in such manner or in such circumstances as to be likely to cause annoyance to the woman (or any of the women) solicited, or nuisance to other persons in the neighbourhood.

The SOA 2003 has not simplified the law. Sections 33–40 of the SOA 1956 have not been repealed, nor have s 1 or 2 of the SOA 1985. What the Act does is create a number of new offences, particularly in relation to the abuse of children through prostitution and to the trafficking in people for sexual exploitation. There is a new offence of 'causing or inciting prostitution for gain' (s 52), and existing gender-specific offences are extended to protect male as well as female prostitutes.

10.32 There is a large literature on prostitution (see, for example, Lacey, Wells, and Quick (2010)) and, in considering the rightful ambit of the criminal law (there is no doubt that the law should protect people from unwelcome sexual exploitation), you might like to consider whether you think the law is cast too wide. Consider the Government's recommendations in their prostitution strategy published in

2006 (available on the Home Office website), which has resulted in the new strict liability offence of paying for the sexual services of a prostitute subjected to force, threats, or any other form of coercion or any form of deception (committed by a third person (see **3.40**)). Here is another example of a strict law, if not strict liability:

Paul v DPP (1989) D picked up a known prostitute in his car. There were no other pedestrians or cars around at the time, apart from the police car which followed him. He was convicted of an offence of soliciting under the SOA 1985, s 1 (now s 51A of the SOA 2003, added by s 19 of the Policing and Crime Act 2009).

CA (Woolf LJ): dismissed his appeal. There was no need for evidence that anyone was actually offended: a likelihood of nuisance to others in the neighbourhood was sufficient. In determining that issue, the magistrates could use their knowledge of the locality as a residential area, its frequentation by prostitutes, and its population density.

Bigamy

10.33 Bigamy, while not a common offence, is worth mentioning since it is an example of an offence where the circumstances surrounding the act (of marrying) are more important than the act itself. What is the rationale for the offence: protection of the victim, or upholding the institution of marriage? The OAPA 1861, s 57 provides:

> Whosoever, being married, shall marry any other person during the life of the former husband or wife, whether the second marriage shall have taken place in England or Ireland or elsewhere, shall be guilty of [an offence], and being convicted thereof shall be liable to [imprisonment] for any term not exceeding seven years ... : provided, that nothing in this section contained shall extend to any second marriage contracted elsewhere than in England and Ireland by any other than a subject of Her Majesty, or to any person marrying a second time whose husband or wife shall have been continually absent from such person for the space of seven years then last past, and shall not have been known by such person to be living within that time, or shall extend to any person who, at the time of such second marriage, shall have been divorced from the bond of the first marriage, or to any person whose former marriage shall have been declared void by the sentence of any court of competent jurisdiction.

10.34 Thus P needs to prove that D got married when he or she was already married; that the first spouse was alive; and in respect of certain categories of people, that the second marriage took place in England or Ireland. The section does not specify the requisite *mens rea*, and this may cause difficulties in relation to the various different circumstances.

Tolson **(1889)** D believed in good faith and on reasonable grounds, but mistakenly, that her husband was dead, and she remarried.

CCCR (by a majority of 9 to 4): held that her conviction for bigamy should be quashed. Cave J:

> At common law, an honest and reasonable belief in the existence of circumstances, which, if true, would make the act for which a prisoner is indicted an innocent act has always been held to be a good defence.

This decision, that mistaken beliefs should excuse, was confirmed in *DPP v Morgan* (1976, see **10.13**), though since *B (a minor) v DPP* (2000, see **3.40** and **5.28**) it is no longer necessary that the mistake should have been reasonable.

10.35 There are many, many more sexual offences not discussed in this chapter: voyeurism, sexual penetration of a corpse, or sexual activity in a public lavatory, etc. But this book is primarily concerned with 'general principles'. Perhaps the most important questions to be asked about the major reforms of the SOA 2003 are:

- Has it had any effect in encouraging victims to report sexual offences and in increasing conviction rates (as the Government hoped)?

- Does the new law on consent work?

- Is the law now too complex and over-inclusive?

- Why did the Government enact such a convoluted and complex scheme?

Try drafting your own code of sexual offences. How many different offences would you want?

FURTHER READING

Buxton, R., 'Sitting En Banc in the New Supreme Court' (2009) 125 LQR 288.

Finch, E. and Munro, V., 'Breaking Boundaries? Sexual Consent in the Jury Room' (2006) 26 *Legal Studies* 303.

Home Office, *Review of Sexual Offences: Setting the Boundaries* (2000).

Lacey, N., Wells C., and Quick, O., *Reconstructing Criminal Law* (4th edn, 2010).

Leigh, L., 'Two Cases on Consent in Rape' (2007) 6 *Archbold News* 6.

Miles, J., 'Sexual Offences: Consent, Capacity and Children' (2008) 10 *Archbold News* 6.

Munday, R., *Evidence* (5th edn, 2009).

Munro, V. and Stychin, C. (eds), *Sexuality and the Law* (2007).

Rook, P. and Ward, R., *Sexual Offences: Law and Practice* (4th edn, 2010).

Spencer, J. R., 'The Sexual Offences Act 2003: Child and Family Offences' [2004] Crim LR 347.

Spencer, J. R., 'Three New Cases on Consent' (2007) 66 Camb LJ 490.

Stern, V., A Report of an Independent Review into How Rape Complaints are Handled by Public Authorities in England and Wales (Home Office, 2010).

Temkin, J. and Ashworth, A., 'The Sexual Offences Act 2003: Rape, Sexual Assaults and the Problems of Consent' [2004] Crim LR 328.

Walby, S. and Allen, J., 'Domestic Violence, Sexual Assault and Stalking', Findings from the British Crime Survey (Home Office Research Study 276, 2004).

Williams, R., 'Deception, Mistake and Vitiation of the Victim's Consent' (2008) 124 LQR 132.

SELF-TEST QUESTIONS

1   What offences are committed in the following circumstances:

   (i)   Dee persuades Phil aged 15 to have sex with her.

   (ii) Dee encourages Dave to have sex with Viola (aged 15). Dave presumes without thinking that Viola is consenting. In fact, Viola only allows him to have sex with her because Dee has threatened to beat her up if she does not.

2   Dave, angry that one of his lovers has infected him with the AIDS virus, has sex with as many people as he can. Discuss his liability in the following circumstances:

   (i)   He informs Ann that he has AIDS, and she decides to have sex with him anyhow.

   (ii) He does not tell his wife, Beth, that he has the virus, and she says that she would not have consented to have sex had she known the truth.

   (iii) He has anal sex with Charles, who says that while he consented to rough sexual play with Dave, he never consented to the intercourse.

3   At a wild party, Dee encourages Dave to have sex with Violet. Violet is dragged screaming and kicking by Dave into a bedroom, where he pulls off most of her clothes. Dee stands around laughing, but others arrive to save Violet before intercourse takes place. Discuss.

4   In what respects, if at all, does the law of sexual offences still need reform?

11

Theft, fraud, and other property offences

SUMMARY

Theft: the main problems centre on the meaning of the words 'appropriation' (does it imply consensual appropriation? Can you steal your own property? *Gomez; Hinks*) and 'dishonesty' (the *Feely* test).

Robbery: only minimum 'force' is required.

Burglary: distinguish the two separate offences under TA 1968, s 9. Are either or both of these offences necessary?

Blackmail: unwarranted demands with menaces.

Handling stolen goods and offences of 'deception': does the overlap between the various offences (and theft) matter? The Fraud Act 2006 abolished the eight existing offences of deception, and replaced them with two 'new offences':

- fraud, which can be committed three ways;

- obtaining services dishonestly.

Note that common law conspiracy to defraud lives on. And the large overlap between offences.

Introduction

11.1 Most of the offences that we study in this chapter concern 'property'. Some of the problems are not caused by unclear criminal law, but by civil law uncertainties concerning ownership. Criminal law adapts to the civil framework: land law, contract, gift, succession, and intellectual property issues may all be relevant here. This reflects a key difficulty—where the line is to be drawn between those who are sufficiently 'naughty' to be criminally liable and those who are not. If I ask a plumber to mend my dripping tap and then say (falsely) that I cannot pay him this month, should I be guilty of a crime? Should all those people who delay paying their bills as long as possible be guilty of a crime?

Starting afresh, how would you distinguish different crimes in this field? The basic one would probably be stealing. In ordinary language this involves 'taking' other people's property. But the current law of theft is much wider than this: you may be guilty of theft without taking anything, just because you infringe one of someone's property rights (as long as you have the appropriate dishonest intent): see **11.8**. Property itself is a difficult concept: what is the property involved in a mortgage fraud, for example? Working on from here, would you specify various aggravated forms of theft (e.g. burglary, robbery), or would you merely give those thieves who use violence, or who steal from houses, higher sentences for theft? Then you have to face the problem of whether thieves and cheats are different: how does or should the law of fraud and deception vary from the law of theft? You face the same problem with offences of fraud as you faced with theft: do you break fraud into a number of different offences, or should there be just one offence of 'obtaining a benefit by fraud'? How does 'white-collar crime' fit into this picture? Should we be concerned that it seems to be easier to convict petty thieves and conmen than those who defraud the tax and social security systems, or those who carry out major commercial frauds? Finally in this chapter we will come to those who help or encourage thieves. They are normally convicted not of aiding and abetting theft, but of a separate (and more serious) offence of handling stolen goods. Why?

Theft

11.2 Despite the fact that we have a statement of the law of theft in the TA 1968, s 1, the law is far from clear. Theft replaced larceny (grand and petit), which could be defined as 'the felonious taking and carrying away of personal goods'. The CLRC (1966) sought to bring common sense, clarity, comprehensiveness, coherence, and consistency to the law. You may judge to what extent they succeeded! Section 1 provides a general definition:

(1) A person is guilty of theft if he dishonestly appropriates property belonging to another with the intention of permanently depriving the other of it; and 'thief' and 'steal' shall be construed accordingly.

It is an offence triable either on indictment or summarily, and is subject to a maximum penalty of seven years' imprisonment (though only six months if tried summarily: see **1.13**). The *actus reus* may be seen as 'the appropriation of property belonging to another' and the *mens rea* as 'dishonesty plus an intention to permanently deprive'. Most elements have proved difficult to interpret.

Meaning of property

11.3   Property is partially defined in the TA 1968, s 4:

> (1) 'Property' includes money and all other property, real or personal, including things in action and other intangible property.

Money (coins and banknotes) is clearly property which can be stolen. Land in general can't be stolen (see s 4(2)), unless a trustee or some other authorized person sells it in breach of the confidence reposed in him. Picking wild mushrooms, fruit, or flowers from land is not theft unless done for commercial reasons (s 4(3)). Personal property includes goods such as the piece of paper on which a cheque or exam paper is written. A thing in action (or 'chose in action') is a property right which can only be claimed by action and not physically taken. The most common thing in action is a debt for a fixed sum. An account held at a bank or building society is a thing in action: but once the account is overdrawn there is no thing in action which is capable of being stolen. Intangible property which can be stolen includes patents, copyrights, and electronic transfers (see *Mensah-Lartey* (1996)).

Oxford v Moss **(1978)** D, a civil engineering student, copied an exam paper and then returned it.

CA: quashed his conviction for theft since confidential information cannot be stolen.

Williams (Roy) **(2000)** D, a builder, was convicted of 23 counts of theft for overcharging clients.

CA: dismissed appeal. D stole a chose in action when he cashed the cheques. His presentation of a cheque caused a diminution of V's credit balance in his bank account, amounting to an appropriation of V's property.

11.4   The Law Commission's Consultation Paper No. 150 (1997), *Misuse of Trade Secrets*, provisionally proposed that it should be an offence to use or disclose a trade secret without authority (the Law Commission point out that theft of a boardroom table is currently punished more severely than theft of boardroom secrets). Other property which cannot be stolen includes electricity and human bodies, but other specific offences cover those who abuse those two things (for the former see **11.31** and for the latter, the Human Tissue Act 1961, Anatomy Act 1984, etc.). The Computer Misuse Act 1990 created specific offences related to those who dishonestly enter other people's computer systems.

Belonging to another

11.5 According to the TA 1968, s 5:

(1) Property shall be regarded as belonging to any person having possession or control of it, or having in it any proprietary right or interest (not being an equitable interest arising only from an agreement to transfer or grant an interest).

The following subsections raise specific situations where property may be deemed to belong to another: where property is subject to a trust, the persons to whom it belongs shall be regarded as including any person having a right to enforce the trust (s 5(2)); where a person receives property for or on account of another and is under an obligation to deal with it in a particular way, the property shall be regarded as belonging to the other (s 5(3)); where a person gets property by mistake and is under an obligation to make restoration (in whole or in part) the property shall be regarded as belonging to the person entitled to restoration (s 5(4)).

11.6 Thus although a classic case of theft involves taking something from the owner, it can also be committed against those with lesser interests. A partner can steal from his co-partners, or a director can steal from his company. D may even steal from himself:

Turner (No. 2) **(1971)** D took his car home from a garage where it had been repaired without paying for the repairs. He was convicted of theft.

CA: dismissed the appeal. It was sufficient that the person from whom the property was appropriated was in fact at the time in possession or control.

(But note *Preddy* (1996) where D supplied false information on a mortgage application to a building society.)

HL, reversing CA: quashed his conviction under s 15 of the TA 1968 (since repealed: see **11.35**), since nothing which had belonged to V now belonged to D. A thing in action belonging to V had been diminished or extinguished, and a thing in action belonging to D had been enlarged or created. Lord Jauncey: 'In Scotland common law and common sense rather than Parliamentary wisdom still prevail.'

Hinks **(2000)** D, a 38-year-old woman, was friendly with a 53-year-old man of limited intelligence, who over an eight-month period withdrew about £60,000 from his building society account and gave it to her. She was convicted of five counts of theft.

CA: dismissed appeal.

HL (by a majority of 3 to 2): dismissed the appeal, answering the certified question ('whether the acquisition of an indefeasible title to property is capable of amounting to an appropriation of property belonging to another for the purposes of s 1(1) of the TA 1968') in the affirmative. Lord Steyn was clear that Professor Sir John Smith's research into the intentions of individual members of the Larceny Sub-Committee of the CLRC 'could not conceivably be relevant' as an aid to the construction of the TA 1968. There were no convincing reasons to narrow the definition of appropriation, and he stressed the beneficial consequence that the wider definition eliminates the need for trial judges to explain overly complex civil law concepts to the jury. The mental elements of the offence are an adequate protection against injustice. Lord Slynn and Lord Jauncey agreed with the speech of Lord Steyn, Lord Slynn stating that he did not think it 'right in this case to depart from the decisions in *Lawrence* (1971) and *Gomez* (1991).

Lord Hobhouse and Lord Hutton dissented. Lord Hutton agreed with Lord Steyn on the question of appropriation, but concluded that the trial judge's summing up on dishonesty was defective. He argued that it follows from s 2(1)(b) of the Act that a person's appropriation of property belonging to another should not be regarded as dishonest if the other person actually gives the property to him:

> In a case where the prosecution contends that the gift was invalid because of the mental incapacity of the donor it is necessary for the jury to consider that matter. I further consider that the judge must make it clear to the jury that they cannot convict unless they are satisfied (1) that the donor did not have the mental capacity to make a gift and (2) that the donee knew of this incapacity... in a case where the defendant contends that he or she received a gift, a direction based only on *Ghosh* (1982) (**11.15**) is inadequate because it fails to make clear to the jury that if there was a valid gift there cannot be dishonesty...

For Lord Hobhouse, ss 1–6 of the TA should be read as a cohesive and coherent whole, and with a consideration of the law of gift. This led him to conclude that Rose LJ's proposition in the Court of Appeal that a valid gift is fully consistent with theft was 'seriously inconsistent' with the scheme of ss 1–6 and with other parts of the Act:

> What must be erroneous is to treat as 'belonging to another' property which at the time of the alleged appropriation belongs to the defendant in accordance with section 5(4). Similarly it must be wrong to treat as dishonest 'appropriation of property belonging to another' under s 2(1) an appropriation for which the defendant correctly knows (as opposed to mistakenly believes) he actually had (as opposed to would have had) the other's consent, the other knowing of the appropriation and the circumstances of it (as opposed to the other person only hypothetically having that knowledge)... Theft is a crime of dishonesty but dishonesty is not the only element in the commission of the crime.

11.7 Lord Steyn stated that one must retain a sense of perspective, and that what he calls 'the tension between the civil and criminal law' is not a factor which justifies a departure from the law. But the result of this case is another example of English criminal law becoming more difficult to define with any precision: the criminal law appears to be reduced to little more than a moral judgment. Already the boundary of manslaughter is according to Lord Mackay in *Adomako* (1995) (**8.29**) 'supremely a jury question'. As Lord Hobhouse states, an essential function of the criminal law is to define the boundary between what conduct is criminal and what merely immoral. The boundaries of manslaughter and now the law of theft are extraordinarily unclear.

The HL in *Hinks* seems to accept that there can be theft where there are no stolen goods. Yet, as J. C. Smith (at [1998] Crim LR 906) says, 'the TAs assume the existence of the civil law of property...TA offences exist for the purpose of protecting those interests.' Gardener (1998), on the other hand, argues that there may be good reasons for contract and criminal law not to coincide: the civil law is there to protect property rights, even if they were unsatisfactorily acquired, whereas the criminal law rightly concentrates on the unsatisfactory manner of acquisition. Compare these decisions with *Preddy* (1996) discussed at **11.35**, and:

A-G's Reference (No. 1 of 1985) **(1986)** A publican sold his own beer in a tied house, keeping the profit.

CA (Lord Lane CJ): upheld his acquittal. The manager had a civil obligation to the brewery, but there was no theft. Despite the wording of s 5(2), the concept of theft by importing the equitable doctrine of constructive trust is so obtuse and so far removed from ordinary people's understanding of what constitutes stealing, that it should not amount to it.

Actus reus: appropriation

11.8 Section 3 provides:

> **s 3** (1) Any assumption by a person of the right of an owner amounts to an appropriation, and this includes, where he has come by the property (innocently or not) without stealing it, any later assumption of a right to it by keeping or dealing with it as owner.
>
> (2) Where property or a right or interest in property is or purports to be transferred for value to a person acting in good faith, no later assumption by him of rights which he believed himself to be acquiring shall, by reason of any defect in the transferor's title, amount to theft of the property.

Appropriation involves any usurpation of the rights of the owner. It is much wider than merely 'taking'. If you give me your chocolate to look after and I eat it, I have usurped your rights as the owner. In that case, I have usurped all your rights, but any interference with your rights as the owner may constitute usurpation. Even if all I do is fail to return your chocolate to you when you ask for it (having dishonestly decided to keep it), I have stolen it. This is a form of liability by omission which, as discussed in 2.5, is rare in criminal law.

Appropriation and consent

11.9 The HL has made a difficult issue more difficult:

Lawrence **(1971)** An Italian tourist on his first visit to the UK was taken by taxi from Victoria Station to an address in central London. The taxi driver, when offered £1 from V's wallet, took a further £6 from the wallet, although the correct fare should have been less than £1.

CA and HL: upheld D's conviction. Viscount Dilhorne:

> I see no ground for concluding that the omission of the words 'without the consent of the owner' was inadvertent and not deliberate, and to read the subsection as if they were included is, in my opinion, wholly unwarranted. Parliament by the omission of these words has relieved the prosecution of the burden of establishing that the taking was without the owner's consent. That is no longer an ingredient of the offence.

Morris; Anderton v Burnside **(1984)** In both these cases Ds took price labels from lower-priced articles and substituted them for the price labels on higher-priced articles. In one case, D paid the lower price at the checkout and was then arrested; in the other, D was arrested before he reached the checkout.

HL (Lord Roskill): upheld their convictions, but introduced a narrower view of appropriation. The concept involves 'an act by way of adverse interference with or usurpation of' any of the rights of the owner. Thus a shopper was not appropriating goods by taking the goods from the shelf: he was doing what the shop wanted him to do. Only when the interference was 'adverse' was it an appropriation.

11.10 To many commentators this case was a disappointment. Spencer (at (1984) 43 Camb LJ 10) called it a depressing decision 'not even competent in technical respects'. Here, he suggests, was the HL, clearly bored by theft, concurring in a single speech which flatly contradicted *Lawrence* (1971) without saying whether that decision was distinguished or overruled. There followed a whole series of cases which added confusion upon confusion. For example, in *Fritschy* (1985) the CA held that a man who agreed to take krugerrands from London to Geneva for the owner only appropriated the money once he had deviated from the authorized route, even though from the beginning he had never intended to deliver them to their correct destination. In *Dobson v General Accident Fire and Life Assurance Corporation* (1990), a civil case, the CA drew a distinction between authorization and consent in order to try and reconcile the cases: an act which is authorized could constitute appropriation (following *Morris* (1984) but an act which was consented to could not (following *Lawrence* (1971)). The best thing about the next decision is that it at least clarified the law:

> **Gomez (1991)** D persuaded the manager of the shop where he worked to sell £16,000 worth of electrical goods to a rogue by accepting a cheque that was subsequently dishonoured. He pleaded guilty to theft when the judge refused to accept a submission that there was no appropriation since the manager had expressly authorized the removal of the goods.
>
> CA: allowed D's appeal, but HL (by a majority of 4 to 1) allowed the Crown's appeal. Lords Jauncey, Browne-Wilkinson, and Slynn agreed with the speech of Lord Keith. Lord Keith accepted that no 'sensible distinction can be made in this context between consent and authorisation', and that *Lawrence* (1971) was authoritative and correct. This speech should be contrasted with the vociferous dissent of Lord Lowry. He relied heavily on the 8th Report of the CLRC (1966), and also on the fact that s 15 becomes redundant if s 1 is given the meaning accepted by the majority.

11.11 The *Gomez* solution has the merit of simplifying the law. It has also, though, widened the law quite extraordinarily. Any assumption of a right of an owner, even with her consent, may constitute the *actus reus* of theft (see *Hinks* (2000) at **11.6**). That case turned on the question whether a valid gift was capable of being 'an appropriation' of property belonging to another. A majority of the HL held that it could. Does this go a step further than *Gomez*, or is it simply a logical conclusion from the reasoning in *Gomez*? Nor did the decision in *Gomez* resolve other potential problems:

> **Gallasso (1992)** D, a nurse caring for mentally handicapped adults, had the responsibility of drawing money from their bank accounts for their living expenses. She opened a separate bank account for V, a patient, and subsequently transferred some of the money in it into her own account and some into a cash card account.

> CA: quashed her conviction for theft based on the opening of the account in V's name, since paying the cheque into a trust account could not be regarded as an appropriation since it was evidence of D affirming V's rights rather than assuming them for herself.

Is this an appropriate interpretation of *Gomez* (1991)? Surely merely by handling the cheque she was 'appropriating' it: the question then remains as to whether she was dishonest.

> **Briggs (2003)** D appealed against her conviction of theft. She had been involved in the sale of a house and the purchase of another by Vs, an elderly couple. In a letter of authority written by D but signed by Vs, Vs had instructed licensed conveyancers to apply £49,950 from the proceeds of sale of the first house towards the purchase of the second. Vs believed that the money would be used to ensure that the second house was conveyed to them. However, the title in the second house was transferred to, and later registered in, the names of D and her father. P's case was that D had appropriated the money when she had caused it to be transferred for her own purposes, and that Vs' consent to the transfer had been induced by fraud. D argued that the transfer could not amount to an appropriation as it was made in accordance with, and as a result of, Vs' instructions, and that a party did not appropriate an item if, by fraud, she had induced the owner to part with it.
>
> CA: allowed appeal. Where V caused a payment to be made in reliance on deceptive conduct by D, there was no appropriation by D within the meaning of the TA 1968: the word 'appropriation' connoted a physical act rather than a more remote action triggering the payment giving rise to the charge of theft. Although in the instant case the appropriate charge might have been one of an offence of deception, a verdict of guilty of a deception offence would not be substituted under the Criminal Appeal Act 1968, s 3 as there had been a deliberate decision by P not to charge deception.

Can you distinguish this case from *Hinks* (2000)? Or do you think it was wrongly decided?

11.12 Can property be appropriated more than once? Section 3(1) appears to say that where someone has come by property without stealing it, he may still commit theft by some later act. Can one person therefore commit theft of an item more than once? If so, this may pose problems for the law of handling (see **11.52**) since handling can only be committed once the stealing is complete. For the complex overlap between handling and theft, see **11.52**. Even larger is the overlap between theft and fraud (see **11.40**). Does this matter? Glazebrook (1991) argues (supporting the approach taken by the majority in *Gomez (1991)*) that it should not. He points out that if one accepted the argument of Lord Lowry's dissent in *Gomez*, D would not be guilty of theft simply because he was guilty of a more serious offence. Many cases of theft nowadays involve D obtaining goods by trickery. In strict contract law, D becomes the owner of the goods in these circumstances: the contract is valid until and unless the victim chooses to avoid the contract. In which case, can one argue that D is appropriating his own property?

11.13 Another problem is whether appropriation is a one-off, or continuing event.

Atakpu **(1994)** Ds hired cars in Belgium and Germany using false documents. They then brought them to England intending to sell them. They were arrested within the hire period, and charged with conspiracy to steal.

CA: quashed their conviction. If goods have once been stolen, they cannot be stolen again by the same thief. Courts should:

> ...leave it for the common-sense of the jury to decide that the appropriation can continue for so long as the thief can sensibly be regarded as in the act of stealing or, in more understandable words, so long as he is 'on the job' as the editors of *Smith and Hogan*...suggest the test should be.

There was therefore no conspiracy to steal in England.

Note that this particular problem would not arise today: the CJA 1993, s 5 provides that conspiracies to defraud may be tried in this country if some part of the conspiracy arose in this country (see **7.3**).

Mens rea: dishonesty

11.14 Section 2 of the TA 1968 provides no definition of dishonesty, simply some examples of behaviour which is not dishonest:

s 2 (1) A person's appropriation of property belonging to another is not to be regarded as dishonest—

    (a) if he appropriates the property in the belief that he has in law the right to deprive the other of it, on behalf of himself or a third person; or

    (b) if he appropriates the property in the belief that he would have the other's consent if the other knew of the appropriation and the circumstances of it; or

    (c) (except where the property came to him as trustee or personal representative) if he appropriates the property in the belief that the person to whom the property belongs cannot be discovered by taking reasonable steps.

  (2) A person's appropriation of property belonging to another may be dishonest notwithstanding that he is willing to pay for the property.

This gives no guidance on whether the test for dishonesty should be subjective or objective, nor whether it is a matter of fact for the jury or a question of law for the judge.

Feely **(1973)** D, a branch manager of a firm of bookmakers, borrowed £30 from the 'float'. Four days later he was transferred to another branch, and the new manager discovered the loss. D then gave an IOU to cover the deficiency and, when questioned by the police, he said that he intended to pay it back and that he was owed by the firm in wages more than he had borrowed.

CA (five judges, but only Lawton LJ gave a judgment): quashed his conviction. Because the word 'dishonestly' is in common use, judges should not define it.

> Jurors when deciding whether an appropriation was dishonest can be reasonably expected to, and should, apply the current standards of ordinary decent people. In their own lives they have to decide what is and what is not dishonest. We can see no reason why, when in a jury box, they should require the help of a judge to tell them what amounts to dishonesty.

It was a defence that should have been left to the jury that he intended to repay the money and that he had reasonable grounds for believing that he would be able to do so.

11.15 Thus the test for dishonesty is left as a question of fact for juries to apply, using ordinary standards and with no help from the judge. Griew (1985) was highly critical of this, giving a long list of criticisms such as the danger of inconsistent verdicts, the fiction of community norms, the danger of longer and more expensive trials, and the problem of the ordinary dishonest juror. Guest (1987) went further, arguing that if the judge hands over a question of interpreting the law to the jury he is abdicating his constitutional responsibility. It is for judges to identify the state of affairs which were envisaged to be within the scope of the relevant law. Particular difficulties arise where D says he did not think that his act was dishonest:

Ghosh **(1982)** D, a locum hospital consultant, falsely claimed that money was owing to him for an operation, but later explained that the money was in any case owing to him in fees.

CA (Lord Lane CJ): upheld his conviction. Dishonesty describes a state of mind, not conduct, and therefore the test is subjective. However the standard to be applied is that of the reasonable and honest man, not that of the accused.

> It is no defence for a man to say 'I know that what I was doing is generally regarded as dishonest, but I do not regard it as dishonest. Therefore I am not guilty.' What he is

> however entitled to say is 'I did not know that anybody would regard what I was doing
> as dishonest'. He may not be believed…but if he is believed, or raises a real doubt
> about the matter, the jury cannot be sure that he was dishonest.

11.16 Thus the *Ghosh* test is a two-stage test. First the jury ask themselves whether D's behaviour was dishonest by the standards of the honest and reasonable person. Only if the answer to the first question is yes, should they then ask whether D realized it was dishonest in this sense. Spencer (at (1982) 41 Camb LJ 222) criticizes the test for being too sophisticated ('clearly intelligence tests for juries will soon be needed'), and for allowing in effect a mistake of law to act as a defence. The CA has made clear (in *Price* (1989), for example) that the *Ghosh* test should only be applied in *Ghosh*-like situations, that is, where D might have believed that what he is alleged to have done was in accordance with the ordinary person's idea of honesty. Otherwise all that is necessary is a *Feely* (1973) direction. But if you think that a definition of dishonesty would be useful, what would it say? Glazebrook (1993) had a proposal:

> A person's appropriation of property belonging to another is to be regarded as dishonest unless—
>
> (a) done in the belief that he has in law the right to deprive the other of it, on behalf of himself or a third person; or
>
> (b) done in the belief that he would have the other's consent if the other knew of the appropriation and the circumstances of it; or
>
> (c) done (otherwise than by a trustee or personal representative) in the belief that the person to whom the property belongs is unlikely to be discovered by taking reasonable steps; or
>
> (d) he received it in good faith and for value; or
>
> (e) the property is money, some other fungible, a thing in action or intangible property, and is appropriated with the intention of replacing it, and in the belief that it will be possible for him to do so without loss to the person to whom it belongs; or
>
> (f) it consists in picking (otherwise than for reward or for sale or other commercial purpose) mushrooms, flowers, fruit or foliage growing wild.

Would this resolve the difficulties? Would the person who keeps a £50 note found in the gutter be dishonest under this test? The Law Commission in their Consultation Paper No. 155 (1999) seemed to want to go yet further: exploring the proper role of dishonesty in the law, they pointed out that the CLRC in their 8th Report (1966) intended that the word 'dishonesty' should do little more than preserve the old defence of claim of right, and they criticized both the *Feely* and the *Ghosh* tests for 'their assumption of, and dependence on, a shared moral standard' (para. 5.8). 'The fact-finders are required not merely to place D's conduct at an appropriate point on the scale, but to construct their own scale' (para. 5.13). They provisionally concluded that dishonesty should not be a separate element in deception offences (see **11.38**). However, as we shall see at **11.48**, the new fraud offence of the Fraud Act 2006 keeps dishonesty as a key element.

Intention permanently to deprive

11.17 The biggest problems here are evidential: all rogues when caught are likely to say that they intended to pay back/give back the property in due course. But add to this evidential difficulty the huge legal problem of interpreting s 6, which, in Spencer's words, 'sprouts obscurity at every phrase':

> **s 6** (1) A person appropriating property belonging to another without meaning the other permanently to lose the thing itself is nevertheless to be regarded as having the intention of permanently depriving the other of it if his intention is to treat the thing as his own to dispose of regardless of the other's rights; and a borrowing or lending of it may amount to so treating it if, but only if, the borrowing or lending is for a period and in circumstances making it equivalent to an outright taking or disposal.
>
> (2) Without prejudice to the generality of subsection (1) above, where a person, having possession or control (lawfully or not) of property belonging to another, parts with the property under a condition as to its return which he may not be able to perform, this (if done for purposes of his own and without the other's authority) amounts to treating the property as his own to dispose of regardless of the other's rights.

11.18 Spencer (1977) traces the uncomfortable passage of this section through Parliament: the moral of the story seems to be that a criminal code should not be over-specific. The approaches taken to the interpretation of this section by different courts, too, have not been entirely consistent:

> *Lloyd* (1985) D, a cinema projectionist, borrowed films from the cinema where he worked in order to make unlawful copies of them. He was convicted of conspiracy to steal.
>
> CA (Lord Lane CJ): quashed his conviction. Section 6:
>
> > …must mean, if nothing else, that there are circumstances in which a D may be deemed to have the intention permanently to deprive, even though he may intend the owner eventually to get back the object which has been taken…A mere borrowing is never enough to constitute the necessary guilty mind unless the intention is to return the thing in such a changed state that it can be truly said that all its goodness or virtue has gone.
>
> Here the films were not diminished in value at all, so there could have been no theft.

11.19 If I borrow your football season ticket and return it after I have seen the first match of the season, have I stolen it?

***Coffey* (1987)** D obtained machinery by a worthless cheque in order to put pressure on V to resolve a dispute between them. He was convicted of obtaining property by deception.

CA: quashed his conviction. If the jury thought that D might have intended to return the goods, they would not have convicted unless they were sure that he intended that the period of detention should be so long as to amount to an outright taking. Even if the jury concluded that D had in mind not to return the goods if V failed to do what he wanted, they would still have to consider whether he had regarded the likelihood of this happening as being such that his intended conduct could be regarded as equivalent to an outright taking.

> ...the reference in s 6(1) to 'borrowing' (plainly used in a loose sense to denote non-consensual assumption of possession coupled with an intention ultimately to restore the object taken) shows that the 'deprivation' can be 'permanent' even if it is meant to be temporary.

***DPP v Lavender* (1994)** D took two doors from one council house and installed them in another.

CA: upheld his conviction for theft.

***Mitchell* (2008)** D was convicted of robbery. He was one of four men who seized V's vehicle after crashing their own in a police chase. They abandoned V's car and took another one which they subsequently abandoned and burnt out. P conceded that the second vehicle had not been stolen. The trial judge rejected a submission of no case, finding that the taking of the first car and abandoning it was sufficient evidence capable of amounting to an intention to dispose of property regardless of the owner's rights pursuant to s 6(1) of the Act.

CA: allowed the appeal. Section 6(1) was not intended to dilute the definition of theft in s 1(1). A car that is taken as a getaway car and then abandoned is not stolen. Not every conversion amounts to theft, otherwise every taking of a vehicle without authority contrary to s 12 of the Act would amount to theft. (See also Ormerod's comment at [2008] Crim LR 995.)

***Raphael* (2008)** Ds appealed against their convictions for conspiracy to rob (and D2 also appealed against his separate conviction for murder). V's car was taken from him by force, and later D1 contacted him and offered to get his car back in return for a sum of money. The car was subsequently recovered by police.

CA: dismissed the appeals. Even though V was offered the opportunity to buy back his car, this did not prevent the jury from concluding that an intention to permanently deprive him of it was established. The express language of the TA 1968, s 6 specified that the subjective element necessary to establish the *mens rea* for theft included an intention on the part of the taker 'to treat the thing as his own to dispose of regardless of the other's rights'. There was clearly such an intention here given that an offer was made to V to sell the car back to him subject to a condition inconsistent with his right to possession of his own property.

This decision must be right: even if D made a genuine invitation to V to buy back his property that did not preclude a finding that D had an intention permanently to deprive.

Vinall (2011) D1 punched V from his bicycle. V ran away, and the Ds walked off with the bicycle which was later found abandoned by a bus shelter 50 yards away, on a main road. They were convicted of robbery (see 11.22).

CA: quashed the convictions. The jury could not be sure of theft unless they were also sure that at the time of taking the bicycle either the Ds had an intention permanently to deprive (s 1) or they intended to treat the bicycle as their own to dispose of regardless of the other's rights (s 6). The jury did not receive these directions.

If the charge had been theft only, and the jury was not sure that at the moment of taking the Ds dishonestly appropriated the bicycle with intent (actual or deemed) permanently to deprive, they could next consider whether there was a later appropriation at the time of the abandonment. In that event, the question for the jury would be: *did the appellants, when they abandoned the bicycle (1) assume the rights of an owner, (2) intending permanently to deprive the owner of it or intending to treat the bicycle as their own to dispose of regardless of the other's rights?* If so, the offence of theft was committed at the time of the abandonment. This, however, was a charge of robbery. The judge left to the jury the option of concluding that the act of theft was completed not at the time of taking but at the time of abandonment. If the theft was committed only at the moment of abandonment, P could not prove that force or the threat of force was used before or at the time of and *in order to* steal.

It was open to the judge to invite the jury to consider whether the later abandonment of V's bicycle was evidence from which they could infer that Ds intended *at the time of the taking* to treat the bicycle as their own to dispose of regardless of V's rights. If that was the way the judge had chosen to leave the issue of intent to the jury, an explicit direction would have been required explaining that an intention formed only upon abandonment of the bicycle at the bus shelter was inconsistent with and fatal to the allegation of robbery. This was not a case in which the court should substitute a conviction for theft or taking a pedal cycle.

11.20 Would Parliament have been wiser to leave the interpretation of an 'intention permanently to deprive' to case law? Some statutory provisions create more problems than they solve. Is this concept one that could simply be left to juries or magistrates as a question of fact? Or perhaps you prefer Glazebrook's (1993) simpler definition:

> A person is to be regarded as having the intention of permanently depriving the person to whom the property belongs of it if he realises that
>
> (a) the person may be permanently deprived of it, or
>
> (b) it may not be returned to that person before it has become worthless.

11.21 Perhaps the requirement of an intent to deprive permanently should simply be removed, and the law of theft should include unlawful borrowings. Parliament decided in 1968 that such unlawful borrowings could be dealt with under the civil law, or by specific crimes such as removal of articles from places open to the public (TA 1968, s 11) and taking a motor vehicle without authority (s 12). However, Ashworth (PCL, p. 393) argues that since the value of many objects lies in their use, and that they may have relatively short lives, there is a strong argument for penalizing temporary deprivations generally: see also Glanville Williams (1981).

Robbery

11.22 Robbery is stealing with force. It could be as easily classified as an offence of violence as a property offence. Section 8 of the TA 1968 provides:

> **s 8** (1) A person is guilty of robbery if he steals, and immediately before or at the time of doing so, and in order to do so, he uses force on any person or puts or seeks to put any person in fear of being then and there subjected to force.
>
> (2) A person guilty of robbery, or of an assault with intent to rob, shall on conviction on indictment be liable to imprisonment for life.

11.23 Thus the *actus reus* of robbery is that of theft combined with the use of force or fear of subjection to force. The courts have accepted that only minimal force is required:

Dawson **(1976)** Three men, including D, approached V who was 'nudged' by one of them. As V stumbled, his wallet was stolen.

CA: the word 'force' had been deliberately used in the TA 1968 rather than the word 'violence' which had appeared in the Larceny Act 1916. It was a word in ordinary use which juries could apply appropriately.

Clouden **(1987)** D pulled on a lady's shopping bag in order to wrench it from her. He appealed from his conviction for robbery on the basis that he had not used force on any person.

CA: dismissed his appeal. Whether force was 'used on any person' should be left to the jury. It may be sufficient for D to use force on V's possessions in a way which affects V.

The CLRC (1966) considered that they 'would not regard mere snatching of property, such as a handbag, from an unresisting owner as using force for the purpose of definition.' Does the decision in *Clouden* dilute the offence of robbery too much, offending the principle of fair labelling (see **1.2**)? The offence is indictable only, subject to a maximum of life imprisonment. The Crime (Sentences) Act 1997 included robbery with a firearm (including an imitation firearm) amongst those offences, which for a second conviction, resulted in an automatic life sentence (now replaced by the 'dangerousness' provisions of the CJA 2003). The Sentencing Guidelines Council's *Definitive Guideline on Robbery* (2006) identified five different sorts of robberies:

1. Street robbery or 'mugging';
2. Robberies of small businesses;
3. Less sophisticated commercial robberies;
4. Violent personal robberies in the home;
5. Professionally planned commercial robberies.

Should these all be labelled simply 'robbery', or should the offence itself be broken down further?

11.24 The *mens rea* of robbery is the *mens rea* for theft: dishonesty (see **11.14**) plus an intention permanently to deprive V of the property (see **11.17**), as well as at least recklessness as to the force used: since D must use the force in order to steal, more than accidental or negligent use of force is necessary.

Burglary

11.25 Stealing from buildings has long been treated differently to other forms of stealing. The word 'burglary', deriving from 'burge breche', an old English term, used to mean breaking into a house by night with intent to commit a felony. Section 9 of the TA 1968 creates two distinct offences:

> **s 9** (1) A person is guilty of burglary if—
>
> > (a) he enters any building or part of a building as a trespasser and with intent to commit any such offence as is mentioned in subsection (2) below; or
> >
> > (b) having entered any building or part of a building as a trespasser he steals or attempts to steal anything in the building or that part of it or inflicts or attempts to inflict on any person therein any grievous bodily harm.
>
> > (2) The offences referred to in subsection (1)(a) above are offences of stealing anything in the building or part of a building in question, of inflicting on any person therein any grievous bodily harm therein, and of doing unlawful damage to the building or anything therein.

The two separate offences are (i) entering a building with the necessary intent and (ii) having entered a building as a trespasser, committing one of the specified offences. Both are triable either way, though burglary is generally tried summarily (unless the unrecovered value of property is at least £10,000). When it comes to sentencing, burglary from domestic premises is taken more seriously than burglary from shops or businesses: the maximum penalty for domestic burglary is 14 years' imprisonment; whereas if the burglary is from a non-dwelling the maximum penalty is only ten years. It is not clear whether D has to know he is in a dwelling to incur a higher penalty.

The meaning of 'building'

11.26 Something will not qualify as a building unless it has a certain degree of permanence. Thus a 25-foot-long freezer weighing three tons which had sat in a farmyard for more than two years qualified as a building (*B and S v Leathley* (1979)) whilst a disconnected articulated container did not (*Norfolk Constabulary v Seekings and Gould* (1986)).

Walkington **(1979)** D walked into the till area in a department store but found it to be empty.

CA: dismissed his appeal against conviction for an offence under the TA 1968, s 9(1)(a). The jury were entitled to conclude that the counter area was a 'part of a building' from which members of the public were excluded. He also had an intention to steal, although this was conditional upon him finding something worth stealing.

'Trespasser'

11.27 Perhaps the greatest difficulty of the pre-1968 law on burglary was the requirement of a 'breaking and entry'. In order to get rid of these difficult and somewhat technical rules, Parliament introduced a new test that entry must be as a trespasser. The courts have been keen to avoid all the technicalities of the tort of trespass:

Collins (1973) D, who was drunk, saw a ladder leaning against a house at 3.30 am. He climbed the ladder and saw V, a naked woman, asleep. He descended, removed his clothes, and climbed up again. As he climbed on to the window sill, V woke up and invited him in, believing him to be her boyfriend. They had sexual intercourse before V realized her mistake (NB: this was at a time when s 9(2) included rape amongst the list of ulterior offences D may intend: it was removed in the SOA 2003 as s 63 of the SOA 2003 creates a more appropriate sexual offence (see 10.30)).

CA (Edmund Davies LJ): quashed D's conviction for s 9(1)(a) burglary. There cannot be a conviction for entering premises as a trespasser unless the person entering does so knowing that he is a trespasser and nevertheless deliberately enters, or, at the very least, is reckless whether or not he is entering the premises of another without the other party's consent.

Smith and Jones (1976) D1 and D2 were arrested having removed two television sets from D1's father's house. D1 argued that since he had a general permission to enter his father's house, he could not be a trespasser. Both Ds were convicted of s 9(1)(b) burglary.

CA (James LJ): dismissed their appeal. A person is a trespasser if he enters premises knowing that he is entering in excess of the permission that has been given to him, or being reckless as to whether he is entering in excess of the permission that has been given to him to enter, provided the facts are known to D which enable him to realize that he is acting in excess of the permission given.

Does *Smith and Jones* widen the law of burglary too far? It suggests that all shoplifters are in fact burglars: why then are they charged with theft? Presumably burglary has a higher penalty than theft because Parliament felt that people need especial protection from intruders in their own homes. Should this protection be limited to uninvited intruders?

'Entry'

11.28 Not all of the burglar's body need enter the building:

Brown (1985) D broke a shop window and rummaged around with the top half of his body inside the window.

CA: dismissed his appeal. His entry had been both effective and substantial.

J. C. Smith in his commentary to this case (at [1985] Crim LR 212) suggests that the words 'effective' and 'substantial' should be in the alternative, otherwise the law requires too much.

11.29 The *mens rea* of burglary depends on which offence is charged: for s 9(1)(a) an intention to commit one of the ulterior offences must be proved; for s 9(1)(b) the *mens rea* for the ulterior offence must be proved. In both cases, D must know or be reckless as to whether he is entering as a trespasser. The main problem that has arisen in the case law is whether conditional intent is sufficient. If D only has a conditional intent, he may still be liable for attempted burglary. Why is a person who enters with intent to do an ulterior offence not guilty simply of an inchoate offence (whether attempted burglary or an attempt at the ulterior offences specified in s 9(2))? This raises another fair labelling question (see 1.2): is the crime of burglary necessary, or could we rely simply on prosecutions for the ulterior offence, or an attempt at these offences? Parliament's answer is clear where the ulterior offence is theft, personal violence, or criminal damage: burglary is a more serious version of these ulterior offences since D has intruded into V's home. Until the SOA 2003, another ulterior offence which constituted s 9(1)(b) burglary was rape. You may well agree that it is better to deal with that offence as a sexual offence (see **10.30**). Should trespass with intent to commit grievous bodily harm really constitute the offence of burglary?

Aggravated burglary

11.30 Section 10 of the TA 1968 creates an aggravated form of burglary:

...if he commits any burglary and at the time has with him any firearm or imitation firearm, any weapon of offence, or any explosive...

Aggravated burglary is triable only on indictment and has a maximum penalty of life imprisonment. The offence poses few problems, except perhaps in defining a 'weapon of offence'. The maximum penalty for 'plain' domestic burglary is 14 years' imprisonment (see **11.25**), and sentences of more than 14 years are extremely rare even for aggravated burglary. If the burglar has real weapons with him, and uses them, he will be charged with offences against the person as well as (or rather than) burglary. It is therefore questionable whether aggravated burglary is required as a separate offence.

Abstracting electricity

11.31 As we saw at **11.4**, electricity is not property so the TA 1968 provides a separate (triable either way) offence of abstracting electricity in s 13:

> A person who dishonestly uses without due authority, or dishonestly causes to be wasted or diverted, any electricity shall on conviction on indictment be liable to imprisonment for a term not exceeding five years.

A person is guilty of an offence under s 13 if she abstracts electricity by tampering with a meter, or by diverting electricity in any way without the consent of the owner. It looks as though merely leaving the lights on wastefully could be an offence! Would it be more straightforward to decide that electricity was property which could be stolen?

Blackmail

11.32 A close cousin to robbery is blackmail, the extortion of money by threats rather than by violence. Section 21 of the TA 1968 provides:

> **s 21** (1) A person is guilty of blackmail if, with a view to gain for himself or another or with intent to cause loss to another, he makes any unwarranted demand with menaces; and for this purpose a demand with menaces is unwarranted unless the person making it does so in the belief—
>
> (a) that he has reasonable grounds for making the demand; and
>
> (b) that the use of the menaces is a proper means of reinforcing the demand.
>
> (2) The nature of the act or mission demanded is immaterial, and it is also immaterial whether the menaces relate to action to be taken by the person making the demand.
>
> (3) A person guilty of blackmail shall on conviction on indictment be liable to imprisonment for a term not exceeding 14 years.

The meaning of the words 'unwarranted demands with menaces' causes some difficulties. Menaces are serious threats, but when are they unwarranted demands? Where a person who takes back his own property from someone who borrowed it is not guilty of stealing it, if he threatens violence in order to recover it, he may be guilty of assault but is not guilty of robbery. However, since his threats of violence are improper, he may still be guilty of blackmail.

Lawrence and Pomroy (1971)   D1 and D2 went round to V's house to obtain money that V was refusing to pay for building repairs which he said had been inadequately carried out. D1 said, 'Step outside the house and we will sort this out', and D2 said menacingly, 'Come on mate, come outside'. A flick knife was later found in D1's coat pocket.

CA: affirmed D1 and D2's convictions for blackmail.

The word 'menaces' is an ordinary English word which any jury can be expected to understand and only in exceptional cases where, because of special knowledge in special circumstances, what would be a menace to an ordinary person is not a menace to the person to whom it is addressed, or where the converse applies, is it necessary for the trial judge to spell out the meaning of the word.

11.33   The gain or loss concerns only money or other property (see s 34(2)). If D by menaces gains other benefits, then there is no blackmail. If the benefit is sexual intercourse, then D may be charged with rape, since V does not consent within the definition of the SOA 2003, s 74 (see **10.12**). What about other favours? Suppose D manages to gain a place at his chosen school for his child by threatening to reveal secrets about the head teacher: should this be blackmail? The demand may take any form and need not be explicit. It need not even reach the intended victim.

Mens rea

11.34   D must intend to make an unwarranted demand with menaces, with a view to gain for himself or another or with intent to cause loss to another. The section provides that a demand is not unwarranted if the use of menaces is a proper way of reinforcing the demand. In deciding what is 'proper', the court faces the ambiguity and potential for inconsistency of the *Ghosh* (1982) test (see **11.15**).

Deception offences

11.35   In the original TA 1968, the two main offences of deception were found in s 15 (obtaining property by deception: maximum sentence, ten years' imprisonment) and s 16 (obtaining a pecuniary advantage by deception: maximum sentence, five years' imprisonment). A third deception offence was procuring the execution of a valuable security by deception (s 20(2)). Major problems were apparent very quickly with the interpretation of s 16: Edmund-Davies LJ in *Royle* (1971) called it 'a judicial nightmare' and asked for it to be replaced by a simpler provision. The most significant part of it (s 16(2)(a)) was repealed, but the TA 1978, passed to plug the gap, was certainly no simpler. Section 1 introduced the offence of obtaining services by deception and s 2, three separate and overlapping offences of evasion of liability by deception. We have already noted the '*Preddy* problem' (see **11.6**) and the Theft (Amendment) Act 1996 was passed to deal with this. It inserted ss 15A and 15B (obtaining a money transfer by deception) into the TA 1968. These offences have all been repealed by the Fraud Act 2006. Why?

The nature of deception

11.36 The main problem was defining 'deception'. The CLRC (1966) had preferred the term 'deception' to 'false pretence'. It meant any deception (whether deliberate or reckless) by words or conduct as to fact or as to law, including a deception as to the present intentions of the person using the deception or any other person. Someone could be deceived by silence:

> *Silverman* **(1987)** D charged elderly customers excessive amounts for repairs to their flat. He had not pressurized them to accept his quotation.
>
> CA: quashed his conviction because of an inadequate summing up, yet stressed that where there is a situation of mutual trust, an excessively high quotation could constitute a representation of the D's state of mind, that he did not intend to make an excessive profit. Consider this case in the context of our discussion of liability for omissions generally (see **2.10**).

It had to be proved that D actually deceived someone and that this caused V to act. Only people could be deceived, not machines. Thus it appeared that if you used someone else's PIN to obtain money from the bank you were guilty of theft but not of obtaining the money by deception. The ordinary meaning of 'to deceive' is 'to induce someone to believe that a thing which is false is true'. However, in the criminal law it may be a deception to persuade someone falsely that something only *may* be true.

> *Lambie* **(1982)** D had been asked by the bank to return her credit card having exceeded her credit limit. Instead she continued to use it. She bought goods in a shop

with it, the assistant having made the usual checks against the credit card. The shop manager gave evidence that she was not concerned about what went on between D and Barclaycard.

HL (reversing CA): upheld D's conviction under s 16. By tendering the credit card, D was making a representation of actual authority to make the contract with the shop on the bank's behalf that the bank would honour the voucher when it was presented by the shop. Had the assistant known that the customer did not have the authority to make such representation, the inference was irresistible that she would not have allowed D to take the goods away.

The HL were obviously concerned by the enormous potential for fraud created by credit cards, but does this overcome the logical difficulty that the victim of the deception was genuinely indifferent whether or not she was deceived? The shop knew that they would be paid as long as they checked the signature, the current 'stop-list', etc. The banks introduced credit cards not for the convenience of their customers but because they knew that they were a wonderful way in which the banks could make more profit. Should it not be for the banks to control the abuse of their own inventions? The case of *Lambie* illustrates well the difficulty of drawing a line between civil and criminal law. Mrs Lambie never pretended to the bank that she was anyone but Mrs Lambie, nor did she deny her civil debt to the bank. What is it that makes her conduct criminal? If I lie to the plumber who comes and mends my dripping tap that I have lost my cheque book and have no cash on me, and I ask him to come back next week for the money, am I a criminal? If he contacted the police, they would probably tell him that it sounded simply like non-payment of a debt and that the plumber should sue me through the small claims court (at his own expense). What is it that is different about *Lambie* which allowed the banks to sue for their bad debts at taxpayers' expense through the mechanism of the criminal justice process?

11.37 Another difficulty was the overlap between these various offences. The Law Commission's Consultation Paper No. 155 (1999) on *Fraud and Deception* considered, amongst other things, 'whether a general offence of fraud would improve the criminal law'. We noted their comments on dishonesty (**11.16**), which led them to conclude that proof of dishonesty should not be a separate element in deception offences. This would (of course) necessitate a new defence that D secured the requisite consequence in the belief that he or she is legally entitled to do so, whether by deception or otherwise. For this reason, perhaps, 'dishonesty' continues to be a key ingredient of the new offences (see **11.48**). The Law Commission in 1999 recommended a number of reforms: the *Preddy* problems (**11.35**) could be avoided if, for the purposes of the offence of obtaining property by deception, it was sufficient that the person to whom the property belongs is deprived of it by deception, whether or not anyone else obtains it. They proposed that the 'intention permanently to deprive' in theft should be removed. This would have inevitably criminalized certain trivial conduct and would have increased reliance on prosecutorial discretion not to prosecute in appropriate cases.

11.38 Most importantly, the Law Commission in 1999 deprecated the association of deception with false representations: it argued that the question should simply be: did D, by what he did, induce in the other a mistaken belief? Non-disclosure alone should not count as deception, whether or not there is a legal duty to disclose. Similarly, it criticized the 'constructive deception' applied in cases such as *Lambie*: 'we believe that deception should be understood as the inducing of a false belief—a psychological fact—rather than as something which by abstract analysis can be *deemed* to have occurred' (para. 8.16). It therefore proposed that the misuse of payment cards should form the subject matter of a new offence, adopting the suggestion of J. C. Smith (1996):

> A person commits an offence if he intentionally causes a legal liability to pay money to be imposed on another, knowing that the other does not consent to his doing so and that he has no right to do so (pp. 40–1).

In the Consultation Paper, the Law Commission questioned whether the *mens rea* of this proposed offence should be intention, or whether recklessness would suffice. The development of e-commerce reinforces the difficulties that arise from the fact that a machine cannot be deceived. The Law Commission provisionally concluded that it should be criminal to obtain a service without the permission of the person providing it, albeit without the deception of a human mind. This change, it suggests, should be effected by extending the offence of theft, rather than by extending the concept of deception.

11.39 By the time the Law Commission published its final Report on *Fraud* (Law Com No. 276 (2002)), it had come down in favour of a general fraud offence. It recommended that the eight offences of deception created by the Theft Acts 1968–96 (ss 15, 15A, 16, and 20(2) of the TA 1968, and ss 1 and 2 of the TA 1978) should be repealed, and that the common law conspiracy to defraud should be abolished. In their place it recommended the creation of two new statutory offences—one of fraud, and one of obtaining services dishonestly. The offence of fraud would be committed where, with intent to make a gain or to cause loss or to expose another to the risk of loss, a person dishonestly (1) makes a false representation, (2) wrongfully fails to disclose information, or (3) secretly abuses a position of trust. The offence of obtaining services dishonestly would be committed where a person by any dishonest act obtains services in respect of which payment is required, with intent to avoid payment. Deception would not be an essential element of the offence, which would therefore extend to the obtaining of services by providing false information to computers and machines. In May 2004, the Home Office published a consultation document based on these proposals. The main result of the consultations was that the Government then decided to keep the common law offence of conspiracy to defraud (see **7.24–7.25**. Read those pages carefully now: think about why prosecutors often prefer to charge conspiracy rather than the substantive offences.)

The Fraud Act 2006

11.40 The Fraud Act 2006, which came into force on 15 January 2006, created a general offence of fraud, with three (overlapping) ways of committing it:

> **s 1 Fraud**
>
> (1) A person is guilty of fraud if he is in breach of any of the sections listed in subsection (2) (which provide for different ways of committing the offence).
>
> (2) The sections are—
>
>   (a) section 2 (fraud by false representation),
>
>   (b) section 3 (fraud by failing to disclose information), and
>
>   (c) section 4 (fraud by abuse of position).

The maximum sentence for the offence of fraud, when tried on indictment, is ten years' imprisonment. It can be committed in one of three ways:

Fraud by false representation

11.41 Section 2 provides that:

> **s 2** (1) A person is in breach of this section if he—
>
>   (a) dishonestly makes a false representation, and
>
>   (b) intends, by making the representation—
>
>   (i) to make a gain for himself or another, or
>
>   (ii) to cause loss to another or to expose another to a risk of loss.
>
> (2) A representation is false if—
>
>   (a) it is untrue or misleading, and
>
>   (b) the person making it knows that it is, or might be, untrue or misleading.
>
> (3) 'Representation' means any representation by words or conduct as to fact or law, including a representation as to the state of mind of—
>
>   (a) the person making the representation, or
>
>   (b) any other person.

(4) A representation may be express or implied.

(5) For the purposes of this section a representation may be regarded as made if it (or anything implying it) is submitted in any form to any system or device designed to receive, convey or respond to communications (with or without human intervention).

Thus we see that here P must prove that D:

- acted 'dishonestly', which will presumably be defined as before: see *Feely* (1973) (11.14) and *Ghosh* (1982) (11.15);

- made the representation with the intention of making a gain *or* causing loss *or* risk of loss to another. The gain or loss does not actually have to take place. Gain and loss are defined in s 5:

  (1) The references to gain and loss in sections 2 to 4 are to be read in accordance with this section.

  (2) 'Gain' and 'loss'—

     (a) extend only to gain or loss in money or other property;

     (b) include any such gain or loss whether temporary or permanent; and 'property' means any property whether real or personal (including things in action and other intangible property).

  (3) 'Gain' includes a gain by keeping what one has, as well as a gain by getting what one does not have.

  (4) 'Loss' includes a loss by not getting what one might get, as well as a loss by parting with what one has.

- made a false representation: see s 2(2). A representation is defined as false if it is untrue or misleading and D must know that it is, or might be, untrue or misleading. This is (surprisingly?) broad.

Representation: see s 2(3)–(5). It means any representation as to fact or law, including a representation as to a person's state of mind. It may be express or implied. It can be stated in words or communicated by conduct. It may be written or spoken or posted on a website. Misusing a credit card is clearly caught. And 'phishing' (i.e. where a person disseminates an email to large groups of people falsely representing that the email has been sent by a legitimate financial institution. The email prompts the reader to provide information such as credit card and bank account numbers so that the 'phisher' can gain access to others' assets.) The main purpose of s 2(5) is, according to the Explanatory Notes published with the Act, 'to ensure that fraud can be committed where a person makes a representation to a machine and a response can be produced without any need for human involvement' (e.g. where a person enters a number into a 'CHIP and PIN' machine). Section 2(5) is expressed in 'fairly general terms', we are told, because it would be artificial to distinguish situations involving modern technology, where it is doubtful whether there has been a 'representation', because the only recipient of the false statement is a machine or a piece of software, from other situations not involving modern technology where a false statement is submitted to a system for dealing with communications but is not in fact communicated to a human being (e.g. postal or messenger systems). This is a very wide offence: it is a wholly inchoate offence which appears to criminalize lying or 'lying for economic purposes' (see Dennis at [2007] Crim LR 2). Here is an example:

> *Idrees v DPP (2011)* D had failed on 15 occasions to pass the theory driving test. A 16th test was booked online in his name, and the Driving Standards Agency had sent a confirmation letter detailing the date, time, and location of the theory test to him. X, a person known to have impersonated other people in test centres, appeared to take the test, with D's driving licence. When he was spotted and not allowed to take the test, he left. D was arrested, and in due course convicted of fraud, contrary to ss 1 and 2 of the Fraud Act: making a false representation, namely that an unknown person impersonated him for the purpose of taking and passing a theory driving test for his benefit.
>
> DC: on an appeal by way of case stated, the evidence of D's guilt was overwhelming, and the appeal dismissed. The court had rightly focused on the fact that the only person who could have benefited from the attempt by X to impersonate D was D himself and no other sensible explanation had been advanced.

Fraud by failing to disclose information

11.42 Section 3 provides:

> **s 3** A person is in breach of this section if he—
>
> (a) dishonestly fails to disclose to another person information which he is under a legal duty to disclose, and
>
> (b) intends, by failing to disclose the information—
>
> (i)   to make a gain for himself or another, or
>
> (ii) to cause loss to another or to expose another to a risk of loss.

Here P must prove that D:

- acted 'dishonestly', which will presumably be defined as before: see *Feely* (1973) (**11.14**) and *Ghosh* (1982) (**11.15**);

- failed to disclose the information with the intention of making a gain *or* causing loss *or* risk of loss to another. The gain or loss does not actually have to take place. Gain and loss are defined in s 5 (**11.41**);

- was under a legal duty to disclose information, which may include duties under oral contracts as well as written contracts. According to the Law Commission's Report on *Fraud* (Law Com No. 276 (2002)):

> *Such a duty may derive from statute (such as the provisions governing company prospectuses), from the fact that the transaction in question is one of the utmost good faith (such as a contract of insurance), from the express or implied terms of a contract, from the custom of a particular trade or market, or from the existence of a fiduciary relationship between the parties (such as that of agent and principal) (para. 7.29).*
>
> *For this purpose there is a legal duty to disclose information not only if the defendant's failure to disclose it gives the victim a cause of action for damages, but also if the law gives the victim a right to set aside any change in his or her legal position to which he or she may consent as a result of the non-disclosure. For example, a person in a fiduciary position has a duty to disclose material information when entering into a contract with his or her beneficiary, in the sense that a failure to make such disclosure will entitle the beneficiary to rescind the contract and to reclaim any property transferred under it (para. 7.29).*

The Explanatory Notes suggest that the failure of a solicitor to share vital information with a client within the context of their work relationship, in order to perpetrate a fraud upon that client, would be covered. Similarly, an offence could be committed under this section if a person intentionally failed to disclose information relating to his heart condition when making an application for life insurance.

Fraud by abuse of position

11.43   Section 4 provides:

> **s 4** (1) A person is in breach of this section if he—
>
> (a) occupies a position in which he is expected to safeguard, or not to act against, the financial interests of another person,
>
> (b) dishonestly abuses that position, and
>
> (c) intends, by means of the abuse of that position—
>
> (i) to make a gain for himself or another, or
>
> (ii) to cause loss to another or to expose another to a risk of loss.
>
> (2) A person may be regarded as having abused his position even though his conduct consisted of an omission rather than an act.

P must prove that D:

- acted 'dishonestly', which will presumably be defined as before: see *Feely* (1973) (**11.14**) and *Ghosh* (1982) (**11.15**);

- intended to make a gain *or* causing loss *or* risk of loss to another. The gain or loss does not actually have to take place. Gain and loss are defined in s 5 (**11.41**);

- abused his position. The Law Commission (Law Com No. 276 (2002)) explained the meaning of 'position' (and this is not further clarified in the statute):

    The necessary relationship will be present between trustee and beneficiary, director and company, professional person and client, agent and principal, employee and employer, or between partners. It may arise otherwise, for example within a family, or in the context of voluntary work, or in any context where the parties are not at arm's length. In nearly all cases where it arises, it will be recognised by the civil law as importing fiduciary duties, and any relationship that is so recognised will suffice. We see no reason, however, why the existence of such duties should be essential. This does not of course mean that it would be entirely a matter for the fact-finders whether the necessary relationship exists. The question whether the particular facts alleged can properly be described as giving rise to that relationship will be an issue capable of being ruled upon by the judge and, if the case goes to the jury, of being the subject of directions (para. 7.38).

The term 'abuse' is not defined (or as the Explanatory Notes put it 'not limited by a definition'!). Note that s 4(2) makes clear that the offence can be committed by omission as well as by positive action. The Explanatory Notes give the following examples: an employee who fails to take up the chance of a crucial contract in order that an associate or rival company can take it up instead at the expense of the employer; an employee of a software company who uses his position to clone software products with the intention of selling the products on; a person who is employed to care for an elderly or disabled person has access to that person's bank account and abuses his position by transferring funds to invest in a high-risk business venture of his own. Would this catch *Hinks* (2000) (**11.6**)? Collins (2011) argues that this offence is 'under-theorised'. As she says, those 'who have half a mind to manipulate a situation will relatively easily satisfy the dishonesty and intention requirements of the offence' and so abuse a position. She justifies the broad drafting of the offence by saying that otherwise 'it would not be able to uphold effectively the basic public good of protecting trust relationships in dealing with another's financial interests.' The bottom line is the need to criminalize the risk that the moral wrong of disloyalty poses to trust relationships. Do you agree?

11.44 The Act goes on to create a number of other offences.

s 6 Possession, etc. of articles for use in frauds:

(1) A person is guilty of an offence if he has in his possession or under his control any article for use in the course of or in connection with any fraud.

The offence is triable either way. This broad preliminary offence is similar to s 25 of the TA 1968 (without the need for D to be absent from his place of abode). P must prove that:

- D possessed or controlled the article(s). 'Article' is defined in s 8 (and includes any program or data held in electronic form);

- although not expressly stated, it would appear that D must possess the article for the purpose or with the intention of using it in the course of fraud. (It is not necessary to prove that he intended to use it in a specific fraud, or that he intended to use it himself: *Ellames* (1974). Does this catch the Ds in *Hollinshead* (1972)? Is there really a need for common law conspiracy as well?)

Montague **(2013)** D and 3 co-Ds were charged with having articles in their possession in connection with fraud, contrary to FA 2006, s 6. The evidence included driving licences in false names and with D's photograph attached. P's case was that D was not the principal fraudster, but that his involvement was demonstrated by his photographs on the driving licences, since he was the only person who could have used them. The trial judge directed the jury that someone might be in possession of something not physically on his person if it was part of a common pool to which he had the right to draw at will or say what should be done with it, or if the possession was part of a joint enterprise, although mere presence at the scene was not enough to prove guilt. D was convicted and appealed.

CA: dismissed the appeal. The judge had directed the jury that D was not to be convicted if he had done no more than provide the photographs. That direction ensured that D could only be convicted on the basis that he had participated in the plan to possess or control articles for use in fraud.

---

s 7 Making or supplying articles for use in frauds:

(1) A person is guilty of an offence if he makes, adapts, supplies or offers to supply any article—

(a) knowing that it is designed or adapted for use in the course of or in connection with fraud, or

(b) intending it to be used to commit, or assist in the commission of, fraud.

11.45 The offence is triable either way.

For this preliminary offence, P must prove that:

- D makes, adapts, supplies, or offers to supply any article. 'Article' is defined in s 8 (earlier) and includes any program or data held in electronic form. The Explanatory Notes give the example of someone who makes devices which when attached to electricity meters cause the meter to malfunction;

- D intends or knows that it will be used in connection with fraud.

s 9 Participating in fraudulent business carried on by sole trader, etc.:

(1) A person is guilty of an offence if he is knowingly a party to the carrying on of a business to which this section applies.

11.46 The offence is triable either way. This offence is similar to that under the Companies Act 1985, s 458, but extends the offence to non-corporate traders. (Section 10 of the Fraud Act 2006 increases the maximum custodial sentence for fraudulent trading under the companies' legislation to ten years.) Under s 9, P must prove:

- dishonesty, which will presumably be defined as before: see *Feely* (1973) (**11.14**) and *Ghosh* (1982) (**11.15**);

- an intention to defraud;

- that D exercised some kind of controlling or managerial function within the company.

Obtaining services dishonestly

11.47 After these various fraud offences, we find the other main offence (s 11):

s 11 (1) A person is guilty of an offence under this section if he obtains services for himself or another—

(a) by a dishonest act, and

(b) in breach of subsection (2).

(2) A person obtains services in breach of this subsection if—

(a) they are made available on the basis that payment has been, is being or will be made for or in respect of them,

(b) he obtains them without any payment having been made for or in respect of them or without payment having been made in full, and

(c) when he obtains them, he knows—

(i) that they are being made available on the basis described in paragraph (a), or

(ii) that they might be,

but intends that payment will not be made, or will not be made in full.

11.48 The maximum sentence for this offence is five years' imprisonment. The offence is triable either way. This offence replaces the offence under s 1 of the TA 1978 (though there is no longer any need for a deception). P must prove that D:

- acted 'dishonestly', which will presumably be defined as before: see *Feely* (1973) (**11.14**) and *Ghosh* (1982) (**11.15**);

- obtained services for himself or another. The Explanatory Notes give the example of someone who attaches a decoder to her TV to enable access to satellite TV channels for which she has no intention of paying;

- knew that the services were to be paid for or knew that they might have to be paid for;

- had the intent to avoid payment in whole or in part.

Let us reach a conclusion on the Fraud Act 2006 even before we have much significant case law (the reported cases focus on evidential and sentencing issues): it would be difficult not to agree with Ormerod (2007) that the Act has the potential to create serious practical problems because of the excessive breadth of the offences and a lack of definition of key terms, resulting in undue emphasis placed on dishonesty and the prospect of the criminal courts becoming entangled in complex civil law issues.

False accounting

11.49 In view of the publicity given to the prosecution of three MPs and a peer for false accounting, it seems appropriate to add a reference to the TA 1968:

s 17 False accounting

(1) Where a person dishonestly, with a view to gain for himself or another or with intent to cause loss to another,—

(a) destroys, defaces, conceals or falsifies any account or any record or document made or required for any accounting purpose; or

(b) in furnishing information for any purpose produces or makes use of any account, or any such record or document as aforesaid, which to his knowledge is or may be misleading, false or deceptive in a material particular;

he shall, on conviction on indictment, be liable to imprisonment for a term not exceeding seven years.

(2) For purposes of this section a person who makes or concurs in making in an account or other document an entry which is or may be misleading, false or deceptive in a material particular, or who omits or concurs in omitting a material particular from an account or other document, is to be treated as falsifying the account or document.

Chaytor **(2011)** Ds (members of the House of Commons and House of Lords) were charged with false accounting, contrary to the TA 1968, s 17(1)(b) for allegedly fraudulently submitting claims over a number of years for the payment of allowances and expenses to compensate them for expenditure in carrying out their parliamentary duties. They appealed unsuccessfully to the SC against a decision that criminal proceedings against them for allegations of dishonestly claiming expenses as MPs were not precluded by parliamentary privilege. They then pleaded guilty, and appealed only against their sentences.

CA: upheld the custodial sentences.

> It is difficult to exaggerate the levels of public concern at the revelation of significant abuse of the expenses system by some MPs. Some of those elected representatives, vested with the responsibility for making the laws which govern us all, betrayed public trust. There was incredulous consequent public shock. The result was serious damage to the reputation of Parliament, with correspondingly reduced confidence in our priceless democratic system and the process by which it is implemented and we are governed. This element of damage caused by D (and others) cannot be valued in monetary terms, but it is nonetheless real, and the impact of what has been done will not dissipate rapidly (para. 28).

The case is not important for our purposes, except as an illustration of this broad offence. In reality, this section of the TA 1968 is much more commonly used to prosecute those who make false statements on mortgage applications or in applications for housing benefit.

Making off without payment

11.50 This is an important offence, and one which need involve no trickery. Section 3 of the TA 1978 defines the offence of making off without payment:

s 3 Making off without payment

(1) Subject to subsection 3 below, a person who, knowing that payment on the spot for any goods supplied or service done is required or expected from

him, dishonestly makes off without having paid as required or expected and with intent to avoid payment of the amount due shall be guilty of an offence.

(2) For purposes of this section 'payment on the spot' includes payment at the time of collecting goods on which work has been done or in respect of which service has been provided.

(3) Subsection (1) above shall not apply where the supply of goods or the doing of the service is contrary to law, or where the service done is such that payment is not legally enforceable.

(4) Any person may arrest without warrant anyone who is, or whom he, with reasonable cause, suspects to be, committing or attempting to commit an offence under this section.

Making off without payment is triable either way, and has a maximum penalty when tried on indictment of two years' imprisonment. Since no deception need be proved it is a more minor offence than those discussed earlier. However, there is clearly a wide overlap with theft and fraud: where someone leaves a restaurant without paying, he may be prosecuted for theft or fraud if it can be proved that he never intended to pay. However, if D does not admit the offence, or does not admit that it was his intention at the time he obtained the food not to pay, P may instead charge him with making off without payment.

11.51 The *mens rea* of the offence is dishonesty plus knowledge that payment on the spot is required plus an intent to avoid payment permanently. It was not clear from s 3 whether D has to intend to avoid payment permanently but the HL decided that this was so:

> *Allen* **(1985)** D left a hotel leaving an unpaid bill of £1,286. He rang the hotel two days later to explain that he was in financial difficulties but hoped to pay the bill a month later. When he returned a month later to collect his possessions he was arrested.
>
> HL (Lord Hailsham): upheld the CA's decision to quash his conviction for an offence under s 3. Whilst there might be something to say for a summary offence to punish those who abscond without paying as required, this was not what this offence did. At the very least it provided an equivocation which had to be resolved in D's favour.

More recently, the CA has decided that D is not guilty even if he may have obtained an agreement to defer payment by deception:

> *Vincent* **(2001)** D left two hotels without paying his bill in full. He maintained that he had reached agreements with the proprietors of each hotel, that payment would be postponed and that payment had therefore not been 'expected' of him for the

purposes of s 3(1). The judge directed the jury to consider whether any agreement to defer payment had been procured by his deception. He was convicted of two offences under s 3.

CA: quashed his convictions. The usual expectation, for the purposes of s 3(1), that 'payment on the spot' would be made had been defeated by the alleged agreements, even though those agreements might have been obtained by deception. Section 3 did not stipulate or allow for an examination as to whether an agreement had been obtained through deception. It followed that the judge had erred when directing the jury.

J. C. Smith comments (at [2001] Crim LR 488) on the legislative history of this section, describing 'a deep-seated hostility to criminalising non-payment of debts'. Should the Ds in these cases be guilty of a crime?

Handling stolen goods

11.52   By the TA 1968, s 22:

(1) A person handles stolen goods if (otherwise than in the course of the stealing) knowing or believing them to be stolen goods he dishonestly receives the goods, or dishonestly undertakes or assists in their retention, removal, disposal or realisation by or for the benefit of another person, or if he arranges to do so.

Tunkel's diagram (**Figure 11.1**) illustrates the different modes by which handling can be committed. The penalty for this triable either-way offence is up to a maximum of 14 years' imprisonment. Why is the maximum double the maximum for theft? The rationale is that some handlers are particularly culpable: those who commission specific offences of theft for example, or who are professional organizers or distributors of stolen goods. Without handlers, it is often said, there would be few thieves.

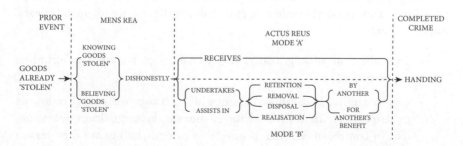

Figure 11.1   Modes of handling
Source: Reproduced with permission from (1983) 13 NLJ 844.

11.53 As Ashworth points out the offence of handling is drafted so widely as to 'cast a net around the main Theft Act offences' (PCL, p. 396). He points out that in doing so, the offence assumes the role normally played by the doctrine of complicity and the inchoate offences, and since these doctrines still apply here, the scope of criminal liability is widened yet further.

Pitham **(1976)** M decided to steal and to sell an acquaintance's furniture, knowing the acquaintance was in prison. D1 and D2 paid a sum considerably less than they knew the furniture was worth.

CA (Lawton LJ): as soon as M had assumed the rights of the owner, the appropriation was complete and the Ds were not dealing with the goods in the course of stealing.

Bloxham **(1983)** D innocently purchased a car, and then later realized that it must be stolen so sold it on to someone else. He was charged with handling, and convicted.

HL (Lord Bridge): allowed his appeal. A purchaser could not be 'another person' for whose benefit goods were realized or sold since it was the purchase, not the sale, that was for the purchaser's benefit. The purchase of goods by a person could not be described as a disposal or realization of the goods 'by' him.

Money laundering

11.54 Offences of 'money laundering' are now covered by the Proceeds of Crime Act 2002. A range of provisions had been inserted into the CJA 1988 by the CJA 1993, Part III, originally to deal with the proceeds of drug trafficking, but later extended to cover the proceeds of crime generally. Part 7 of the Proceeds of Crime Act 2002 (as amended by the Serious Organised Crime and Police Act 2005) created three principal money laundering offences, punishable with sentences of up to 14 years' imprisonment:

- concealing, disguising, converting, transferring, or removing criminal property (s 327);

- entering into or becoming concerned in an arrangement which he knows or suspects facilitates (by whatever means) the acquisition, retention, use, or control of criminal property by or on behalf of another person (s 328);

- acquiring, using, or possessing criminal property (s 329).

There are also important 'tipping off' offences (see ss 330–333) to encourage the reporting of known or suspected money laundering. See also the Money Laundering Regulations 2003 and 2007, which require the financial, accountancy, legal, and other business sectors to put in place systems to prevent the use of their services for money laundering or terrorist financing. Clearly there is a vast overlap between money laundering offences and the more traditional offence of handling stolen goods.

Serious fraud

11.55 Much publicity has been given in recent years to the significant problem of serious fraud. The Serious Fraud Office was set up in 1987 to investigate and to prosecute serious frauds, but has had a disappointing record in securing convictions in high-profile (and costly) cases. These failures, however, are not so much a result of inadequate criminal law, but stem from difficulties in securing convincing evidence, despite the fact that the Office has wide powers to compel suspects to answer questions (which were initially struck down by the ECtHR in *Saunders v United Kingdom* (1996)). The CJA 2003 took the controversial step of abolishing trial by jury for certain fraud cases, but the Government undertook not to bring this into force without a further vote in Parliament. The abolition of jury trial (and its replacement by a mixed tribunal of lay and professional judges) has been recommended by many individuals and bodies such as the Roskill Committee on Fraud Trials (1986), but would the abolition of juries in this area lead to their abolition altogether? In any case, is fraud innately more 'difficult' than, say, rape? It is worth considering what constitutes 'serious' fraud: if it is just the amount of money involved, why does this merit a different criminal procedure?

Recently, attention has switched to the need to recover the proceeds of serious crime by both criminal sanctions and civil recovery (see the Proceeds of Crime Act 2002) and to strengthen the powers of those who investigate serious fraud (see the Serious Organised Crime and Police Act 2005). Do you think the major reforms to the substantive law of fraud of the Fraud Act 2006 (see **11.41**) will contribute usefully to the vitally important task of reducing fraud? A few years ago, the police estimated that *reported fraud alone* cost the economy and society at least £13.9 billion a year (Levi *et al* (2007)). How would you deal with this huge problem?

FURTHER READING

Beaton, J. and Simester, A., 'Stealing One's Own Property' (1999) 115 LQR 372.

Collins, J., 'Fraud by Abuse of Position: Theorising Section 4 of the Fraud Act 2006' [2011] Crim LR 513.

Criminal Law Revision Committee, Eighth Report, *Theft and Related Offences* (Cmnd 2977, 1966).

Gardener, S., 'Property and Theft' [1998] Crim LR 35.

Glazebrook, P., 'Thief or Swindler: Who Cares?' (1991) 50 Camb LJ 389.

Glazebrook, P., 'Revising the Theft Acts' (1993) 52 Camb LJ 191.

Griew, E., 'Dishonesty: the Objections to *Feely* and *Ghosh*' [1985] Crim LR 341.

Guest, S., 'Law, Fact and Lay Questions' in *Criminal Law and Justice* (1987).

Law Commission, *Fraud and Deception* (LCCP No. 155, 1999).

Law Commission, *Fraud* (Report No. 276, 2002).

Levi, M., Burrows, J., Fleming, M., and Hopkins, M., *The Nature, Extent and Economic Impact of Fraud in the UK* (ACPO, 2007).

Ormerod, D., 'The Fraud Act 2006—Criminalising Lying?' [2007] Crim LR 193.

Smith, J. C., 'Reforming the Theft Acts' (1996) 28 Bracton LJ 27.

Smith, J. C., *The Law of Theft* (8th edn, 1997).

Spencer, J. R., 'The Metamorphosis of s 6 Theft Act 1968' [1977] Crim LR 653.

Spencer, J. R., 'The Theft Act 1978' [1979] Crim LR 24.

Spencer, J. R., 'Theft—Appropriation and Consent' (1984) 43 Camb LJ 7.

Williams, G., 'Temporary Appropriation Should Be Theft' [1981] Crim LR 129.

SELF-TEST QUESTIONS

What offences have been committed in the following scenarios?

1   Dee persuades Jo to buy Phil's hotdog stand for £1,000 by persuading her that it is Dee's own. Phil, knowing nothing about the agreement, takes the stand round to Jo's house where he leaves it, believing that Jo is going to carry out some minor repairs for him. Dee meanwhile enters Phil's house because she is curious to see whether he has a large supply of hotdogs. She trips and breaks a vase.

2   Dee takes Phil's season ticket for the football club, uses it twice, and then returns it, but Phil has missed the match he most wanted to see.

3   Dee promises to mend Phil's bicycle tyre and asks for £5 in advance. She spends the money on beer and never does the repair. Would it make any difference if she had asked Phil for the £5 saying that she needed it to buy materials?

4   Dee breaks into Phil's office, and removes a copy of an exam paper that Phil has just set for the forthcoming exams. She photocopies it and returns the original. She shows the copy to her friend Ann. She then makes an imaginary paper, and sells a copy of it to Belinda for £5, pretending that it is a copy of the real paper.

5   Dee obtains a student railcard by falsely representing that she is a student.

6   Dee finds Phil's credit card and takes it to the bank. She inserts it into the cash machine and the first PIN she invents works. She asks the machine for £100 cash which it gives to her, and then she transfers £50 from Phil's account to her own at the same bank.

12

Criminal damage and public order offences

SUMMARY

Criminal damage and arson: distinguish simple and aggravated criminal damage. If the offence is committed by fire, it is arson. Wide definition of destroying or damaging property. *Mens rea*—objective recklessness.

Offences under the POA 1986: but what is 'public order'?

Riot: 12 or more people using or threatening unlawful violence for a common purpose.

Violent disorder: three or more people using or threatening unlawful violence for a common purpose.

Affray: using or threatening violence in a group.

Other offences (e.g. fear or provocation of violence; causing harassment, alarm, or distress): are they necessary or could public order be maintained simply by the enforcement of other criminal laws?

Introduction

12.1 A discussion of criminal damage could easily sit within a chapter on theft, since it is an offence against property. Yet criminal damage in everyday speech is often simply vandalism, which can be seen as an offence against good order. Not all syllabuses include public order offences (so check!), but they are included briefly in this book in order to provide an important comparison with other offences of violence. And the crimes dealt with in this chapter are numerically very significant: see the annually published Criminal Statistics (available at <www.justice.gov. uk/publications/statistics-and-data/criminal-justice/criminal-justice-statistics. htm>). Given the existence of the offences of violence discussed in Chapter 9, do we need these substantive public order offences? Whilst the offences found in the Public Order Acts are primarily designed to deal with group offending, there is nothing to stop the prosecution of 'rioters' under the OAPA 1861. A rioter who seriously injures someone, for example, may be guilty of an offence under the OAPA 1861, s 20 (see **9.8**). The POA 1986 consolidated and strengthened existing public order law. It abolished a number of common law offences (including riot, unlawful assembly, and affray) and replaced them with statutory offences. It also extended controls over processions and public assemblies. The language of the POA seems somewhat confrontational. It starts: 'Part I: New Offences'. Part II then deals with the new rules surrounding processions and assemblies. Think how you would draw up such a statute. For example, the Immigration Act 1971, whilst severely limiting immigration into the UK, started with a section of 'General Principles' which specifies that all those who have the right of abode in the UK shall be free to live in, and to come and go into and from, the UK (subject of course to the limitations described later in the Act). Should the POA have started with a general right to protest and to demonstrate, before proceeding to the limitations on these rights?

12.2 Whilst it is clearly a vital police function to maintain public order, do the police have sufficient powers to prevent disorder without the need for these additional offences? You might argue that what the POA adds to the 'armoury' of criminal law is more symbolic than real: the police will often choose to rely on other powers. Their common law powers include the power to arrest for a breach of the peace, and they have other statutory powers beyond the offences in the OAPA: the power to ban wilful obstructions of the highway, contrary to the Highways Act 1980, s 137, for example. It is also an offence under the Police Act 1996, s 89 to assault a constable in the execution of his duty. One 'weapon' which is used is the power to 'bind people over to be of good behaviour' despite the fact the power was struck down by the ECtHR:

> *Hashman and Harrup v United Kingdom* **(1999)** Ds, who had been disrupting a hunt by shouting and sounding horns, were bound over to keep the peace and to be of good behaviour for 12 months.
>
> ECtHR (by a majority of 16 to 1): there was a violation of Art 11 of the ECHR (see **1.25**). Ds did not breach the peace, and it could not be said that what they were being bound over not to do must have been apparent to them.

Law Com No. 22 (1994) had previously recommended that binding over orders should be abolished without replacement. But in 2003, the Home Office published a Consultation Document entitled 'Bind Overs: A Power for the 21st Century' which recommended that a Practice Direction should be issued by the Lord Chief Justice clarifying the use of the power. Now see the Consolidated Criminal Practice Direction, Part III.31: the individual is bound over to do or to refrain from doing specific activities, and the terms must be evidenced by a written order of the court.

12.3 The POA 1986 was reinforced by a welter of additional provisions in the CJPOA 1994. Many people, including police officers, argued at that time that what were needed were not more powers but greater resources. The 'criminals' in this area are often football hooligans, travellers, strike pickets, and those generally at the bottom of the social hierarchy. Here we are in the most obviously political area of criminal law: who is to define what is order and what is not, who is acting lawfully and who unlawfully? Do you think the POA and the CJPOA 1994 are useful reactions to people's legitimate fears of public disorder, or do the media and politicians encourage a moral panic? Criminal law is often not the best weapon to use in seeking to reduce serious social problems. At **9.29**, we asked whether the Protection from Harassment Act 1997 was an appropriate response (with its mixture of civil and criminal sanctions) to the public's concern about harassment. Then at **9.38** the racially aggravated offences added to the Crime and Disorder Act 1998 were discussed: s 30 introduced a new offence of racially aggravated criminal damage; and s 31 created three racially aggravated offences based on the offences in ss 4, 4A, and 5 of the POA 1986 (see **12.17–12.20**), that is:

- racially aggravated fear or provocation of violence;
- racially aggravated intentional harassment, alarm, or distress;
- racially aggravated harassment, alarm, or distress.

Would better community policing and more effective sentences deal with the problem more usefully than the enactment of more legislation? What do you understand to have been the cause of rioting in England in August 2011? Another key and current issue is the police decision frequently to issue fixed penalty notices (Penalty Notices for Disorder) to many Ds who might have expected to be prosecuted. See *Gore and Maher* (2009) and *R (Guest) v DPP* (2009) and Padfield (2010).

12.4 Many of the most interesting cases in this area are not strictly criminal, but have involved people using judicial review proceedings to challenge the decisions of the police, or other bodies, to use their powers in what is considered by another person or body to be an improper way.

12.5 Drawing the line between who is and who is not acting lawfully in these situations is a near impossible task. In *R v Chief Constable of Devon and Cornwall, ex p Central Electricity Board* (1982) Lord Denning MR said:

> There is a breach of the peace whenever a person who is lawfully carrying out his work is unlawfully and physically prevented by another from doing it.

Of course people have a right to go about their lawful business. But you also have a right to demonstrate. If your demonstration is to bring your cause successfully to the public attention it may well be inevitable that people are prevented from crossing the road for a minute or two, or are prevented from taking their lorry where they want for a short while. Are you inevitably breaking the law? Anyone who attends a peaceful demonstration should be aware that they are at risk of finding themselves on the wrong side of the criminal law. Where does this leave the right to demonstrate lawfully? (See also on police powers at demonstrations the decisions of the HL in *R (Laporte) v Chief Constable of Gloucestershire Constabulary and others* (2006) and in *Austin v Commissioner of the Police of the Metropolis* (2009), and the CA in *R (Moos) v Commissioner of Police of the Metropolis* (2012) which uphold the legality of police 'kettling' (or the confining of protesters) at demonstrations.)

Criminal damage and arson

12.6 The Malicious Damage Act 1861 was replaced by the CDA 1971. Section 1 provides:

> (1) A person who without lawful excuse destroys or damages any property belonging to another intending to destroy or damage any such property or being reckless as to whether any such property would be destroyed or damaged shall be guilty of an offence.

An aggravated form of the offence is to be found in s 1(2):

> A person who without lawful excuse destroys or damages any property, whether belonging to himself or another –
>
> (a) intending to destroy or damage any property or being reckless as to whether any property would be destroyed or damaged; and
>
> (b) intending by the destruction or damage to endanger the life of another or being reckless as to whether the life of another would be thereby endangered;
>
> shall be guilty of an offence.

If the offence is committed by fire, it is charged as arson (s 1(3)). The maximum penalty for simple or aggravated arson is life imprisonment; whereas the maximum sentence for 'simple' criminal damage is ten years' imprisonment.

Actus reus

12.7 Destroying or damaging property has been defined very widely: in *Whiteley* (1991), which concerned interference with a computer disk, Lord Lane CJ said that 'any alteration to the physical nature of the property concerned may amount to damage within the meaning of the section'. Property is defined for the purpose of this Act in s 10: it is wider than the definition in the TA 1968 (**11.3**) in that it does not exclude land, but it is narrower in that it does not include things in action or intangible property.

Mens rea

12.8 The *mens rea* of criminal damage is recklessness. For many years this was interpreted objectively for, as Lord Diplock said in *Metropolitan Police Comr v Caldwell* (1982, see **3.22**):

> …a person charged with an offence under section 1(1) of the Criminal Damage Act 1971 is 'reckless as to whether any such property would be destroyed or damaged' if (1) he does an act which in fact creates an obvious risk that property will be destroyed or damaged and (2) when he does the act he either has not given any thought to the possibility of there being any such risk or has recognised that there was some risk involved and has nonetheless gone on to do it … Neither state of mind seems to me to be less blameworthy than the other; but if the difference between the two constituted the distinction between what does and what does not in legal theory amount to a guilty state of mind for the purpose of a statutory offence of damage to property, it would not be a practicable distinction for use in a trial by jury.

However, as we saw at **3.22–3.28**, the HL overruled *Caldwell* in *G* (2004), preferring to adopt the subjective definition of recklessness to be found in the DCC of 1989.

Thus, the JSB's Model Direction for judges now merely suggests for s 1(1):

> P will have proved that D was reckless if, having regard to all the available evidence, you are sure that he was aware of a risk that property would be destroyed/damaged; and that in the circumstances which were known to him it was unreasonable for him to take that risk.

For s 1(2), they suggest:

> P will have proved that D was reckless as to whether the life of V would be endangered if, having regard to all the evidence, you are sure that he was aware of a risk that the destruction/damage would endanger V's life and that in the circumstances that were known to him it was unreasonable to take that risk.

The defence of lawful excuse

12.9 See **4.25** for details of how s 5 provides a defence of lawful excuse. By s 5(2), D has a lawful excuse for causing criminal damage:

(a) if at the time of the act or acts alleged to constitute the offence he believed that the person or persons whom he believed to be entitled to consent to the destruction of or damage to the property in question had so consented, or would have so consented to it if he or they had known of the destruction or damage and its circumstances; …

Kelleher (2003) D knocked the head off a statue of Lady Thatcher causing £50,000 of damage and was convicted of criminal damage. He asserted that his actions were a political protest against globalization and motivated by fears for his infant son's future and that the judge was wrong to rule as a matter of law that the statutory defence of lawful excuse under CDA 1971, s 5(2) was unavailable.

CA: dismissed the appeal. The trial judge was right to conclude that D's stated purpose in damaging the statue did not raise the defence of lawful excuse for the jury's consideration, since when applying an objective test, D's act of damage was not done in order to protect property belonging to another.

A more complex version of this defence was argued in *Jones* (2006), which is discussed in detail at **5.39**.

In this context, the defence of lawful excuse leads to the acquittal of those whose mistaken beliefs may be caused by their own drunkenness, particularly since s 5(3) states that:

For the purposes of this section it is immaterial whether a belief is justified or not if it is honestly held.

Jaggard v Dickinson (1981) D, who had been drinking, mistook V's house for that of her friend, with whom she had planned to stay. Finding the house locked and no one at home, she broke a window in order to get in. She was convicted of criminal damage.

DC (Mustill J): quashed her conviction. The defence under the CDA 1971, s 5(2)(a) was still available although D was drunk.

The court is required by s 5(3) to focus on the existence of the belief, not its intellectual soundness; and a belief can be just as much honestly held if it is induced by intoxication, as if it stems from stupidity, forgetfulness, or inattention.

See **4.25–4.26** for a discussion of this defence.

Public order offences

12.10 Public order offences typically penalize group offending. Does this offend against the principle that criminal responsibility is generally personal and individual?

Compare these offences with comments made in Chapter 6 on accomplices on the common purpose rules (see **6.20**). You might have thought that another characteristic of public order offences would have been that they must take place in public but this is not so: *DPP v Orum* (1988, see **12.20**) is an example of the POA 1986 being enforced in a domestic matter, and against one single offender. Is this appropriate?

Riot

12.11 Section 1 of the Public Order Act 1986 provides:

> **s 1** (1) Where 12 or more people who are present together use or threaten unlawful violence for a common purpose and the conduct of them (taken together) is such as would cause a person of reasonable firmness present at the scene to fear for his personal safety, each of the persons using unlawful violence for the common purpose is guilty of riot.
>
> (2) It is immaterial whether or not the 12 or more use or threaten unlawful violence simultaneously.
>
> (3) The common purpose may be inferred from conduct.
>
> (4) No person of reasonable firmness need actually be, or be likely to be, present at the scene.
>
> (5) Riot may be committed in private as well as in public places.

Riot is triable only on indictment and the maximum sentence is ten years' imprisonment or a fine, or both. The *mens rea* is intention or awareness. Should this awareness be replaced by a subjective form of recklessness as recommended by the DCC (in clause 198)? This would involve, in addition to awareness of the relevant risk, an awareness that it is unreasonable to take it. However, it is difficult to see how a person could claim that it was reasonable for him to take the risk that his conduct might be violent or his behaviour threatening, so the difference is not great. It is noted at **4.26** that the POA 1986, s 6(5) makes clear that awareness impaired by self-induced intoxication is no defence. This avoids the need to apply the difficult *Majewski* (1977) rule (see **4.19**). The section places on D the burden of proving that his intoxication was involuntary: is this appropriate?

12.12 How does riot vary from an offence under the OAPA? The key must be the concept of collective violence. An offender is only guilty under the POA 1986 if the 12 were together using or threatening violence. Should the fact that several people are involved make it a different offence or should it merely affect the sentence? While it is clearly an aggravating feature of an offence that there was a group of people who put others in fear, these factors would justify a higher sentence if the offender were simply charged under the OAPA.

***Sallis* (1993)** D prisoners were convicted of riot after disturbances at a prison remand centre, during which two prison officers were badly injured and damage of £1.3 million was caused.

CA: upheld sentences of four-and-a-half and five years on two prisoners who had been ringleaders.

Do you think riot was the appropriate offence to charge in this case?

Violent disorder

12.13   Section 2 of the POA 1986 provides:

s 2 (1) Where three or more people who are present together use or threaten unlawful violence for a common purpose and the conduct of them (taken together) is such as would cause a person of reasonable firmness present at the scene to fear for his personal safety, each of the persons using or threatening unlawful violence is guilty of violent disorder.

(2) It is immaterial whether or not the three or more use or threaten unlawful violence simultaneously.

(3) No person of reasonable firmness need actually be, or be likely to be, present at the scene.

(4) Violent disorder may be committed in private as well as in public places.

Although violent disorder is triable either way (see **1.13**), it is generally committed for trial in the Crown Court. The maximum penalty is five years' imprisonment, a fine, or both. The key again is the number of people present: three or more people using or threatening violence. Section 6(7) provides that where one or more Ds are acquitted because they lack *mens rea*, the determination of the number of people involved is unaffected.

***NW* (2010)** D, a 15-year-old girl, was with a friend who was asked by two police officers to pick up litter she had dropped. She refused, the police took hold of both girls, and an incident developed, with a large crowd gathering, and several members of the public becoming involved in making threats of violence to the police. D was convicted of violent disorder.

CA: dismissed her appeal. The term 'present together' in the POA 1986, s 2 meant no more than being in the same place at the same time; there was no requirement that there was a common purpose among those using or threatening violence:

> Three or more people using or threatening violence in the same place at the same time whether for the same purpose or different purposes, are capable of creating a daunting prospect for those who may encounter them simply by reason of the fact that they represent a breakdown of law and order which has unpredictable consequences (Moore-Bick LJ at para. 19).

Affray

12.14 Section 3 of the POA 1986 provides:

s 3 (1) A person is guilty of affray if he uses or threatens unlawful violence towards another and his conduct is such as would cause a person of reasonable firmness present at the scene to fear for his personal safety.

(2) Where two or more persons use or threaten the unlawful violence, it is the conduct of them taken together that must be considered for the purposes of subsection (1).

(3) For the purposes of this section a threat cannot be made by the use of words alone.

(4) No person of reasonable firmness need actually be, or be likely to be, present at the scene.

(5) Affray may be committed in private as well as in public places.

The maximum punishment for affray is three years' imprisonment, but since it is a triable either-way offence, which is normally tried summarily, the penalties are usually much less.

12.15 Since a threat cannot be made by words alone (see s 3(3)), there must be some conduct on the part of the accused but this may be minimal.

> ***Dixon* (1993)** When the police arrived at a domestic incident, D ran away accompanied by his Alsatian-type dog. He encouraged the dog to attack the policemen who eventually cornered him. Two officers were bitten before reinforcements arrived and the man was arrested.
>
> CA: upheld his conviction for an offence under the POA 1986, s 3.

If the dog had not attacked, do you think that the court would have held that the order to the dog constituted conduct?

12.16 Note in s 3(4) that no person of reasonable firmness need be present at the scene.

***Davison* (1992)** The police were called to a domestic incident at a house. D waved an eight-inch knife at a police officer saying 'I'll have you'.

CA: upheld his conviction for an offence under the POA 1986, s 3.

Is this a suitable case for the application of s 3, or should affray typically be charged in cases of street battles between gangs, or fights outside pubs?

***I v DPP; M v DPP; H v DPP* (2001)** Ds were members of a gang which, armed with petrol bombs, was waiting for a rival gang. No one else had been present and the group dispersed when the police arrived, throwing away their petrol bombs.

HL: allowed their appeal from DC, thereby quashing the decision of the stipendiary magistrate to convict them of affray. Lord Hutton, with whom the other Law Lords agreed, held that an affray can only be committed where the threat was directed towards another person or persons actually present at the scene. In a wide-ranging review which included pre-1986 common law authorities and substantial quotation from Law Commission Report No. 123 on *Offences Relating to Public Order* (1983), he concluded that:

> …as a matter of law the carrying of dangerous weapons such as petrol bombs by a group of persons can constitute a threat of violence within the meaning of section 3(1). Whether it does so in a particular case is a matter for the tribunal of fact to decide having regard to the facts of the case.

However, the overt carrying of petrol bombs could not on the facts of this case constitute a threat of violence to anyone in the vicinity since the magistrate had found that no one other than the police was present at the scene. Similarly, on the facts, they were of no threat to the police since the group dispersed as soon as the police carrier came into view.

***Plavecz* (2002)** D was charged with affray which was alleged to have been committed inside a club when D was ejecting a woman who had been asked to leave.

CA: conviction quashed. Affray is a public order offence, not a supplementary offence against the person. Here the relatively minor, 'indeed trifling', assault could not be categorized such as would cause a bystander to fear for his personal safety.

These decisions have brought much needed common sense into what is after all public order law. As Lord Hutton pointed out in *I v DPP*, these young men should have been prosecuted under s 1 of the Prevention of Crime Act 1953 or s 4 of the Explosive Substances Act 1883. In 2000, there were 1,891 offences of affray charged in the Metropolitan Police area: it seems that little has changed since Brown and Ellis (1994) argued that it would be more efficacious if public order offences were reserved for cases in which the public genuinely suffer significant fear. Here is a borderline case:

Freeman v DPP **(2013)**

CCTV evidence showed D delivering a single kick to V, and four bystanders could be seen witnessing the assult—one put their head in their hands and another ran away. D appealed (by way of case stated) against convictions for assault and affray.

DC: the magistrates had been right to conclude that the nature of the violence was sufficient to cause a hypothetical person of reasonable firmness to fear for their safety, even though the violence was clearly solely aimed at one person. *Plavecz* could be distinguished as there the physical contact was minimal and caused no injury and V didn't appear to fall to the ground.

Note *Carey* (2006) (discussed at **8.24**) where the CA held that, whilst there might be circumstances in which a verdict of unlawful act manslaughter could properly be entered where the unlawful act was affray, on the evidence and basis on which the P case had been put in that case, none of the Ds were guilty of manslaughter.

Fear or provocation of violence

12.17   Section 4 of the POA 1986 states:

s 4 (1)   A person is guilty of an offence if he:

(a)   uses towards another person threatening, abusive or insulting words or behaviour, or

(b)   distributes or displays to another person any writing, sign or other visible representation which is threatening, abusive or insulting,

with intent to cause that person to believe that immediate unlawful violence will be used against him or another by any person, or to provoke the immediate use of unlawful violence by that person or another, or whereby that person is likely to believe that such violence will be used or it is likely that such violence will be provoked.

(2) An offence under this section may be committed in a public or a private place, except that no offence is committed where the words or behaviour are used, or the writing, sign or other visible representation is distributed or displayed, by a person inside a dwelling and the other person is also inside that or another dwelling.

This offence is triable summarily only, and is subject to a maximum of six months' imprisonment (though the racially aggravated version of the offence, mentioned at **12.3**, has a maximum sentence of two years' imprisonment). It can be committed in four different ways. D uses threatening words or behaviour, or distributes or displays such threatening, abusive, or insulting material and, either:

   (i) D may intend his victim to believe that immediate unlawful violence will be used against him or another person; or

   (ii) D may intend to provoke immediate unlawful violence by that person; or

   (iii) the victim is likely to believe that violence will be used; or

   (iv) simply, it is likely that violence will be provoked.

12.18   The phrase 'threatening, abusive or insulting words or behaviour' is not defined. However, the words are not the creation of this Act.

Brutus v Cozens **(1972)** D ran on to a tennis court during a match at Wimbledon blowing a whistle and distributing leaflets against apartheid in South Africa. The whole protest lasted two or three minutes. He argued that he had no intention to break the law: it was an entirely peaceful protest. He was charged (and acquitted by magistrates) of insulting behaviour, whereby a breach of the peace was likely to be occasioned, contrary to the POA 1936, s 5 (since repealed).

HL: 'insulting' was to be given its ordinary meaning and the question whether words or behaviour are insulting is a question of fact.

It has been held that masturbating in a public lavatory in the sight of another person, or homosexuals kissing at a bus stop, can constitute insulting behaviour. Whilst these acts may be offensive to some people, does this mean they are 'insulting'? Should the judge or jury decide the issue? Remember Guest's argument discussed at **11.15**, in relation to the meaning of the word 'dishonesty', that judges should identify the state of affairs which was envisaged to be within the scope of the relevant law. A judge who hands over a question of interpreting the law to the jury is abdicating her constitutional responsibility. But is this a question of law or fact?

Intentionally causing harassment, alarm, or distress

12.19 Section 4A (inserted by the CJPOA 1994, s 154) reads:

> **s 4A** (1) A person is guilty of an offence if, with intent to cause a person harassment, alarm or distress, he—
>
> (a) uses threatening, abusive or insulting words or behaviour, or disorderly behaviour, or
>
> (b) displays any writing, sign or other visible representation which is threatening, abusive or insulting,
>
> thereby causing that or another person harassment, alarm or distress.
>
> (2) An offence under this section may be committed in a public or a private place, except that no offence is committed where the words or behaviour are used, or the writing, sign or other visible representation is displayed, by a person inside a dwelling and the person who is harassed, alarmed or distressed is also inside that or another dwelling.
>
> (3) It is a defence for the accused to prove—
>
> (a) that he was inside a dwelling and had no reason to believe that the words or behaviour used, or the writing, sign or other visible representation displayed, would be heard or seen by a person outside that or any other dwelling, or
>
> (b) that his conduct was reasonable.

This too is a summary offence, punishable with up to six months' imprisonment or a fine (though the racially aggravated version of the offence, mentioned at **12.3**, has a maximum sentence of two years' imprisonment). The offence is similar to the offence under s 5, except that s 4A is more serious: D must be proved to have intended to cause harassment, alarm, or distress.

Harassment, alarm, or distress

12.20 Section 5 of the POA 1986 provides that:

> **s 5** (1) A person is guilty of an offence if he—
>
> (a) uses threatening, abusive or insulting words or behaviour, or disorderly behaviour, or

(b) displays any writing, sign or other visible representation which is threatening, abusive or insulting, within the hearing or sight of a person likely to be caused harassment, alarm or distress thereby.

(2) An offence under this section may be committed in a public or a private place, except that no offence is committed where the words or behaviour are used, or the writing, sign or other visible representation is displayed, by a person inside a dwelling and the other person is also inside that or another dwelling.

(3) It is a defence for the accused to prove—

(a) that he had no reason to believe that there was any person within hearing or sight who was likely to be caused harassment, alarm or distress, or

(b) that he was inside a dwelling and had no reason to believe that the words or behaviour used, or the writing, sign or other visible representation displayed, would be heard or seen by a person outside that or any other dwelling, or

(c) that his conduct was reasonable.

The maximum sentence is a level 3 fine, with a guideline fine of £180 (though the racially aggravated version of the offence, mentioned at **12.3** has a maximum sentence of a level 4 fine). The person who is likely to be caused harassment, alarm, or distress may be the police officer called to the scene of a domestic disturbance:

DPP v Orum **(1988)** D was having an offensive and public argument with his girl-friend. He was abusive to a police officer who intervened and was arrested for breach of the peace. He assaulted the police officer in the back of the police van, and was later charged with, and convicted of, offences under the POA 1986, s 5 and with assaulting a police officer in the execution of his duty.

DC (Glidewell LJ): a police officer may be a person who would be likely to be harassed, alarmed, or distressed for the purposes of s 5(1).

Is this a surprising use of a public order offence? Brown and Ellis (1994) doubt whether grossly insulting abuse would cause alarm and distress except to unduly sensitive officers. Their study of the policing of low-level disorder suggests that many incidents follow a spiral of warning/abuse/arrest, and they conclude that s 5 should not be used merely to restore order by removing drunk participants from the streets: for that purpose, the police should arrest people for being drunk and disorderly or for causing a breach of the peace. They argue that it is more efficacious if s 5 is reserved for cases in which the public genuinely suffer significant harassment. What of this case?:

Hammond v DPP (2004) D, an evangelical preacher, held up a sign saying, 'Stop immorality; stop homosexuality; stop lesbianism' and was convicted under the POA 1986, s 5.

QBD: interference with D's rights under Arts 9 and 10 of the ECHR was justified by the pressing social need to show tolerance to others. It had not been perverse for the magistrates to hold that the words used on the sign were insulting within the meaning of s 5 of the 1986 Act and the appellant had no defence of reasonable conduct.

Holloway v DPP (2005) D was convicted of the offence of disorderly conduct contrary to the POA 1986, s 5. He had used a video recorder to film a group of schoolchildren. While doing this, he stood naked in view of the camera whilst the children were in the background some distance away. The District Judge found that anyone seeing D naked would be likely to be caused harassment, alarm, or distress, and that D must have been aware of the likely effect of his naked state on others in a public place. The question for the court was whether a person who had not been seen but could have been seen by anybody had committed an offence under s 5.

DC: allowed D's appeal. Section 5 required the insulting words or behaviour to be 'within the ... sight of a person'. Those words meant that some person must have actually seen the abusive or insulting words or behaviour. It was not enough that somebody merely might have seen or could possibly have seen that behaviour. If Parliament had intended that an offence under s 5 would have been committed if the offensive behaviour could have seen by somebody, even if not actually seen, then it would have inserted a provision to that effect in s 5. In contrast, a person could be convicted of an offence of affray under s 3 if a notional person would have seen the conduct complained of, but the legislature did not adopt such wording in s 5, indicating that the parliamentary intention was that the two provisions should be construed differently. The view that someone would have committed an offence under s 5(1) if somebody could have seen him or her entailed a rewriting of the section and there was no reason why it should be rewritten or construed in that way.

Other offences of public order

12.21 The POA is far from comprehensive. D may be prosecuted for common law offences such as public nuisance, outraging public decency, seditious and criminal libel. See the cases of *Rimmington; Goldstein* (2005) discussed at **1.24** and **3.31**:

***Rimmington; Goldstein* (2005)** R was alleged to have caused a public nuisance by posting strongly racist communications to numerous people. He unsuccessfully challenged the indictment preferred against him at a preparatory hearing and his appeal to the CA was heard with that of G, who had been convicted of causing a public nuisance, having admitted sending a small quantity of salt through the post to a friend. A small quantity of salt had leaked on to the hands of a postal worker and the sorting office had been temporarily closed. Both appeals were dismissed by the CA.

HL: unanimously allowed both appeals. The reasons are discussed at **3.31**.

Not all of the POA 1936 has been repealed: for example, it remains an offence under the POA 1936, s 1 to wear a uniform for a political objective. The CJPOA 1994, ss 70 and 71 inserted into the POA 1986 new ss 14A, 14B, and 14C, creating offences in connection with organizing or participating in a trespassory assembly, or incitement to an offence.

***DPP v Jones* (2002)** In 1995 the Chief Constable of Wiltshire obtained an order banning trespassory assemblies within four miles of Stonehenge for four days. On the last day, 21 people gathered on the grass verge on the main road near Stonehenge. Ds were convicted of an offence under s 14B(2) of the 1986 Act.

HL (by a majority of 3 to 2): held the assembly had not been shown to be trespassory, largely because Ds had not exceeded the public's right of access but also because of their right to peaceful assembly protected by Art 11 of the ECHR (see **1.25**).

The CJPOA 1994, s 68 creates an offence of aggravated trespass:

(1) A person commits the offence of aggravated trespass if he trespasses on land in the open air and, in relation to any lawful activity which persons are engaging in or are about to engage in on that or adjoining land in the open air, does there anything which is intended by him to have the effect—

    (a) of intimidating those persons or any of them so as to deter them or any of them from engaging in that activity,

    (b) of obstructing that activity, or

    (c) of disrupting that activity.

This summary offence, subject to a maximum sentence of three months' imprisonment or a fine or both, was designed to deal with people who are interrupting such activities as hunting or the construction of controversial roads. The Anti-Social Behaviour Act 2003 extends it to cover trespass in buildings as well as in the open air, to cover 'animal rights' activists who invade the building of a targeted company. Section 63 of the CJPOA 1994 created offences in relation to raves: it is an offence for a person who knows that the police have given a direction ordering people to leave land to fail to leave as soon as is reasonably practicable. The original 1994 offences were limited to raves where 100 or more persons were present: this is reduced to 20 in the 2003 Act. Even stranger is the definition of a public assembly, which in the 2003 Act is defined to include groups of two or more people, whereas previously there had to be 20 or more to constitute a public assembly.

12.22 In conclusion, reconsider these offences. If you were drawing up a Criminal Code would you include a separate category of 'public order offences'? Note that the DCC gathered together offences concerned with the preservation of public order and safety under the title 'Offences against public peace and safety'. Is this a better description? Criminal damage and arson are included by the drafters of the DCC in a separate chapter called 'Other offences relating to property' (immediately following the chapter on theft, fraud, and related offences, as in this book).

FURTHER READING

Brown, D. and Ellis, T., *Policing Low Levels of Disorder* (HORS No. 135, 1994).

Padfield, N., 'Out-of-Court (Out of Sight) Disposals' (2010) 69 Camb LJ 6.

Parpworth, N., *Constitutional and Administrative Law* (8th edn, 2014).

Smith, A. T. H. and Hare, I., *Offences Against Public Order* (2nd edn, 2010).

Stone, R., *Textbook on Civil Liberties and Human Rights* (10th edn, 2014).

Thornton, P., *Law of Public Order and Protest* (2010).

SELF-TEST QUESTIONS

1   Are the offences in the Public Order Act 1986 necessary?

2   A large crowd gathers at the docks to protest against the export abroad of young animals in small crates. Dee and Bee, peace-loving vegetarians, wave banners saying, 'You lorry drivers are murderous bastards' and 'Anyone who works in this trade deserves to be eaten'. Many others in the crowd, including Fee, throw bottles at lorries which arrive at the dock. Discuss the criminal liability of Dee, Bee, and Fee.

Index